| OX | 06/09 | | | | | |

CENTRAL LIBRARY, WESTGATE, OXFORD OX1 1DJ
Renewals: (01865) 241718 - Enquiries: (01865) 815509

To renew this item please quote your reader ticket number, or the number on the bar code above

To renew this book, phone 0845 1202811 or visit
our website at www.libcat.oxfordshire.gov.uk
You will need your library PIN number
(available from your library)

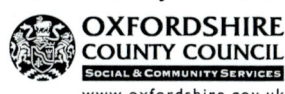

www.oxfordshire.gov.uk

The Sikhs

The Sikhs
Ideology, Institutions, and Identity

J.S. GREWAL

OXFORD
UNIVERSITY PRESS

OXFORD
UNIVERSITY PRESS

YMCA Library Building, Jai Singh Road, New Delhi 110 001

Oxford University Press is a department of the University of Oxford.
It furthers the University's objective of excellence in research, scholarship, and education by publishing worldwide in

Oxford New York

Auckland Cape Town Dar es Salaam Hong Kong Karachi Kuala Lumpur
Madrid Melbourne Mexico City Nairobi New Delhi Shanghai Taipei Toronto

With offices in

Argentina Austria Brazil Chile Czech Republic France Greece Guatemala
Hungary Italy Japan Poland Portugal Singapore South Korea Switzerland
Thailand Turkey Ukraine Vietnam

Oxford is a registered trademark of Oxford University Press
in the UK and in certain other countries

Published in India
by Oxford University Press, New Delhi

© Oxford University Press 2009

The moral rights of the author have been asserted
Database right Oxford University Press (maker)

First published 2009

All rights reserved. No part of this publication may be reproduced,
stored in a retrieval system, or transmitted, in any form or by any means,
without the prior permission in writing of Oxford University Press,
or as expressly permitted by law, or under terms agreed with the appropriate
reprographics rights organization. Enquiries concerning reproduction
outside the scope of the above should be sent to the Rights Department,
Oxford University Press, at the address above

You must not circulate this book in any other binding or cover
and you must impose this same condition on any acquirer

ISBN 13: 978-0-19-569494-9
ISBN 10: 0-19-569494-5

Typeset in Garamond Premier Pro 11/13.2
by Excellent Laser Typesetters, Pitampura, Delhi 110 034
Printed at Ram Printograph, Delhi 110 020
Published by Oxford University Press
YMCA Library Building, Jai Singh Road, New Delhi 110 001

*Dedicated to Harjinder, my wife,
who remained the main support in
my academic pursuits for half a century*

Contents

Preface ix
Introduction xi

PART I: IDEOLOGICAL UNDERPINNINGS

1. Guru Nanak and his Panth — 3
2. 'Raj Karega Khalsa' — 22
3. Martyrdom in Sikh History and Literature — 42

PART II: SOCIO-POLITICAL INSTITUTIONS

4. The Sikh State — 79
5. The Darbar Sahib and the Akal Takht — 95

PART III: CONCERNS OF SIKH LITERATURE

6. An Early Eighteenth Century Janamsākhī — 123
7. The *Prem Sumārg*: A Sant Khalsa Vision of the Sikh Panth — 158

PART IV: NORMS OF EQUALITY

8. Caste and the Sikh Social Order — 189
9. Sikhism and Gender — 206

PART V: NEW SOCIO-CULTURAL ORIENTATIONS

10. Contest over the Sacred Space — 229
11. Colonial Rule and Cultural Reorientation — 261
12. The Akalis and Khalistan — 287

Part VI: Cross-cultural Debates

13. Empathy with the Sikh Past: J.D. Cunningham — 315
14. The Contemporary Controversy in Sikh Studies — 334

Glossary — 369
Bibliography — 391
Name Index — 407
Place Index — 412
Subject Index — 415

Preface

There are fourteen essays in this volume. Some of them were given their present shape over the past few years. Others are slightly or thoroughly revised versions of articles published in the past four decades or so. The main argument of each essay is kept clear even at the cost of some repetition. Unless otherwise stated, the translation from Persian or Punjabi into English is my own. The 'Introduction' is meant to provide a context for each essay in relation to the growing concerns in Sikh studies.

These essays are based on primary sources seen in the context of received wisdom and my own understanding of historical methodology. Much in these essays is new in terms of information and interpretation. Altogether, they present a comprehensive perspective on Sikh tradition as a whole from the time of Guru Nanak to the present.

Since these essays are the result of research covering several decades, I am indebted to a large number of institutions and individuals in India and abroad. I am grateful to all of them. My main support in academic pursuits for half a century was my wife, Harjinder. This book is dedicated to her.

For giving this collection its present form, I am indebted to Professors Indu Banga and Gurinder Singh Mann. I am thankful to Karamjit K. Malhotra for her help in preparing the press copy and Sheena Pall for preparing the index.

J.S. Grewal

Introduction

In the late 1960s, I taught 'Punjab History' at the Panjab University, Chandigarh. In the prescribed syllabus it was virtually equated with Sikh history. The most respectable work on early Sikh history at that time was Indubhusan Banerjee's *Evolution of the Khalsa*.[1] After a detailed discussion of the teachings of Guru Nanak, Banerjee had come to the conclusion that he was not 'a revolutionary' but a radical reformer. This was Banerjee's way of saying that Guru Nanak did not found a new religion; he was a great Vaishnava reformer. The *Evolution of the Khalsa* was meant to explain how Sikhism became a distinct and militant faith in the course of its later history. Whether or not Guru Nanak was 'a revolutionary' was a popular question in the Master's examination and even the students showed great interest in the issue. I was keen to find an answer for myself on the basis of my own research.

The quincentenary of the birth of Guru Nanak gave me the opportunity. The Panjab University invited me to write a book on Guru Nanak. The book I wrote was formally divided into 'the milieu' and 'the response'. The study of the milieu in terms of politics, society, and religion (Islam and Hinduism) was based on sources other than the compositions of Guru Nanak. His response to the politics, society, and religion of his period was obviously based entirely on his own compositions.

This approach, to be followed later by Owen Cole[2], resulted in a few major surprises. The first was the comprehensive character of Guru Nanak's response. It embraced nearly all important aspects of his environment, making it distinct from the response of other religious figures of the medieval period. The second was the qualitative significance of Guru Nanak's response. He had little appreciation for the contemporary systems of religious beliefs and practices. The *mullā* and the *qāzī* as the representatives of orthodox Islam, the Gorakh Nathi *jogī* as the representative of the Indian ascetic tradition, and the pandit as the representative of the Vaishnava, Shaiva, and Shakta systems, were categorically rejected. What was more surprising, Guru Nanak's relative appreciation for the Sūfīs was qualified by a serious criticism of some of their assumptions, attitudes, and practices. Notable among these was their alignment with the state, which had gone totally unnoticed before. Equally surprising was his criticism of the worshippers of Krishna and Rama, the great representatives of Vaishnava bhakti. A thorough analysis of the compositions of Guru Nanak made it clear that he did not invoke the authority of any known scripture. In fact, he claimed to be a herald of God to deliver His message and a minstrel of God to sing His praises. Evidently, Guru Nanak did not identify himself with any of the traditional systems or any of the contemporary movements.[3]

Guru Nanak did not refer to any historical figure of medieval India, not even Kabir, but his appreciation for *sādh*s and *sant*s in general was quite explicit. Therefore, the possibility of Guru Nanak's approval of the sants in general remained open. Some scholars of the bhakti movement make a distinction between *saguṇa* and *nirguṇa* bhakti, the former addressed to incarnations and the latter to an attributeless God. This distinction enables them to gloss over the differences between figures like Chaitanya and Kabir. Some others equate the nirguṇa bhakti with the sant tradition of northern India as distinct from Vaishnava bhakti. W.H. McLeod places Guru Nanak squarely in the sant tradition, bracketing him with Kabir.[4]

My own study of Kabir and Guru Nanak suggests, however, that though there are important similarities between them, particularly in terms of ideas, there are significant differences even in the realm of ideas. Furthermore, while concentrating on ideas or concepts, scholars have excluded other relevant dimensions of the situation. They have considered only what Kabir and Guru Nanak said and not what they did during their lifetime. This raises the question of institutionalization and the formation of their following. In the essay entitled 'Guru Nanak and his Panth', the relationship between ideology, institutions, and the *panth*s is explored to account for both the similarities and differences between Kabir and Guru Nanak, and to see the implications of the differences for the history of the Kabir Panth and the Panth of Guru Nanak.

Before I wrote on Guru Nanak, I was introduced to perhaps the most fascinating figure of Sikh history, Guru Gobind Singh, through a book written for the Panjab University as a part of the celebration of the tercentenary of his birth. The chapter on the institution of the Khalsa was deliberately based on contemporary and near contemporary evidence.[5] It had provoked some debate as a fresh interpretation of the institution of the Khalsa. For the purpose of including it in the present collection, I have written it all afresh entirely on the basis of contemporary evidence. It is entitled 'Raj Karega Khalsa', a belief that became current in the early years of the seventeenth century, emphasizing the political identity of the Khalsa Panth.

Scholarly interest in the tradition of martyrdom in Sikh history began to emerge in the late 1960s when the tercentenary of Guru Gobind Singh's birth was celebrated. The recent debate in Sikh studies has accentuated this interest and by now a doctoral thesis on the subject has also been published. Two different views have been taken of the relevance of Sikh ideology for the tradition of martyrdom: one, that this tradition was an integral part of Sikh ideology from the very beginning and two, that the concept of martyrdom developed later in Sikh history. However, the scholars who have written on the subject have not studied the pre-colonial Sikh literature in a systematic manner. The essay included in this collection, 'Martyrdom in Sikh History and Literature', takes into account a wide range of Sikh literature for a proper historical perspective.

My study of historical writings on medieval India suggested that the bulk of this writing in the early twentieth century related to political history, but without serious interest even in political institutions. While teaching at Chandigarh, I proposed a seminar on the medieval Indian state. It was approved by the University Grants Commission. The scope of the seminar was not confined to the Sultanate of Delhi and the Mughal empire. A number of senior historians participated in this seminar, writing on several states of the medieval period. My paper was on 'The Eighteenth Century Sikh Polity' which had been characterized by J.D. Cunningham as 'theocratic confederate feudalism'. The later historians had generally looked upon this polity as 'republican' in contrast with the monarchical state established by Ranjit Singh in the early nineteenth century. They seemed to have concentrated more on the acquisition of power than on its use and the structural arrangements for its maintenance. The idea of equality, which was central to Guru Gobind Singh's institution of the Khalsa, appeared to have been operative for the acquisition of power, but power seemed to be exercised by individuals who behaved like sovereign rulers in the territory under their administration from the very beginning of territorial occupation.

Since this was a tentative interpretation, I focused on all kinds of evidence on Sikh polity: literary (both historical and non-historical), documentary, and numismatic. Some of the works in Persian, like Ahmad Shah's *Tārīkh-i Hind*, Sohan Lal Suri's *Umdat ut-Tawārīkh*, and Ganesh Das', *Chār Bāgh-i Punjab* were analysed from the viewpoint of Sikh polity. The work of Ram Sukh Rao on Fateh Singh Ahluwalia of Kapurthala was also studied in detail. Persian documents in the form of orders from Sikh rulers of the late eighteenth and the early nineteenth centuries, and in the form of legal deeds executed in the court of the qāzī, during Sikh rule, were studied from the angle of Sikh polity. A number of articles on different aspects of Sikh polity were written and published.[6] Finally, on invitation from the Aligarh Group of Historians recently to a seminar on the Indian state I thought of contributing a paper on 'the Sikh State as a Political Institution'. This appears in the present collection in a slightly modified form as 'The Sikh State'.

The earliest and the most important institution in Sikh history has been the Gurdwara, known in the beginning as *dharmsāl*. It is frequently referred to in the compositions of the Gurus, the *Janamsākhīs* and the *Vār*s of Bhai Gurdas. Surprisingly, however, not much had been written on this institution. Writing an article on the Gurdwara as the Sikh sacred space I discovered a whole range of literature celebrating the Harmandar, popularly known as the Golden Temple, as the foremost place of Sikh pilgrimage.[7] Sikh literature of the period of Sikh rule refers equally frequently to the Akal Bunga, popularly called the Akal Takht, as the place where the Khalsa took some of the most vital decisions affecting the whole Panth and the history of the region. The centrality of these two institutions, the Golden Temple and the Akal Takht, is generally taken for granted. The emergence of these two institutions was the result of a long historical process. The essay entitled 'The Darbar Sahib and the Akal Takht' outlines the process by which they emerged as the central institutions of the Sikhs.

The Janamsākhī form of Sikh literature has been studied by a number of scholars. One of their major concerns has been their relevance for the life of Guru Nanak. Much debate has also revolved around this issue. W.H. McLeod has studied the Janamsākhī traditions more thoroughly than others and he has underlined that the Janamsākhīs present the 'myth' of Guru Nanak. However, he has not analysed in detail this 'myth', or rather 'myths', because all the different traditions do not present exactly the same 'myth'. The essay entitled 'An Early Eighteenth Century Janamsākhī' presents an analysis of the contents of the *B40 Janamsākhī* to see how some of the Sikhs liked to look upon Guru Nanak and his mission in the early eighteenth century.

In the *rahitnāma* genre of Sikh literature, the *Prem Sumārg* has attracted perhaps the greatest attention despite its anonymous authorship and uncertain date. What is fascinating about this work is the scope of its contents. I analysed it in 1965 as 'a Theory of Sikh Social Order'. Its English translation has been published by W.H. McLeod as 'The Testimony of a Sanatan Sikh'. My reading of the work is different. Its detailed analysis appears in this collection as 'The *Prem Sumārg*: A Sant Khalsa Vision of the Sikh Panth'.

The term Nanak Panth is almost as old as the Sikh movement. The author of the *Dabistān-i Mazāhib*, writing on the Nanak Panthis around the mid-seventeenth century, talked of their presence in the towns and cities of the Mughal empire, and of their major occupations. Writing a few decades earlier, Bhai Gurdas talked of the eminent Gurus of the Sikhs in different parts of the Punjab and in the cities of the Mughal empire, often mentioning their caste background or occupation. For a systematic demographic information on the Sikhs, however, we have to wait for the census reports of the colonial period. For the pre-colonial period, scholars have talked about the composition of the Sikh Panth in terms of the traditional social background, raising the issue of caste in the Sikh social order, an issue linked up with the egalitarian character of Sikh ideology. Two extreme views have been taken: one, that there were no distinctions of caste in the Sikh Panth, particularly the Khalsa; the other, that the caste system remained operative in the Sikh Panth. A few scholars have appreciated the operation of an egalitarian ethos in the sphere of religion but without seeing much relevance of the idea of equality in the social or political spheres. The essay on 'Caste and the Sikh Social

Order' relates to the idea of equality, its institutional forms, and its limitations in application.

The increasing interest in gender relations is reflected in Sikh studies too. Apart from a few monographs of descriptive nature and some analytical articles, a doctoral thesis has also been published. However, the pre-colonial period of Sikh history has not received serious attention from the perspective of gender. 'Sikhism and Gender' takes into account the bearing of a wide range of pre-colonial Sikh literature on gender relations, bringing out the tension between the ideal of equality and acceptance of the inegalitarian institution of the patriarchal family.

The essay on 'Contest over the Sacred Space' is a continuation of 'The Darbar Sahib and the Akal Takht'. The colonial rulers were keen to maintain their control over these institutions for political reasons, going to the extent of making it the sole example in British India. There is hardly any doubt that both the institutions deteriorated under British control. The rise of the Singh Sabha movement in the late nineteenth and early twentieth centuries resulted in a demand for the control of historic Gurdwaras by the true representatives of the Sikh Panth. A clash was inevitable: it took the form of the Akali movement. As a result, the Shiromani Gurdwara Parbandhak Committee came into existence as a statutory body of its own kind. The essay presents a comprehensive view of the developments from 1849 to 1925.

I was invited by the Cambridge University Press to write a volume on the Sikhs for *The New Cambridge History of India* in 1980. Ten years later came out *The Sikhs of the Punjab*, covering the contemporary and the colonial periods as well as the earlier Sikh history which had remained the main focus of my interest in Sikh studies. British administrators of the Punjab had mostly written about their own administration and policies during the period of colonial rule, providing the context in which the history of the people of the region could be studied. In the post-colonial period, some North American historians turned to the response of the Punjabis to the colonial environment, producing monographs on the Arya Dharm, the Ahmadiyas and the Sikhs. For the Sikh response to the colonial environment, more work was done subsequently by G.S. Dhillon, Fauja Singh, Nripinder Singh, N. Gerald Barrier, John C.B. Webster, W.H. McLeod and Harjot Oberoi, concentrating on the religious movements among the Sikhs during the colonial period: the Nirankari, the Namdhari, and the Singh Sabha. Most of these writers show a preoccupation with the issue of the relationship between the earlier Sikh tradition and the developments in the colonial period. Three views have been projected on the Singh Sabha movement: one, that it was a revival of the early Sikh tradition; two, that it was a re-formation and, therefore, both old and new; three, that it was basically a rupture, making 'modern' Sikhism a new kind of faith. All the scholars agree, however, that the Singh Sabha movement revitalized the Khalsa or the Singh tradition. The essay entitled 'Colonial Rule and Cultural Reorientation' provides a clue to the greater success of the Singh Sabha as a movement that invoked the most vital features of the earlier Sikh tradition to promote 'modern' outlook and attitudes in matters cultural, social, and political, involving both continuity and change. However, the Singh Sabha response was not the only Sikh response to the colonial environment. There were more secular responses too in politics, literature, and art.

Nevertheless, Bhai Kahn Singh Nabha's exposition of Sikh identity became the basis of 'Sikh politics' for a growing number of Sikhs during the colonial period, culminating in the idea of a sovereign Sikh state before 1947. During the twentieth century, all the Sikh leaders did not pursue politics based on Sikh identity. It is true that some of the Sikh Ghadarites could derive inspiration from their faith but all of them stood for the freedom of the country as a whole. This was true of the Babbar Akalis as well. The nationalist ideal was even more evident in the case of the Naujawan Bharat Sabha and the Kirti Kisan Party. Two major parties to survive into the post-colonial era are the Communists and the Congress, each having a considerable number of Sikhs but with no special concern for Sikh identity. However, the protagonists of 'Sikh politics' on the basis of Sikh identity have been more active in the Punjab even after Independence. Before the rise of militancy and the movement for Khalistan, the leaders of Sikh politics had espoused two political objectives: the Punjab as a linguistic state in a federal system, and a 'Sikh homeland' with a special constitution and a special relationship with the Indian Union. The declared objective of the movement for Khalistan, on the other hand, was a sovereign Sikh state. There has been a general tendency among scholars and politicians to make no distinction between the supporters of these three objectives partly because the basis of all the three was Sikh identity. The essay entitled 'The Akalis and Khalistan' relates to these blurred lines in Sikh politics.

Working for my doctoral thesis on British historical writing on medieval India upto the time of Mountstuart Elphinstone, I came upon the classic works of James Grant Duff and James Todd on the Marathas and the Rajputs. It was not difficult to identify their counterpart for the Sikhs because the only British historian known to have produced a classic on the Sikhs was Joseph Davey Cunningham. His work had influenced both Sikh and non-Sikh historians during the twentieth century. The article I wrote on his *A History of the Sikhs* was published in 1964, incidentally, the first publication in my academic career. It appears here in a revised form as 'Empathy with the Sikh Past: J.D. Cunningham'. His work acquires a new kind of significance in the cross-cultural dialogue that is now becoming increasingly important.

The last essay in this collection describes the emergence of a prolonged controversy in Sikh studies in recent decades. It involves a number of Sikh and non-Sikh scholars and raises a number of issues: the nature and character of Janamsākhīs and their relevance for the life of Guru Nanak; the nature and character of the faith enunciated by Guru Nanak and its status in the history of religion in India and the world; the role of ideology and environment in the history and politicization of the Sikh movement; the relevance of the ideal of equality for the Sikh social order; the issue of Sikh identity; the making of Sikh scripture and its authenticity; and relevance of the historical method for religious studies. The essay on 'The Contemporary Controversy in Sikh Studies', based largely on my *Historical Perspective on Sikh Identity* and the *Contesting Interpretations of the Sikh Tradition*, which I wrote as a National Fellow of the Indian Council of Historical Research,[8] can serve as a kind of introduction to the contemporary state of Sikh studies.

Notes

1. Indubhusan Banerjee, *Evolution of the Khalsa*, 2 vols, Calcutta: A Mukherjee & Co., 1962, 1963 (rpt).
2. W. Owen Cole, *Sikhism and its Indian Context*, London: Darton, Longman and Todd, 1984.

3. J.S. Grewal, *Guru Nanak in History*, Chandigarh: Panjab University, 1969, 1979, 1998 (rpts).
4. W.H. McLeod, *Guru Nanak and the Sikh Religion*, New Delhi: Oxford Paperbacks edition, 2001, pp. 150–8; W.H. McLeod, *The Sikhs: History, Religion and Society*, New York: Columbia University Press, 1989, pp. 22–7.
5. J.S. Grewal and S.S. Bal, *Guru Gobind Singh: A Historical Biography*, Chandigarh: Panjab University, 1967, 1987 (rpt).
6. J.S. Grewal, *Sikh Ideology, Polity and Social Order*, New Delhi: Manohar, 1996, pp. 73–126.
7. J.S. Grewal, 'Gurdwara', in J.S. Grewal, ed., *Religious Movements and Institutions in Medieval India*, New Delhi: Oxford University Press, 2006.
8. J.S. Grewal, *Historical Perspectives on Sikh Identity*, Patiala: Punjabi University, 1997; J.S. Grewal, *Contesting Interpretations of the Sikh Tradition*, New Delhi: Manohar, 1998.

PART I
Ideological Underpinnings

1. Guru Nanak and his Panth*

Unity and Diversity in Bhakti

John Stratton Hawley and Mark Juergensmeyer regard the saint-poets of medieval India as 'the fount of the Hindi language'. Their songs, though religious in content, are universal in themes. They speak of 'the trials of life in society' as well as 'the pains and exaltations of love'. Hawley and Juergensmeyer refer to the distinction made between the *bhakta*s who worship God 'with attributes' (*saguṇa*) and the *sant*s who worship God 'without attributes' (*nirguṇa*), and argue that all bhaktas and sants belonged to 'a single family'. Surdas and Mirabai were primarily devotees of Krishna, and Tulsidas was primarily a devotee of Rama. Kabir, Ravidas, and Nanak disapproved of worship through image and myth. However, all of them were committed to the value of personal experience in religion. They questioned the ritualistic worship superintended by Brahmans, and criticized caste conceits. Regional languages were used for the appropriate expression of faith. They composed poetry in a petitionary genre called *vinaya* (humble submission), and their poems were included in common anthologies irrespective of their conception of God.[1]

Karine Schomer appreciates the great importance of the bhakti movement in the history of the systems of religious belief and practice in India as a personal faith that profoundly changed both the quality and structure of religious life, but goes on to say that it is more appropriate to conceive it as 'a cluster of individual bhakti groups, each with its particular emphases'. These groups were strongly regional and, therefore, distinguished not only by their doctrinal content but also by their separate histories. Furthermore, whereas in Maharashtra

---

*'Guru Nanak and his Panth' is a revised version of the 'S.C. Misra Memorial Lecture' delivered at Mysore to the Indian History Congress in 2003. It was published by the Congress as *Religious Ideologies, Institutions and Panths: Kabir and Guru Nanak*, 2003.

the sant tradition may be seen as clearly represented by the Varkari saints from Jnaneshvar in the thirteenth century to Tukaram in the seventeenth century, the sant tradition of northern India presents a more fragmented picture. Instead of one there are many *panth*s, each with its separate history going back to a particular founding figure. The north Indian sants were not bound to one another by any historical connection or institutional focus. Schomer believes, nonetheless, that there was a strong sense of spiritual unity among them due to the similarity in their teachings.

The fountainhead of the sant movement in the North, according to Schomer, was Kabir. Two other prominent sants who came after him were Nanak (1469–1539) and Dadu Dayal (1544–1603). They were unquestionably influenced by Kabir's thoughts, though they reworked them in unique ways of their own. The panths founded or inspired by Kabir, Nanak, and Dadu were the oldest surviving sant communities in the late twentieth century. The Sikh community was by far the most important, with over 13 million members and a distinctly religious way of life that removed it from the Hindu fold and distanced it considerably from its sant origins. The Kabir Panth with its 2.5 million adherents was 'a religious community of the dispossessed'. The Dadu Panth was influential in Rajasthan because of its special historical connection with the State of Jaipur.[2]

Thus, whereas Hawley and Juergensmeyer underscore the unity of the bhakti movement from the viewpoint of literature produced by the saint-poets, Schomer makes a clear distinction between the Vaishnava bhaktas and the sants in terms of their doctrines and institutions. The sant panths of northern India followed different trajectories, raising the issue of relationship between the origins of a panth and its later history.[3]

Kabir's Ideological Independence

David N. Lorenzen sets out 'to examine the role of social and religious dissent in the bhakti movement associated with the name of Kabir'. He states at the outset that no ideology can be properly understood without analytically locating it in its specific historical context. This commonsensical view has often been ignored in academic discussions of the systems of religious belief and practice in India. Consequently, continuity of the Hindu tradition is assumed or asserted at the cost of discontinuities, resulting in anachronistic or de-contextualized analysis. To understand any particular manifestation of bhakti religiosity, it is necessary to ask a number of specific questions about 'both content and context'.

Kabir has been commonly portrayed as a religious and social reformer who sought 'a spiritual reconciliation and purification of Islam and Hinduism', propounding at the same time an exalted mystical religion which would do away with vulgar exterior rites and noxious social practices and prejudices. However, Kabir's satires against both Islam and Hinduism go beyond mere attacks on the hypocrisy of their external rites, and suggest that he was attempting 'to stake out an ideological position basically independent of both'. Born in a family of Muslim weavers, Kabir could not hope to improve his status by joining the Hindu fold even if he was allowed to do so. This was also true of the people he addressed. His social position appears to explain his choice of an impersonal deity as the sole object of worship. Kabir's ideological independence was thus linked to his social position. His conception of liberation entailed both spiritual and social dimensions.

The earliest known legends of Kabir make him 'more Hindu and less Muslim'. He descends from heaven onto a lotus leaf as an *avtār* of Vishnu or, alternately, he is born to a Brahman virgin; he becomes a disciple of Ramanand; he is persecuted by a Muslim ruler and he disputes with a Muslim *shaikh*; he saves the temple of Jagannath in Puri from the wrath of the Lord of the Ocean. The monks of the Kabir Panth insist that he remained an unmarried ascetic all his life. All this clearly illustrates the 'Hinduization' of Kabir and his tradition. Lorenzen suggests that 'the panth has functioned primarily as a Hinduizing agent for marginal groups, mainly Untouchables, Shudras and Tribals'.

Whatever the original intent and function of the strong element of social and religious dissent in Kabir's teachings, it was used by the adherents of the Kabir Panth to express their rejection of certain aspects of hierarchical caste ideology and, at the same time, to foster their assimilation within the traditional social order. The adoption of 'Sanskritized' customs did not raise their caste ranking dramatically. 'Even so, the more egalitarian ideology of the Kabir Panth does provide them with a positive self-image, one which rejects the innate and absolute character of the inferior status to which they were relegated by more orthodox Brahmanical Hinduism'. The Untouchable in their vision was not intrinsically inferior to the Brahman, and human beings were judged on their merit rather than birth in a particular family. Thus, the social ideology of Kabir expressed in a sense the 'liberating moment' in the bhakti tradition.

Lorenzen points out that the Kabir Panth was generally classified with the indigenous movements of social dissent and protest. This classification, though justified, tends toward oversimplification. The monks of the Kabir Panth turned it clearly into a Vaishnava Hindu sect. Most of its low-caste members distinguished themselves from others of their caste by their vegetarianism and abstention from alcohol. Kabir's rejection of idolatry and other external religious practices was only partly honoured. Some of the monks rejected the caste system itself, though they gave verbal support to Kabir's attack on caste pride. The religious insight and biting social criticism of Kabir's verses was thus reduced to little more than vegetarianism.

Lorenzen makes the general observation that no influential religious and social critic in pre-colonial India directly questioned the overall legitimacy of the Hindu socio-religious order. The only exceptions are Basava in the south and Kabir and Nanak in the north. Even in their case, 'the extent to which they questioned the legitimacy of the system is debatable'. The implication is clear: the overt verbal criticism has to be seen in relation to the actual practice of the critic and his followers. The ideology and actions of the real or putative founder of a panth and its later development have to be examined together for a proper understanding of the social dimensions of a religious movement.[4]

LATER VAISHNAVIZATION OF KABIR

Only a dozen *shloka*s, or *sākhī*s, are common to the Guru Granth Sahib, the *Bījak*, and the *Kabir Granthāvalī*. In these verses we find some of the basic ideas of Kabir: concern with *Brahm-giān*; dying unto self to subsist in God; *maya* as the snare and pride as the impediment to liberation from transmigration; rejection of the Brahmanical way and denunciation of evil company. There are some common *pada*s or *shabad*s too in which the unity of God is emphasized. Har and Hari, Ram and Allah are the same. The multiplicity of epithets for God reinforces the idea of His oneness. God is the creator of the universe. He is within every living being as much as in the universe.

He is also the creator of *māyā* which lures human beings to earthly pursuits and sensual pleasures; pride keeps them bound to the chain of transmigration. Kabir does not identify himself with any of the existing systems of religious beliefs and practices. He is critical of the representatives of Hinduism and Islam, their scriptures, their beliefs, and their practices. There was only one path to liberation: Kabir's own path. God is equated with the name. He is also the True Guru. To turn to him is to be a *Gurmukh*. Another term for the true devotee of God is sant.

In the *Bījak*, there is great emphasis on *ahimsa* and on the mutual wrangling of the self-styled representatives of Hindus and Muslims. According to the *Bījak*, they are both wrong and they mislead others. Bracketed with them in this respect is the yogī. The idea of incarnation is totally rejected and no sanctity is attached to places traditionally regarded as the most sacred. Māyā appears very prominently in the *Bījak*. It is God's creation but almost as important as God. Some of the verses appear to refer to monistic Reality rather than personal God. The emphasis on knowledge is greater than on the union with the Divine.

In the Ādi Granth, Kabir figures as a householder. His criticism of the prevalent systems of religious beliefs and practices, both Hindu and Muslim, is quite comprehensive. The scriptures, beliefs or practices of Mullās and shaikhs, Brahmans and Jogīs, Vaishnavas and Shaktas, and others are denounced and discarded. There is no merit in practices like idol worship, pilgrimage, and the *shradhs*, and in the notions of purity or pollution, auspicious or inauspicious time. Kabir's conception of God here is more of a personal deity than in the *Bījak*. The idea of divine self-revelation, related to the concepts of *sachch* (truth), *nām* (name), shabad (word), guru (preceptor), *hukam* (order), and *kripa* (grace), is far more important in the Ādi Granth than in the *Bījak*. Transmigration is a concept that figures both in the *Bījak* and the Ādi Granth. However, ahimsa and māyā figure far less prominently in the Ādi Granth. Asceticism, renunciation, and mendicancy do not receive the short shrift that is given to many other contemporary practices.

Kabir contests caste in strong and unambiguous terms to establish the point that the path of liberation is open to all, including the lowest of the low. A severe indictment of the contemporary social order is built into this egalitarian ideal. However, poverty is not contested in the same way as caste. Women are generally seen as members of the patriarchal family in their subordination to men, or even as māyā. However, the ideal of *suhāgan* makes the Lord accessible to women in theory. Satī is appreciated as a metaphor for total dedication. The idea of impurity attached to women is discarded, and women can be seen as devotees of God in their own right. Kabir's metaphors come from his physical and social environment, including battles and sieges. The drum is beaten and the warriors enter the field. 'The brave warrior is he who fights for righteousness (*dīn*) and does not leave the field even if he is cut into pieces'. Political power is transitory; the real power is with 'the true king' who lasts forever. He can turn a king into a beggar and a beggar into a king, a fool into a learned pandit and a learned pandit into an idiot. Kabir's metaphors from the administration of revenue can be taken as evidence of the oppression of the peasantry.[5]

We may agree with David Lorenzen that Kabir carved out a path of salvation that was independent of the systems represented by Hindus and Muslims of his times. His rejection of incarnation on the one hand and his acceptance of transmigration on the other underscore his distinction from both the Vaishnava bhaktas and the Sūfis. Also, as mentioned by Lorenzen, Kabir rejected the principle of inequality embodied in the *varnashrama* ideal. His path was open to men and women irrespective of their social background. However, the image of Kabir as a householder in the Ādi Granth is compromised by his ambivalence toward renunciation and mendicancy. This could justify the Kabir Panthi monks who present him as a celibate ascetic. In any case, monkhood was not opposed by Kabir. Similarly, the vegetarianism of the Kabir Panthis could be justified by Kabir's insistence on ahimsa. The predominance of Shudras and Untouchables in the Kabir Panth may be viewed as a compliment to Kabir's total rejection of distinctions based on caste, occupation or family for the purpose of liberation. The political comment made by Kabir also lends itself to the possibility of the lowest being raised in the social scale. But there is nothing in the compositions of Kabir to make him a Vaishnava.[6]

There is no evidence to suggest that Kabir himself founded any institution. The earliest references to him talk of his personal achievement. Ravidas, who lived in Benares, refers to Kabir as one of the lowly who was 'saved' and a Muslim who attained liberation through devotion to God and one who is revered in the three worlds.[7] Guru Amar Das, in the third quarter of the sixteenth century, refers to the *julāhā* Kabir as one who attained liberation through the Guru's grace and whose *bāṇī* was sung by the people. Towards the end of the century Abul Fazl talks of Kabir as being revered by both Hindus and Muslims for the catholicity of his doctrine and the illumination of his mind so much so that when he died the Hindus wished to cremate him and the Muslims wanted to bury him. For Abul Fazl, Kabir was a Unitarian (*muwāhid*) who discarded the effete doctrines of his time (whether Hindu or Muslim). Numerous verses of Kabir in the Hindi language 'containing important theological truths' are still extant. There is no reference to his successors, or to an organized body of his followers.

Around 1600, Nabha Das said:

Kabir refused to acknowledge caste distinctions or to recognize the authority of the six Hindu schools of philosophy, nor did he set any store by the four divisions of life (*ashrama*s) prescribed for Brahmans. He held that religion (*dharma*) without devotion (*bhakti*) was no religion (*adharma*), and that asceticism, fasting and alms-giving had no value if not accompanied by adoration (*bhajana*). By means of *ramāinī*s, shabdas, and sākhīs, he imparted religious instruction to Hindus and Turks alike. He showed no partiality to either but gave teaching beneficial to all. With determination he spoke and never tried to please the world.[8]

This statement remains very close to our own impressions from the compositions of Kabir. However, Nabha Das makes him a disciple of Ramanand, carrying the implication that Kabir was a Vaishnava. In the middle decades of the seventeenth century, the author of the *Dabistān-i Mazāhib*, who refers to himself as Mobad looks upon Kabir as a *muwāhid*, makes him a *bairāgī* and a disciple of Ramanand. Vaishnavization of Kabir is more evident in Priyadas' commentary on Nabha Das' *Bhaktamāl* in 1712. The formation of Kabir Panth and the process of Vaishnavization probably happened simultaneously.[9] In the absence of institutionalization by Kabir himself, those who invoked his authority later to institutionalize his message had a large degree of freedom in interpreting it and giving it a concrete shape. They used Kabir's ideology rather selectively for their own purposes. In the process, they moved away from some of its basic features.

W.H. McLeod's View of the Sikh Panth

W.H. McLeod maintains that the sant doctrine, with its strong emphasis upon the interior quality of religious devotion, offers no overt encouragement to the emergence of religious institutions or formally organized communities. 'On the contrary, one learns to expect from its proponents a persistent attack on the futility of institutional loyalties or sectarian allegiance'. Indeed, to be a sant was 'to be freed from the institutional obligations of organized religion'. Speaking logically, there should be no panth of the sants. But for most people, actual practice differs from any theory which seeks to minimize the value of institutional forms. 'The first gathering of any group of disciples may flourish without acknowledging any formal organization, but if this first generation is followed by continuing family loyalties and widening influence, the pressure to institutionalize becomes irresistible'.

The emergence of the Nanak Panth took place in the early sixteenth century during the last phase of Guru Nanak's life. He settled at Kartarpur (Dera Baba Nanak) and the appeal of his teachings and his lifestyle attracted disciples. Nanak became Baba Nanak and those who were thus attracted to him became his disciples or *sikh*s. 'The Nanak Panth was born'. Guru Nanak was outspoken in his denunciation of caste. Consequently, membership of the Panth was seen to be open to people of all castes. Three features made significant contribution to its 'strength and longevity': the impact of Guru Nanak's personality, the hymns he composed to communicate his message of salvation through devotion to the divine name, and the nature of his early following. The effect of Guru Nanak's charismatic personality is reflected in the Janamsākhīs. His compositions had started being used for communal singing (*kīrtan*) even in his lifetime. However, the nature of his early following was 'perhaps the most important of all'. McLeod thinks that 'a significant measure of the initial response came from the Jats of rural Punjab' due largely to the egalitarian message of Guru Nanak and his successors. It helps to explain not merely 'the strength and longevity' of the Panth but also its subsequent transformation.

Whereas for Guru Nanak the Guru was the inner voice of God, the supreme guide for Guru Angad (1539–52) was Guru Nanak himself. The panth now had a clear identity, but it was still 'an informal organization'. The Guru alone provided a focus for a continuing devotion to the memory and teachings of the Panth's founder. A more formalized structure began to appear under Guru Amar Das (1552–74) with two 'major innovations': the appointment of territorial deputies (*masand*s), and the conferring of a distinctively Sikh status upon a specific place, specific occasions, and specific rituals. These two 'innovations' represent a distinct shift in emphasis, though in the compositions of Guru Amar Das there is no ideological shift. McLeod suggests that the pressure produced by the growth of the Panth could 'only be relieved by institutional means'. Guru Amar Das' third contribution was a proto-scripture, the collection of works known as 'Goindwal *pothīs*', which can be regarded as 'yet another step towards panthic definition and independence'.

The trends established in the time of Guru Amar Das were further strengthened during the time of Guru Ram Das and Guru Arjan. The sacred scripture known as the Ādi Granth was compiled in 1603–4. The Panth now possessed a growing number of holy places, distinctive rituals, and a line of Gurus. Its coherence was emphasized by challenge to the *gaddī* by rival contestants because a successful resistance to these challenges involved a heightened loyalty on the part of those who adhered to the orthodox line. The same effect was produced by the execution of Guru Arjan in 1606 which was seen as martyrdom by his followers. 'Sikhs were now united by a common threat as well as by a common devotion'. The execution of Guru Tegh Bahadur in 1675 strengthened panthic cohesion. The growing hostility finally led to open war in the time of Guru Gobind Singh (1675–1708).

Concepts of panthic destiny were thereafter intertwined with traditions of rights attained and protected through the exercise of arms. Warfare extending to the eighteenth century greatly strengthened this self-awareness. The Panth which emerged from that turbulent century confidently affirmed its identity as a society built upon the exercise of military power. Three other issues of fundamental importance explain the identity of the Panth at the end of the eighteenth century: the formal pattern of discipline and organization bestowed upon the Panth during the period of Guru Gobind Singh (the Khalsa and the *rahit*), the social constituency of the Panth, and the question of authority after the termination of the line of personal Gurus in 1708.

The most fundamental of all these issues was the social constituency of the Panth. In its early history there was representative caste distribution of its more prominent members, and the Khatris as a caste group held a particular prominence. At the less conspicuous levels of membership, the Nanak Panth had a substantial Jat constituency from the very earliest days. In the early seventeenth century, Jat strength within the Panth is clearly indicated by the author of the *Dabistān-i Mazāhib*. The Jats were unquestionably a distinctive group, manifesting a distinctive range of ideals and conventions which included 'strong martial traditions' and 'the regular use of arms'. McLeod argues that 'the Khalsa philosophy and code of discipline bear a striking resemblance to Jat ideals and conventions'. An explanation of the rise of the Khalsa should be sought in the Panth's dominant constituency. Combined with the experience of extended conflict in the eighteenth century, the social constituency of the Panth produced the all important rahit. The Khalsa can be seen as having 'absorbed strong influences from its Jat connections and its experience of struggle without renouncing its avowedly religious inheritance from the early Nanak-panth'. There was a non-Khalsa component of the Sikh Panth but 'the eighteenth-century Khalsa had asserted a claim to orthodoxy which it has never since relinquished'.

Until the first decade of the eighteenth century, the nature of authority within the Panth had presented no problem. The personal leadership of the Guru was acknowledged by all who believed in him. This authority could be delegated to deputies but never transferred. The scriptures too acquired a sanctity which implied divine authority. During the years following Guru Gobind Singh's death, there was a phase of confusion. Apart from claimants to personal Guruship, there was the dual authority of the Granth as the Guru and the Panth as the Guru. During the eighteenth century, the doctrine of Guru Panth evidently possessed a measure of genuine authority which was consciously exercised in the presence of the sacred scripture. This authority was eventually superseded by an assertion of personal power on the part of Maharaja Ranjit Singh. The doctrine of Guru Granth was now advanced and came to stay.[10]

In his account of the development of the Sikh Panth, McLeod gives primacy to the increasing number of the Sikhs in the sixteenth century and the increasing number of Jats within the Sikh Panth during the seventeenth century. The first phase was marked by a large measure of institutionalization and the second by a large measure of transformation. In combination with external threat, the dominant constituency of the Sikh Panth largely explains the form and philosophy as well as the orthodox status of the Khalsa. The scripture retained its importance but only next to that of the corporate body of the Khalsa as the Guru until the early nineteenth century.

In this presentation of the development of the Sikh community, the time of Guru Nanak and Guru Angad is treated as merely the background for the development of the Sikh Panth and that too rather cursorily. In fact, McLeod talks of 'innovations' from the time of Guru Amar Das. In his understanding, the ideology of Guru Nanak and what he did in his lifetime appear to be the least important factors in the historical development of the Sikh Panth.

Early Institutionalization of the Sikh Panth

We know more about the life of Guru Nanak than about the life of Kabir. Guru Nanak's comment on the political, social, and religious life of his times is also more comprehensive. There is a direct denunciation of contemporary rule in his compositions. The rulers discriminated against their non-Muslim subjects by extorting *jizya* and pilgrimage tax. The ruling class, which was non-Muslim at the lower rungs, oppressed the peasantry and the common people nonetheless. Justice was administered by the *qāzī* on the basis of bribery. Thus, the contemporary state was discriminatory, oppressive, and unjust. That Guru Nanak's political comment was relevant for the attitudes of his followers is evident from the fact that his comment was seldom forgotten. In socio-religious terms, caste distinctions were equally discriminatory, oppressive, and unjust. Therefore, Guru Nanak rejected the distinctions of caste as emphatically as Kabir, if not even more categorically. Though a Khatri, he identified himself with the lowest of the low. The socio-political role of the Brahmans and Khatris of the days of Guru Nanak was far removed from the role ascribed to them in the *varna* ideal. Therefore, the social order as such appeared to have lost its legitimacy.

The basis for social regeneration advocated by Guru Nanak was essentially spiritual and ethical. That it was different and distinct from the prevalent systems of religious beliefs and practices becomes evident from his comment on them. Brahma, Vishnu, and Mahesh are created by the God of Guru Nanak's conception. Thus, even if Brahma created the Vedas, they did not represent divine revelation. The authority of the Puranas, Smritis, and Shastras was even weaker. Guru Nanak claimed to derive his authority directly from God. With the virtual rejection of traditional deities and religious texts went the repudiation of traditional modes of worship and religious practices. Rejection of the idea of incarnation left no room for appreciation of Vaishnava bhakti. Guru Nanak's references to the worship of Krishna and Rama indicate his disapproval of their practices. Guru Nanak's attitude towards the *ulamā* and the shaikhs is no different from his attitude towards the pandit and the jogī. He refers to thousands of entities like Brahma, Vishnu, Shiva, and Muhammads as created by God. The *Qur'ān* and the other Semitic scriptures were no more authoritative than the Vedas or the Puranas. Allah is inscrutable and therefore his grace cannot be taken for granted. Mere allegiance to Islam could not 'save' a person. Guru Nanak shows preference for the Sūfis over the ulamā but this relative appreciation does not mean unqualified approval of the Sūfis. They received revenue-free lands from the rulers and, thus, aligned themselves with a state that was unjust. They also infringed their own doctrine of complete trust in God. They presumed to have reached the goal and authorized others to guide still others.

God, for Guru Nanak, is the unchanging Formless One. He is the only one; there is no second; there is no other. He possesses unqualified power and absolute authority. He can confer rule upon an ant, and he can reduce whole armies to dust. It is his light that shines in the creation. His light is everywhere and in everyone. He is everywhere and there is no other. He is within everything and yet outside the universe. He is immanent and transcendent at one and the same time. He stands revealed in his creation. To attribute all creation to him is to recognize the Truth. To accept his will is to live in accordance with the divine order. Guidance comes from him, and liberation comes through his grace. All presumption to liberation through self-effort was to be discarded, but it was absolutely necessary to make incessant effort. Remembrance of God, meditation on the nature of his creation, singing his praises, leading ethical life as householders, and helping others were some of the commendable forms of action. The liberated-in-life lived in accordance with God's will as socially committed persons.[11]

Guru Nanak claimed to be God's herald (*tabal-bāz*) to proclaim his Truth, and assumed the formal position of a guru (guide). He admitted disciples through a formal rite of initiation and gave them regular instruction. A regular discipline was evolved for the adoration of God. All the disciples joined Guru Nanak for singing the praises of God in the morning and in the evening. The ideal of equality was given concrete form in the community meal (*langar*) even more than in the congregational worship (*sangat*). Contribution to the langar came from individual members in cash, kind or service. The place of their meeting (*dharmsāl*) was regarded as sacred. An important aspect of the mode of worship was the use of the compositions of Guru Nanak. The followers of Guru Nanak belonged to a large number of castes and occupations. Prominent among them were many Khatris and a few Jats.

They were all householders. Their ideal was to live detached amidst the attachments of the world. To live in accordance with the Truth was more important than to realize the Truth. To make willing sacrifice for the true way of life was an essential ingredient of the faith. Guru Nanak chose one of his followers (sikhs), named Lehna, to occupy the office of the Guru in his lifetime. Installed by Guru Nanak himself, Lehna became Guru Angad. A disciple became the Guru, and the Guru became a disciple. By now, a new socio-religious group had come into existence with an acknowledged Guru to guide its social and religious life according to the pattern set by the founder and in the light of the ideas expounded by him. The stage was set for the expansion and consolidation of the Sikh Panth.[12]

Guru Nanak stands distinguished from Kabir in several important ways. He shows much greater awareness of politics and government. His criticism of the traditional social order goes deeper into its very structure. His criticism of the contemporary systems of religious belief and practice springs from a coherent system of ideas which serve as the conscious criteria for judgement. Guru Nanak explicitly claims divine authority for what he says, which makes him patently independent of known earthly authorities. He is categorically opposed to renunciation and mendicancy. His ideal is self-reliance to a degree that enables one to help others. He attaches great importance to ethical life, and his values are meant to be universal. His message is not merely of liberation through the name but also of social action for and through liberation-in-life. Above all, his concern for institutionalization contrasts him with Kabir. McLeod's view that the sant doctrine offers no overt encouragement to the emergence of religious institutions or formally organized communities does not hold good in the case of Guru Nanak. His definition of the sant does not apply to Guru Nanak.

The organizational and institutional axes of the Sikh Panth were provided by Guru Nanak himself in the form of three Gs: the Guru, the Granth, and the Gurdwara. At one level God is the Guru; at another, Nanak is the divinely commissioned Guru. The human Guru is not God but has in him an element of divinity due to his commission. This office is passed on to his successors who remain one with him. The belief is reflected in the use of the epithet 'Nanak' in their own compositions. The office is one and continuous. What the successors say and do is legitimized by virtue of their office. They represent a series of interpretations and extensions of Guru Nanak. Guruship undoubtedly was an institution of the highest significance in the development of the Sikh Panth. Guruship did not end with the death of Guru Gobind Singh. Instead of choosing one Sikh to the office he chose the collective body of his Khalsa.

Believed to be divinely inspired, Guru Nanak's own bāṇī was a form of revelation. It was meant to serve as an alternative to the known scriptures. Significantly, Guru Nanak equates the Shabad with the Guru, and his successors equate his bāṇī with the Shabad. Guru Ram Das makes the explicit statement: '*bāṇī* is Guru, Guru is *bāṇī*'. The compositions of Guru Nanak had begun to be recorded in his lifetime in a script that came to be known as Gurmukhi. This was the background for the *pothīs* compiled by Guru Amar Das which served as a major source for the compilation of the Granth by Guru Arjan in 1604. He himself says that the Granth compiled by him was the abode of God. The equation of God with the Guru, of the Guru with the Shabad, and of the Shabad with Gurbaṇī enables us to appreciate Guru Arjan's reference to the Granth as the abode of God. Guru Gobind Singh vested Guruship in the shabad-bāṇī embodied in the Granth so that it became Guru Granth Sahib.

McLeod says virtually nothing about the Gurdwara which was by far the most important institution of the Sikh Panth. The sacred space of the Sikhs, called dharmsāl, had three distinct but interrelated components: shabad, sangat, and langar. This institution became increasingly important with the increasing number of Sikhs and local Sikh communities. The dharmsāl where the Guru was personally present was more important than others. However, in view of the equation of bāṇī with the Guru, the recitation of Gurbāṇī in a dharmsāl gave it great importance. Furthermore, the Guru was believed to be present in the sangat in which kīrtan was performed through Gurbāṇī. To serve the sangat in the dharmsāl was to serve the Guru. The term Gurdwara was used by Guru Nanak as a metaphor for the door of God. It came to be used for a dharmsāl. With the vesting of Guruship in the Granth and the sangat, every dharmsāl with a recension of Guru Granth Sahib logically became a Gurdwara. From the eighteenth century onwards the term Gurdwara began to replace the term dharmsāl for the sacred space and the sacred institution of the Sikhs.[13]

In McLeod's hypothesis, external threat and internal influence in the form of Jats as the dominant component of the Sikh Panth become operative in the seventeenth century. We may leave his hypothesis alone for the present and turn to the sixteenth century Sikh Panth. There is credible evidence for the increasing number of Sikhs and the proliferation of local Sikh communities called sangats. Organizationally, they were linked with the Guru through his representatives called masands. They brought offerings from the sangats at the time of Baisakhi and Diwali when many of the Sikhs also came to see the Guru. The place where the Guru lived became a place of pilgrimage, with the potential of developing into a town. With their increasing resources, the Gurus founded towns. By definition, they were places where traders, shopkeepers, artisans, and labourers were numerically dominant. The affairs of the town were administered by the Guru directly or indirectly. As Guru Arjan says of Ramdaspur (later Amritsar), there was no fear of the tax-gatherers of the state in these autonomous places. Built by the resources of the Sikhs, they added to the resources of the Guru in both human and material terms.

The evidence available on the composition of the Sikh Panth in the sixteenth century indicates the presence of a wide range of castes, subcastes, and occupations. Among the eminent Sikhs of Guru Arjan, there was a *chandāl* who represented the lowest social background. There were Brahmans, too, among the eminent Sikhs of the Guru. There were Khatris and Suds, ironsmiths and carpenters. There were Jats too. The low castes figure prominently in the compositions of Guru Ram Das. If the eminent Sikhs of the Gurus are taken to be an index of the composition of the sixteenth century Sikh Panth, the Khatris rather than the Jats would appear to form the most important component. The Sikhs were not confined to the towns and villages of the province of Lahore. They were found in Kabul and Kashmir, Delhi and Agra, and other provinces of the Mughal empire. It may be safe to assume that the Sikhs living in the provincial capitals and other cities and towns of the Mughal empire were not agriculturists. In fact, they were mostly traders and shopkeepers. Their offerings in cash and kind contributed much to the Guru's treasury. Guru Ram Das refers to the wealth of his Sikhs and blessed them with earthly riches as much as with faith and liberation. The mansions which they occupied were sanctified; the caparisoned horses which they rode were sanctified. Obviously, there were affluent individuals among the Sikhs.[14]

Guru Nanak's Contrast with Kabir

In retrospect, we can see that the idea of bhakti was common to all the Vaishnavas and the sants but they cannot be treated as a single family. There were important differences between the Vaishnavas and the sants in terms of their doctrines and the social implications of their religious ideas. Indeed, there was significant differentiation even among the so-called sants in north India. A common core of teachings does not wholly account for the ideological systems they propounded. Their differences come into high relief if we keep in view the links between what they said and actually did in their lifetime, and between the origins and the development of the Panths associated with them.

The compositions of Kabir clearly indicate that he occupied a position independent of Islam and Hinduism. He was neither a Sūfī nor a Vaishnava. The link between his spiritual independence and his low social position has the merit of plausibility, but there is no evidence that he founded any institution or appointed any successor in his lifetime. He appears to conform to the sant of McLeod's definition. Institutionalization in his case appears to have started at the same time as his Vaishnavization after 1600. Those who invoked his authority had considerable freedom to accept or reject ideas according to their needs. Even so, the Kabir Panth was not wholly unrelated to Kabir's ideology. The 'liberating moment' was at least partially captured, even though he was Vaishnavized to fit into the traditional Hindu social order.

Guru Nanak presents a contrast to Kabir. Far from being opposed to institutionalization, he created institutions which served as the basis of later development. The institutions of Guruship, the sacred scripture, and the sacred space largely account for a well-organized Panth. McLeod's assumption that the sants were opposed to institutionalization is contradicted partly by his own statements about what Guru Nanak did in his lifetime. Instead of revising his definition of the sant, or placing Guru Nanak outside the sant tradition, McLeod postulates an increasing proportion of Jats in the Sikh community to explain the institutionalization of the Sikh Panth in the sixteenth century and its transformation later, minimizing the importance of both ideology and institutions. Despite some of their common concepts, Kabir and Guru Nanak appear to present a study in contrast in terms of organization, institutionalization and identity. At the beginning of the seventeenth century, when a panth in the name of Kabir had not yet come into existence, the Panth of Guru Nanak had already become 'a state within the state'.

Notes

1. John Stratton Hawley and Mark Juergensmeyer, *Songs of the Saints of India*, New York: Oxford University Press, 1988, pp. 3–7.
2. Karine Schomer and W.H. McLeod, eds, *The Sants: Studies in a Devotional Tradition of India*, Delhi: Motilal Banarsidass, 1987, pp. 1–6.
3. Generally, the sant tradition in the south is equated with the Varkari movement in Maharashtra. As the term Varkari itself suggests, pilgrimage to Pandharpur, with its temple dedicated to Vithoba, provided the common bond for the followers of the major and minor saints of Maharashtra. Despite the Vaishnava leanings of the Varkari movement, Namdev in particular is regarded as a sant to suggest a common ground of ideas and attitudes for the sants of the south and the north. If Kabir is regarded as the typical sant of the north, then the Sant tradition of the north can be seen as clearly moving away from Vaishnavism. Kabir rejected not only the incarnations of Vishnu but also Vishnu himself as the Supreme Deity. Worship of idols in temples was rejected equally emphatically. Though Kabir's influence on Guru Nanak is assumed by many, there was no link between them or their followers. In other words, the movements known after Kabir and Guru Nanak were independent of each other.

4. David N. Lorenzen, 'The Kabir-Panth and Social Protest', in Schomer and McLeod, eds, *The Sants*, pp. 281-303.
5. Linda Hess and Shukdev Singh, *The Bijak of Kabir*, San Francisco: North Point Press, 1983. Charlotte Vaudeville, *The Weaver Named Kabir*, New Delhi: Oxford University Press, 1997. J.S. Grewal, 'Kabir and the Kabir-Panthis', in J.S. Grewal, ed., *Religious Movements and Institutions in Medieval India*, New Delhi: Oxford University Press, 2006, pp. 383-409.
6. On the question of Kabir's ideology, especially whether it was Hindu or Islamic, there is the contemporary or near contemporary evidence of Ravidas, who lived in Benares itself, that Kabir was born in a Muslim family. But this does not mean that his ideology was Islamic. He subscribed to the idea of transmigration which was regarded as categorically heterodox even among the Sūfīs. Kabir was opposed to the killing of animals in ritual sacrifice, whether by a Mullā or a Brahman. Neither the *Qur'ān* nor the Vedas held for him a scriptural authority. He believed neither in Islam nor in Hinduism as a system of religious beliefs and practices (if we assume for the sake of argument that Hinduism was one system). Nevertheless, if we look at the whole set of Kabir's ideas it is possible to maintain that most of his ideas were closer to the Indic than to the Islamic tradition. But this is not the same thing as to say that he was a Hindu.
7. Sahib Singh, *Bhagat Bāṇī Steek Hissa Dūjā* (*Bāṇī Bhagat Ravidas Ji*), Amritsar: Singh Brothers, 1993 (7th rpt), p. 158.
8. Quoted by David N. Lorenzen, 'The Kabir Panth: Heretics to Hindus', in David N. Lorenzen, ed., *Religious Change and Cultural Domination*, Mexico: El Colegio de Mexico, 1981, p. 155.
9. For later legends about Kabir, including a reference to Priyadass commentary on Nabha Das' *Bhaktāmala*, see Lorenzen, ibid., pp. 156-60.
10. W.H. McLeod, 'The Development of the Sikh Panth', in Schomer and McLeod, eds, *The Sants*, pp. 229-49.
11. There is no doubt that Guru Nanak was thoroughly familiar with the beliefs and practices of the Jogīs. He refers to their ear-rings (*mundā* or *mundrā*), their cloak (*khinthā*), their blowing horn (*singī*), their object of concentration (*samyā*), their loin-cloth (*jangotā*), their bodies smeared in ash (*bhasam* or *bhabūt*), their objective of attaining to supranatural powers (*riddhī* or *siddhī*), their interest in herbs and alchemy (*rasāyaṇa*), their mode of salutation, their common meal (*bhandār*), and their twelve orders (*bhekh*). This does not mean that Guru Nanak appreciated the Jogīs. There is a longish composition of Guru Nanak, known as the *Siddh-Gosht*, in which he refutes the Jogīs on all possible points and presents his own path as the only valid one. Guru Nanak has no appreciation for

renunciation: 'Jog does not consist in the cloak, nor in the staff, nor in smearing the body with ash; it does not consist in wearing the ear-ring, nor in shaving the head, nor in blowing the horn. Living pure amidst the impurities of attachment is real *jog*'. To be liberated-in-life so as to take up social responsibilities was the most commendable objective for Guru Nanak. The idea of attaining liberation through physico-psychic practices was repugnant to Guru Nanak who believed in God's grace as the ultimate source of liberation. Ethical considerations remained relevant for Guru Nanak's conception of liberation.

12. J.S. Grewal, 'The Sikh Movement', in Grewal, ed., *Religious Movements and Institutions*, pp. 450–73.
13. J.S. Grewal, 'The Gurdwara', in Grewal, ed., *Religious Movements and Institutions*, pp. 533–47.
14. On the question of equality and differentiation among the followers of the protest movements of medieval India, both in the north and the south, the idea of equality was embodied in the conception of God as the sole creator of human beings: in theory, all had access to God and to liberation, irrespective of their religious, social or racial background. In the case of several movements, the path of liberation was open to women. In the case of the movement initiated by Guru Nanak, congregational worship and community kitchen were open to all his followers. Just as human beings were equal in the eyes of God, so were they equal in the eyes of the Guru. The Sikh sacred space remained an egalitarian space. The extent to which the idea of equality was translated into social and political terms is not clear. There was no restriction on change in occupation. There was no injunction against intercaste marriage and commensality. However, the patriarchal family and the monarchical form of government were taken as the given social and political institutions. All new spaces had to be created within their framework, and there was a tension between an egalitarian ideology and the inegalitarian institutions.

2. 'Raj Karega Khalsa'*

Much has been written on Guru Gobind Singh and his Khalsa but largely on the basis of later evidence. The first critical account of the Khalsa, based on contemporary and near contemporary evidence was published nearly four decades ago.[1] A chapter on the 'Chastening Baptism' raised a number of issues for a comprehensive treatment of the Khalsa: Guru Gobind Singh's position in the history of the Sikh movement, his world view, the purpose of instituting the Khalsa, the Baisakhi of 1699, the *rahit* prescribed for the Khalsa, and the question of Guruship. Our present purpose is to revisit the Khalsa on the basis of contemporary evidence.

GURU GOBIND SINGH'S IDENTIFICATION WITH HIS PREDECESSORS

Evidence from the *Dasam-Granth* leaves no doubt that Guru Gobind Singh identified himself with his predecessors, and with the Sikh tradition which appeared to be threatened by external forces. He was prepared to fight for its protection and propagation.

Guru Gobind Singh's consciousness of his position in the Sikh movement is reflected in the opening lines of the Sikh *Ardās* which come from the *Chandī di Vār*:

Remembering Bhagauti first, I invoke the name of Guru Nanak. Then I seek the aid of Guru Angad, Guru Amar Das and Guru Ram Das. I remember Guru Arjan, Guru Hargobind and Guru Har Rai. I meditate on Sri Guru Har Krishan whose sight removes all sorrow. All the nine treasures are obtained by remembering Guru Tegh Bahadur. In all situations they come to our aid.[2]

---

* 'Raj Karega Khalsa' has turned out to be very different from 'The Chastening Baptism', in *Guru Gobind Singh: A Biographical Study* (written jointly with S.S. Bal and published by the Panjab University, Chandigarh, in 1967, pp. 103–26, 182–9, 225–30) which I had thought of revising.

Another composition underlines that all the Gurus from Guru Nanak to Guru Tegh Bahadur were one. 'Nanak assumed the form of Angad and spread *dharm* in the world. Then he was named Amar Das, as one lamp is lighted from another. Before leaving the world, Amar Das passed on the gift he had received', and Ram Das became the Guru. Thus, Guru Nanak was regarded as Angad, and Angad was seen as Amar Das. Then Amar Das was called Ram Das. The fools regarded them as separate from one another, but the discerning *sādh*s (Sikhs) saw them all as one, and attained the highest spiritual state. Before Ram Das mingled with God, he gave Guruship to Arjan, and before Arjan left for the next world he made Hargobind the Guru who seated Har Rai in his position. Then his 'son' Har Krishan became the Guru and then Tegh Bahadur.[3] They were all one and, by implication, Guru Gobind Singh himself was one with them.

There is something special about Guru Tegh Bahadur. He wrought a great event in the Kaliyuga, laying down his life for the sake of sādhs without betraying any pain. He wrought this event for the sake of his faith or dharm, giving his head but not giving up his commitment. A display of supranatural powers does not behove the devotees of God. Breaking the pitcher of his body on the head of the master of Delhi, Guru Tegh Bahadur went to the abode of the True Master. He did something that no one else could do. The world became full of sorrow, and cries of grief were heard everywhere. In the heavens, however, there were shouts of praise.[4]

In the verses about Guru Tegh Bahadur occur the words '*tilak janjū rākhā prabh tā kā*'. One view is that these words refer to Guru Tegh Bahadur's own sacred mark and sacred thread. Another is that they refer to the sacred thread and sacred mark of the Brahmans who had come to him for help in the face of an offensive launched by Aurangzeb against the Hindus. There is a common belief among both Sikhs and Hindus that Guru Tegh Bahadur sacrificed his life for the protection of Hindu dharma.

However, the use of the words dharm and sādhs in the verses about Guru Tegh Bahadur would cover the Sikh faith and the Sikhs. It is stated explicitly in the *Bachittar Nātak* that Guru Nanak started his dharm in the Kaliyuga, showing the right path to all sādhs. Those who adopt his path do not suffer the misery of sins. Those who join his *panth*, their sins and miseries are washed away. Sorrow and suffering never trouble them and they do not get caught in the net of death and rebirth.⁵ This was the path propagated by Guru Nanak's successors and upheld by Guru Tegh Bahadur at the cost of his life. This was the tradition that had been handed down to Guru Gobind Singh, and this was the tradition he was duty bound to defend and propagate as a successor of Guru Nanak.

It is important to note here that Guru Gobind Singh was acutely conscious of external threat. In the *Benatī Chaupaī* there are expressions like 'destroy all our enemies'; 'kill all the enemies today'; 'save our *sevak*s and Sikhs and kill our enemies one by one'; 'give me protection now, save the Sikhs and destroy the un-Sikh'; 'kill all the enemies and the *mlechh* in the field of battle'. The author hammers the point that God alone is the refuge of all and devotion to him is the only right path. He explicitly states that God feels pain if the sants are in pain and he feels pleasure if the sādhs are happy.⁶ There is hardly any doubt that Sikhs are among these sants and sādhs, if not actually synonymous with them.

LITERARY USE OF VAISHNAVA AND SHAKTA TRADITIONS

For Guru Gobind Singh's determination to use physical force against his enemies we may turn to the 'incarnation' literature in the *Dasam-Granth*. The standard text of the *Dasam-Granth* has 1,428 pages. Over 600 of these are given to tales meant more to instruct than to please. About thirty-four pages are given to *Giān Prabodh* which relates to legendary kings and their *yajna*s, and the letter of Guru Gobind Singh, called the *Zafarnāma,* which was addressed to Aurangzeb in Persian verse. There are forty-six pages of devotional literature in the form of *Jāp, Akāl Ustat, Shabad*s, and *Savvyyā*s. As many as 455 pages are given to *Chaubīs Avtār* (twenty-four incarnations of Vishnu), mostly to Krishna, followed by Rama and Kalki. About 100 pages are given to the incarnations of Brahma and Rudra (Shiva). More than fifty pages cover the three versions related to Chandi and Durga. Closely related to incarnation literature are the *Bachittar Nātak* (Guru Gobind Singh's autobiographical account) and the *Shastar Nām Mālā* which relates to weapons of war. Together, they cover 126 pages. Thus, 733 pages of the *Dasam-Granth* get related directly or indirectly to incarnation. It is quite obvious that much of the *Dasam-Granth* is concerned with avtārs.

It must be underlined that Guru Gobind Singh did not subscribe to the idea of divine incarnation. At the opening of the *Chandī Charitra Ukti Bilās*, God is the primal being, eternal, limitless, unknowable, indestructible, and garbless. He is the creator of Shiva and Shakti, the four Vedas, the day and the night, the sun and the moon, the three *guṇa*s and the five elements. He is the creator of strife between gods and demons, and their incessant struggle. He himself remains aloof and enjoys the show.[7] At the opening of the *Vār Srī Bhagautī Jī Kī* (better known as *Chandī dī Vār*), it is stated that God created the double-edged sword (*khaṇḍā*) first and then he created the universe. He created Brahma, Vishnu, and Mahesh. He created the earth and the sky, the oceans and the mountains. He created gods and demons, and their mutual strife. Then comes the statement:

You yourself created Durga to destroy the demons. From you Rama received the strength to kill the ten-headed (Ravana) with his arrows. From you Krishna received the strength to catch Kansa by the hair and to dash him to the ground.[8]

At the end of the *Ram Avtar* it is stated: 'Leaving all other doors I have come to your door; it is for you to honour the hope of protection: Gobind is your slave'. This statement is preceded by the well-known stanza which says:

Ever since I have caught hold of your feet, I have found none worthy of my glance. Many talk of Ram and Rahim, of the Puranas and the *Qur'ān*, but I do not believe anyone. The Smritis, Shastras and Vedas talk of many mysteries but not for me.

It is through the grace of 'the wielder of the sword' (*sri asipāni*) that the work has been completed.[9]

Towards the end of the *Krishan Avtār* it is stated that what matters in life is not renunciation but loving devotion to God. The son of a 'Chhatrī' in particular should have nothing to do with asceticism; his cherished wish should be to die fighting on the battlefield. The tenth book of the *Bhagvata Purana* was rendered into *bhākhā* with no other purpose than that of inspiring *dharmyudh*. Worthy of praise in the world is he who has God on his lips and the intent of war in his heart.[10]

The *Jāp* states at the outset that God has no physical form or features, and he has no caste. None can describe His form, complexion or garb;

He is the eternal and self-effulgent being whose power has no limit. The *Jāp* ends with the statement that God pervades all the four directions; He is self-created, eternal, compassionate and omnipresent.[11] The *Akāl Ustat* opens with the statement: 'I have the protection of the immortal being (*akāl purkh*), the protection of all-steel (*sarbloh*).' It ends with the statement that God is the king of all vegetation, land and water, and He is everywhere as the treasure of compassion; the light of His perfection shines everywhere, and His grace embraces all the seven skies and the seven worlds below the earth.[12]

The *Akāl Ustat*, in praise of the immortal being, gives expression to the idea that everything in the universe emanates from Him and is finally absorbed in Him. Just as millions of sparks rise from the fire and fall back into it, as millions of particles rise from the dust and fall back into it, as millions of waves rise in water and merge in it again, so the multitudinous forms in the universe arise from the one eternal being and are absorbed in Him.[13] Without remembering God, no means are of any avail: neither bathing at sacred places, charities and modes of meticulous worship, nor the recitation of Vedas, Puranas, the Qur'ān, and other Semitic scriptures; neither ascetical practices nor knowledge.[14]

In the *Shabad*s, metaphors from *sanyās* and *yogā* are used to express Sikh religious ideas and values. The Sikh is instructed to practise such a sanyās that the house becomes a forest and *udās* (detachment) enters the mind and to practise such a yogā that truth becomes the blowing horn (*singī*), good conduct the rosary, and meditation the ashes with which the body is smeared. Appropriate the feet of the Primal Being and wake up from the sleep of attachment.[15] Pray to God that He may preserve your honour. Regard none other than God as the creator who does not take birth and who is eternal.[16] How can He be conceived in a human form whom the *siddha*s have failed to see despite their deep meditation? Recognize none other than God who alone creates and destroys and who knows everything. There is no refuge without the Name; there is no escape from Him who has mastered the fourteen worlds. From Guru Gobind Singh's point of view, every known deity was God's creation. Therefore, he underscores the oneness of God in rather strong terms. Ram and Rahim, whose name you recite, cannot lead you to liberation; Brahma, Vishnu, and Rudra, the sun and the moon, are subject to annihilation. The Vedas, the Puranas, and the

Qur'ān call him unknowable; Indar, Phunindar, and Munindar meditated on Him for ages but without seeing Him. He who has no form and no colour, how can He be called Sham? You will escape death only when you catch hold of the Lord's feet.[17]

One particular shabad has a special significance. The idea of God's incarnation as Krishna brings no honour to God and adds nothing to His greatness or glory. Kal alone is the doer who creates and destroys innumerable forms from the beginning to the end, to whom praise and blame are alike, who knows no friend or enemy, why would He become the charioteer of Arjan? He who has no father, no mother, and no caste, He who has no son or grandson, why would He become Devki's son? He who has created all gods and demons, who is pervasive in all directions, what praise would it be if He is called Murari?[18]

To underline the exclusive validity of his own faith, Guru Gobind Singh in his savvyyās talks of futile beliefs (*phokat dharm*) and futile acts (*phokat karm*), which include the belief in traditional scriptures, deities, and religious practices. The Vedas and the Semitic scriptures have not understood the mystery of the formless and the eternal, the merciful and the compassionate one who is lodged in every human frame.[19] Why do you worship stones? There is no God in stones. The jogī begs from door to door to be disillusioned in the end, for nothing is gained without loving devotion.[20] Some have tied *thākur* to their necks and others regard Mahesh as God; some insist that God is in the temple and others that He is in the mosque; some call Him Rama or Krishna, and believe in avtārs. These futile beliefs should be discarded: the creator alone should be regarded as God.[21] They who claimed to be avtārs on this earth died in the end with regret.[22] What the Vedas and the Semitic scriptures could never understand was revealed by God as the Guru.[23]

Evidently, Guru Gobind Singh believes in one God who is transcendent and immanent at one and the same time, who is omnipotent and omnipresent, who is just and compassionate towards all, and who is specially concerned with His devotees. The traditional deities like Brahma, Vishnu, Shiva, and Durga are seen as God's creatures who are subject to destruction. The idea of divine incarnation is discarded as fantastic and futile. The so-called avtārs like Rama and Krishna are seen as God's creatures, like human beings, and not as divine incarnations.

It is absolutely clear that the relevance of gods and goddesses in general and of Krishna, Rama, and Chandi or Durga in particular for the mission of Guru Gobind Singh did not arise from any belief in their divinity. They are commendable for three reasons. In the struggle between good and evil, they supported the forces of good. They used physical force in their fight against evil. They demonstrated the physical and moral qualities of great warriors on the battlefield. All these three aspects are emphasized in the *Krishan Avtār*, the *Rām Avtār*, and the three versions related to Chandi or Durga.

Declaration of Guru Gobind Singh's Mission

The autobiographical part of the *Bachittar Nātak*, called *Apnī Kathā*, acquires a special relevance in this context. It opens with an invocation to 'Sri Kharag', the power of God symbolized by the sword. The praise of God is presented in terms which occur in the works already cited. He created and destroyed millions of Krishnas and Ramas; millions of Muhammads appeared on the earth and died in the end. All gods and demons who came into the world eventually died, and so did, Ramas, and Krishnas. There is only one refuge for all created beings. Nothing else and no one else can save you: neither Krishna nor Vishnu, neither Rama nor Rahim, neither Brahma nor Shiva, neither austerities nor *mantras*.[24]

The author traces the genealogical antecedents of the Bedis and the Sodhis to Rama in order to make the point that the Bedis owed a debt of rulership to the Sodhis, which was to be repaid in the Kaliyuga. The Guruship (spiritual rulership) that started with the Bedi Nanak and came to the Sodhi Ram Das, and remained in his family, was in accordance with this legend which explained and justified the development.[25] Nevertheless, the author (who is supposed to be Guru Gobind Singh) had a special mission to undertake.

In Guru Gobind Singh's presentation of mythology, God tells him that he first created the demons who became so intoxicated with power that they forgot their creator. In their place, the gods were created but they too got entangled, and adopted the position of God, like Mahadev, Vishnu, and Brahma. Similarly, the Siddhas and Sadhs started their own panths. The Rishis compiled their own Smritis and made them current. Brahma created the four Vedas and people followed the mode of worship prescribed by them. Others who find specific mention in this context are Datt, Gorakh, Ramanand, and Muhammad. They all ignored the true Name, and failed to recognize God.[26]

God called the author to his presence in order to send him into the world, saying: 'I have made you my son and assigned to you the task of propagating the panth. Spread true dharm everywhere and stop the people from doing foolish things'. The author made the humble submission that the Panth could be propagated in the world only with the divine support. Significantly, he gives the warning: 'they who call me God shall fall into the pit of hell'. 'Regard me as his slave; make no mistake about it. I am the slave of the Parm Purkh and I have come to see his sport. I shall proclaim what he has told me to, and I shall not remain silent (for fear of anyone) in this mortal world'. The author makes it very clear that God has sent him into the world for the sake of dharm: 'spread dharm everywhere; destroy the enemy and the oppressor'. The sādhs should understand very clearly why he has taken birth: 'I have come to spread dharm, to raise the sants and to root out all their enemies'.[27] This becomes virtually a declaration of waging war against the enemies of the Sikh tradition.

When the author reached the age of *dharm-karm*, his father left for the other world. The *rāj* and *sāj* became his responsibility and he propagated dharm according to the best of his capacity. Then he shifted to Paonta and Fateh Shah attacked him. The Guru was victorious in the battle at Bhangani which is described in detail. He returned to Kahlur and founded Anandpur. Those who did not fight at Bhangani were turned out and those who had fought valiantly were well rewarded. Later, the author personally took part in a battle against the Mughal *faujdār*s, using his musket first and then the bow and arrows. This battle was followed by the expeditions of the Khānzādah and Husain Khan against the author. Both of them failed and Aurangzeb sent Prince Mu'azzam to Madar Des. Many people left the author and went into the hills. Those who remained with the Guru came to no harm whatever. 'They who turn away from the Guru, their faces are blackened in this world and the next'. The Guru's opponent dies the death of a dog and goes to hell. The sādhs who take refuge in God remain safe like the tongue between the teeth. Their enemies are destroyed.[28]

The dharmyudh of the *Bachittar Nātak* is similar to the struggle between the gods and the demons. 'The person whose deeds are that of a *sādh* is called *devtā* in the world. They who perpetrate misdeeds in the world, they are called *asur* by all'.[29] The author is on the side of sādhs and sants, and they are all under God's protection. 'In all ages God has raised the *sādhs* and killed their enemies'. He has revealed his concern for the *bhagat*s and resolved all their crises. 'He has supported me as his slave and has saved me with his own hand'.[30] Divine protection, as much as divine sanction, is behind the mission of Guru Gobind Singh. The sādhs, sants, and bhagats of the *Bachittar Nātak* are his Sikhs. They are already in the dharmyudh.

The evidence of his *hukamnama*s reveals clearly that in the 1690s Guru Gobind Singh was supported by Sikhs from far and near with human and material resources. In May 1691, he acknowledged that a *hundī* worth 900 rupees, eight pieces of cloth, turbans, and swords sent by the *sangat* of Dhaka had been duly received. Over a score of Sikhs are named in this hukamnama and they were asked to send forty embroidered turbans worth 1600 rupees, 30 shields worth 300 rupees and two shields worth a hundred rupees. It is added that 'Dhaka is our house'. In February 1694, Bhai Sangatia was asked to come at the time of Baisakhi with the sangat and to bring with him a musket-maker (*tupak-saz*). At the beginning of August in 1696, Bhai Taloka and Bhai Rama, the sons of Phul, are asked to come with a body of horsemen, adding that 'your house is my own'. At the same time Bhai Sukhia (of Bhai Rupa) was asked to come with foot musketeers and horsemen, adding that 'the house of Bhai Rupa is my own'.[31]

In this context, the stanzas written by Guru Gobind Singh about his followers acquire a new significance. 'I have won battles with their support. With their support have I disbursed charities'. The Guru goes on to add that all his enemies had been killed with their support. There were millions of ordinary men like him but the support of his followers had ensured for him a position of eminence. He liked to serve them, and no one else. All his charities were meant for them. Everything that he possessed belonged to them.[32]

Removal of the Masands

There is no indication in the *Bachittar Nātak* as to who among the Sikhs were supporting Guru Gobind Singh in his dharmyudh. In the last decade of the seventeenth century, there were three broad categories of Sikhs: the followers of the rival claimants to Guruship, the followers of Masands, and the *khalsa* Sikhs. The rival claimants would certainly not support him. The followers of the Masands too were unlikely. It was probably the third category of Sikhs who gave support to Guru Gobind Singh.

The term khalsa occurs in a composition of Kabir included in the Granth Sahib. It expresses disillusionment with the pandit's *karmkand* based on the Vedas and the Puranas, the jogī's ascetic practices and renunciation, and the Vaishnava practice of ritual dance and music as a form of worship. All of them were alien to the way of bhakti. 'They who know the way of loving devotion (*prem-bhakti*) have become *khālsā*'. Only they can attain to liberation.[33] The khalsa of Kabir is thus a bhakta or a sant, a liberated person, as distinguished from the pandit, the jogī, and the Vaishnava.

The word *khālas* occurs in a Savvyyā of Guru Gobind Singh. He who remembers throughout day and night the master of light and thinks only of him, who is adorned with perfect love and trust and does not believe in fasting, tombs or *marhī*s, who recognizes the Only One and does not perform conventional practices like pilgrimage, charity, austerities or ritual worship, in whose heart burns the light of the Perfect One—he is the purest of the pure (*khālas*).[34] This comes very close to Kabir's conception of the khalsa.

However, this was not the only connotation of the khalsa in the seventeenth century. In a hukamnama of Guru Hargobind, 'the sangat of the east' is 'the khalsa of the Guru'. A hukamnama of Guru Tegh Bahadur refers to the sangat of Pakpatten as 'the khalsa of Sri Guru ji'. This sangat was in existence before the time of Guru Tegh Bahadur. In a hukamnama of Guru Gobind Singh, dated 12 March 1699, the sangat of Machhiwara is called 'my khalsa'. Significantly, the sangat of the village Phaphre is referred to as *sahlang* in a hukamnama dated 25 April 1699.[35] The khalsa and sahlang, thus, refer to two categories of Sikhs in the time of Guru Gobind Singh.

The evidence of the *Dabistān-i Mazāhib* clarifies the distinction. In the time of Guru Arjan, people had begun to be enrolled as Sikhs of the Guru through the mediation of the masands. In the time of Guru Hargobind, the Jatt masands had Brahmans and Khatris as their sahlangs and *melī*s who were initiated into the Sikh faith by the masands.[36] The term khalsa, therefore, was reserved for individuals or sangats directly affiliated to the Guru, having been initiated into the Sikh faith by one of the Gurus in the acknowledged line of succession from Guru Nanak to Guru Gobind Singh.

The followers of Masands were a new category of Sikhs added to the khalsa in the seventeenth century. Introduced into the organization by Guru Amar Das, the representatives of the Guru had become important in the time of Guru Ram Das and Guru Arjan. The use of the term 'Ramdas' for the Guru's representative reflects the importance he acquired in the time of Guru Ram Das. The use of the term masand in the time of Guru Arjan indicates his enhanced status. According to the *Dabistān*, 'since the Sikhs regarded the Guru as the *Sachcha Padshah*, that is, the True King, the latter's representative is known as *masand*, and also Ram Das'. The author goes on to add that the word masand was derived from *masnad-i 'āla* or the elevated seat used by the Afghan rulers for their nobles.[37]

In the early seventeenth century, the masands played an important role among the Sikhs. According to the *Dabistān*, every Sikh used to put together money according to his resources and take it to the masand for being passed on to the Guru as a part of the offerings or *bhet* for him. The masand was not expected to keep anything for himself if he had his means of livelihood. He took the offerings to the Guru in the month of Baisakh when all the masands used to assemble at the Guru's court. 'Of their *melīs*, whoever so desires and is possessed of the means of travel, goes with the *masand* to the Guru. At the time of departure, the Guru confers a turban on each of the *masands*'.[38] Their services were thus suitably acknowledged and appreciated. The author of the *Dabistān* knew some of the masands of Guru Hargobind personally. The information he gives on them indicates their importance, their dedication to the Guru, and their autonomy.[39]

By the time of Guru Gobind Singh the attitude of the masands had changed. He bracketed them with jogīs and others, and criticized them very severely. If anyone went to the masands they told him that if he brought everything in his house as offering they would enable him to meet God. If anyone wished to serve the masands, they would tell him to bring everything in his kitchen to them as food; they expected that he should think of them all the time and never think of anyone else. They were not pleased without receiving, but when it came to giving they ran away during the night. They put oil in their eyes and shed tears before the people. They served dainty food to their rich followers, but they did not offer anything to the poor even if they begged. They did not show their face to the poor Sikhs. They never sang the praises of God, but fleeced the ignorant people. In constant pursuit of wealth, they lost merit in this world and the next.[40]

The evidence of the hukamnamas issued from March 1699 to February 1702 suggests that Guru Gobind Singh dispensed with the mediacy of the masands. The khalsa of Machhiwara were told not to recognize the authority of the masands and Bhai Kalyan Rai was asked to bring *golak, dasvandh,* and *mannat* personally to the Guru. The Sikhs of the sangat of Sarangdeo were told that they had become 'my khalsa' and they should come to the Guru at the time of Diwali; they should themselves bring their offerings and should not hand them over to someone else. The Sikhs of the sangat of Patan Faridke (Pakpattan), who were the Guru's khalsa, were told to bring their offerings personally to the Guru at the time of Baisakhi and not to recognize the authority of any masand. Three turbans were also sent to them with 'robes of honour' or *sirpāo*. They were again instructed not to hand over their offerings to any masand; whatever they had put together they were to keep with themselves and bring it personally when they came to the Guru's presence; those who could not come, were to send the amount through a hundī. 'The Sikh of the Guru shall not condole with any *masand* or *masandia*'. The khalsa sangat of Naushehra was told to bring their offerings personally at the time of Holi and not to condole with any masand or masandia. The khalsa sangat of Dasuha was given the same instructions. Bhai Mihar Chand, the *peshkār* of a *khufia-navīs*, who was a khalsa of the Guru, was told to have no association with a masand or a masandia. Similarly, Bhai Mihar Chand, Dharam Chand, and Karam Chand were told not to have any association with any masand or masandia, nor to give any recognition to them. A similar hukamnama was sent to the khalsa sangat of Pirag. Bhai Bindraban and Gulal Chand of Dhaka were given similar instructions. The same instructions were sent to the khalsa sangats of Naushehra and Rupayana.[41]

The Khalsa shall Rule

Before the death of Guru Gobind Singh, 'the Khalsa of the Guru' became 'the Khalsa of Sri Vaheguruji'. This rather imperceptible transformation had something to do with the political status of the Khalsa. In any case, there is contemporary evidence on both these points.

In a hukamnama of Guru Gobind Singh, dated 3 February 1708, the sangat of Benares is referred to as *'Vaheguruji da Khalsa'*. In the hukamnamas of the time of Banda Bahadur, the sangats of Bhai Rupa and Jaunpur are referred to as *'Akal Purkh jio da Khalsa'*. In the hukamnamas of Mata Sundari, the phrase used is *'Sri Akal Purkh ji ka Khalsa'* as well as *'Sri Vaheguruji ka Khalsa'*. In the hukamnamas of Mata Sahib Devi the phrase used is *'Sri Akal Purkh ji ka Khalsa'*. A hukamnama issued from Ramdaspur on 12 April 1759, refers to *'Sat Sri Akal Purkh ji ka Khalsa'* as the issuing authority. Thus, whereas in the seventeenth century the khalsa were 'the Guru's khalsa' or 'my khalsa', before the death of Guru Gobind Singh they became *'Vaheguruji da Khalsa'* and subsequently the Khalsa of Vaheguruji, Akal Purkh, Sri Akal Purkh or Sat Sri Akal Purkh. Related earlier to the Guru directly, the Khalsa were now related directly to God.[42]

There is a manuscript in the Library of Guru Nanak Dev University, Amritsar, that was compiled in 1718–19. It contains, among others, a work called *Nasīhatnāma*, professedly the answer given by Guru Gobind Singh to the question posed by Bhai Nand Lal about what the Sikhs should and should not do. It has been suggested by W.H. McLeod that the original *Nasīhatnāma* was composed within a few years of Guru Gobind Singh's death. Like many other scholars, he had believed for a long time that the genre called Rahitnama came into currency several decades after the death of Guru Gobind Singh. Therefore, he calls the *Nasīhatnāma* 'a dramatic find'. It has been argued more recently, that the *Nasīhatnāma* contains nothing to go against the assumption that it was composed in the lifetime of Guru Gobind Singh between 1699 and 1708. Addressed to the Sādh, the Sikh, the Khalsa, and the Singh at one and the same time, it underlines the importance of *nām*, *dān*, and *isnān* for the followers of the Guru who held a crucial importance for the Sikhs. The Shabad and Gurbāṇī are next in importance to the Guru. Daily kīrtan and *kathā* in the *dharmsāl* is followed by the performance of *bhog* and *ardās* and distribution of *kaṛhā parshād*. The *Nasīhatnāma* emphasizes the importance of ethics as well as the necessity of right belief and the right mode of worship. There is hardly any doubt that it embodies the ethical and religious norms of the Sikh tradition going back to the time of Guru Nanak.

However, there is a new feature in the *Nasīhatnāma*. The duties of the Khalsa include bearing arms, riding the horse, fighting in the front, killing *khāns* and subduing the Turks. The aspiration is clearly political. Significantly, the well-known lines of the Sikh anthem occur in the *Nasīhatnāma*:

> *Rāj karegā khālsā ākī rahe nā koī*
> *Khuār hoe sabh milenge bache saran jo hoe*

'The Khalsa shall rule and none shall remain obdurate. Humbled in the end, all shall join (the Khalsa) and only they shall be saved who take refuge (in the Khalsa)'. Almost certainly, this prophecy comes from the days of Guru Gobind Singh.[43]

Numismatic evidence confirms this inference. The first Sikh coin was struck in 1710 as a declaration of Sikh sovereignty within two years of Guru Gobind Singh's death. The inscription on the coin of the second year refers to the sword of Nanak as the helper and the victory of Gobind, the king of kings, due to the grace of God. It refers also to the throne of the Khalsa.[44] It is unlikely that the idea of the sovereignty of the Khalsa originated with Banda Bahadur. The idea had become familiar to the Khalsa in the time of Guru Gobind Singh and they tried to give it a tangible form in the inscription of the first Sikh coin.

The Evidence of Sainapat

Finally, we may consider the evidence of an author who was a contemporary of Guru Gobind Singh and wrote his work within three years of his death, namely Sainapat, the author of the *Gursobha*. He equated the institution of the Khalsa with the removal of the Masands first of all. Their removal amounted to purification of the (Sikh) world. Guru Gobind Singh proclaimed that 'the *sangat* as a whole from the beginning to the end is my Khalsa'. The offerings or *kār bhet* meant for the Guru were not to be given to anyone else. Those who refused to become the khalsa of the Guru were 'non-believers' or *dharia*s. One became a khalsa by abandoning the masand, and taking refuge with the Guru. The khalsa sangat was the only true sangat. When the Mughal authorities in Delhi asked the Sikhs to explain what was meant by khalsa, the Sikhs told them that the Gurus used to have deputies or *nāib*s called masands; they were all removed by Guru Gobind Singh and, consequently, all the Sikhs became his Khalsa.[45]

The removal of masands was inseparably linked with the institution of the Khalsa. On the day of Baisakhi, Guru Gobind Singh gave *khande kī pahul* (baptism by the double-edged sword) to his Khalsa to increase their charismatic splendour or *tej* and to make them powerful as Singhs. They were to keep their *kesh* uncut and discard the practice of *bhaddar* (as a part of the mourning rites). The Khalsa Singhs were to remain armed with five weapons: the matchlock, the bow, the spear, the sword (*shamsher, tarwar, teg*), and the dagger. The proof of becoming a true Khalsa was to die fighting on the battlefield. It is interesting to note the gradual, almost imperceptible, transition from the Sikh to the Khalsa, the Khalsa Sikh, the Khalsa Singh, and eventually to the Singh, so that the Sikh and the Singh are equated. The Khalsa Singh has no equal. His salutation is '*Vaheguruji ka Khalsa, Vaheguruji ki fateh*'.[46] The Khalsa belong to God and their victory is God's victory.

The institution of the Khalsa in Sainapat's presentation is linked with what came to be known as the rahit of the Khalsa. Apart from taking the pahul, keeping unshorn hair, bearing arms and the epithet Singh, the Khalsa were not to smoke. Significantly, the essential features of the earlier Sikh way of life are emphasized in the Khalsa rahit. Sainapat underlines the importance of singing the praises of God in congregation. The Khalsa recite the Name and they are dedicated to the Name. They take refuge with God, the sole creator of the universe who is all pervasive. Remembering God is the source of liberation for the Khalsa. No liberation is possible without the Guru. One meets the Guru in the *sat-sangat*. Contemplation of the shabad and love of the Name remove sorrow and illusion. No liberation is possible without loving devotion to God and the Name. Hence, by serving the true Guru, one gains peace; the perfect Guru is found in the sat-sangat.[47]

Guru Gobind Singh instructed the Khalsa not to have any association with 'the five', and never to join them in their funerals and marriages. Among 'the five' would obviously be the masands and their followers. One category specifically mentioned by Sainapat is that of *sir-gumman* (those who pluck their hair?).[48] The others in all probability were the followers of Prithi Chand and his successors, known as the Miṇas, the followers of Dhir Mal and his successors, called Dhir Mallias, and the followers of Ram Rai and his successors, called Ram Raiyas. They did not belong to the khalsa category, but they could not be removed. They could only be excommunicated.[49]

Sainapat has no hesitation in referring to the activity of the Khalsa as political. Towards the end of his work, he refers to the rehabilitation of Anandgarh in terms suggestive of political power. It can be argued that Sainapat is reiterating the prophecy of '*raj karega khalsa*' which had become current in the time of Guru Gobind Singh.

According to the *Gursobha*, only a day before his death the Khalsa wanted to know from Guru Gobind Singh as to who would guide them in his place. The Guru referred to Shabad-Bāṇī as the eternal Guru and to Khalsa as the Guru's visible form.[50] Personal Guruship, thus, yielded place to Guruship of the Granth and the Panth before Guru Gobind Singh's death in 1708.

Continuity and Change

Contemporary evidence does not provide detailed information on all aspects of the Khalsa but it provides enough evidence on its salient features. Evidence from the *Vār Srī Bhagautī Jī Kī*, *Bachittar Nātak*, and *Benatī Chaupaī* reveals Guru Gobind Singh's identification with his predecessors and the Sikh tradition, and his acute awareness of external threat to this tradition. His great appreciation for Guru Tegh Bahadur's martyrdom reveals his own determination to defend the Sikh tradition at all costs. The ideal of martyrdom was built into the institution of the Khalsa.

As stated earlier, evidence from the *Chandī Charitra Ukti Bilas*, *Vār Srī Bhagautī Jī Kī*, *Rām Avtār*, *Krishan Avtār*, the Jāp, the *Akāl Ustat*, the Shabads, and the Savvyyās leaves no doubt that Guru Gobind Singh believed in One Supreme Being who created entities like Brahma, Vishnu, Shiva, and Durga, and who did not appear in the form of any avtār. The so-called avtārs like Rama and Krishna were human beings, like Guru Gobind Singh himself. Like Durga, they represented the forces of good, used physical force against the forces of evil, and showed martial prowess. These aspects were relevant for Guru Gobind Singh's own position.

The autobiographical part of the *Bachittar Nātak* makes it absolutely clear that the only object of worship for Guru Gobind Singh was the One Supreme Being. The worship of the One Supreme Being was established by Guru Nanak for the Kaliyuga and this tradition was cherished by his successors, including Guru Gobind Singh. He was divinely commissioned to spread this dharm and to destroy its enemies. The process had already started and he had divine protection for his dharmyudh. He patronized those who supported him and punished those who betrayed his cause. The evidence of his hukamnamas makes it evident that he received support from the category of Sikhs known as the khalsa, that is, the Sikhs who were initiated into the faith by Guru Nanak and his acknowledged successors and whose descendants were linked with Guru Gobind Singh directly. The stanzas written in praise of the Sikhs embody Guru Gobind Singh's appreciation for this category of Sikhs. Their welfare and their future was his primary concern.

Evidence from the Guru Granth Sahib shows that the term khalsa was used by Kabir for a person liberated through loving devotion to God. In a Savvyyā of Guru Gobind Singh the word khālas is used in the same sense. However, in the hukamnamas of Guru Hargobind, Guru Tegh Bahadur, and Guru Gobind Singh, the term khalsa is used for the Sikh as against the sahlang. The evidence of the *Dabistān-i Mazāhib* shows that the term sahlang, or meli, was used for a person who was initiated into the Sikh faith by a masand. The masands formed an important link between the Guru and the Sikhs, and their services were suitably acknowledged and appreciated. Some of the known masands of the time of Guru Hargobind were dedicated to him but they also enjoyed a large degree of autonomy, presumably due to their considerable resources. Evidence from the Savvyyās of Guru Gobind Singh shows that the masands were no longer dedicated to the Guru and they were neglecting their religious duties as well as the poor Sikhs. The hukamnamas of Guru Gobind Singh make it very clear that the mediacy of the masands was dispensed with. In other words, all the Sikhs were made the khalsa of Guru Gobind Singh. By implication, the Minas, the Dhir Mallias, and the Ram Raiyas were not recognized as Sikhs.

The evidence of a hukamnama of Guru Gobind Singh shows that 'the Khalsa of the Guru' had become 'the Khalsa of Sri Vaheguruji' before his death. This is confirmed by the hukamnamas of Banda Bahadur, Mata Sundari, Mata Sahib Devi and the Khalsa. The *Nasīhatnāma* indicates that the establishment of Sikh rule had become a belief of the Khalsa during the lifetime of Guru Gobind Singh.

The *Gursobha* leaves no doubt about the removal of the masands for establishing Guru Gobind Singh's direct link with all the Sikhs, making them his Khalsa. A fresh initiation through khande dī pahul was introduced. The baptized Khalsa was given the title 'Singh'; he was to bear arms and to keep his hair uncut; his salutation was *Vaheguruji ka Khalsa, Vaheguruji ki fateh*. Loving devotion to God was the primary duty of the Khalsa. They were not to smoke. They were not to have any association with five categories of people. The masands with their followers and the sirgum are specifically mentioned. The other three categories could almost certainly be the Miṇas, the Dhir Mallias, and the Ram Raiyas. Before his death, Guru Gobind Singh declared that Guruship henceforth was vested in Shabad-Bāṇī and the Khalsa. The Khalsa were meant to be sovereign.

Thus, contemporary evidence on the Khalsa clarifies a number of issues. Guru Gobind Singh identified himself completely with the Sikh movement, so completely indeed that he was determined to carry it forward against all odds. In his uncompromising monotheism there was no room for gods and goddesses and no scope for incarnation. But he appreciated the legendary and heroic figures for their martial prowess and their fight against evil. He declared that his own mission was to protect the pious and to destroy the wicked. His followers belonged to the first category and their enemies to the second. The chances of success lay in transforming his followers into a political community. The removal of intermediaries and the excommunication of the sectarians made the Khalsa a coherent entity. A new form of initiation, a new appearance, new aspirations, and a new sense of unity transformed the Khalsa into a political community with a strong conviction that their destiny was to hold political power for protecting and promoting the dispensation of Guru Nanak. The end of personal Guruship with the vesting of Guruship in Shabad-Bāṇī and Khalsa came as the culmination of the Sikh movement to enable the Khalsa to stand on their feet as a political community committed to uphold and propagate the Sikh tradition in the world.

Notes

1. J.S. Grewal and S.S. Bal, *Guru Gobind Singh: A Biographical Study*, Chandigarh: Panjab University, 1967, pp. 103–26.
2. Rattan Singh Jaggi and Gursharan Kaur Jaggi, eds, *Sri Dasam-Granth Sahib*, 5 vols, New Delhi: Gobind Sadan, 1999, vol. I, p. 314.
3. Ibid., vol. I, pp. 142, 144. The idea that all Gurus were one had become current by the early seventeenth century. Bhai Gurdas gives expression to this idea, and the author of the *Dabistān-i Mazāhib* takes notice of its prevalence among the Sikhs.
4. *Sri Dasam-Granth Sahib*, vol. I, p. 144.
5. Ibid., p. 142.
6. *Sri Dasam-Granth Sahib*, vol. V, p. 670.
7. *Sri Dasam-Granth Sahib*, vol. I, p. 172.
8. Ibid., p. 314.
9. Ibid., p. 682.
10. *Sri Dasam-Granth Sahib*, vol. II, p. 792.
11. *Sri Dasam-Granth Sahib*, vol. I, pp. 2 and 28.
12. Ibid., pp. 30 and 102.
13. Ibid., p. 54. The stanzas which precede this one are well known for underscoring the unity of mankind in all diversity. *Sri Dasam-Granth Sahib*, vol. I, p. 52. Quoted by themselves they give a different impression. They make better sense if read in conjunction with the idea of emanation and absorption.
14. *Sri Dasam-Granth Sahib*, vol. I, pp. 40, 42, 48, 68, 94.
15. *Sri Dasam-Granth Sahib*, vol. III, p. 382.
16. Ibid., p. 384.
17. Ibid., p. 386.
18. Ibid., p. 384.
19. Ibid., p. 388.
20. Ibid., p. 394.
21. Ibid., p. 392.
22. Ibid., p. 394.
23. Ibid., p. 392.
24. *Sri Dasam-Granth Sahib*, vol. I, pp. 108, 116, 118, 120. The term *Bachittar Nātak* in the *Dasam-Granth* is used for a number of compositions, including *Apnī Kathā*.
25. *Sri Dasam-Granth Sahib*, vol. I, pp. 138–44.
26. Ibid., pp. 146–8.
27. Ibid., pp. 148–50, 152.
28. Ibid., pp. 156–88.

29. Ibid., p. 126.
30. Ibid., pp. 188–90.
31. Ganda Singh, ed., *Hukamnāme Guru Sāhibān, Mātā Sāhibān, Banda Singh Ate Khalsa Ji De*, Patiala: Punjabi University, 1967, pp. 140–1, 144–9.
32. *Sri Dasam-Granth Sahib*, vol. III, p. 400.
33. Bhai Jodh Singh, ed., *Bāṇī Bhagat Kabir Ji Steek*, Patiala: Punjabi University, 1993 (3rd edn), p. 124.
34. *Sri Dasam-Granth Sahib*, vol. III, p. 382.
35. Singh, ed., *Hukamnāme*, pp. 66–7, 76–7, 152–3, 155.
36. J.S. Grewal and Irfan Habib, eds, *Sikh History from Persian Sources*, New Delhi: Tulika and Indian History Congress, 2001, p. 67.
37. Ibid., pp. 66 and 72.
38. Ibid., p. 67.
39. Ibid., pp. 72–6.
40. *Sri Dasam-Granth Sahib*, vol. III, pp. 396–9.
41. Singh, ed., *Hukamnāme*, pp. 152–3, 159, 160–9, 170–3, 175–7, 179.
42. Ibid., pp. 190–7, 200–3, 205–7, 214–17, 222–3, 226–7, 232–3.
43. For a study of the *Nasīhatnāma* in some detail, see Karamjit K. Malhotra, 'The Earliest Manual on the Sikh Way of Life', in Reeta Grewal and Sheena Pall, eds, *Five Centuries of Sikh Tradition: Ideology, Society, Politics and Culture*, New Delhi: Manohar, 2005, pp. 55–81.
44. For inscriptions on the earliest Sikh coins, see Surinder Singh, *Sikh Coinage: Symbol of Sikh Sovereignty*, New Delhi: Manohar, 2004, p. 41.
45. *Sri Gursobha*, pp. 29–30, 33–8, 53.
46. Ibid., pp. 29, 33, 42–3, 51, 60–1, 63, 66, 78–81, 85, 87, 90, 96, 103, 105, 131.
47. Ibid., pp. 31, 35–6, 40, 140–3, 146–9, 151.
48. Ibid., p. 31.
49. The Miṇas were descendants and followers of Prithi Chand who had refused to acknowledge Guru Arjan's son Hargobind as the Guru. The Dhir Mallias were the descendants and followers of Dhir Mal, the elder grandson of Guru Hargobind, who had refused to acknowledge his younger brother, Har Rai, as the Guru after Guru Hargobind. The Ram Raiyas were the successors and followers of Ram Rai, the elder son of Guru Har Rai, who had refused to recognize his younger brother Har Krishan as the Guru. All these dissenting groups were patronized by the Mughals to retain their support for the state.
50. *Sri Gursobha*, p. 132.

3. Martyrdom in Sikh History and Literature*

Sikh Martyrdom from Sikh Ideology

Talking about 'the joining of Heaven and Earth, and the role, in this joining of dead human beings' in the Christian tradition, Peter Brown argues in *The Cult of the Saints* that the analogy of 'the cult of the hero' with 'the Christian cult of the martyrs' breaks down because of the crucial distinction that the Christian martyrs 'enjoyed close intimacy with god'. 'This was the *sine qua non* of their ability to intercede for and, so, to protect their fellow mortals'. The martyr was an intercessor in a way in which 'the hero could never have been'. Furthermore, the heroism of the martyr had always been strictly dissociated from normal human courage, and the death of the martyr was vibrant with a miraculous 'suppression of suffering'. The celebration of the memory of the martyrs was a reassurance that 'good power' overcomes 'evil power'.[1] Martyrdom in the Christian tradition, thus, stands linked with ideology, metaphysics, and social function.

Bhai Jodh Singh looked upon the Sikh tradition of martyrdom as grounded firmly in Sikh ideology. In his view, Guru Gobind Singh's *'jin prem kiyo tin hī prabh pāyo'* was an echo of Guru Nanak's *'jau tau prem khelan kā chāo'*. The Sikh conception of love or *prem*, according to Bhai Jodh Singh, involves the willing acceptance of God's will or *bhāṇā*.

---

* 'Martyrdom in Sikh History and Literature' is a slightly revised version of 'Martyrdom in the Sikh Tradition' in my *Lectures on History, Society and Culture of the Punjab* (Punjabi University, Patiala, 2007, pp. 247–86). It was first published as 'Martyrdom', *Sikh Studies Quarterly*, vol. II, no. 3 (July–September 2000, pp. 10–20). A revised version was later published as 'The Sikh Tradition of Martyrdom', in J.S. Grewal, ed., *Sikh Ideology, Polity and Social Order* (New Delhi: Manohar, 2007, pp. 126–37).

This conception of love, according to Bhai Jodh Singh, was reiterated by Guru Arjan by saying that if love could be purchased with gold then Ravana, master of the golden Lanka, would not have given his head to Shiva. The gift of love cannot be obtained without sacrifice. For Bhai Jodh Singh, this is the meaning of Guru Gobind Singh's verse. For instituting the Khalsa, he invoked the principle of sacrifice in love. Standing before the congregation on the Baisakhi day he gave the call: 'is there anyone who loves the Guru so much that he is ready to give his head for the sake of *dharm*?' Thus, both the martyrdom of Guru Arjan and the institution of the Khalsa are linked with Guru Nanak's conception of sacrifice in love, equating martyrdom with dying for the cause of faith.[2]

Another Sikh scholar has argued recently that the goal of life for Guru Nanak was not a passive state of bliss but a life of action in accordance with the will of God who is All Love. Struggle against oppression was a logical corollary of this commitment. Guru Arjan provided the first landmark in Sikh history with his martyrdom as 'an open act of confrontation with the state'. Guru Tegh Bahadur responded to 'the oppression in Kashmir' by opting for martyrdom. The principle of 'total commitment' and sacrifice for 'the cause' was implied in the selection of volunteers by Guru Gobind Singh. A fundamental feature of the Khalsa tradition was to make sacrifice for 'the cause of righteousness, love and truth'. In other words, the Khalsa tradition of martyrdom was linked with the ideology of Guru Nanak which had inspired the martyrdom of Guru Arjan and Guru Tegh Bahadur.[3]

J.P.S. Uberoi has given serious attention to martyrdom in the Sikh tradition in his *Religion, Civil Society and the State*. In his view, Niharranjan Ray gave 'a hint as to the Sikh theory of martyrdom', stating with reference to the Sikh movement that for the first time in history, 'fear of death, the darkest and greatest of all fears, was taken out of man, death not merely in the heat and tumult of war, but death in silent defiance of the most painful and tortuous tyranny'. Guru Arjan was the first 'modern' martyr of India, and he established an unending line of men and women martyrs for the faith. His life, work, and death perfectly represented all that Guru Nanak had founded and anticipated. As a matter of conscience, Guru Arjan urged 'the claims of pluralism' against imperialism which stood for 'one single central rule in culture as well as power, religion, civil society, and political economy'. To self-abnegation and self-sacrifice, he added the conflict of 'martyrdom versus kingdom'. In 1675, the whole pattern of the grammar of conflict was exemplified in the voluntary martyrdom of Guru Tegh Bahadur. Then at the end of the seventeenth century, Guru Gobind Singh asked every Sikh 'to forfeit life rather than faith'. The free Sikh of the new commonwealth was ever to try not like the soldier and the hero to be stronger than the other 'but like a martyr or a saint to be stronger than oneself'.[4]

The story of martyrdom in the Sikh tradition did not end with the eighteenth century. Uberoi quotes Gandhi on the Gurdwara Reform Movement from 1921–5 to show that the movement involved martyrdom and ended in legislation to Gandhi's 'entire ideological satisfaction'. Uberoi suggests that, in theory and practice, martyrdom as a creed was more or less equivalent to non-violence as a creed in the making of 'the Indian modernity' from the birth of Sikhism up to Gandhism. An examination of the period of collaboration between Sikhism and Gandhism calls for 'a recognition among students of human culture of the figure of the martyr, rather than of the hero or the victim, as the universal foundation of civil society'. For J.P.S. Uberoi, thus, martyrdom is not only an essential feature but also an integral part of the Sikh tradition, embedded in the life and theology of Guru Nanak.[5]

MARTYRDOM AS A HEROIC TRADITION

With a limited interest in martyrdom, Harjot Oberoi strikes a different note. He sees the relevance of 'martyrs' for the construction of religious boundaries in Sikhism during the late nineteenth and early twentieth centuries. He states that appropriation of the body was a powerful symbolic system that reflected Sikh beliefs and ideals. The external symbols recommended in the eighteenth century *rahitnāma* literature were rigidly enforced by the radical reformers (Tat Khalsa) of the late nineteenth and early twentieth centuries as the most important symbolic expression of corporate Sikhism. The rahitnāma tradition was consolidated by arguing that only those individuals who upheld *rahit* injunctions, particularly the rules of external appearance and Khalsa initiation through baptism by the double-edged sword, had the right to call themselves Sikhs. Since this was a new claim the Tat

Khalsa encouraged the rewriting of history, which was done through two kinds of texts: histories of martyrs and historical fiction.[6]

In popular biographies of martyrs, Sikh heroic figures from the eighteenth century were shown to have been punished, tortured, and killed for desiring to retain cultural markers. Several Sikh 'martyrs' became household names: Bhai Tara Singh, Bhai Mani Singh, Bhai Bota Singh, Bhai Mahtab Singh, Bhai Taru Singh, Bhai Subeg Singh, Baba Dip Singh, and Nihang Gurbakhsh Singh. The most salient of the meanings generated by such tales of martyrdom was martial bravery. Underneath their bloody surface lay a corpus of multivocal *signata* conveying among other things the ideal Sikh modes of bodily comportment. Oberoi cites the example of Bhai Taru Singh as portrayed by Bhagat Lakshman Singh in his *Sikh Martyrs*. Imbued with the spirit of the eighteenth century Khalsa, Bhai Taru Singh could not submit to the insult of having his *kesh* being cut. The minions of the provincial governor and a shoemaker proved to be a failure. Then a carpenter was called to cut off Bhai Taru Singh's head. Oberoi goes on to underline the message embedded in such narratives: 'if the Sikhs of the eighteenth century could uphold the Five Ks at a time when they had to lay down their lives in their defence, why should the contemporary Sikhs lack will to follow their illustrious forefathers'. Those who failed to live up to the high standards of the past had no right to the membership of the community. That 'the martyr's blood provided the Tat Khalsa with unlimited potential to recast the façade of Sikhism in a form very desirable in the nineteenth century' was evident also from the historical novels of Bhai Vir Singh.[7]

Harjot Oberoi does not talk about martyrdom in the Sikh tradition. He merely refers to the Sikh heroic figures of the eighteenth century and their martial bravery. In his opinion, the Tat Khalsa treated them as martyrs and dwelt on their acts of sacrifice to underline that the external symbols of the Khalsa were an essential feature of Sikh identity.

A little more elaborate is W.H. McLeod's treatment of martyrdom in the Sikh tradition. He introduces the theme in connection with 'the militant aspect' of the Sikh tradition. It can be seen as the heroism of the warrior Khalsa and it can also be observed from the closely related angle of martyrdom. The two perspectives are two ways of viewing the same obligation to be supremely brave and undaunted, never to yield to an enemy under any circumstance. This ideal of militant bravery runs through Sikh history from the early seventeenth century and emerges with particular force from the founding of the Khalsa onwards. McLeod says that the term used for the martyr was *shahīd*, an Arabic word brought in by Muslims and originally introduced into Punjabi to express an important feature of Islamic culture. It served as the source of derivation for the Sikh usage. A significant part in its development was played by Punjabi folklore. The traditional bards or *dhādīs* began to sing of the courage and sacrifices of the Sikh martyrs in the eighteenth century. They continued to sing of the two 'martyr Gurus', of Baba Dip Singh and a host of other martyrs from the eighteenth century, and of the noble souls who in the early 1920s gave their lives for the freedom of the sacred Gurdwaras. In recent times a new chapter has been added and Sikh martyrology now lists names of Sant Jarnail Singh Bhindranwala and others like him who laid down their lives in the 1980s and the early 1990s for defending the Panth against the 'designs of evil men and women' from Delhi.[8]

According to McLeod, the ideal of militant bravery became a central theme of the Tat Khalsa during the Singh Sabha movement in the late nineteenth century. As a result of their preaching, it remains at the heart of orthodox Sikhism. Since the time of Guru Arjan to the present day, there have been phases of Sikh history marked specially by martyrdom. For the individual they meant pain and death, steadfastly endured. For the Khalsa they brought triumphant glory. The martyr ideal has lived on in the Panth and provided much inspiration to Sikhs. It is not a passive ideal; whenever evil returns weapons are to be used, even though as a last resort. Swords can be brandished or guns fired in the interest of justice, not for the benefit of an individual. 'For justice and Panth, all Sikhs should be prepared to undergo suffering, even to the point of martyrdom'. Though this message was not new to the Panth, it was clearly spelt out by the Tat Khalsa and it received 'a force and a coherence which previously it had not attained'.[9]

McLeod emphasizes that Khalsa Sikhism is 'a militant faith'. The Khalsa prayer or *ardās* refers to 'those loyal members of the Khalsa' who laid down their lives for the Panth. This impression is reinforced by the Sikh museums in Delhi and Amritsar. Together with the collection of weapons, the art work convincingly demonstrates 'the related themes of heroism and martyrdom'. In the popular posters, Baba Dip Singh figures as frequently as Guru Nanak or Guru Gobind Singh. Indeed, there are three dominant themes of popular Sikh art: the doctrine of the Divine Name, the heroism of the Panth in the fight for justice, and martyrdom or the conviction that bravery is not sufficient unless it extends to the ultimate stage of death.[10]

As presented by McLeod, the eighteenth century was marked by heroism, and dhādīs began to sing of the heroic deeds of the Khalsa. The death of a hero made him a martyr for whom the term shahid was used. The ideal of martyrdom acquired a new force and coherence from the Tat Khalsa in the late nineteenth and the early twentieth century. The Sikh tradition is emphatic about the status of Guru Arjan and Guru Tegh Bahadur as martyrs, but they do not fit into McLeod's understanding of martyrdom as the culmination of militant bravery. McLeod does not see any significant connection between Sikh ideology and the ideal of martyrdom in the Sikh tradition.

Martyrdom as a Historical Development

McLeod's hypothesis has been elaborated with some modifications by Louis E. Fenech in a revised version of his doctoral dissertation published as *Martyrdom in the Sikh Tradition: Playing the 'Game of Love'* and dedicated 'in gratitude' to his mentor, W.H. McLeod. Fenech states at the outset that for many contemporary Sikhs the concept of martyrdom is a fundamental feature of the Sikh tradition, representing a doctrine which has been in place for the last five centuries, but 'the concept of martyrdom has not always been as fundamental to Sikhism as the Sikh people and popular histories suggest'.[11]

In his exposition of the concept and tradition of martyrdom in Sikhism and Sikh history, Fenech adopts a historical approach. Therefore, we may follow the drift of his argument in a broad chronological order and not in the order in which he has presented it. Fenech argues that there is no conception of martyrdom in the compositions of Guru Nanak and his four successors, nor in the *Vārs* of Bhai Gurdas. The contemporary and near contemporary sources do not substantiate the popular claim that Guru Arjan died the glorious death of a martyr. The three sources examined by Fenech in some detail are the *Dabistān-i Mazāhib*, the *Maktūbāt-i Imām-i Rabbānī* of Shaikh Ahmad Sirhindi, and the *Tuzuk-i Jahāngirī*. This evidence shows nothing more than the fact that Guru Arjan incurred the enmity of the Mughal state by appearing to support the rival claim of Khusrau. He was imprisoned by the emperor's minions and he subsequently died in Mughal custody in Lahore. At this point in Sikh history, there was no concept of martyrdom.[12]

According to Fenech, the well-known passage in the *Bachittar Nātak* on Guru Tegh Bahadur's martyrdom is the first statement in Sikh literature to aver that the 'great deed' of stoically sacrificing one's life for the 'purpose of righteousness' ensures 'a spot in paradise'. Fenech goes on to add that this is 'something entirely new to the Sikh tradition'. Never before had such courage been absorbed into a conceptual system which rewarded the heroic sacrifice of one's life for a righteous cause with liberation. In Sainapat's *Gursobha*, according to Fenech, the concept of martyrdom can easily be inferred from the text, though the poet does not use the word shahīd or shahīdī. Fenech notices in a footnote the use of the word *shahīdganj* as a place 'where Sikhs have given their heads for the sake of Sikhism' in Chaupa Singh's *Rahitnāma* but adds that 'the term does not directly relate to the killed Sikh but rather to the spot on which he or she falls'.[13] The later works in the *gurbilās* and rahitnāma genres refer to the Khalsa imbued with a tremendous martial prowess, bravery and ability to sacrifice, along with their 'particular devotion to the goddess'.[14]

For Fenech, there is no contemporary or near contemporary evidence on the 'martyrs' to judge whether or not any ideals were operative in their case. There was only one exception. The Persian accounts of the execution of Banda and his men dwell on the stoic composure and cheerful countenances of the Sikhs when they were led to the place of execution. Fenech surmises that this 'extraordinary heroism' was highlighted by the Persian writers in order to underscore the courage and daring of their Mughal captors. Surman and Stephenson explicitly state that none of the captives 'apostatized from his new-formed religion'. This evidence seems to indicate that the choice of Islam was offered to at least some of the captives. Fenech says that the difference between being offered the choice and 'not apostatizing' was 'a crucial one'. He is inclined to think that, since the concept of martyrdom had emerged by this time, the contemporary Sikhs could feel that these deaths warranted the status of martyrdom.[15]

Some of the early British writers made comments on the Sikhs of the eighteenth century. George Forster, for example, recorded in 1782 that 'an invincible perseverance' of the Sikhs enabled them to rise superior in a contest with the most potent prince of his age. This could be based on the oral tradition current in the late eighteenth century. Malcolm refers to the Sikhs seeking 'the crown of martyrdom'. Determined to bathe in the sacred tank in Amritsar, if a Sikh was captured on the way, he never abjured his faith. Cunningham refers specifically to Bhai Taru Singh in terms which remind the reader of Ratan Singh Bhangu's statement on Bhai Taru Singh's martyrdom. It is likely that an oral tradition was accessible to both Bhangu and Cunningham. As dhādīs wandered from village to village, Sikh heroes and martyrs were brought to life, along with a number of other popular warriors. Presumably, a number of Gurdwaras associated with a Sikh Guru or a martyr had their own dhādīs, like the Golden Temple. The crux of this argument is that there is no direct evidence on motivation. The role of the dhādīs is underscored for turning 'heroes' into 'martyrs'. They transmitted the tradition of martyrdom within Sikhism orally from generation to generation.[16]

According to Fenech, Seva Singh's *Shahīdbilās* is the first work to clearly project the shahīd as a martyr 'who provides testimony to injustice, heroically witnessing to the truth with his blood'. This understanding of the martyr was grafted upon the concept of martyrdom in the *Bachittar Nātak* and the *Gursobha*,[17] and it was reflected in Ratan Singh Bhangu's *Guru Panth Prakāsh* in which the term shahīd is frequently used.[18]

Fenech tries to depict the pre-colonial tradition of martyrdom within Sikhism in order to show how it was different from the Tat Khalsa projection of Sikh martyrdom. In his view, in the passage on Guru Tegh Bahadur in the *Bachittar Nātak,* the sacred thread and the frontal mark are seen as a part of the Sikh religious culture. He quotes Malcolm's statement based on the evidence of Bhai Gurdas that Guru Gobind Singh and his son Ajit Singh had laid aside the sacred thread.[19] It does not occur to Fenech that Bhai Gurdas wrote much earlier than the birth of Guru Gobind Singh. Nor does it occur to him that in the *bāṇī* of Guru Tegh Bahadur himself there is no appreciation for any Brahmanical belief and practice.

For a composite picture of the shahīd Fenech talks of popular martyrolatry in the Punjab and then cites the *Sau Sākhiān,* an anonymous work of the mid-nineteenth century, for an exposition of the martyr's role. Guru Gobind Singh tells the Sikhs that shahīds lived in the world, in the realm of Kuber (the god of riches) and in the realm between the sun and the sky in which dwell the munīs and siddhas. 'All that which the martyrs desire comes to pass'. The spirits called *bhūt*s, *pret*s, *rākshasa*s, *yaksha*s, *gandharva*s, and *apasara*s as well as humans, birds, and serpents are under their command. The messengers of Yama consult the martyrs. In the Shastras they are called *baitāl* and *vidyādhar*. Worshipped by their congregations, the shahīds fulfil all their wishes. Parmeshwar has placed them in positions of power. The Guru protects them, and watches over them like a shepherd. This *sākhī* is seen as reflecting the Sikh participation in popular martyrology in which the Sikhs venerated the martyrs of other religious faiths as well as their own.[20] Elsewhere, however, Fenech contradicts himself by saying that the Sikh martyrs were not associated with the martyrs and demi-gods of other traditions, such as Sakhī Sarvar, Guggā Pīr, and Ghāzī Miān.[21]

Fenech thinks that there are instances in Ratan Singh Bhangu's text where the term shahīd implies far more than the pious witness to the glory of Sikhism: one, for example, that Guru Tegh Bahadur's martyrdom led to the downfall of the Mughal empire and two, that Shahid Gurbakhsh Singh was born as Maharaja Ranjit Singh.[22] This actually means that Bhangu linked Sikh martyrdom with metahistory and metaphysics, and not that he entertained a popular, or composite concept of martyrology. According to Fenech, Bhai Vir Singh transformed the martyr of Ratan Singh Bhangu into the Singh Sabha martyr while editing his *Guru Panth Prakāsh*. For Bhangu, the Sikhs were essentially Hindu. Bhai Vir Singh replaced the term 'Hindu' in Bhangu's text with 'Sikh' or 'Singh' wherever he felt that it was used for a Sikh. In the narratives of martyrdom, where the extant manuscripts of Bhangu's work show 'Sikhs happily sacrificing their lives for the Devi', the version supplied by Vir Singh shows these same Sikhs 'sacrificing themselves for their Guru and for the benefit of the Panth'. Even Guru Gobind Singh is not spared. 'While he offers his four sons as a sacrifice to the goddess in the manuscripts he is presented as sacrificing all he holds dear for the sake of the Panth in the printed version'.[23] Fenech makes this statement on the basis of an article by Chopra and Hans, and not on the basis of a direct study of the manuscripts. The statements of Bhangu can be appreciated better if the role assigned to the goddess in his work as a whole is properly understood.

Notwithstanding his insistence on the 'Hindu understandings' of Ratan Singh Bhangu, Fenech finds one martyr narrative in Bhangu's original where a specific Sikh identity, as opposed to Hindu, appears to be assumed. Taru Singh chooses death over having the sacred kesh shaved from his head. Though an exception, it seems to demonstrate 'the inherent element of identity' which could be exploited by the Tat Khalsa. A close reading of Bhangu's text would show that Bhai Taru Singh was not an exception. Fenech's statement that Bhangu's Khalsa Sikh is set within the Sanatan Sikh paradigm put forth by Harjot Oberoi does not clarify the issue. Oberoi's exposition of 'Sanatan Sikhism' in *The Construction of Religious Boundaries* is vague and it is based on a part of the contemporary evidence used rather selectively. His hypothesis is wide open to debate. Essentially, the Sanatan Sikhs or the traditional Sikhs are seen as tolerant of or indifferent to diversity in religious beliefs and practices among the Sikhs and the Tat Khalsa or the radical Singhs are regarded as standing for uniform beliefs and practices of the Khalsa as defined by them. For a keen similarity between the original text and Vir Singh's edition in respect of martyrdom, Fenech says that both the texts were meant to inspire and enthuse Sikhs of the periods to which Bhangu and Vir Singh belonged. There were compelling reasons for both for writing in the way they did. Fundamental to both were the heroic ideals in a situation of conflict with the British.[24] However, there was no conflict with the British when Bhai Vir Singh edited Bhangu's text.

Finally, the enormous devotion which the Sikhs have towards the Tat Khalsa interpretation of Sikh tradition is as much due to the Akalis of 1920–5 as to the nineteenth century reformers. 'The power of the reformers was that of ideas, but the power of the Akalis was putting such ideas into practice. Speaking, writing, and touring were replaced by the ideals enunciated therein: suffering, standing true to vows, and dying'. Consequently, the Tat Khalsa message penetrated the very heart of the Punjab due largely to the Singh Sabha rhetoric of martyrdom.[25]

The strongest feature of Fenech's work is its historical approach. For him, the art of the historian lies in questioning traditions about the past in the light of empirical evidence for a better understanding of the past. However, a historical approach by itself does not ensure adequate interpretation. The evidence Fenech uses for the pre-colonial conception and tradition of martyrdom within Sikhism is limited to a few works. His reading of this limited evidence is also open to question. The inadequacies of his work oblige the historian to use a wider range of evidence and to interpret it more systematically for a proper perspective on the Sikh tradition of martyrdom.

Implications of Sikh Ideology

We may notice first of all that Guru Nanak was aware of the tradition of shahīd in Islamic culture. The word occurs in one of his compositions:

Baba! Allah is inscrutable and boundless. His names are holy, His abode is holy, and He is the true sustainer. His will (*hukam*) cannot be comprehended; none can describe it. Not even a hundred poets together can describe its smallest fraction. None knows His worth though all hear and talk about Him. There are *pīrs, paighambars, sāliks, sādiqs, shahīds, shaikhs, mashāikh, qāzīs, mullās,* and adept *darveshes*. They read prayers (*darūd*) in the hope of His grace. He consults none to make or unmake, to give or take away. He alone knows his power (*qudrat*) and He alone does whatever is done. He watches everyone and bestows His grace on whomever He pleases.[26]

This stanza shows Guru Nanak's familiarity with the categories of religious persons who were believed to hold a recognized status in the Indo-Muslim society. Among them were shahīds. Ravidas mentions them as being worshipped like pīrs by Muslims.[27] They were important enough to be taken notice of. But they had no sanctity in the eyes of Guru Nanak. For him, the shahīd of Islamic culture was merely a descriptive category.

Bhai Gurdas refers to people going to the places of shahīds for pilgrimage in the context of Muslim beliefs and practices. He has no appreciation for them. In another stanza, several new categories of Muslims are mentioned along with shahīds. It is made absolutely clear that no category of devotees is comparable with the Gurmukh who is indifferent to death and remains hopeless-in-hopefulness or *āsā vich nirās*. The Islamic categories of religious persons, including shahīds, are mentioned in yet another stanza which actually underlines the idea that none gets liberated without the Guru and none gets rid of *haumai* without joining the *sādh-sangat*. Finally, the term shahīd is used by Bhai Gurdas to express a Sikh ideal in a stanza in which a dozen other words of Perso-Arabic origin are used. The ideal put forth in this stanza is that of becoming dead in life to serve the Guru.[28] It is clear therefore that the word shahīd is given a Sikh connotation at the same time as the shahīd of Islamic culture is virtually rejected.

The scholars who have written on martyrdom in the Sikh tradition have tried to look for a direct statement in the Gurbāṇī. The relevant question to ask is whether or not the idea of martyrdom is implicit in Sikh ideology. The path of *sikhī* is underlined as a hard path. Guru Nanak refers to the path of liberation as 'sharp like the edge of a double-edged sword (*khandedhār*). The extremely narrow lane of love is compared to the oil-press that crushes the sesame seed.[29] Guru Amar Das says that the path of devotion is sharper than the edge of a double-edged sword and narrower than the width of a hair. One has to sacrifice haumai to follow this path.[30] The metaphor of the double-edged sword for the difficulty of the path and sacrifice of the self involved in following the path have a suggestive bearing on martyrdom.

The path of sikhī demands sacrifice. In the familiar words of Guru Nanak, 'If you wish to play the game of love, enter my lane with your head on the palm of your hand. Without the slightest hesitation, give your head if you set your foot on this path'.[31] The smooth transition from a metaphysical to a literal meaning is evident from the use of the words 'prem khelan kā chālo', (keenness to play the game of love) '*sir dhar talī*' (having placed the head on the palm) and '*sir dījae*' in later Sikh literature for actual martyrdom. Elsewhere Guru Nanak himself says that only God enables men to render service for him; they who give their head attain to liberation and find honour in God's court.[32] The phrase used here is '*sir de*'. It is a metaphor for sacrifice but a telling metaphor.

The concept of liberation-in-life or *jivan-muktī* is relevant for martyrdom. Essential for liberation-in-life are fear and love of God, that is, *bhau-bhagtī*. Guru Nanak makes it absolutely clear that only they who cultivate bhau (fear) can appropriate *bhav* (love).[33] Without *bhai* there can be no bhagtī.[34] Guru Amar Das says that there can be no bhagtī without bhai, and no love for the Name.[35] The fear of God lodged in the heart eradicates haumai, and the love of God leads to complete dedication. Through the instruction of the Guru one experiences God as the Fearless One.[36] The state of liberation is a state of fearlessness. Guru Nanak says that all fears are removed by the fear of

God.[37] Guru Angad says that they who have fear of God have no other fear.[38] God is *achint*, without anxiety. Therefore, Guru Amar Das says that they who lodge *achintā* in their mind have no *chintā* whatever.[39] Guru Ram Das says that all fears are removed by meditating on one who is *nirbhau*[40] who alone is free of fear .[41] Guru Arjan prays for the boon of *abhai-pad*, the state of fearlessness.[42] He advises others to strive for the gift of fearlessness by singing God's praises in association with others.[43] Guru Tegh Bahadur prays for *abhaidan*, the boon of fearlessness.[44] Death is shorn of its fear for the one who has attained to the state of liberation.

An essential element in Sikh ideology was the renunciation of renunciation. Guru Nanak refers to the householders who, through the Guru's instruction, have awakened to God and pursue the life of *nām, dan*, and *isnān*.[45] The house-holder who prays for *jap, tap*, and *sanjam* and who practises *punn* and dān is pure like the water of Ganga.[46] Guru Arjan says that by meeting the True Guru one attains liberation while laughing, playing, dressing, and eating.[47] For Guru Nanak, true conduct was higher in scale than the realization of truth.[48] Without an occupation that enables one to earn honestly, whether profits or wages, even charity brings discredit.[49] Guru Nanak has no respect for those who live on charity or mendicancy: only he recognizes the true path who works hard to earn his living and gives something to others.[50]

The liberated-in-life pursued life's activities in a spirit of detachment. Guru Nanak refers to this state as *āsā mahi nirās* (hopeless in hope), a state in which one remains hopeful that God will take care of everything and there is no desire of one's own. It is a state of selfless optimism.[51] Guru Amar Das refers to this state as *ghar hī mahi udās* (renunciation in the home itself). There is no attachment (*moh*) or desire (*piyas*) in this state.[52] He who meditates on the shabad gets rid of haumai and becomes detached in action or *nih karmi*.[53] Service or *seva* is a supreme criterion of good conduct.[54] The epithet used by Guru Ram Das for the Gurus is *par-upkārī* (one who does something for others).[55] To work for the welfare of others is an essential concern of the liberated-in-life.

According to Guru Nanak, acceptance of God's will enables one to get rid of haumai.[56] To accept his will is to affirm one's faith in him. Guru Nanak says that he remains happy in whatever condition he is kept by God.[57] Guru Amar Das says that he who recognizes God's hukam receives all kinds of happiness. Therefore, he advises everyone to act in accordance with God's hukam and to accept whatever he does.[58] Guru Arjan addresses God as: 'Whatever you do, tastes sweet'.[59] The liberated-in-life live in accordance with His will.

Finally, a self-oriented person (*manmukh*) has *kathnī* (verbal profession) but no rahit; his talk is tall but his actions do not correspond to what he says. But a person who has attained *giān* and *dhiān* (meditation) through the Guru has a true rahit.[60] True happiness lies in true rahit.[61] True rahit (*sachchi rahit*) is the whole way of life advocated by Guru Nanak. This way of life is prized by his followers and his successors above everything else. A total commitment to this ideology involves sacrifice for the faith. The metaphor of the double-edged sword and carrying one's head on one's palm to play the game of love symbolize total commitment. Self-sacrifice without self-interest was, thus, built into the Sikh ideal of life.

From Bhai Gurdas to the Early Eighteenth Century

The *Vārs* of Bhai Gurdas are regarded as the key to Guru Granth Sahib. He was nurtured on Gurbāṇī. Sikh ideology is amply reflected in his *Vārs*. Since he was closely associated with Guru Arjan and Guru Hargobind, his *Vārs*, paradoxically, are a little more relevant even than Gurbāṇī. Bhai Gurdas talks of the Sikh Panth as a unique development in human history. He underlines the greatness of the Name in the Kaliyuga. There is no other means of liberation. The Nirmal Panth is the coin struck by Guru Nanak in the world as a distinct or *nirālā* Panth of his own. The whole world was 'drowning' without the Guru and he appeared in the world to redeem it in the Kali Age. There is only one shop in the world for the shabad. The Gurmukh Panth is distinct from all others and cannot be confused with any other. The True Guru is the True King and he has shown the highway or *gādī rāh*. The Gurmukh *mārg* is the path of truth (*sachch*) and they who appropriate it become true followers (*sachiār*).[62]

According to Bhai Gurdas, the Sikh of the Guru pursues sikhī which is known to be narrower than the width of a hair (*vālon nikkī*). The Sikh of the Guru quafs the cup of love (*pirm piālā*). The path of Gursikhī is hard in the extreme; it is like licking a saltless slab; it is sharper than the edge of a double-edged sword; it is narrower than the width of a hair.[63] Bhai Gurdas mentions several categories of paths and practices to assert at the end that they bear little fruit in comparison with Gursikhī.[64] The cup of love enables them to see the unseeable.[65] The Sikhs of the Guru taste the cup of love, like the moth that burns itself on the flame, like the deer that gets killed while absorbed in the sound of the hunter's bell, like the black bee stuck to the flower, and like the fish in water.[66] Absorbed in the shabad in association with other Sikhs, they drink the cup of love and bear the unbearable.[67] The preoccupation of Bhai Gurdas with 'the cup of love' is quite remarkable. In later Sikh literature, it would come to mean 'martyrdom'.

Bhai Gurdas talks of love and fear (bhau-bhav) as the means of liberation.[68] The True Guru shows the way to dedicate oneself to love and to tread in fear; the Sikh remains intoxicated and alert at the same time.[69] God alone is without fear (nirbhau).[70] The True Guru, who is eternally free from fear, removes the fear of death and rebirth.[71] The Gurmukh is born in fear, lives in fear and walks in fear.[72] The Sikhs of the Guru are born in fear, live in fear and die in fear to live for ever.[73] In fear, they become liberated-in-life (jīvan-mukt) and accept the bhāṇā of God.[74] As instructed by the True Guru, they accept God's will and abandon their own 'self'.[75] Bhai Gurdas uses the term *hukmī bandā* for the Sikh of the Guru who follows the Sikh way of life by cherishing the bhāṇā of the Master.[76] He lives in accordance with the Divine Order.[77]

As for Guru Nanak, the earth for Bhai Gurdas is the place of dharm.[78] It is the place where one attains liberation and helps others attain it too. Bhai Gurdas talks of liberation-in-life at many places in his *Vārs*. A Sikh of the Guru should become the dust of his feet, die unto himself and live for God.[79] The Gurmukh dies unto 'self' and becomes liberated-in-life.[80] Bhai Gurdas makes it clear that liberation-in-life is to live in hope without any desire of one's own (āsā vich nirās).[81] The liberated-in-life is a householder who is not affected by attachment.[82] To die unto oneself is to get rid of the haumai; to live in accordance with the instruction of the Guru is to discard haumai so as to be dead in life.[83] The Gurmukh dies unto himself and lives for God.[84]

Like Guru Nanak, Bhai Gurdas underscores the importance of honest living. He talks of manual work and *kirt* (earning through honest work, especially manual) of dharm.[85] There is hardly any doubt that *ghāl khāṇā* (to eat on the basis of hard work) and *sukirt karnā* are linked up with āsā vich nirās in the life of a Gursikh.[86] Bhai Gurdas lays much emphasis on remaining detached-in-attachment. He uses the familiar phrases: ghar hī vich udās, āsā vich nirās, māyā vich udās. Such phrases are used repeatedly.[87] The Sikh of the Guru does not cry in suffering, just as he does not laugh in comfort.[88]

The Gurmukh who discards his 'self' and becomes a jīvan-muktā serves the Sikhs of the Guru and looks upon them as his mother and father, brother and friend.[89] Bhai Gurdas himself wishes that a Sikh of the Guru may wear shoes made from his skin.[90] It is expected of the Sikhs of the Guru to serve the Sikhs.[91] They serve the sādh-sangat and reap the fruit of service.[92] The liberated Sikh enables other Sikhs to attain liberation.[93] The Sikhs of the Guru are par-upkārī: while others return good for good, they return good for evil.[94] The identifying mark of the Sikh is that he is never oblivious to the welfare of others.[95] The par-upkārī Sikhs meet everyone with a smile.[96]

Finally, the Gurmukh spreads knowledge in the world. He discards ego and purifies his inner self. He cultivates truth and contentment and discards lust and anger. Being devoid of enmity (*nirvair*) he entertains enmity towards none. He gives instruction to all the four *varna*s to lead them to liberation (*sahaj*). Praise be to the mother who has given birth to this supreme warrior.[97] The supreme warrior of Bhai Gurdas is not only a fighter of battles but also a Gurmukh who is committed to the welfare of humanity. The warrior (*sūrā*) is thus redefined.

It is important to know how Bhai Gurdas looks upon Guru Arjan, the first Guru who was the son of a Guru. Thenceforth, Guruship was to remain in the house of the Sodhi Guru Ram Das. Like Guru Ram Das, Guru Arjan is one with all his predecessors, with the same light and the same status. Bhai Gurdas talks of the eminent Sikhs of Guru Arjan who belonged to a large number of varnas, jātīs, and occupations. Among them was a former Chandāl and a former Muslim who was a *huzūrī* Sikh. Highly visible in the Punjab, the Sikhs were also found in many cities of the Mughal empire. In line with Guru Nanak, Guru Angad, Guru Amar Das, and Guru Ram Das, Guru Arjan represented eternal intoxication (*abchal arkheo*). He enabled all the four varnas to follow the path of truth. He filled the storehouse of Gurbāṇī and remained absorbed in kīrtan in the sādh-sangat. His court was true, his *nīsān* was true, and true was his strength and his honour; his *rāaj* was to stay for ever. Innumerable Sikhs flocked to him from all four directions; he transformed them into true devotees who, like Janak, lived detached amidst the attachments of the world.[98]

In the stanza which relates to Guru Arjan's martyrdom, he exhorted the Sikhs till the end that they should never forget the *updes* of the Gurus. He regarded the sādh-sangat as the source of comfort, love and the blissful state (*sahaj smādhī*). Bhai Gurdas is a sacrifice to Guru Arjan who did not think of anything but God bearing the severest of physical tortures. The metaphors used are those of a fish that remains alive only in water, a moth that burns itself on the flame, a deer that remains absorbed in the sound of the hunter's bell, a black bee that remains wrapped inside the lotus, and a rain bird that constantly cries for union. All the metaphors relate to love to the point of self-sacrifice.[99] All these metaphors occur in a composition by Guru Arjan.[100] Guru Nanak had taught how to die the death of a warrior-hero: to accept God's will in life and in death.[101] This was the game of love.

Significantly, the martyrdom of Guru Tegh Bahadur was a deliberate act. We have a contemporary comment on the event. The relevant verses in the *Bachittar Nātak*, generally attributed to Guru Gobind Singh, are translated as follows:

> For their frontal mark and their sacred thread
>   he wrought a great deed in this Age of Darkness.
> This he did for the sake of the pious, silently
>   giving his head.
> For the cause of truth he performed this deed,
>   giving his head in obedience to his resolve.
> Bogus tricks are for counterfeit conjurors, deceits
>   which God's people must spurn.
> Dashing himself on the ruler of Delhi, he
>   departed for God's abode.
> Such was the achievement of Tegh Bahadur,
>   the feat which he alone could perform.
> At the death of Tegh Bahadur lamentation
>   swept the earth.
> From below came anguished wailing,
>   from heaven triumphant cries.[102]

These lines indicate that Guru Tegh Bahadur was asked to perform a miracle as a proof of his nearness to God, but he rejected the notion that miracles were proof of the veracity of one's faith. It is equally clear that he gave his head deliberately in confrontation with the ruler of Delhi for the cause of truth and for the sake of the pious. The religious import is obvious enough. The use of the words 'the frontal mark and the sacred thread' (*tilak, janjū*) has to be seen in this context. There can hardly be any doubt that these words refer essentially to Brahmans.[103]

However, Guru Tegh Bahadur did not give his head for the sake of Hindus alone. The sādhs and dharm mentioned in the *Bachittar Nātak* refer to Sikhs and the Sikh faith. In the *Gursobha* are mentioned *karm-dharm*, dharmsāl and *sarb-dharm*, along with tilak and janjū as protected by Guru Tegh Bahadur. We know that Guru Tegh Bahadur is generally called *Hind dī chādar* (the protector of Hind) and the saviour of Hinduism. But Sainapat calls him *jagg chādar* (the protector of the world) as well.[104] 'Hind' is not excluded from 'the world' and 'Hinduism' is not excluded from 'sarb-dharm'. Therefore, Guru Tegh Bahadur may be seen as defending the principle of the freedom of conscience. This principle was implied in Guru Nanak's denunciation of the discrimination practised by the state which taxed gods and their temples.[105] Since Aurangzeb was using political power to promote the interests of Sunni Islam at the cost of others, the conflict between the principle of freedom and the practice of coercion was inevitable.

The *Gursobha* is important in another way too. Its author does not refer to the call given by Guru Gobind Singh for sacrifice in the cause of dharm but he takes it for granted. At one level the Khalsa represents direct affiliation with Guru Gobind Singh. This affiliation is affirmed by the baptism of the double-edge sword. The choice of *khandā* carries a great significance: '*khandedhār pahul*' symbolizes the determination to lay down one's life in a righteous cause. After the first evacuation of Anandpur, when Guru Gobind Singh and his Khalsa were attacked at Nirmoh, Sahib Chand died fighting in the field. The author of the *Gursobha* makes the general statement that the perfectly fortunate ones proved themselves to be the *khalsa* by sacrificing their life. When Sahibzada Ajit Singh died fighting in the battle of Chamkaur, Guru Gobind Singh himself remarked: 'today he has become the Khalsa in the court of the True Guru'. The reference to 'the cup of love' in this context is highly significant. The younger

Sahibzadas are seen as following the example of their grandfather, Guru Tegh Bahadur, in preferring their faith over their life. They too are regarded as martyrs.[106]

The term shahīdganj is used in the *Rahitnāma* of Chaupa Singh for the place 'where Sikhs have given their heads for the sake of sikhī.' Such places were sacred. The Sikhs are told to 'light a lamp there'.[107] The word shahīd for the Sikh martyr makes its appearance in the early eighteenth century, and the sanctity of the place of martyrdom is recognized.

The *Rahitnāma* of Chaupa Singh is generally placed in the mid-eighteenth century but the possibility of an earlier date for its text cannot be ruled out. In any case, this work suggests a close connection between pahul, kesh, and martyrdom. Its author talks of two categories of Sikhs: *keshdhārī* and *sahajdhārī*. The term keshdhārī is used for the Khalsa who have taken the pahul. Obviously, thus, kesh and khandedhār pahul go together.[108]

The sanctity of the kesh is underlined in a number of ways. The Sikh of the Guru should take good care of his kesh, combing them twice a day and washing them with curd. He should not touch the kesh with unclean hands and should ensure that no lice grow in his hair. He should not uproot grey hair and should not dye them. He should not insult another Sikh by catching his kesh, beard or turban. Ten more injunctions regarding the kesh make it absolutely clear how important they are for the Sikhs. The kesh are the outward symbol of the inner faith of the Sikh. Through the Guru's grace the kesh symbolize sikhī. The Sikhs of the Guru should preserve sikhī till the end of their life. The Sikh Panth is the *panth* of dharm. The muktā Sikhs are defined as those who sacrifice their life in battles against the Turks. This definition postulates a close link between martyrdom and liberation. The muktās preserve their sikhī. Thus, pahul, kesh, and martyrdom go together. No wonder, the removal of hair is as heinous as incest.[109]

In the *Rahitnāma* of Chaupa Singh and the *Sākhī Rahit Kī*, the kesh serve as the marker of a distinct Sikh identity. Just as Guru Arjan prepared a scripture distinct from all others, so did Guru Gobind Singh create a Panth distinct from all others. The Keshdhārī Sikhs, according to Chaupa Singh, are like a particle of stone in the eyes of Hindus and Musalmans: it cannot be removed, it does not get dissolved, and it remains a source of constant irritation. According to the *Sākhī Rahit*

Kī, the Khalsa have been given such a marker that even a single Sikh stands out in a crowd of lacs of Hindus and Musalmans. How can he with his kesh, turban, and flowing beard be concealed?[110] Thus, pahul, kesh, and martyrdom not only go together but also serve as the markers of Sikh identity.

In the Late Eighteenth Century Sikh Literature

Several Sikh writers of the late eighteenth century introduce the episode of the Goddess in connection with the Khalsa. We may look at their treatment of martyrdom. Kesar Singh Chhibber brings in the law of karma to explain the enmity between Guru Arjan and his elder brother Prithi Chand. Nevertheless, Guru Arjan was conscious of his impending martyrdom. Deliberately, therefore, he installed Hargobind as the Guru and told the Sikhs that the time had come to stake his 'head'. He had to face the Turks but he had no fear. Welcome to him was the bhāṇā of the Master. He was subjected to tortures. Guru Arjan's death brought moral discredit to his oppressors. The Turks were unjust in supporting his enemies. However, Jahangir had no hesitation later to pacify Guru Hargobind. The Sahi Khatris of Lahore were delivered to him for punishment. The whole family of Chandu Sahi, except his daughter-in-law who was sympathetic to Guru Arjan, was killed. Furthermore, Guru Hargobind took up the sword and the khaṇḍā in accordance with the will of Guru Nanak: to fight and to die without any fear. In a situation of confrontation, Guru Har Krishan refused to see Aurangzeb's face and chose to sacrifice his life.[111]

The enmity of Aurangzeb with Guru Tegh Bahadur was due to the law of karma, and the old enmity of some Khatri families with the Gurus. Aurangzeb asked the Guru to show a miracle or accept Islam. Otherwise, he should be prepared to get his head cut off. Guru Tegh Bahadur said that one should not become an apostate or *be-dīn* by changing one's faith. To show a miracle was to draw God's wrath upon oneself. The head was not everlasting; its removal depended on God's will. Finally, however, Guru Tegh Bahadur said that he would tie a thread to his neck to make the sword ineffective. When the sword was struck, his head was cut off. This was how he gave his head deliberately. Had he not done so, all Hindus would have been converted to Islam.

He preserved his faith (dharm) and earned the praises of the whole world. Chhibber quotes two lines from the *Bachittar Nātak* which imply that Guru Tegh Bahadur made this sacrifice to save the sacred thread and the sacred mark, and for the sake of sādhs. Other lines from the *Bachittar Nātak* are quoted a little later. Chhibber goes on to add that only two Sikhs, Mati Das and Sati Das, stayed with the Guru to sacrifice their life. Guru Gobind Singh decided to give such a marker to the Sikhs that they would never be able to conceal their identity. As Chhibber tells us later, this marker was the uncut hair or kesh.[112]

The narrative of the goddess is more elaborate in Kesar Singh Chhibber's *Bansavalinama* than in any other work of the eighteenth century. It is important, therefore, to see its relevance for the Khalsa. Guru Gobind Singh told the Brahmans that he had been commissioned by God to establish dharm by protecting the pious and destroying the wicked. For this purpose, he was to create a panth for sovereign rule. The Sikhs of the Guru were to be made distinct in the world to pursue both Rāj and Jog. After a long discussion with Pandit Kalikdas, the goddess was invoked through an elaborate ceremony. The eight-armed Mata Devi appeared in all her splendour and Guru Gobind Singh could not look at her after the first glimpse. Kalikdas received a khandā from her. This was presumably used for preparing *amrit*. Furthermore, the goddess exempted the Khalsa from janjū, *tikkā, bhaddan,* and *kirya*. Their place was taken by the kesh, the arms, and the epithet Singh. The Khalsa adopted the blue dress of Mata Kali. Their objective was to fight the Turks and to remove them forever. Hukamnamas were issued to promulgate the new rahit. The *masand*s, who were opposed to the new programme, were punished and removed. For waging a righteous war (*dharmyudh*), the third panth was to be made distinct from both Hindus and Musalmans. Pahul was administered to create the Keshdhārī panth which was to wield the sword in the cause of righteousness. The Sikhs who were prepared to give their head for the goddess were chosen for rulership. The rule of the Shudras was sanctified through this mode of selection. To fight for dharm and sovereignty involved death and whosoever died fighting went to heaven. Thus, pahul, kesh, *kirpan*, dharm, rāj, and *sīs dena* are sanctified by the goddess. For Kesar Singh Chhibber, the rulers of the land in his own time were the martyr Singhs of the time of

Banda Bahadur.[113] If anything, the episode of the goddess enhances the significance of martyrdom.

In Sarup Das Bhalla's account of Guru Arjan's death, the enmity of Chandu Sahi figures prominently. Chandu made much of the hospitality offered by Guru Arjan to Prince Khusrau at Tarn Taran. Aware of the consequences, Guru Arjan told Arth Mal that the time had come for his light to mingle with the Light. Then the Guru alluded to his confrontation with the Turks, and told the Sikhs to return to Goindwal and look upon Hargobind as the Guru, saying that 'there is no difference between me and him'. Then Guru Arjan deliberately went to the abode of dharm to assume the *nirbāṇ* form. The body of Guru Arjan was cremated on the bank of the Ravi. Rāj-Jog was made manifest by Guru Hargobind in the context of confrontation with the state. Guru Har Rai agreed to help Dara Shukoh. Aurangzeb called the Guru to Delhi but he refused to go. Eventually, he sent Ram Rai to Aurangzeb, with the instruction that he should take a dignified stand and should not reveal his supranatural power. He infringed this injunction, and Guru Har Rai installed Har Krishan as the Guru.

Sarup Das Bhalla goes on to state that Aurangzeb called Guru Har Krishan to Delhi. On the pretext of having his *darshan*, the emperor offered him the insignia of spirituality and many valuable articles. Guru Har Krishan accepted the former but rejected the latter. When Aurangzeb expressed the wish to see him again, Guru Har Krishan said that there was no possibility now of a meeting with the Turks: this was God's bhāṇā. Guru Har Krishan asked the messenger to tell the emperor that he was suffering from small pox. Consequently, smallpox appeared on his body. After five days he told his mother that he would now go to *dharm-dhām* and his light would mingle with the Light. The *sangat* was told that they would find his successor in Bakala.[114]

The sangat discovered Guru Tegh Bahadur. Dhir Mal complained to Aurangzeb and he called Guru Tegh Bahadur to Delhi. The emperor was keen to see a miracle but the Guru did not believe in revealing such powers. He told Aurangzeb that by demonstrating supranatural powers one became *mushrik* (one who associates someone else with God) and this was not to the liking of the *lāsharīk* (the one without a partner). Servanthood behoved men, just as justice behoved the ruler. The Hindus and Turks had the same Master and the King should be kind to both. God liked justice and not oppression. Nothing happened without His will. Aurangzeb kept quiet but later on demanded a miracle. Mati Das argued that the 'men of God' did not perform a miracle. He was sawn into two, but his head still recited the *Japuji*. This was nothing short of a miracle.[115]

Guru Tegh Bahadur went towards the east to meet the Sikh sangats, visiting sacred places on the way. The tenth Nanak was born at Patna. The Guru went to Monghyr, Dhaka, and Kamrup where he established peace between the local chief and Raja Bishan Singh. Before returning to Delhi with the Raja, Guru Tegh Bahadur installed his son Gobind as the Guru. The time had come for sacrificing his life for the sake of dharm and to save the sacred thread and the sacred mark. He demonstrated in the Kaliyuga how to retain faith rather than save the head. The borrowing from the *Bachittar Nātak* is obvious.[116]

The twentieth sākhī in the sākhīs of Guru Gobind Singh is actually the *Bachittar Nātak*, a declaration of his mission. This sākhī is preceded by the institution of the Khalsa. The masands were exposed and removed. In their place, five Sikhs administered pahul. The congregation of the Khalsa at Anandpur was not liked by Hindus and Turks. The Guru asked the Sikhs to come with arms. There were armed conflicts, and many Sikhs were killed, sacrificing their life in dedication to the Guru. Not to reveal his own supranatural power, Guru Gobind Singh thought of Chandi to establish the dharm of Chhatris in order to destroy the *mlechh*. The ceremony called *kharag-jagg* was performed at the top of the hill. The pandit who acted as the priest could call Chandi but he could not face her. The *hom* was performed for the sake of dharm. The eight-armed Mother appeared but the pandits lost their senses and Guru Gobind Singh made the offering to her. She left a khanda in the fire pit. It was taken out and named 'Sri Sahib'. It was used for preparing pahul to be administered to Sikhs. They became Keshdhārī Singhs, and the Guru adopted the same form. Both *deg* and *tegh* were bestowed upon them. The Hindus and Turks felt as if a mote had entered their eyes. Without wealth and without any territory yet, the Singhs became sovereign like rulers.[117]

The younger Sāhibzādas were asked by Jhutha(Suchcha) Nand to do '*salām*' to the Subedar of Sirhind and they replied: 'we have done *salām* to the True King (*sachchā pātshāh*) and we do salām to no one else'. The Subedār ordered the executioner (to slaughter them). At that spot now stands the *dehurā* of the two Sāhibzādās. The two elder Sāhibzādās had died fighting. Thus, all the four sons of Guru Gobind Singh became shahīd. Banda Bahadur was appointed later by Guru Gobind Singh for vengeance (upon the Subedār of Sirhind).[118]

In the sākhīs of Sarup Das Bhalla there is a long confrontation between the Gurus and the Mughal emperors leading to deliberate sacrifices for the faith. Bhalla refers to the distinct identity of the baptized Sikhs and their sovereign status; he talks of the righteous war and the sacrifices involved in it. In this general context, he makes explicit references to martyrdom. The goddess serves a limited purpose in the righteous war. Her role comes after the commission by Akāl Purkh. To him goes the allegiance of the Sikhs.

Sukha Singh invokes Guru Nanak and Guru Gobind Singh in the opening *dohra* of his *Gurbilās Pātshāhī 10*. At the end of the Chaupai that follows he refers to Kalka. Then, for getting the gift of the sword for the Khalsa, Guru Gobind Singh decides to invoke Shakti Mata, the destroyer of the wicked. The Brahmans advise him to meditate on Kalka and worship Chandi as Adi Bhavani. Kalka appears after two and a half years and Guru Gobind Singh receives the boon from her. This gift came from the Wielder of the Sword for creating the Khalsa Panth. The masands were opposed to the idea of creating the Khalsa Panth. They were punished and removed. At Keshgarh then Guru Gobind Singh addressed the Sikhs: 'is there any Sikh who can offer his head to the Guru?' On the third call, a Sikh volunteered himself. He was taken into a tent, given a sword, and asked to slaughter a goat. Its blood flowed out for everyone to see. Nevertheless, other Sikhs responded to the call till the number reached five. The people began to attribute the sacrifice of these five men to the baneful effect of getting a boon from Kali. However, Guru Gobind Singh came out of the tent with all 'the five beloved'. They were dressed afresh and armed with weapons. Amrit was prepared and administered to them. In this way 'Sri Khalsa' was made manifest. Guru Gobind Singh made an earnest request to them to administer amrit to him.[119]

This was an extraordinary request. Therefore, 'the five beloved' wanted to know how they could presume to do such a thing. The explanation given by Guru Gobind Singh is extremely significant. The eternal and formless creator of the universe intervened in its affairs to redress the imbalance between the *bhagat*s and the *dusht*. In the

Kaliyuga the mlechh Turks had become predominant. The sants were oppressed. The whole earth groaned in pain and God sent Guru Gobind Singh to destroy the Turks root and branch. For this purpose the Khalsa Panth was created. They represented the Eternal Guru as the form of the eternal Master. After this explanation 'the five beloved' prepared amrit and administered it to Guru Gobind Singh. They discarded the false thread and put on the sword to take refuge in God. The others were then initiated into the fold and the entire body of the Khalsa asked for rahit. Guru Gobind Singh said many things. Sukha Singh mentions the most important: appropriation of nām and dān, seva and bhagti, and the *mantar* of the True Name; not to believe in anyone other than the Wielder of the Sword; to remain fully armed; to destroy the dusht and to promote the sants; to fight battles with the Turks; not to smoke and not to observe bhaddan; not to recite anything other than the shabad; to associate with the sādh-sangat all the time. The goddess figures nowhere in the rahit of the Khalsa. Strictly speaking she is out. Her position in relation to God is of no consequence whatsoever.

Sukha Singh is emphatic about the unique identity of the Khalsa and its totally egalitarian character as much as about the unity of the Supreme Being. Having imbibed amrit, the Khalsa roared like lions in battle and never stepped back. They died fighting in battle and went to the eternal abode. Their heroism was inspired by dharm-yuddh. By giving up their life for the sake of dharm they became immortal. The death of the younger Sāhibzādās in their firm commitment to the faith made them immortal and cut at the very roots of the mlechh. Even at the time of his departure from the world, Guru Gobind Singh told the Khalsa to fight against the Turks. Without using the term martyr (shahīd), Sukha Singh talks of sacrifices made for the faith which included the fight for sovereignty so far as the Khalsa were concerned. The ideal of martyrdom was built into its institution.[120]

Talking of the same light in all the ten Gurus, Sukha Singh refers to Guru Arjan as the bestower of the gift of fearlessness on the world. Guru Tegh Bahadur gave his head in sacrifice for saving the Bharat Khand. It was relevant for Sukha Singh to note that Guru Tegh Bahadur's father had put on two swords, he had created the Takht Bunga, and he was the destroyer of armies. Guru Tegh Bahadur went to Delhi, destroyed the mlechh through his sacrifice, and went to the eternal abode. He had been asked to accept Islam but he refused with contempt and remained steadfast in his faith. Deliberately, he ordered a Sikh to cut off his head. Nevertheless, Sukha Singh looks upon Guru Tegh Bahadur as a martyr. What is relevant for Sukha Singh is the essential commitment and not the mode of death.[121]

Bhangu's Portrayal of Sikh Martyrs

In Ratan Singh Bhangu's *Guru Panth Prakāsh*, martyrdom appears as the core of the Sikh tradition. He expected his work to reaffirm the faith of the reader, the reciter and the listener. Those who listen to it never turn their back; they die on the field of battle and mingle with the shahīds as water mingles with water.[122] Bhangu talks of the martyrdom of Guru Tegh Bahadur, the Sāhibzādās, Bhai Tara Singh, Bhai Mani Singh, Bhai Bota Singh, Bhai Mahtab Singh, Bhai Taru Singh, Bhai Sukha Singh, and Nihang Gurbakhsh Singh, among others. In the process he reveals his own theory of martyrdom.

Guru Tegh Bahadur gave his head for the sake of others, that is, *parsuārth*: he saved the dharm-karm of the Hindus. The Brahmans of Kashmir and other Hindus were being forcibly converted to Islam. Fear spread everywhere and Brahmans from several places came to Guru Tegh Bahadur as their only hope for help. It was decided that the Turks should be asked to convert the Guru first. He went to the Turks on his own initiative. They asked him to perform a miracle or *karāmāt* or to accept Islam. Guru Tegh Bahadur asserted that karāmāt invited God's wrath or *qahr*. Eventually, however, to save his *dharm-karm* he said that he would show a miracle: he would tie a thread to his neck and they would not be able to cut off his head. They were taken in. He was beheaded. This was how he gave his head for the sake of others. The pīrs and *paighambar*s of the Turks were removed by the True Lord from the Abode of Truth or Sachch-Khand: 'from that moment the *pātshāhī* of Delhi began to decline, from that moment the power of the Turks began to diminish'.[123] History and cosmology got linked up through martyrdom.

The Sāhibzādās and the other Singhs who died fighting after the final evacuation of Anandpur are presented as shahīds. The idea of parsuārth is reiterated and martyrdom diminishes the power of the Turks. Where did the status of shahīd come from? Guru Gobind Singh tested his Sikhs: 'is there any Sikh who can give his head?', he asked the congregation. The Sikhs who thought of Bhai Gurdas' reference to the 'Guru's *sāng*' offered themselves. The Guru slaughtered goats instead. For their readiness to lay down their lives, the five volunteers were given the status of shahīd or *shahīdī pad*.[124] Bhai Tara Singh 'used to carry his head on his palm', standing for justice and defying the Turks. He believed that martyrdom led to pātshāhī. By his deliberate acts he invited attack from the Mughal administrators. With twenty-two other like-minded Sikhs he faced the enemy undaunted, refusing to take the chance to escape. He courted martyrdom, living up to the words of the Guru: 'give your head but never give up your resolve'.[125]

Bhai Mani Singh unbound the Guru Granth and changed the order of its contents. A Sikh commented that his limbs too would be hacked. Believing that this would come true, Bhai Mani Singh approached the sangat, which is no different from the Guru, to pray that his body may be cut into pieces but his faith (sikhī) may remain safe. Years later, Bhai Mani Singh was hacked limb by limb but his head remained one piece with its kesh. Thus, his sikhī was saved. After his martyrdom Bhai Mani Singh became the *deorīdār* of the Sāhibzādās. Bhangu quotes a *kabitt* of a contemporary Bhatt which refers to Bhai Mani Singh as the 'foundation of Sikhī'. In utter fidelity to his faith, he allowed his body to be cut into pieces. He was unparalleled in the way in which he lived and died as a Gursikh.[126]

Bota Singh sacrificed his head to protect the honour of the Singhs. When the Singhs were virtually eliminated by the Mughal administrators someone saw him and remarked, 'how is this Singh still alive'? Others commented that he could be an imposter, or a coward, because the Khalsa fought in the front, unafraid of death, and defied the state to stake his head. As if stung by a scorpion, Bota Singh resolved to defy the Mughals, to give his head, to prove his Khalsahood, and to justify the Khalsa's claim to pātshāhī. He began to collect duty at one *anna* a cart and one *paisa* a donkey. He was joined by a Ranghreta Singh. Troops were sent against them by the Mughal governor, and the two Singhs were asked to surrender in the face of an overwhelming force. They refused to submit, fought stubbornly with simple weapons till their last breath, and attained martyrdom. They joined the *dera* of shahīds who were holding the pīrs and paighambars (of the Turks) under a siege.[127]

Even more emphatically than the martyrdom of Bhai Mani Singh, the martyrdom of Bhai Taru Singh underscores the sanctity of the kesh. His scalp was removed with his hair intact while he was alive. Bhangu gives some detail to show that, as a true Sikh, Bhai Taru Singh supported the Khalsa with his modest means without giving any offence to the administration. For the sake of the Panth, and to expose the Turks, he bore all kinds of hardships. He told the Sikhs gathered around him when he was being taken to Lahore that 'the true Guru had given his head for the sake of the Sikhs. As the Sikhs of the Guru, how can we save our heads'? Taru Singh and Subeg Singh saved the honour of the Panth as true Sikhs by courting martyrdom. Mahtab Singh did not wish to lag behind in giving his head to weaken the Turks. This was his way of being faithful to dharm and to sikhī. Not to lose faith and not to forget the Guru while giving one's head was his ideal too. How else could one attain the status of shahīd? Offering himself voluntarily to be broken on the wheel, he attained martyrdom. Bhangu narrates the story of the martyrdom of Mitt Singh to explain how a shahīdganj was raised and the wishes of those who made offerings there were fulfilled.[128]

Zain Khan, the Afghan governor of Sirhind, was defeated and killed and the fort of Sirhind was occupied by the Khalsa in 1763. They decided to build a dehurā at the spot where the two younger Sāhibzādās were beheaded. The old men of the place were consulted to identify the exact location. The Khalsa resolved to erect a *darbār* there, with standards and a drum or *nagārā*. Some Sikhs were appointed for worship (*pūjā*). The Panth held a *dīwān* in the morning and constructed a platform. Five weapons were placed at this *takht*, regarding them as a form of the Guru (*gur-sarūp*). A Singh was appointed as the custodian (*mukhtiyār*) of this place. A *rabābī* was appointed for reciting shabads. Jāgīrs were assigned for the maintenance of this dehurā. Offerings were made there by many who circumambulated the place and recited bāṇī. All their wishes were fulfilled.[129]

A shahīdganj was raised at the spot where Nihang Gurbakhsh Singh was cremated along with other martyrs just behind the Akal Bunga in Amritsar. Prayers offered there found a sure response and many Sikhs distributed *karhā parshād* there for their wishes having been fulfilled. Nihang Gurbakhsh Singh had always led the Khalsa in battle. Now he was the leader of the Singhs who died fighting to defend the

Harmandar Sahib against an overwhelming number of Afghans. They had resolved not to leave the place and offered the prayer (ardās) that they may preserve Sikhī with the kesh on their heads. Gurbakhsh Singh was exultant like a bridegroom and observed all the rites of marriage (with death). All the members of 'the marriage party' resolved to die with him. 'May we attain to martyrdom' (shahīdī) was their constant prayer, and they were determined not to show their backs. On their martyrdom they were welcomed by Bhai Mani Singh and Bhai Taru Singh and presented to the True Guru. Nihang Gurbakhsh Singh was later reborn as Ranjit Singh with the blessing that his authority would be recognized by the entire Khalsa.[130]

There is hardly any doubt that martyrdom for Ratan Singh Bhangu was the core of the Khalsa tradition which he equated with 'the Sikh tradition'. It was linked with parsuārth or selfless sacrifice. In the case of Guru Tegh Bahadur the sacrifice was made for the 'Hindus'; in the case of others it was made for the Panth. Commitment to the Sikh faith and concern for its visible emblem, the kesh, was common to all Sikh martyrs. Martyrdom was linked closely with the idea of the sovereignty of the Panth. In this connection Bhangu presents the myth or metaphysics of martyrdom. From this metaphysics flowed the sanctity of the places of martyrdom and the efficacy of the prayers offered there. Logically, monuments were raised to be known as shahīdganj and maintained as sacred spaces. The Sikh faith and the Sikh Panth provide the basis and the purpose of martyrdom.

THE PRE-COLONIAL TRADITION

The tradition of martyrdom is enshrined in the Sikh ardās. Among other things, the Khalsa are asked to turn their thoughts to:

The Cherished Five, the Four Sāhibzādās, and the Forty Muktās: all who were resolute, devout and strict in their self-denial; they who were faithful in their remembrance of the divine Name and generous to others; they who were noble both in battle and in the practice of charity; they who magnanimously pardoned the faults of others: reflect on their merits, O Khalsa, and utter Vāheguru. Those loyal members of the Khalsa who gave their heads for their faith; who were hacked limb from limb, scalped, broken on the wheel or sawn asunder; who sacrificed their lives for the protection of hallowed Gurdwaras, never forsaking their faith; and who were steadfast in their loyalty to the uncut hair of the true Sikh: reflect on their merits, O Khalsa, and utter Vāheguru.[131]

The martyrs of this ardās belong almost entirely to the pre-colonial period of Sikh history. Whatever the date of this part of the ardās, it breathes the spirit of the eighteenth century.

Bhai Kahn Singh Nabha was familiar with much of the pre-colonial Sikh literature. He defines shahīd as a person who sacrificed his life in dharmyudh, and shahīdī as the act of laying down one's life for the sake of dharm. The place of martyrdom was called shahīdganj. The best known of these places were in Lahore, Amritsar, Anandpur, Fatehgarh and Muktsar. Among the shahīds venerated at these places were the younger Sāhibzādās, the Forty Muktās, Bhai Mani Singh, Bhai Taru Singh, Nihang Gurbakhsh Singh and a large number of unnamed shahīds. They all belonged to the seventeenth and eighteenth centuries. Like the ardās, Bhai Kahn Singh's entries in the *Mahān Kosh* make a historical statement, a statement about an essential feature of the past Sikh tradition. The protagonists of the Singh Sabha movement cherished this feature of the tradition. In the works of the Sikh writers of the pre-colonial period there is much detailed information on the Sikh martyrs and the Sikh conception of martyrdom. Among other things, what comes out clearly from this literature is the close link of martyrdom with the Sikh faith, of the Sikh faith with the kesh, of the kesh with the baptism of the double-edged sword (khandedhār pahul), and of all of these with Sikh identity. Martyrdom, thus, becomes an integral part of the Sikh tradition.

Notes

1. Peter Brown, *The Cult of the Saints: Its Rise and Function in Latin Christianity*, Chicago: The University of Chicago Press, 1981, pp. 1, 5–6, 79–80, 101.
2. Bhai Jodh Singh, 'Jin Prem Kiyo Tin Hi Prabh Payo', in S.S. Amol ed., *Ek Murit Anek Darsan*, Jalandhar: Lyallpur Khalsa College, 1967, pp. 44–5. The lines quoted from Guru Nanak are:

   Jau tau prem khelān ka chāo,
   Sir dhar talī gali merī āo.
   It mārag paer dharījae,
   Sir dījae kāṇ nā kījae.

   The title of the article comes from a line of Guru Gobind Singh, meaning 'only he who loves deeply finds the lord.'
3. Kharak Singh, 'Martyrdom in Sikhism', *Abstracts of Sikh Studies*, Chandigarh: Institute of Sikh Studies, January 1994.

4. J.P.S. Uberoi, *Religion, Civil Society and the State,* New Delhi: Oxford University Press, 1996, pp. 61, 88–9, 93–4, 96–7.
5. Ibid., pp. 114–23, 135, 151.
6. Harjot Oberoi, *The Construction of Religious Boundaries: Culture, Identity and Diversity in the Sikh Tradition,* New Delhi: Oxford University Press, 1994, pp. 328–30.
7. Ibid., pp. 330–3.
8. W.H. McLeod, *Sikhism,* Harmmondsworth: Penguin Books, 1997, pp. 128–30.
9. Ibid., p. 129.
10. Ibid., pp. 130–1.
11. Louis E. Fenech, *Martyrdom in the Sikh Tradition: Playing the 'Game of Love',* New Delhi: Oxford University Press, 2002, pp. 1, 23.
12. Ibid., pp. 63–102, 117–23.
13. Ibid., pp. 7, 27–8.
14. Ibid., pp. 123–9.
15. Ibid., pp. 129–32.
16. Ibid., pp. 41, 53–5, 132–7.
17. Ibid., pp. 11, 20, 22.
18. Ibid., pp. 11, 148, 150.
19. Ibid., pp. 151–3, 172.
20. Ibid., pp. 154–70.
21. Ibid., p. 193.
22. Ibid., pp. 11, 148, 150.
23. Ibid., pp. 189–91, 217–18.
24. Ibid., pp. 191–6.
25. Ibid., pp. 275, 297.
26. Ādi Granth (AG), p. 53.
27. Ibid., p. 1,293.
28. Giani Hazara Singh, ed., *Vārān Bhai Gurdas,* Amritsar: Khalsa Samachar, 1962 (7th edn), Vār 8, *pauṛīs* 8, 24; Vār 21, pauṛī 13. An English translation of the Vārs is now available in Jodh Singh, *Varan Bhai Gurdas: Text, Transliteration and Translation,* 2 vols, Patiala: Vision and Venture, 1998.
29. AG, p. 1028.
30. AG, p. 918.
31. AG, p. 1412.
32. AG, p. 421.
33. AG, p. 465.
34. AG, p. 831.
35. AG, p. 788.

36. AG, p. 1288. For the combination of love and fear, also see pp. 357 and 722.
37. AG, p. 151.
38. AG, p. 788.
39. AG, p. 587.
40. AG, p. 11.
41. AG, p. 464.
42. AG, pp. 701–2.
43. AG, p. 820.
44. AG, p. 703.
45. AG, p. 419.
46. AG, p. 952.
47. AG, p. 522.
48. AG, p. 62.
49. AG, p. 472.
50. AG, p. 1245.
51. AG, p. 243.
52. AG, p. 26.
53. AG, p. 128.
54. AG, p. 992.
55. AG, p. 749.
56. AG, p. 141.
57. AG, p. 421.
58. AG, pp. 440–1.
59. AG, p. 94.
60. AG, p. 831.
61. AG, p. 1343.
62. *Varan Bhai Gurdas,* Vār 1, pauṛīs 16, 23, 29, 31, 45; Vār 3, pauṛīs 5, 7; Vār 5, pauṛī 13; Vār 9, pauṛī 17; Vār 18, pauṛī 20; Vār 23, pauṛī 17.
63. Ibid., Vār 4, pauṛī 18; Vār 6, pauṛī 5; Vār 9, pauṛī 2; Vār 28, pauṛī 1.
64. Ibid., Vār 28, pauṛī 18.
65. Ibid., Vār 20, pauṛī 13.
66. Ibid., Vār 28, pauṛī 17.
67. Ibid., Vār 16, pauṛī 21.
68. Ibid., Vār 3, pauṛī 13.
69. Ibid., Vār 11, pauṛī 1.
70. Ibid., Vār 18, pauṛī 5.
71. Ibid., Vār 26, pauṛī 19.
72. Ibid., Vār 18, pauṛī 17.
73. Ibid., Vār 28, pauṛī 17.
74. Ibid., Vār 20, pauṛī 20.

75. Ibid., Vār 20, paurī 13.
76. Ibid., Vār 28, paurī 16.
77. Ibid., Vār 29, paurī 13.
78. Ibid., Vār 12, paurī 13.
79. Ibid., Vār 3, paurī 19.
80. Ibid., Vār 5, paurī 2.
81. Ibid., Vār 6, paurī 15.
82. Ibid., Vār 6, paurī 18.
83. Ibid., Vār 20, paurī 3; Vār 28, paurī 9.
84. Ibid., Vār 9, paurī 19; Vār 13, paurī 14.
85. Ibid., Vār 1, paurī 3.
86. Ibid., Vār 28, paurī 15.
87. Ibid., Vār 3, paurī 2; Vār 5, paurī 5, 13; Vār 6, paurī 2, 15; Vār18, paurī 14, 20; Vār 19, paurī 8; Vār 20, paurī 3; Vār 28, paurī 15.
88. Ibid., Vār 28, paurī 14.
89. Ibid., Vār 5, paurī 2.
90. Ibid., Vār 9, paurī 18.
91. Ibid., Vār 14, paurī 17.
92. Ibid., Vār 20, paurī 10.
93. Ibid., Vār 1, paurī 3.
94. Ibid., Vār 28, paurī 11.
95. Ibid., Vār 28, paurī 13.
96. Ibid., Vār 6, paurī 14.
97. Ibid., Vār 19, paurī 18.
98. Ibid., Vār 1, paurī 47; Vār 11, paurī 18–28; Vār 13, paurī 25; Vār 24, paurī 18, 19, 20; Vār 27, paurī 34; Vār 38, paurī 20.
99. Ibid., Vār 24, paurī 23.
100. AG, p. 462.
101. AG, pp. 579–80. On the themes of abhaidan, abhaipad, bhau, jivanmukt, par-upkar, and sadachar, there are useful entries in Ratan Singh Jaggi, *Guru Granth Vishvkosh,* 2 vols, Patiala : Punjabi University, 2002, vol. I, pp. 44, 141–3; vol. II, pp. 31–3, 207–8, 313–15.
102. McLeod, *Sikhism,* pp. 45–6.
103. McLeod refers to an 'alternative Sikh tradition' in Chaupa Singh's *Rahitnāma* in which the first arrest of Guru Tegh Bahadur takes place due to complaints by close relatives (*sanbandhī sāk*): W.H. McLeod, *The Chaupa Singh Rahit-Nama,* Dunedin: University of Otago Press, 1987, pp. 79–80, 167–8. There is no reference to Brahmans in this version but the deliberate decision of Guru Tegh Bahadur to give his head to expose the injustice of the ruler of Delhi is underscored.

104. Sainapat, Shamsher Singh Ashok, ed., *Shri Gur Sobha*, Amritsar: Shriomani Gurdwara Parbandhak Committee, 1967, pp. 10–11, 15.
105. J.S. Grewal, *Guru Nanak in History*, Chandigarh: Panjab University, 1969, pp. 157–8.
106. Sainapat, *Gur Sobha*, pp. 29–30, 33, 40–2, 63–4, 90, 94.
107. McLeod, *The Chaupa Singh Rahit-Nama*, p. 110.
108. Ibid., pp. 63–4, 68, 83. The alternative use of the phrase 'kesān dī pahul' leaves no doubt about the inevitable link.
109. Ibid., pp. 65, 68, 77, 88–9, 112, 120, 133.
110. Ibid., pp. 80, 134.
111. Kesar Singh Chhibber, *Bansāvalīnāma Dasān Pātshāhiān Kā*, Ratan Singh Jaggi, Chandigarh: Panjab University, 1972 (vol. II of *Research Bulletin of Panjabi Language and Literature*, S.S. Kohli), pp. 52–5, 65, 69, 78–9.
112. Ibid., pp. 87–97, 126.
113. Ibid., pp. 128, 129, 132, 134, 138, 143, 148, 151, 153, 157, 176.
114. Sarup Das Bhalla, *Mahima Prakash*, vol. II, Gobind Singh Lamba, ed., Patiala: Punjab Language Department, 1971, pp. 410–16, 420, 423–5, 435, 590, 598, 601–7, 641–3, 646–7.
115. Ibid., pp. 656, 660–6, 673–9.
116. Ibid., pp. 682, 709, 760–1.
117. Ibid., pp. 797–806, 815–28, 832–70.
118. Ibid., pp. 877–8, 882, 888–9, 892.
119. Sukha Singh, *Gurbilas Patshahi 10*, Gursharan Kaur Jaggi, ed., Patiala: Punjab Language Department, 1989, pp. 1–2, 130, 134, 136, 145, 160, 170–8.
120. Ibid., pp. 77–9.
121. Ibid., pp. 180–1, 185, 198, 207, 319–21, 323, 333, 441.
122. Ibid., pp. 5, 7, 9, 58, 64–5.
123. Ratan Singh Bhangu, *Prachin Panth Prakash*, Bhai Vir Singh, ed., New Delhi: Bhai Vir Singh Sahit Sadan, 1993, pp. 470–1.
124. Ibid., pp. 34–9.
125. Ibid., pp. 55–9, 61–4.
126. Ibid., pp. 176–8.
127. Ibid., pp. 187–98.
128. Ibid., pp. 223–8. There were other Sikhs who were broken on the wheel at the horse market in Lahore.
129. Ibid., pp. 243–6.
130. Ibid., pp. 268–72, 287–92, 301–2, 352–3.
131. This is my translation of the relevant passage in the Ardās (Sikh prayer). For another translation, see McLeod, *Sikhism*, p. 300.

PART II
Socio-political Institutions

4. The Sikh State*

Generally, the state established by Ranjit Singh in the early decades of the nineteenth century is equated with the Sikh state. For a proper appreciation of the Sikh state, however, we have to take at least two other historical situations into account: the decade after Guru Gobind Singh's death in 1708, when the Khalsa under the leadership of Banda Bahadur established, or claimed to have established, a sovereign state; the late eighteenth century, when a large number of Sikh leaders re-established Sikh rule in the former Mughal province of Lahore and the Sutlej–Jamuna Divide.[1]

DECLARATION OF SOVEREIGN RULE

It is important to note that contemporary writers, both Sikh and non-Sikh, underscore the political aspect of Guru Gobind Singh's life. Muhammad Qasim, for example, refers to his magnificence in terms of his material and martial resources: 'he was not behind the nobles of 5,000 (*zāt*) or even rulers of principalities in anything concerned with greatness of splendour or accumulation of resources'.[2] A Sikh writer of the early nineteenth century projects the idea that Guru Gobind Singh's purpose in instituting the Khalsa was to make them the rulers of the land.[3]

Significantly, the Khalsa established their power within two years of Guru Gobind Singh's death. A report from Bahadur Shah's court refers to their battle with the *faujdār* of Sirhind on 24 May 1710 after which 'the Sikhs of the Khalsa' established their control and government from the River Sutlej upto Karnal. A Jatt named Baz Singh from the *pargana* of Patti Haibatpur in the province of Lahore assumed the *subadārī*

---

* 'The Sikh State' is a slightly revised version of a paper presented at a seminar on 'The Indian State' organized by the Aligarh Group of Historians in 2004. A slightly different version was published in my *Sikh Ideology, Polity and Social Order* (New Delhi: Manohar, 2007, pp. 207–19).

of Sirhind and appointed officers over the parganas.[4] Banda Bahadur established himself in the fort of Mukhlispur (renamed Lohgarh) near Sadhaura.[5]

As a Persian proverb has it, coins are struck in the name of those who strike the sword effectively.[6] A Persian writer refers to a coin struck by the Khalsa. It carried the implication of their claim to have established sovereign rule. Apart from literary evidence, actual coins have been discovered and examined. They refer to the second and the third year of Sikh rule, carrying the implication that the first coin was struck presumably after the conquest of Sirhind in 1710. The Persian inscription on the coins is essentially the same:[7]

Sikka zadd bar har do 'ālam, tegh-i Nanak wāhib ast,
Fateh-i Gobind, shāh-i shāhān, fazl-i sachchā sāhib ast.

Reference to the 'sword of Nanak' as the bestower of power in this inscription is metaphorical. Guru Nanak is believed to be the source of all power. The victory of Gobind, the king of kings, is a mark of the grace of the True Master. No earthly superior or source of authority is acknowledged. The coin clearly symbolizes the declaration of sovereign rule. Reference to the Khalsa on the reverse indicates that the political success of the Khalsa was seen as the victory of Guru Gobind Singh.[8]

The seal used by Banda Bahadur in a *hukamnāma* of 1710 carried the inscription:[9]

Deg-o teg-o fateh-o nusrat bidirang,
Yāft az Nanak Guru Gobind Singh.

Here, again, Guru Nanak is believed to be the bestower of deg, teg, and fateh. These gifts are received by (the Khalsa of) Guru Gobind Singh. Besides 'sword' and 'victory', they have received deg, literally the pot for cooking sacred food and metaphorically 'grace'. The essential significance of this inscription is the same as that of the inscription on the coin. The power has come from Guru Nanak through God's grace. Apart from the fact of striking the coin, the claim to sovereignty is made explicit in the inscriptions. If Banda Bahadur was exercising political power personally, he was seen as doing so on behalf of the Gurus and the Khalsa.[10]

Eighteenth Century Sikh Polity

The idea that the Khalsa were meant to rule is attributed to Guru Gobind Singh. It finds expression in a Sikh work of 1711.[11] In a *rahit-nāma* composed before 1711, the familiar phrase 'rāj karegā khālsā' is used.[12] It became a part of the Sikh anthem recited after the formal Sikh prayer (*ardās*).[13] For half a century after Banda's fall in 1715 and his execution in 1716, the Khalsa waged a relentless struggle for freedom. Confident of their success against Ahmad Shah Abdali, they struck a coin at Lahore in 1765. It bore the inscription that had been used on the seal in the time of Banda Bahadur. Another coin was struck at Amritsar in 1775. It bore the inscription that had been used in the third year of Sikh rule in the time of Banda Bahadur. This coin refers to 'the eternal throne' (*takht akal bakht*).[14] Both the inscriptions remained in use throughout the late eighteenth century when a number of mints were established at places other than Lahore and Amritsar.[15]

It is important to note that these Sikh coins were meant to replace the coinage made current by Ahmad Shah Abdali to symbolize the establishment of his rule in the former Mughal territories. Contested from time to time by the representatives of the Mughal emperor, the authority of Ahmad Shah Abdali had become well established before 1765. Even Nadir Shah had struck his own coins from Peshawar, Lahore, Multan, Sirhind, and Shahjahanabad during his invasion of India in 1739. Ahmad Shah Abdali struck his first coin at Lahore in 1748 and subsequently at several other places. The coins of the Mughal emperors Ahmad Shah and Alamgir II were also struck at Sirhind, Lahore, and even Peshawar from time to time between 1748 and 1759 but no Mughal coin was struck at these places afterwards. The Ahmad Shahi coin had become current in the former Mughal provinces of Kabul, Kashmir, Lahore, and Multan, and in the Sarkar of Sirhind. It bore the inscription:

Hukm shud az qādir-i bechūn b'Ahmad Pādshāh
Sikka zann bar sīm-o zar az auj-i māhī tā b'māh

By deriving his authority from God, Ahmad Shah Abdali was laying claim to sovereignty.[16]

In the same way, the Sikh coins symbolized declaration of Sikh sovereignty. It is asserted sometimes that these coins embody the concept of collective sovereignty of the Khalsa Panth.[17] The doctrines of Guru Panth and Guru Granth, the *gurmatas* (resolutions of the Guru) adopted at the Akal Takht in Ramdaspur (Amritsar), and the collective action of the Sikh forces (*dal khalsa*) on the basis of gurmatas can be seen as supporting the idea of collective sovereignty. It has been pointed out, however, that these doctrines and institutions, like the institutions of *rākhī* and *misl*, were effectively operative during the phase of struggle for the acquisition of power and not for the exercise of power.[18] There was an essential difference between the phase of struggle for territorial occupation and the phase of actual government and administration after territorial occupation. It has been observed that 'the derivation of sovereignty from the Gurus and God enabled each individual to assert his independence of any temporal lord', whether Sikh or non-Sikh. For all practical purposes, the individual Sikh chief became a sovereign ruler 'not in spite of the coin but because of it'.[19]

The orders issued by the Sikh rulers in the late eighteenth century clarify the issue. We may take the example of Jai Singh Kanhiya who was an eminent Sikh ruler of this period. His seal bears the date 1750.[20] The inscription on this seal carries the name 'Jai Singh' without any title. The only other words on the seal are *akāl sahāi* (may God protect, or under God's protection). God alone is the protector of Jai Singh who is wielding power in his own name. His rule is referred to as 'the rule of Khalsa Jio' ('*aml-i khalsa jio*').[21] Jai Singh's writ ran for more than forty years. After his death in the last decade of the century, orders began to be issued in the name of his son, Gurbakhsh Singh, who had died in the 1780s. Power was exercised in his name by his widow, Sada Kaur.[22] Jai Singh is posthumously referred to as 'Singh Sahib, the late Sardar Jai Singh', and the epithet *faiyāz-i zamān* (the generous ruler of the age) is also used for him.[23] Among the Sikh rulers of the late eighteenth century, dynastic succession was the rule which enabled even a widow to wield power on behalf of her deceased husband. Sons had succeeded to the founding fathers as a matter of routine.[24]

The orders we have referred to relate to *dharmarth* grants. It is evident that every Sikh ruler could alienate revenue from land in favour of religious institutions and personages without any reference to others. The ruler confirmed old grants and gave fresh grants in accordance with his own inclination and interests. Revenue from land was alienated also in favour of those who served the Sikh ruler. There is hardly any doubt that he appointed his own *dīwān*s, *kārdār*s, and *qānūngo*s from the very beginning of territorial occupation. The Sikh rulers used their discretion in giving subsistence or *in'ām jāgīr*s as well. That the Sikh ruler of the late eighteenth century was independent in his political relations with others is evident from the polity of suzerain-vassal relationship. There are numerous examples of Sikh rulers collecting tribute from non-Sikh chiefs of the hills and the plains. Among them were the founders of states, like Charhat Singh Sukerchakia, Hari Singh Bhangi, Jassa Singh Ramgarhia, Jai Singh Kanhiya, and Gujjar Singh. Indeed, suzerain-vassal relationship remained an essential feature of polity in the Punjab during the late eighteenth century. Evidently, every Sikh ruler was autonomous in his political relations with others as much as in his internal administration.[25]

The most that can be said about the Sikh rulers of the late eighteenth century is that they professed to rule on behalf of the Khalsa. The use of a common coin could reinforce this impression. They paid homage to the Gurus not only on their coins but also by constructing Gurdwaras at places associated with the Gurus. They assigned revenue-free lands to Gurdwaras and to Granthīs, Rāgīs, Rabābīs, and Ardāsiās. There was hardly a Sikh ruler who did not send regular or occasional offerings to the Harmandar at Ramdaspur which became a common concern of the Sikh rulers as well as the foremost place of pilgrimage for the Sikhs in general. The Sikh rulers gave revenue-free lands to the descendants of the Gurus, notably the descendants of Guru Nanak who were known as Bedis and the descendants of Guru Ram Das who were known as Sodhis. Next to them were the Udasis who claimed to be closely associated with Guru Nanak through his elder son, Sri Chand (whom they regarded as the head of their orders). However, grants were not confined to Sikh, or professedly Sikh, institutions and individuals. Shaiva, Vaishnava, and Shakta temples and their custodians were patronized as well as learned Brahmans and priests. Similarly, *shaikh*s and *sayyid*s, *dargah*s and *masjid*s continued to hold old grants and received some fresh grants. It is difficult to quantify the grants given by the late eighteenth Sikh rulers to various categories of grantees. It is clear, however, that Sikh institutions and individuals received the largest share of fresh grants, while the largest number of the old grants confirmed were those of Muslim individuals and institutions.[26]

Writing in 1769, a conservative Sikh writer advised the Sikh rulers not to trust Khatris and Muslims.[27] Presumably, the Sikh rulers had already begun to associate Hindus and Muslims with the administration of their territories. The dīwāns employed by Charhat Singh Sukerchakia, Gujjar Singh Bhangi, and Milkha Singh of Rawalpindi, for example, were non-Singhs, presumably Khatris, like Shiv Dayal, Gullu Mal, and Sulakhan Mal. There were *qāzīs* in Wazirabad, Gujrat, Gujjranwala, and Batala. Qazi Abdul Rahman was holding a service jāgīr in Ram Nagar in the late eighteenth century. Ismatullah was the qānūngo of Gujrat under Gujjar Singh. Khudadad Khan was given a few villages in jāgīr by Mahan Singh for maintaining twenty horsemen for service, and Mian Khan received a jāgīr worth 15,000 rupees a year from Sada Kaur. Muslim and Hindu *chaudharīs* and *muqaddams* remained associated with the collection of revenues under the Sikh rulers. These known examples make it clear that Hindu and Muslim individuals performed various services for the Sikh rulers of the late eighteenth century and they were paid by the state like its Sikh functionaries. They performed military as well as civil services.[28]

Sikh States in the Sutlej–Jamuna Divide

Turning to the Sutlej–Jamuna Divide we find that there were two categories of Sikh rulers: those who originally belonged to the province of Lahore and those who belonged to the province of Delhi. The former occupied the upper portions of the Divide and the latter occupied the lower portions. The rulers of Patiala, Nabha, Jind, Kaithal, and Faridkot belonged to the latter category. The founders of Patiala, Nabha, and Jind had started their career as zamīndārs of the Mughal empire and made use of its framework to rise into power. None of them is known to have participated in any meeting of the Sarbat Khalsa at Amritsar and none of them joined the Dal Khalsa in operations outside the Divide. When Ahmad Shah Abdali became clearly ascendant in the 1760s, Ala Singh, the founder of Patiala, accepted the title of Raja from him and paid tribute to him. He acknowledged the suzerainty of Ahmad Shah Abdali by striking the coin also in his name. His successor, Amar Singh, received the title of Raja-i Rajgan from Ahmad Shah Abdali to distinguish him from the other rulers of the Divide who had accepted Afghan suzerainty. The Ahmad Shahi coin remained current in the territories of Jind as well as Patiala. The rulers of Nabha struck the coin with the inscription used on the coin of Lahore in 1765. Thus, whereas the founders of Patiala and Jind accepted the status of vassals, the founder of Nabha claimed a sovereign status, though his father too had started his career as a zamīndār under the Mughals.[29]

It is extremely important to note that there was no difference in the government and administration of Nabha and that of Patiala and Jind. Political power was vested in the hands of the individual who used the services of other individuals at subordinate levels. There was no need to make any change in the administrative framework. Hindu and Muslim individuals were associated with government and administration from the very beginning. Patronage was extended to Hindu and Muslim institutions and personages. Thus, on the whole, there was no appreciable difference in the government and administration of the Sikh rulers of the late eighteenth century on the two sides of the River Sutlej.

The State under Maharaja Ranjit Singh

Ranjit Singh was born in 1780. His father Mahan Singh was a Sikh ruler of the second generation. When Mahan Singh died in 1791, Ranjit Singh was recognized as his successor as a matter of course. As we noted earlier, dynastic succession was the rule in Sikh territories in the late eighteenth century on both sides of the Sutlej. In the face of Afghan offensive in the Punjab, Ranjit Singh occupied Lahore in 1799, ousting three Sikh rulers. The event was important in his political career, but it was not the beginning of his rule. Making use of matrimonial and political alliances he started subjugating Sikh, Hindu, and Muslim chiefs on both sides of the Sutlej. In 1809, the East India Company obliged him to confine his activities to the right side of the Sutlej but recognized him as the sole Sikh sovereign. Within ten years then, Ranjit Singh unified the Punjab under his rule and extended his territories towards Multan, Kashmir, and Peshawar at the cost of the Afghans. Eventually, his state became larger than all the Sikh territories of the late eighteenth century put together. The large extent of his dominions, which also meant much larger resources in men and revenues, and more complex politics and administration, distinguished him from his Sikh predecessors. The difference of degree was so large that it could easily be seen as a difference of kind. In the popular idiom, Ranjit Singh the *misldār* became Ranjit Singh the *mahārajā*.[30]

However, Ranjit Singh continued to strike the coins struck at Lahore in 1765 and at Amritsar in 1775. No coin was ever issued in his name. On one exceptional coin he is shown sitting respectfully before Guru Nanak, reinforcing the idea that the Sikh rulers claimed to derive their authority from Guru Nanak. In fact the coins were called 'Nanak Shahi'. These coins were minted in Multan, Kashmir, and Peshawar as well as at Lahore and Amritsar.[31] The inscription on the seal of Ranjit Singh is the simple 'Akāl Sahāi Ranjit Singh'. He is referred to as 'Singh Sahib' or 'Khalsa Jio'. However, he is also referred to as *'sarkār-i 'ālī'* and *'huzūr-i anwar'*. His order is referred to as *'parwāna-i wālā'*. Such phrases are used in the orders of the princes as well, which bear the seal impression of 'Akāl Sahāi Kharak Singh' or 'Akāl Sahāi Tara Singh'. 'Akāl Sahāi' is used on the seals of some Sikh functionaries of the state, like Mangal Singh and Dasaundha Singh. It is interesting to note that Diwan Moti Ram uses 'Daya Karo Bhavani' and Misar Ram Dayal uses 'Bhavani Sahāi' on their seals.[32] In a medal instituted by Ranjit Singh in the 1830s he is called 'Maharaja Ranjit Singh'.[33] But even in his orders of 1834 he is still referred to as 'Khalsa Ji'.[34] There is no doubt that Ranjit Singh used personal discretion in the exercise of his power but, contrary to the general impression, he never assumed the title of Maharaja formally. His position in this respect was close to that of his predecessors.

Ranjit Singh subverted a number of principalities but the number of those which he allowed to exist in subordination to him was larger. Most of them were in the hills. The vassal chiefs paid tribute and bound themselves to place a number of troops at the disposal of Ranjit Singh as their overlord. Their political relations with one another and with other sovereign powers were controlled by the suzerain. It was a common practice of Ranjit Singh to take hostages from the vassal chiefs. Succession to the *gaddī* of vassal principality was controlled by the suzerain. Ranjit Singh created new rājās of his own. The Jamwal bothers—Gulab Singh, Dhian Singh, and Suchet Singh—were given the rāj of Jammu and its neighbouring principalities. In 1827, Raja Dhian Singh was given the title of *'rājā-i rājgān, rājā-i kalān bahādur'*, with the rāj of Bhimbar and Chhibal. His son, Hira Singh, was given the title of 'rājā' in 1837, with the territories of Jasrota and Basohli. All the vassal chiefs enjoyed a large measure of autonomy in the administration of their territories. Significantly, many of the Sikh and Muslim rulers too became tributaries to Ranjit Singh before their territories were taken over. The only Sikh ruler to survive as a vassal chief was Fateh Singh Ahluwalia of Kapurthala.[35]

The vassal chiefs formed an important section of the ruling class. Some of them were among the foremost *jāgīrdār*s of Ranjit Singh, with a large share in the revenues of the state and a considerable role in its administration. Among the jāgīrdārs of Ranjit Singh were some of the former Sikh and non-Sikh rulers, and their jāgīrdārs. However, a larger number were picked up all afresh on the basis of merit and loyalty. They were drawn from different ethnic and religious groups and from different parts of the state. The choice was not confined to the Punjab. Apart from the well-known European officers like Allard, Avitabile, Court, and Ventura, there were important members of the ruling class who did not belong to the Punjab: Diwan Bhavani Das, Diwan Ganga Ram, Diwan Dina Nath, Diwan Ajudhya Prashad, Jamadar Khushal Singh and his nephew Tej Singh, for example. The foremost jāgīrdārs were seen as *sardārs*, *sardārān-i nāmdār*, and *sardārān-i kalān*. Their jāgīrs ranged from Rs 25,000 to Rs 800,000 a year.[36]

The composite character of the ruling class is well reflected in the orders of Ranjit Singh addressed to General Tej Singh in 1834. To figure in these orders are the Europeans like Allard, Avitabile, Court, and Ventura; the Rajas and their kinsmen, like Raja-i Kalan Dhian Singh, his son Raja Hira Singh, Raja Gulab Singh and his son Mian Labha Singh, Raja Suchet Singh, Raja Jodhbir Chand, Mian Naudh Chand, and Wazir Kesari Singh; Prince Kharak Singh and his son Prince Naunihal Singh, and Prince Sher Singh; Diwans Bhavani Das, Kirpa Ram, Prabh Dayal, and Devi Sahai; Misars Beli Ram, Jassa Mal, and Mul Raj; General Sultan Mahmud Khan and Colonels Mahtab Singh, Amir Singh Mann, Mehnga Singh Kakar, Mihan Singh, Gulab Singh Pahuwindia, Mian Ilahi Bakhsh, Shaikh Ilahi Bakhsh and Imam Shah; the Sayyids Faqir Nuruddin Ansari, Faqir Azizuddin Ansari, Faqir Imamuddin Ansari, Faqir Tajuddin Ansari, and Fakir Shah Din Ansari; Bhais Ram Singh and Gobind Ram; Sardars Mangal Singh Ramgarhia, Kahn Singh Nakkai, the Sandhanwalias Atar Singh and Lehna Singh, the Majithias Gujjar Singh and Hem Singh, the Attariwalas Jai Singh and Chatar Singh, the Manns Kahn Singh, Fateh Singh and Sham Singh, the Rangar Nanglias Arjan Singh and Wazir Singh, Sardars Hari Singh Nalwa, Hukma Singh Chimni, Jawala Singh

Padhania, Ishar Singh Sandhu, Gurmukh Singh Lamma, Chatar Singh Kalianwala, and Ratan Singh Garhjakhia; Diwan Sawan Mal and Raja Fazl Dad.[37] Several countries and regions are represented here, and many castes and communities. Amidst all these, the Sikhs appear to have been preponderant and among them the Jatts. But they were not predominant.

A similar pattern appears to emerge when we turn to the grantees. The most conspicuous among them were the Sodhi collaterals of Guru Gobind Singh. Important among them were Bhai Wasti Ram and his sons Bhai Ram Singh and Gobind Ram, Sodhi Sadhu Singh of Kartarpur, and the Sodhis of Anandpur. The Bedis were not far behind the Sodhis. The most prominent among them were Bedi Sahib Singh of Una and his son Bikram Singh. The granthīs, rāgīs, rabābīs, ardāsias, and the *mutasaddī*s of Harmandir Sahib enjoyed grants all over the Punjab. The small establishments around the Golden Temple and shrines of local importance received numerous grants. The Akalis and Nihangs were also the beneficiaries of state patronage. Extensive grants were received by Nirmala *sādh*s. The dharmarth lands of the Udasis were scattered over all the *doāb*s. Then there were Purohits and Brahmans, Shaiva and Vaishnava establishments, the Jwalamukhi Temple, and many other Devidwaras and Thakurdwaras. The descendants of Shaikh Farid received fresh grants. The number of Muslim grantees in Kashmir ran into thousands, the most notable among them being the shrines of Hazratbal, Shah Hamdan and Muhammad Shah Naqshbandi. All the old grants of the sayyids, the '*ulamā*, the *qāzī*s and *faqīr*s were confirmed by Ranjit Singh in the trans-Indus territories. The Gardezi Sayyids of Multan retained much of their wealth and influence. Quantitatively, the revenue-free grants enjoyed by non-Sikh institutions and individuals were almost as important as the grants received by Sikh individuals and institutions. If we keep in view the fact that Sodhis and Bedis held a large proportion of their lands as jāgīrdārs, the purely dharmarth grants of the Sikhs could be less important than those of the non-Sikhs. Qualitatively, Ranjit Singh made no difference between one community and another so far as state patronage was concerned.[38]

The titles used for individuals associated with the state directly or indirectly are not without significance.[39] The epithet *mu'atamid al-khidmat, irādat-nishān, irādat-dastgāh*, and *khusūsiyat-nishān* are used generally for the Punjabi Khatris. However, among them is also a Brahman, the *akhbār-navīs* Misar Bindraban. The epithet reserved generally for Brahmans is *brahm-mūrit*. The term *khāirkhah-i bā-safā* was reserved for the Ansari Sayyids (Nuruddin, Azizuddin, Imamuddin, Tajuddin, and Shah Din). Those who were close to the palace (*deorī-i mubārak*) were referred to as *maqrab-i bārgāh, maqrab-i bārgāh-i khās* or *maqrab-i bārgāh-i khās al-khās*. For Fateh Singh, the ruler of Kapurthala, was reserved the epithet *bhāī* (brother) with reference to the treaty he had signed with Ranjit Singh in 1802. The epithet reserved for Raja Hira Singh, son of Raja Dhian Singh, was *iqbāl āsār*. Two titles were reserved for Sardar Hari Singh Nalwa: *sardār-i kasīr al-iqtidār* and *nusrat jang bahādur*. The titles used for the French General Court were *shujaʻat dastgāh* and *tahhawar panāh*. The latter was commonly used for the army officers.

The epithet generally used for Sikh officers, whether civil or military, was ujjal dīdār. The only non-Sikh for whom this epithet is used is Wazir Kesari Singh. In some cases the epithet *nirmal buddh* is added to *ujjal dīdār*. The only non-Sikh for whom both these epithets are used is Raja Suchet Singh. The epithets used for persons known for their piety are *uttam sarūp, kirpā nidhān, tarn tāran har do jahān* and *ujjal dīdār nirmal buddh bhāī sāhib kirpā nidhān dayā rūp*. For princes the epithets used are *sāhibzāda-i buland iqbāl, shāhzāda-i ʻālamīn, sāhibzāda-i buland akhtar* or *buland iqbāl, farzand-i azīz*, and *sāhibzāda-i sikandar misāl, farzand-i azīz arshad arjmand, sāhibzāda-i buland akhtar farzand-i azīz, sāhibzāda-i iqbal buland* and *sāhibzāda-i nūr al-absār*. Prince Kharak Singh, being the heir apparent, was entitled to a string of epithets: *ghurrah-i nahiya-i jahāndārī, qurrah-i basarah-i kāmgārī, samrah-i shajr-i bakhtyārī, gauhar-i tāj-i nāmdārī, gulshan-i saltnat-i iqbāl, munīr-i sipāh-i hashmat, ajlāl-i shamaʻ-i anjuman-i daulat-i kāmrānī, nūr-i dīdah-i bargāh-i sultānī, barkhurdār-i nūr al-absār*.

As in the titles used for the functionaries of the state, in the epithets used for the orders of Ranjit Singh so we hear echoes of the Mughal times. A common term is *irshād-i wālā*. Another is *irshād-iʻālī* that gets the honour of being issued (*sharf-i sudūr*). Elsewhere, the order is *amr-iʻālam ibtāʻ*, or *hukm-i jahān mutāʻ*, or *hukm-i jahān mutāʻ wa amr-iʻālam ibtāʻ*, or *amr-i jalīl al-qadr*. The *parwāna-i faiz kāshānah* embodies *irshād-i wālā getī minqād ahkām nātiq*.

More tangible continuity with the Mughal times can be found in the administrative arrangements made by Ranjit Singh and his Sikh predecessors. The village remained the smallest unit of administration in the late eighteenth century and pargana the basic unit. Since the territory under every Sikh ruler was rather small, the pargana served as the primary unit, with the exception of Multan in the 1770s when it was treated as a province. When Ranjit Singh conquered the former Mughal province of Lahore, for which the term Punjab was used, he did not treat it as a single unit. However, he did combine a number of parganas into primary units which, though much smaller, could be seen as the counterpart of the Mughal provinces. The provinces of Multan and Kashmir were larger than the other provincial units. With the *nāzim* at the provincial level, the kārdār at the pargana level, supported by chaudharīs and qānūngos, and the muqaddam and the *patwārī* at the village level, the administration of Ranjit Singh was essentially similar to that of the Mughal times. The methods of assessment, that is, *batāi, kankūt,* and *mushakhkhasah* remained the same, though the rates of assessment were somewhat different. Before the end of Ranjit Singh's reign, the practice of *ijāra* was introduced on a considerable scale. In the administration of justice, the qāzī's court continued to function at places. Ranjit Singh appointed new *'adālatīs* as well as qāzīs to cater to the needs of justice. We have already noticed that suzerain-vassal polity, the jāgīrdārī system, and the system of state patronage through grants of revenue or revenue-free lands were strengthened by Ranjit Singh.[40]

One area in which Ranjit Singh was radically different from his Sikh and Mughal predecessors was that of the army. Despite his personal liking for the cavalry, he strengthened the artillery and even more so the infantry. Furthermore, Ranjit Singh modernized his army with the help of Indian officers (trained in the army of the East India Company) first and then with the help of European officers, notably the French. Anticipating aggression eventually from the British, he strengthened the army much beyond the ordinary defensive needs of the state and also beyond the revenue resources of the state. Consequently, the Sikh state got more militarized in character now.

Furthermore, Ranjit Singh ensured numerical dominance of the Khalsa in the army as the defenders of the sovereignty of the state. When his successors felt constrained to compromise on the issue of sovereignty, the army assumed an anti-British role. The Anglo-Sikh wars were fought by the army of Lahore not so much on behalf of the rulers as on behalf of the people. The Singhs and non-Singhs fought gallantly even in the second Anglo-Sikh war in 1848–9. Significantly, the poet who wrote movingly on the fate of the state created by Ranjit Singh was a Punjabi Muslim, Shah Muhammad. He identified himself with the Khalsa, referring to the war as a conflict between the Punjab and the British as foreigners.[41]

CHARACTER OF THE SIKH STATE

In retrospect we can see that the Khalsa claimed to have established sovereign rule and Banda Bahadur exercised power on their behalf in the name of the Gurus. Sovereign status for the Khalsa was claimed in the late eighteenth century as well, deriving authority from the Gurus and God. However, power was clearly exercised by individuals as representatives of the Khalsa under God's protection. In the Sutlej–Jamuna Divide, several states were established by the former zamīndārs of the Mughal empire, making use of its administrative framework. Most of them accepted the suzerainty of Ahmad Shah Abdali, as they had accepted the Mughal authority earlier. However, the government and administration of the Sikh rulers on both sides of the River Sutlej were very much similar. Indeed, it is difficult to think of any appreciable difference.

Ranjit Singh created a large state, but he never adopted the title of Maharaja formally. He continued to strike coins already current, acknowledging the derivation of authority from Guru Nanak, which carried the implication of sovereignty for his state. The simple epithet of Khalsaji continued to be used for him nearly till the end of his reign. But all this does not mean that he did not exercise power without any formal constraint of any kind. This was exactly the position of his late eighteenth century Sikh predecessors. The monarchical pattern was not introduced by Ranjit Singh: he merely strengthened it. His government and administration were much more complex, just as his state was far larger, than that of any of his Sikh predecessors or contemporary Sikh ruler. The ruling class in his reign was composite, and state patronage was extended to all categories of subjects irrespective of their religious affiliation. The Sikhs were represented in a larger proportion in the civil administration and the army than the individuals belonging to other religious communities, but there was no discrimination in principle. Sikh institutions and individuals were the greatest beneficiaries of the state. But state patronage was not limited to the Sikhs. The identification of a large number of people of the region with the state, irrespective their religious creed and social background, may be seen as a measure of its catholic character. Catholicity in relation to non-Sikhs was a common characteristic of the Sikh rulers. The Sikh state, thus, was monarchical in its structure and liberal in its policies.

NOTES

1. In the Sutlej–Jamuna Divide, territories along the hills were occupied by the Sikh leaders of the province of Lahore, but the southern portions were occupied by the Sikh zamīndārs of the province of Delhi. Indu Banga, *Agrarian System of the Sikhs: Late Eighteenth and Early Nineteenth Century*, New Delhi: Manohar, 1978, p. 21.
2. J.S. Grewal and Irfan Habib, eds, *Sikh History from Persian Sources*, New Delhi: Tulika/Indian History Congress, 2001, p. 113.
3. Ratan Singh Bhangu, *Sri Guru Panth Prakash*, Balwant Singh Dhillon, ed., Amritsar: Singh Brothers, 2004, p. 31, et passim.
4. Grewal and Habib, eds, *Sikh History from Persian Sources*, p. 117.
5. Ibid., p. 122.
6. R.B. Whitehead, *Catalogue of Coins in the Lahore Museum*, 3 vols, Lahore: Lahore Museum, 1997 (rpt), quoted on the title page: '*Har keh shamshīr zanadd sikkah b'nāmash khwanand*', translated as 'Men read coins in the name of each one who smites with the sword'.
7. Surinder Singh, *Sikh Coinage: Symbol of Sikh Sovereignty*, New Delhi: Manohar, 2004, pp. 27–47.
8. Ibid., p. 41.
9. Ganda Singh, ed., *Hukamnāme Guru Sāhibān, Mātā Sāhibān, Banda Singh ate Khalsa Ji de*, Patiala: Punjabi University, 1967, pp. 192–5.
10. According to Ratan Singh Bhangu, Banda Bahadur introduced some innovations in opposition to the feelings and practices of the Khalsa. However, his graver fault was that he wanted to exercise political power without consulting the Khalsa. And this proved to be the cause of their alienation from him. *Sri Guru Panth Prakash*, pp. 128–34.
11. Sainapat, *Shri Gur Sobha*, Shamsher Singh Ashok, ed., Amritsar: Shiromani Gurdwara Parbandhak Committee, 1967, pp. 136–8.
12. Karamjit K. Malhotra has argued that this *Nasīhatnāma* could very well have been composed in the lifetime of Guru Gobind Singh between 1699 and 1708: 'The Earliest Manual on the Sikh Way of Life', in Reeta

Grewal and Sheena Pall, eds, *Five Centuries of Sikh Tradition: Ideology, Society, Politics and Culture*, New Delhi: Manohar, 2005, pp. 55–82.
13. 'Raj Karega Khalsa', *Encyclopaedia of Sikhism*, vol. III, Patiala: Punjabi University, 1997, pp. 441–2.
14. Surinder Singh, *Sikh Coinage*, pp. 61–72.
15. Ibid., pp. 73–4.
16. Whitehead, *Catalogue of Coins in the Lahore Museum*, vol. III, pp. 13–48.
17. Surinder Singh, *Sikh Coinage*, pp. 158–98. The author does not take into account all the relevant information available on this theme, and oversimplifies the situation.
18. J.S. Grewal, *Sikh Ideology, Polity and Social Order*, New Delhi: Manohar 1996, p. 96.
19. Banga, *Agrarian System of the Sikhs*, p. 36.
20. B.N. Goswamy and J.S. Grewal, eds, *The Mughal and Sikh Rulers and the Vaishnavas of Pindori: A Historical Interpretation of 52 Persian Documents*, Shimla: Indian Institute of Advanced Study, 1969, pp. 227–9.
21. Ibid., pp. 219–21.
22. There are several documents in the Pindori Collection which bear the name of Gurbakhsh Singh after his death. Ibid., pp. 247–69.
23. Ibid., pp. 267–9.
24. Veena Sachdeva, *Polity and Economy of the Punjab During the Late Eighteenth Century*, New Delhi: Manohar, 1993, Appendix, pp. 163, 167–73, 178, 191.
25. Ibid., pp. 160, 162–5, 167, 169–72, 175–8, 180–5, 188, 190–1.
26. Banga, *Agrarian System of the Sikhs*, pp. 148–67.
27. Kesar Singh Chhibber, *Bansāvalīnāma Dasān Pātshiān Kā* (vol. II of *Parkh*), Rattan Singh Jaggi, ed., Chandigarh: Panjab University, 1972. Chhibber is more hostile to Muslims but he does not spare the Khatris; he brackets them as *tatte* and *khatte*.
28. Sachdeva, *Polity and Economy of the Punjab*, pp. 71–4.
29. Though not concerned with this aspect, Lepel Griffin provides enough information on the founders of Nabha, Jind and Patiala to underline their initial position as zamīndārs of the Mughal empire. *The Rajas of the Panjab*, 2 vols, Patiala: Punjab Language Department, 1970 (rpt).
30. Most of the historians of Ranjit Singh refer to the assumption of the title of 'Maharaja' by him, but there is no contemporary or near contemporary evidence to support this assumption. This fictitious event was celebrated by the Punjab government in 2002 to honour Maharaja Ranjit Singh.

94 THE SIKHS

31. Surinder Singh, *Sikh Coinage*, pp. 93–157.
32. Goswamy and Grewal, *The Mughal and Sikh Rulers and the Vaishnavas of Pindori*, pp. 271–343.
33. B.N. Goswamy, *Piety and Splendour: Sikh Heritage in Art*, New Delhi: National Museum, 2000, p. 187.
34. J.S. Grewal and Indu Banga, eds, *Civil and Military Affairs of Maharaja Ranjit Singh (A Study of 450 Orders in Persian)*, Amritsar: Guru Nanak Dev University, 1987, documents 175, 241.
35. Grewal, *Sikh Ideology, Polity and Social Order*, pp. 121–6.
36. Banga, *Agrarian System of the Sikhs*, pp. 118–47.
37. All these names figure in the orders of Maharaja Ranjit Singh in Grewal and Banga, *Civil and Military Affairs of Maharaja Ranjit Singh*.
38. Banga, *Agrarian System of the Sikhs*, pp. 148–67.
39. Scattered all over in the text of the Orders in Grewal and Banga, *Civil and Military Affairs of Maharaja Ranjit Singh*.
40. Banga, *Agrarian System of the Sikhs*, pp. 63–117.
41. Shah Muhammad in his *Jangnāma* refers to the first Anglo–Sikh war as the war between Hind and the Punjab, and he refers to the English as the third party (*tīsrī zāt*). *Vār Shah Muhammad Athva Jang Hind Punjab* (Pbi.), Sita Ram Kohli and Seva Singh Giani, eds, Ludhiana: Punjab Sahit Academy, 1988, pp. 135, 189.

5. The Darbar Sahib and the Akal Takht*

The Darbar Sahib and the Akal Takht at Amritsar were two central institutions of the Sikhs in the early nineteenth century. They were as much a product of history as the Sikh state. Their centrality was well established before the advent of colonial rule in the Punjab. Our present purpose is to outline the process through which they emerged as central institutions.

THE FOUNDATIONS OF THE DARBAR SAHIB AND THE AKAL TAKHT

The foundations of the Darbar Sahib, popularly called the Golden Temple, were firmly laid by Guru Ram Das and Guru Arjan with the construction of the Harmandar in the midst of a tank called *amritsar* in the town of Ramdaspur. The compositions of the Bhatts included in the *Guru Granth Sahib* compiled by Guru Arjan refer to the *sarovar* of *amrit* as the source of immortality, the true congregation of *sants* for singing God's praises, the union of *rāj* and *jog* in what Guru Ram Das, Guru Arjan did, and divine sanction for the umbrella and throne of Guru Arjan received from Guru Nanak through Guru Ram Das and Guru Amar Das, and Guru Angad.[1] According to Bhai Gurdas, Guru Ram Das received Guruship in return (for the kingship given by the Sodhis to the Bedis in a previous *yuga*). Guru Ram Das is Sodhi *Pātshāh*. He has constructed a perfect pool and, in the midst of this pool of the water of immortality, he spreads the light. In the line of succession from Guru Nanak, Guru Ram Das practises rāj-jog; he is the pillar of both the spiritual and the temporal realm *(dīn-dunī)*.

---

* 'The Darbar Sahib and the Akal Takht' is a revised version of the lecture published in my *Lectures on History, Society and Culture of the Punjab* (Patiala: Punjabi University, 2007, pp. 287–319).

Guruship was to remain in the Sodhi family and his son becomes the fifth Guru. Filling the store house of *Gurbāṇī* to the full, Guru Arjan remains absorbed in *kīrtan* and *kathā* in the *sādh-sangat*. His court is the true court and his rāj is everlasting. Sikhs come to him from all the four directions, and the *langar* of the *shabad* runs with perfection. He teaches detachment-in-attachment and produces innumerable Sikhs who are like Raja Janak.[2] In these compositions, there are explicit references to the sarovar called amritsar, the compilation of the Granth, and kīrtan and kathā. There can be little doubt that these activities were associated with the Harmandar in the town of Ramdaspur.

Though the Bhatts and Bhai Gurdas emphasize the practice of rāj-jog or the mastery of the temporal and spiritual realms in the time of Guru Ram Das and Guru Arjan, the creation of the Darbar Sahib was in a sense, not entirely new. Guru Nanak had established a centre at Kartarpur with a *dharmsāl* for congregational worship and a common kitchen for community meal. A similar establishment was set up by Guru Angad at Khadur. The centre of Guru Amar Das at Goindwal developed into a town and he added a step-well (*bāolī*) to the dharmsāl and langar to cater to the needs of the large number of Sikhs who came to see the Guru personally, especially at the time of Baisakhi and Diwali. By now, there were many local congregations of the Sikhs and, therefore, a large number of dharmsāls. Goindwal became, in a sense, the central dharmsāl. In this context, the foundations of the Darbar Sahib at Ramdaspur can be seen as a logical step forward, and the roots of the institution can be traced to the dharmsāl at Kartarpur.[3]

The compositions of the Gurus refer to the sarovar, the Harmandar and Ramdaspur even more explicitly than those of the Bhatts and Bhai Gurdas. At the same time, their compositions reveal the sanctity and significance of these institutions in the eyes of the Gurus and their Sikhs. It is interesting to note in this connection that *amritsar, harmandar*, and *abchal nagari* (ideal city) are also used as metaphors. In a verse of Guru Nanak the term amritsar is used for the Guru as the ocean of the water of immortality.[4] For Guru Amar Das, the True Guru is the true amritsar that removes all dirt of the mind.[5] In a verse of Guru Ram Das, the True Guru is the pool of nectar which transforms a crow into a swan.[6] Guru Nanak uses the term *harmandar* for the Divine Abode.[7] In a verse of Guru Amar Das, the divine abode is within oneself; it is found through the shabad and the *nām*.[8] In a *shalok* of Guru Amar Das, the human body itself is the harmandar in which resides God.⁹ This is reiterated by Guru Arjan in equally clear terms.¹⁰ Guru Arjan depicts the abchal nagari in terms of the dispensation of Guru Nanak: there is no room for the five adversaries or sins, namely *kām*, *krodh*, *lobh*, *moh*, and *hankār*; all these are removed through the Guru's instruction; the city wall is made of *sachch* and *dharm*; the seed of *nām* is sown here; the *sāhu* and his agents are equally prosperous; the Guru's service day and night is the goods for sale; the shops hold *shantī*, *sahaj*, and *sukh* as merchandise; there is no fine and no taxes; those who trade in the *nām* take large profits home; the True Guru is the sāhu and the Sikhs are his *banjāra*s. This is the eternal city of Guru Nanak Dev.¹¹

These metaphors help us to appreciate the references made by Guru Ram Das and Guru Arjan to Ramdas Sarovar, the Harmandar, and Ramdaspur. In a well known verse of Guru Ram Das, the Sikhs of the True Guru are exhorted to rise early in the morning and meditate on the Name; rising early in the morning they are to bathe, bathe in amritsar, and recite the Name as instructed by the Guru, so as to remove all their sins and suffering. They should sing Gurbāṇī at dawn and remember the Name of God all times. The Sikh of the Guru who remembers God with each breath and morsel is dear to the Guru. Through his grace, the Gursikh is enabled to listen to the Guru's message. Guru Ram Das seeks the dust of the feet of that Gursikh who recites the Name and induces others to recite the Name.¹² The term amritsar in this verse may be a metaphor but it seems to be placed in the context of the morning worship at Ramdaspur. In any case, Guru Arjan makes the point absolutely clear when he says that all sins are washed away by bathing in Ramdas Sarovar. The context appears to be the same. Guru Arjan exhorts the Sikhs to sing the praises of God everyday in congregation: 'all one's wishes are fulfilled by lodging the perfect Guru in the heart'.¹³

This pool is the work of the creator. There was no dearth of money and materials. Such was the will of the Merciful One who completed the perfect design. All the wealth and riches are his.¹⁴ God himself stood amidst the sants to complete their work and to ensure that everything went right. Beautiful is the earth and beautiful is the pool with its nectar-like water. All purposes have been fulfilled and all sorrows have vanished. True to his nature, God bestows all gifts on his devotees. How can He be praised who has constructed this pool? All the merit of bathing at sixty-eight places, all charities, rituals and good deeds is here.[15] All sins are washed away by bathing in Ramdas Sarovar. This source of purification is a gift of the Perfect Guru. Through the Guru's shabad everything is in the right place. The dirt is removed in the sādh-sangat, with God as the kind friend. Significantly, Guru Arjan refers to 'the house having been raised for habitation'. This may be a reference to the Harmandar but it appears to include all important aspects of the situation.[16]

There is a direct reference to the Harmandar. God's temple has been erected for meditation; sants and *bhagat*s sing His praises. Through meditation on the Master they get rid of all their sins. By singing God's praises through the divine *bāṇī* they attain liberation. At an auspicious moment the eternal foundation of God's temple was laid. This could happen only through his grace.[17] In another shabad, God's abode (*ghar*) is mentioned along with the pool and the garden as the sign of God's pleasure. By meditating on God and singing his praises, all wishes have been fulfilled. By attachment to the Guru's feet the mind is filled with joy. Through the Master's grace, our life is blessed in this world and the next.[18]

The sanctity attached to the Darbar Sahib is extended to the town of Ramdaspur. 'I have seen all places', says Guru Arjan, 'but there is none like you. Founded by God himself, you are beautiful'. Thickly populated and spread wide, Ramdaspur is extremely beautiful. By bathing here, all sins are washed away.[19] Through his grace, God has established his own rule in Ramdaspur. The phrase *Rām-rāj* should not be taken in its familiar meaning, that is, the ideal rule of the Rama of Ayodhya. Ram is a familiar epithet for God in the compositions of Guru Nanak and his successors. Ram-rāj refers, therefore, to divine rule. Nothing untoward happens when we meditate on God; the enemy runs away when the nām is praised.[20] Ramdaspur was an autonomous town with which the Mughal administration had nothing to do.

Guru Arjan talks of Abchal Nagari, the eternal city, where peace comes through the nām, which has been established by the creator and where all one's wishes are fulfilled, where the praises of God are sung and everything falls in place, where God himself is the protector, himself the father and the mother, where houses and shops side by side look beautiful, where the gifts of God increase everyday, where all living beings are at peace under God's own care, where the sants of

God discourse, where the noose of transmigration is cut off, and where one discovers God through his grace.[21] Abchal Nagari, thus, represents the dispensation of Guru Nanak and his sucessors.

Guru Arjan refers to the ordinance of the Merciful One that none shall oppress another, that all shall live in peace now that *halemī rāj* or the mild rule has been established. The mild rule is a metaphor for the dispensation of Guru Nanak and his successors. It has a divine sanction. Guru Arjan utters only what the Master bids him to utter. He is a champion wrestler of God. The Master is dear to Guru Arjan. He is sweeter than mother and father, sister and brother, and all his friends. Guru Arjan uses the plough of Truth to sow the seeds of the Name and hopes to harvest a heap of God's grace. God has assigned this task to him and he performs it in accordance with His will. Putting on a robe of honour in His court, God has made him the headman. The village is well settled. Guru Arjan's sole occupation is to serve the Master. There can hardly be any doubt that halemī rāj refers to the entire dispensation headed by Guru Arjan. Significantly, he refers to the dharmsāl of truth that he has established. He seeks Gursikhs to wash their feet and wave the fan over them, and to bow at their feet. Those who hear of the Guru come to him and receive the boon of nām, dān and *isnān*. A whole world has attained liberation by boarding the true boat.[22] Thus, Ramdas Sarovar, the Harmandar and Ramdaspur are the institutions which function as instruments of halemī rāj.

The Mughal emperor Jahangir was unhappy with this halemī rāj. He says that Guru Arjan had 'induced a large number of simple-minded Hindus and even some ignorant Muslims, to become attached to his ways and customs'; he was doing all this openly and people were coming to him from all directions; they reposed full faith in him.[23] In other words, the institutional and material resources of the Sikh community under the leadership of Guru Arjan appeared to be a potential threat. Jahangir ordered his execution on the plea that he had given his blessings to the rebel prince Khusrau. The emperor challenged the halemī rāj.

Guru Arjan's son and successor, Guru Hargobind, became overtly concerned with defending the halemī rāj with his own resources. According to the author of the *Dabistān-i Mazāhib* who knew him personally, Guru Hargobind 'adopted the style of soldiers, and contrary to his father's practice, girded the sword, employed servants and took to hunting'. Jahangir ordered his detention in the fort of Gwalior (which was used generally for detaining political prisoners). Eventually, however, he was released, and he picked up the old threads. After Jahangir's death in 1627, Guru Hargobind had a battle with 'the officers of His Majesty the Emperor Shahjahan, who by His Majesty's orders were sent against him'. His baggage and goods were plundered, and he left Ramdaspur. He established a new centre at Kiratpur in the territory of a Rajput vassal of the Mughal empire. There too he kept 700 horses in his stables, 300 battle-tested horsemen, and sixty musketeers.[24]

The legacy of Guru Hargobind for the town of Ramdaspur accorded well with his martial activities. He built there a fortress called Lohgarh. Far more important, however, was the platform he constructed in front of the Harmandar. It was called Akal Takht, that is, the immortal throne. All temporal activities of Guru Hargobind were conducted from this place. He is remembered as the master of both the temporal and spiritual authority (*mīrī* and *pīrī*). Bhai Gurdas, who was a staunch supporter of Guru Hargobind, refers to him as the king of the spiritual and the temporal realms (*dīn dunī dā pātshāh*) and, as such, the king of kings, the only true king.[25] Quite appropriately, therefore, the Akal Takht could be seen as a symbol of the highest seat of authority for the Sikhs.

Under Sectarian Control

Guru Hargobind's departure from Ramdaspur gave the opportunity to Miharban, son of Prithi Chand, the elder brother of Guru Arjan, Prithi Chand refused to acknowledge Hargobind as the Guru and claimed himself to be the successor of Guru Arjan. After Prithi Chand's death, his son Miharban claimed to be the seventh Guru and took over Ramdaspur with the support of local administrators. The author of the *Dabistān* carried the impression that Prithi Chand succeeded Guru Arjan as 'Guru Miharban' (who was actually his son). In 1645–6, Harji was his successor. They regarded themselves as true devotees of God but the Sikhs of Guru Hargobind referred to them contemptuously as *mīṇā*.[26] According to Bhai Gurdas the opponents of Guru Hargobind contended that unlike the earlier Gurus he did not stay at one place with an established dharmsāl, that the Mughal emperor sent him to Gwalior whereas earlier the emperors used to come to the Gurus, that he roamed fearlessly from place to place and the Sikhs could not have easy access to him, that he went out hunting instead of preaching, that he did not compose, sing or listen to the bāṇī. These charges could easily come from a rival claimant to Guruship, like Prithi Chand, the elder brother of Guru Arjan, who refused to recognize Hargobind as the Guru. Bhai Gurdas denounces them as mīṇās in very strong terms in a number of stanzas.[27]

Like Prithi Chand, Miharban and Harji remained on the right side of the Mughal authorities. Their stance presented a contrast to that of Guru Hargobind. Their activities were essentially religious and literary. The Janamsākhī of Guru Nanak, attributed to Miharban and his sons Harji and Chaturbhuj, shows clearly that they looked upon their literary activity as a strong argument in support of their claim to Guruship. Like Guru Angad, Guru Amar Das, Guru Ram Das, and Guru Arjan, they used 'Nanak' in their compositions, with the implication that they represented the light and the office of Guru Nanak and his four successors. Indeed, Miharban is presented as the seventh Guru after the death of his father around 1620, and Harji as the eighth Guru after Miharban's death in 1639. At one place in the Janamsākhī, Guru Nanak says that his seventh successor would give an exposition of his compositions. Miharban appears to have possessed a volume or *pothī* containing Guru Nanak's compositions. He could use it for the purpose.[28] The form of the expository unit that is the *gosht* used in his Janamsākhī suggests that Miharban used to address his audiences personally.[29]

There is great insistence in Miharban's Janamsākhī on the absolute necessity of remembrance of the divine Name and divine grace. There is insistence also on daily bath in the early hours of the morning. In fact, nām, dān, and isnān are as important in the Janamsākhī as in the *Vārs* of Bhai Gurdas. Opposed to the worshippers of incarnations and Brahmanical orthodoxy in general, the Janamsākhī shows respect for *Siddh*s and Sūfi *pīr*s.[30] The Harmandar was the place where Miharban and Harji could exhibit their learning and their skill in oratory. But they had no use for the Akal Takht. For seven to eight decades Ramdaspur appears to have remained under the control of the Mīṇās. It is most likely, however, that even the Sikhs who were not their followers went to the Darbar Sahib for pilgrimage. According to Muhammad Qasim, who was a government accountant at Lahore before and after

1700, Chak Guru or Ramdaspur was a pleasant and charming place, containing gardens full of trees with sweet fruits, and a big tank known as amritsar where 'lakh upon lakh of people collect on the Baisakhi day' for bathing 'amidst various kinds of spectacles with illuminations'.[31]

Recovered by the Khalsa

The institution of the Khalsa came to have a direct bearing on the town of Ramdaspur, the Harmandar, and the Akal Takht. Guru Gobind Singh gave baptism by the double-edged sword to the five Sikhs who had volunteered to lay down their lives for his cause. 'Gobind Das' himself received baptism from those five Singhs and became 'Gobind Singh'. Many other Sikhs were baptized by 'the five beloved' or the *panj pyārās*. Then any 'five Singhs' could baptize others anywhere. A movement for baptism started at all important places, leading sometimes to tension and conflict within local congregations. The contemporary Sainapat mentions Delhi in this connection and states that this kind of situation developed at many other places.[32] According to Ratan Singh Bhangu, the number of baptized Singhs increased enormously in the central Punjab. Some of them moved from place to place; others built *bunga*s and dharmsāls. Some of the Singhs began to live in Chak Guru to look after the Gurdwara.[33] This clearly refers to the Darbar Sahib.

The Khalsa had to face opposition from time to time. A battle was fought over Ramdaspur in 1709–10. Chaudhari Chuhar Mal Ohri was probably in sympathy with the descendants of Prithi Chand. His son Ramji Mal refused to sell mulberries to some Singhs and they took the fruit forcibly. Ramji Mal complained to the Mughal governor at Lahore who ordered Diwan Har Sahai of Patti and Chaudhari Deva of Naushehra Pannuan to punish the Singhs. But Har Sahai was killed and Deva ran away.[34] According to a report of 24 May 1710, it came to a fight between the Sikhs of the Khalsa and others in Chak Guru and the Khalsa emerged victorious. 'The force that was sent from Lahore failed to control matters'.[35]

After the occupation of Sirhind and the declaration of Sikh sovereignty in 1710, Banda Bahadur discarded the Khalsa salutation of '*Vāheguru ji ka Khalsa, Vāheguru ji ki fateh*' and adopted '*fateh darshan*'. He also discarded the blue dress and non-vegetarian diet. Some of the Khalsa separated from him and went to Ramdaspur with the intention of never joining him again. Their leaders were Kahn Singh and Binod Singh, the Trehan descendants of Guru Angad. According to Kesar Singh Chhibber, Kahn Singh established himself at the Akal Bunga. As long as Banda remained active, the Mughal authorities did not disturb the Khalsa at Ramdaspur. The old practices were revived and Sikhs began to come to amritsar.[36]

After Banda's execution in 1716, his followers began to claim that they were entitled to a share in the offerings that came to the Harmandar. They established themselves near the Jhanda Bunga while the Khalsa were at the Akal Bunga. Both parties mustered strong in the precincts of the Harmandar to assert their right by show of force. Some of the followers of Banda joined the Khalsa when the piece of paper with *'Fateh Vāheguruji ki'* thrown into amritsar rose to the surface before the one with 'fateh darshan'. Many more joined the Khalsa when their nominee won in a wrestling match arranged by way of arbitration. Those who still remained obdurate were driven out. Their leader was killed in a fight.[37] The town of Ramdaspur, the Harmandar, and the Akal Takht came under the control of the Khalsa.

Chhibber, who claims to have been an eyewitness to some of the events at Ramdaspur, talks of the arrangements made in the early eighteenth century. The representatives or *pancha*s of Khatris, Brahmans, Bhabaras, masons, carpenters, and zamīndārs of the town were consulted. The collection of octroi duties was entrusted to Sahaj Singh Trehan; the collection of income from land was entrusted to Dianat Rai. The proceeds from these sources were sent to Mata Sahib Devi at Delhi. Man Singh Arora was appointed as *ardāsia* for offering formal prayers. Kesar Singh's father, Gurbakhsh Singh Chhibber, was made *dārogha* of the cowshed (*gaokhāna*), the workshop (*kārkhāna*), and the treasury (*khazāna*). The offerings in kind received at the *darbār* or Harmandar were measured or weighed and deposited at the shop of Shiam Bhabara. An open kitchen was maintained for all visitors. Daily provisions were given to the old, the disabled, and the needy Sikhs. Monthly allowances from the savings were given to those who worked for the *darbār*. Four masons were employed permanently to work at the Harmandar.[38]

Abdus Samad Khan, the Mughal governor of Lahore who had kept up a policy of persecution till he was transferred to Multan in 1726, was replaced by his son Zakariya Khan who governed the Punjab till his death in 1745. In the early 1730s he decided to placate the Khalsa, 'to kill them with sugar'. Significantly, he offered revenues of a dozen villages adjoining Ramdaspur, recognizing its importance as the political centre of the Khalsa. He also offered the title of 'Nawab' and a robe of honour for their leader in recognition of their political importance. The younger members of the Khalsa were organized into five units or *jathā*s. Each unit with 1,300 to 2,000 men, had its own banner and drum, but there was a common mess, a common store, and a common treasury for all.[39] Organization gave strength to the Khalsa. Their strength gave greater visibility to Ramdaspur, the Akal Takht, and the Darbar Sahib, increasing their importance in the eyes of the Mughal administrators as much as in the eyes of the Sikhs.

Zakariya Khan ended the truce by resuming the villages. Active against the Khasla now was Lakhpat Rai, the Diwan of the province of Lahore. All approaches to Ramdaspur were picketed by troops to prevent the Sikhs from coming to the Harmandar. Bhai Mani Singh, who had made Ramdaspur the rallying centre of the Khalsa, offered to pay Rs 5,000 if the Sikhs were allowed access to amritsar at the time of Diwali. The governor agreed but Lakhpat Rai posted his troops at the nearby Ram Tirath. The festival remained a tame affair and Bhai Mani Singh could not pay the stipulated sum with the limited income accruing from offerings. He was called to Lahore, given the usual alternative of Islam and, on his refusal, was hacked limb by limb.[40]

After the martyrdom of Bhai Mani Singh, Mughal faujdārs and *thānadār*s tried to hold Ramdaspur under their direct control. One of them, called Massa Ranghar, used the precincts of the Harmandar for the performance of professional dancers. For this 'sacrilege' he was assassinated on the spot by Mahtab Singh of Mirankot and Sukha Singh of Mari Kambo. After Zakariya Khan's death, Jaspat Rai, the younger brother of Diwan Lakhpat Rai, was killed by the Khalsa in a battle. The Diwan vowed to exterminate the Sikhs, and filled amritsar with soil in 1746.[41] However, Ramdaspur was recovered by the Khalsa early in 1748.

Role in the Late Eighteenth Century

The phase of intense political struggle of the Khalsa brought the Darbar Sahib and the Akal Takht into sharper focus. On the Baisakhi of 1748 the Khalsa resolved to build a fortress for the protection of Ramdaspur.

On a piece of land near Ramsar to the south of the Harmandar, they threw up an enclosure of mudwall, with watch towers in the corners and a moat around. They themselves supplied the labour and worked as masons and cooks. This fortress, called Ram Rauni, could accommodate about 500 men. It was soon besieged by Adina Beg Khan on orders from the new Mughal governor of Lahore. Jassa Singh, who later became famous as Ramgarhia, abandoned Adina Beg and joined the Khalsa. The siege was lifted after three months due to the invasion of the Punjab by Ahmad Shah Abdali in December 1748.[42]

The Khalsa celebrated the Diwali of 1749 at Ramdaspur and began to occupy territories in the Bari Doab. Mir Mannu (Muin ul-Mulk), the governor of Lahore, heard the news of this disturbance and sent two of his commanders to deal with the Khalsa in the upper Bari Doab. Hard pressed by the Mughal forces, about 900 Sikhs took shelter in Ram Rauni. After a siege they came out to fight. According to Tahmas Khan, a young slave of Mir Mannu, all of them died fighting hand to hand. Mir Mannu himself came to Chak Guru and encamped there for many days. Tahmas Khan talks of Mir Mannu's measures for totally destroying the Sikhs till his death.[43]

With Ramdaspur as their rallying centre, the Khalsa began to assert themselves by occupying territories wherever they could.[44] Taking serious notice of their activities, Ahmad Shah Abdali plundered Ramdaspur in 1757, and demolished its sacred buildings. He appointed Prince Taimur as the governor of Lahore to deal with the Khalsa. On hearing the news that they had gathered in large numbers for bathing at Chak Guru, the Afghan commander Jahan Khan marched towards Ramdaspur, asking Haji Ata Khan to reach there by forced marches. Tahmas Khan, who participated in the battle, says that the victorious Afghans pursued the Sikhs to Chak Guru. Five Sikhs on foot were standing at the gate. They were killed by the Afghan troops, and 'the camp of the victorious army was established there'.[45] The sacrifices made for the Darbar Sahib and the Akal Takht enhanced their sanctity and importance. Bhangu refers to the whole place as 'the door of the Guru' or *Gurdwara*: it was sacred like the land of Kurukshetra; by dying at this Gurdwara as a true Sikh one acquired the merit of a thousand lives.

Ahmad Shah Abdali stayed in India from October 1759 to May 1761, but he remained preoccupied with the Marathas. The Khalsa established their authority all over the province of Lahore.[46] The Maratha reports of the early 1760s explicitly mention the gatherings of the Khalsa at Ramdaspur at the time of Baisakhi and Diwali. There are references to their collective decisions. In a report of July 1763, Jassa Singh Ahluwalia tells Nawab Shujaudaulah: 'we are going for consultation to the place of Chak Guru'. Even important leaders could not take vital decisions without consultation with the others. They turned to Chak Guru 'for mutual deliberation and consultation'. Action was taken on the basis of such collective decisions. At the time of Diwali in 1763, a very large crowd assembled at Chak Guru and buildings were constructed to accommodate them. Some 'conical-hat (*kulah*) wearing Durranis' were employed there as labour. After defeating Ahmad Shah Abdali in 'the great battle' of the Chenab, some of the Sikhs came to Chak Guru for celebrating Holi. In March 1765, Ala Singh of Patiala says that only the Khalsa could 'confront the Shah on equal terms'.[47]

By this time, the doctrines of Guru Granth and Guru Panth had crystallized. These doctrines were based on Guru Gobind Singh's enunciation before his death that Guruship henceforth was vested in Gurbāṇī and the Khalsa. A *hukamnāma* bearing the seal of the Khalsa, issued to the sangat of Patna from Ramdaspur, presumably the Akal Takht, refers to Khalsa as the Guru.[48] Ratan Singh Bhangu makes the general statement that the Khalsa used to converge on Ramdaspur at the time of Baisakhi and Diwali after their campaigns in the country, to sit in the Harmandar to listen to Gurbāṇī, to have a dip in the holy tank so that all their sins were washed away, to hold dīwāns at the Akal Bunga to adopt gurmatas, and to administer justice in order to protect the true Singhs and to punish the un-Sikh. Bhangu refers to a few specific resolutions at the Akal Takht. One gurmata related to the rescue of the wife of a Brahman from the Afghans of Qasur. Another gurmata related to territorial occupation: no one who occupied a place first was to be dislodged by a stronger leader.[49] That this gurmata was regarded as sacrosanct by the majority of the Khalsa is evident from the fact that at the beginning of Sikh rule in the provinces of Lahore and Delhi the number of 'rulers' was very large, many of them holding only a few villages.

Ahmad Shah Abdali attacked Ramdaspur in December 1764. Qazi Nur Muhammad, an eyewitness, states that the Sikhs had repaired the Chak but not completely. The Shah again wished to destroy the Chak and its worshippers 'so that it might again be reduced to dust as he had done earlier'. Ahmad Shah Abdali discovered that a few men had stayed on to 'sacrifice their lives for the Guru'. Coming out of the enclosure, they did not show 'any fear of being killed nor the dread of death'. They all died fighting.[50] Ratan Singh Bhangu tells us that their leader was Nihang Gurbakhsh Singh who used to stay at the Akal Bunga and lead the Khalsa standards in their campaigns. He resolved now 'to court death'. He led his companions to martyrdom. The Khalsa decided to cremate them all together near the Akal Takht and to raise a *shahīdganj* over the spot.[51] The symbols of spirituality, temporal power and martyrdom became intertwined.

After the declaration of Sikh sovereignty in 1765, some of the Sikh rulers constructed forts around the town, like Hari Singh Bhangi, Jassa Singh Ahluwalia, Jassa Singh Ramgarhia, and Jai Singh Kanihya. Several Sikh rulers established their own autonomous localities, known as *katṛa*s. Among these were the katṛas of Hari Singh Bhangi, Desa Singh Bhangi, Karam Singh Dulo, Jassa Singh Ahluwalia, Khushal Singh Faizullapuria, Jai Singh Kanhiya, Amar Singh Bagga, Jaimal Singh Kanhiya, Amar Singh Kingra, and Jassa Singh Ramgarhia. Thus, a number of autonomous localities were created on all sides of Ramdaspur, transforming it into a conglomerate called Amritsar.

The original core of Ramdaspur was regarded as a common heritage of all the Sikhs. The Harmandar and the Akal Takht were reconstructed with the financial resources mainly of the rulers. Bungas were constructed around the tank. The Ramgarhia Bunga is a legacy of the late eighteenth century. The earliest known grants to the Harmandar were given by the Bhangi rulers Hari Singh, Jhanda Singh and Ganda Singh. They were followed by others till nearly every Sikh chief had contributed his share. Their example was followed by the Sikh *jāgīrdār*s who offered revenue-free land to the Darbar Sahib and the Akal Takht.[52]

According to Ram Sukh Rao, Jassa Singh Ahluwalia founded Katra Guru (later known as the Guru Bazar) as a source of income for the Darbar Sahib. Mutasaddīs, ardāsias, and *granthī*s were appointed to work under his general control. Jassa Singh contributed fourteen lakhs of rupees in all, according to the accounts kept by Bhai Des Raj.[53] He appears to have managed the affairs of the Darbar Sahib on behalf of the Sikh rulers, and with the support of the Akalis.

The Attitude of Maharaja Ranjit Singh

The eighteenth century background enables us to appreciate Maharaja Ranjit Singh's attitude towards the Darbar Sahib and the Akal Takht. He could not afford to ignore the city of Ramdaspur which loomed so large in the Sikh imagination. His father and grandfather, Mahan Singh and Charhat Singh, had come to Ramdaspur to bathe in the sarovar, to listen to Gurbāṇī at the Darbar Sahib, to prostrate before the Guru Granth Sahib, and to participate in the political deliberations of the Khalsa at the Akal Takht. According to the *Umdat ut-Tawārīkh*, Maharaja Ranjit Singh visited Ramdaspur (Amritsar) in 1802 after his treaty with Fateh Singh Ahluwalia, and stayed in the fort constructed by Jassa Singh Ahluwalia.[54] On 14 March 1804, he occupied the fort of the Bhangis, dislodging Mai Sukhan, the widow of Gulab Singh Bhangi, and her son Gurdit Singh from their territories as well.[55] This was the beginning of a process that resulted eventually in the unification of the city of Amritsar under the Maharaja. A large number of new katṛas, markets, and bāzārs came up. A new fort, known as Gobindgarh, was constructed by Ranjit Singh himself and a small palace was built in a walled garden called Ram Bagh. An unusually thick wall with strong bastions and a wide moat was built around the city with twelve gates. Amritsar became the premier city of the state and virtually its second capital. For Maharaja Ranjit Singh it was more important than Lahore, primarily because of the sanctity of the Darbar Sahib and the importance of the Akal Takht. To hold Amritsar under control became almost a political necessity.

When Holkar came to Amritsar in 1805, the Maharaja accompanied him to the Darbar Sahib.[56] The terms of the treaty of 1809 with the British were thrashed out with Metcalfe at Amritsar.[57] On the Diwali of 1809, the Maharaja bathed in the sacred tank, and gave cows, horses and other things to the poor.[58] On Dusehra in 1811, effigies of Ravan, Kumbhkaran and others were set up at Amritsar according to the old established custom 'in compliance with the emphatic orders of the Maharaja'. He came personally to the scene with his cavalry and swivels and ordered a mock battle to be fought for the conquest of Lanka. It went out of control and many people were killed and wounded. The

Maharaja ordered Diwan Hukam Singh to come from Lahore to ensure that everyone was properly treated.[59]

It is evident from the *Events at the Court of Ranjit Singh, 1810-1817* that the Maharaja used to visit Amritsar at least three or four times a year, staying in the fort of the Bhangis or in Gobindgarh for a few days or a few weeks. Understandably, he conducted state business from Amritsar during these visits. Princes, vassal chiefs, principal *sardār*s and other *jāgīrdār*s, *ijāradār*s, grantees, and *vakīl*s of ruling chiefs and the Political Agent at Ludhiana would come to Amritsar to meet the Maharaja. The marriage of Prince Kharak Singh in 1812 was a state occasion. Colonel David Ochterlony came as a representative of the Governor General. After the marriage, the Maharaja came to Amritsar, 'rode together with Colonel Sahib to inspect the drill of the English Company in the style in which they would behave in the field of battle'. A few days later, on 11 February, money was distributed among singers and musicians. The Maharaja seems to have taken over the responsibility for the affairs of the Darbar Sahib and the Akal Takht. The Brahmans reminded the Maharaja that it was a Sankrant day. He mounted an elephant, went to the city, bathed in the sacred tank, and offered about five hundred rupees at the Bungas.[60]

The Maharaja continued to visit the Darbar Sahib from time to time, and to ride through the bāzārs. On 13 April 1813, he rode his horse to ramble through the bāzārs to distribute 100 rupees as charity among the poor. In June, the Maharaja told his courtiers that he would offer Rs 2000 rupees in cash and a village in jāgīr to Harmandar Sahib to mark the successful end of the campaign against the Durranis. In January 1814, he rode his special horse to go to the Harmandar Sahib; he climbed up his own Bunga and enjoyed the sight around; he ordered Faqir Imamuddin to see to its repairs. On the Diwali of 1814, he came to his Bunga to watch the festival. In January 1816 he went to the Harmandar Sahib early in the morning, bathed in the tank and presented offerings before the Granth Sahib, and at other shrines. He got himself weighed seven times against articles of food and vessels of copper, bronze, silver, and gold; all of these were distributed among Brahmans, together with some pictures of gold and silver and five cows, worth 2000 rupees. This was a Sankrant day.[61]

Sohan Lal Suri's *Umdat ut-Tawārīkh* contains references to Maharaja Ranjit Singh's visits to Amritsar up to the year of his death.

In August 1834, the Maharaja made an offering of a pearl necklace to the Granth Sahib. Rubbing his forehead before Guru Granth Sahib, he exclaimed: 'Great is the *darbar sāhib* to have enabled me a sacred sight of itself '. As usual, offerings were made at other shrines also. In September, the Maharaja offered his humble offerings or ardās at the Darbar Sahib in thanksgiving for the restoration of his health. One elephant and several horses and cattle were given in charity as the weighing ceremony known as *tulādān*. On 12 May 1838, the Maharaja joyfully entered the Darbar Sahib and made an offering of Rs 525. Then he gave canopied beds, suits of clothes, and large sums of money to the deserving and the needy according to the established custom. It was the day of Sankrant. The Maharaja threw a piece of paper before the Granth Sahib to know whether he should take a cold or a hot bath. In August 1838, the Maharaja arrived at Amritsar and went first to Sri Darbar Sahib to secure the felicity of both the worlds; he made his customary obeisance and offered Rs 1,100.[62]

The days of Diwali and Dusehra were more important than the days of Sankrant. On Diwali in 1835, the Maharaja went to his own Bunga in his special conveyance and entered the Darbar Sahib in a boat; he made a prostration there and offered 511 gold coins by way of ardās in accordance with his usual custom. At night, a graceful and glorious illumination dazzled the eyes of the onlookers. On Dusehra in 1836, the Maharaja made his customary obeisance and offered Rs 12,000 at the Darbar Sahib.[63] A day before his death, he gestured that his special horses should be sent to the Darbar Sahib.

There are references to the 'services' performed by the Maharaja for the Harmandar. In August 1835, he ordered that a marble floor should be prepared for beautifying the Darbar Sahib and its *parkarma*. Bhai Gurmukh Singh, who was associated with the affairs of the Darbar Sahib, was ordered to send reliable persons to Jaipur to procure marble. In January 1838, the Maharaja offered eleven pitchers of gold coins to be utilized in gold-plating of the Darbar Sahib. In April 1839, he ordered Gurmukh Singh to go to Amritsar to make offerings and have an ardās offered for the health of the Maharaja: he offered Rs 500 at the Darbar Sahib, Rs 125 each at Akal Bunga, Jhanda Bunga, Shahid Bunga, Ghariali Bunga, Dukh Bhanjani, Baba Atal, and Manji Sahib. Bhai Gurmukh Singh was also ordered to distribute Rs 11 among the drum-beaters, trumpet-blowers and all the servants and the staff.[64]

Maharaja Ranjit Singh was keen to see that adequate arrangements were made for the Europeans who visited the Darbar Sahib.[65] Elaborate arrangements were made during Lord Auckland's visit in December 1838. Bhai Gurmukh Singh was ordered to arrange illumination and fireworks and *saropa*s for the visitors. Lehna Singh Majithia was ordered to ride with the Governor General to the Ram Bagh Gate. Then the Maharaja took him through the bāzār. They made their obeisance at the Darbar Sahib: the Maharaja offered Rs 700 and Lord Auckland offered Rs 11,250. The Governor General prayed for mutual friendship. They made a public appearance in the Maharaja's Bunga and watched the illumination and fireworks.[66]

For over four years after the death of Maharaja Ranjit Singh in June 1839, his successors continued to give due importance to the Darbar Sahib. On Dushera in 1839, Maharaja Kharak Singh went to the Darbar Sahib, made offerings, and presented all the personal articles of Maharaja Ranjit Singh by way of ardās: suits of clothes, bejewelled ornaments, gold vessels, a gold canopied bed, twenty-five horses with trappings set with jewels and studded with gold coins, three elephants with gold and silver seats, and Rs 1,25,000 in cash. On Diwali in 1839, he made the customary visit to the Harmandar and enjoyed the illumination.[67] In January 1843, Maharaja Sher Singh came to Amritsar and went to the Harmandar for the customary ardās. Early in 1844, he made a *sankalp*, and sent large sums of money and various things to the Darbar Sahib according to the usual custom.[68] This royal tradition suffered a setback under the nominal rule of Dalip Singh.

Writing on the Punjab in Persian for the benefit of the British administrators at the end of Sikh rule, Ganesh Das takes notice of Amritsar as 'a city of distinction'. There were bungas all around the Harmandar, with several places of worship, like the Akal Bunga, Dukh Bhanjani, and Dera Baba Atal. The water of the Hansli canal had been brought to the sacred tank by Ranjit Singh. Every morning and evening a large number of people visited the Harmandar. The gatherings were unusually large on two occasions: Baisakhi and Diwali. Amritsar was the most important centre of pilgrimage for the Sikhs.[69]

Increasing Importance of the Darbar Sahib

State business and other interests brought Europeans to this city of distinction. Some of them recorded their impressions.[70] Baron Charles

Hugel, who came to Amritsar in 1836, visited the 'sacred reservoir'. The pool struck him with surprise as a large body of water. It was surrounded by a pavement which in turn was surrounded by some buildings belonging to the temple and some of the most considerable houses of the city. There were several stone steps by which the bathers descended into the water 'as clear as a mirror'. On returning from his or her ablutions, every bather brought a present for the Harmandar, chiefly of fruit or flowers. The Harmandar was surmounted by a golden roof, very beautifully and skilfully contrived; it was inlaid with marble; a large door of gold opened into the temple, which was surrounded with little vestibules; the ceilings were supported by richly ornamented pillars. The wall of the building was ornamented with a handsome carpet worked in gold. A *chaurī-bardār* waved the fan made of the Tibet cow's tail, while the eyes of the granthi were intently fastened on the Granth. Hugel's presents were duly received and acknowledged, and a shabad was read from the Granth before he left the Darbar Sahib with 'a turban and another cloth' bestowed upon him. There were floral designs painted on the walls of the temple and work in pietra dura was still being carried on.[71]

In 1838, Emily Eden noted that the Sikhs claimed that there was no city like Amritsar. The famous Sikh temple was the only place the Sikhs were supposed to venerate 'in a religious way'. At the time of Lord Auckland's visit, the Bunga of Sher Singh was a sort of volcano of fireworks, and large illuminated fish were swimming about the tank.[72]

Eight years later, W.L. M'Gregor talked of Amritsar as the first city of the Punjab from 'a commercial point of view'. It was also a place of great sanctity owing to its holy tank and temple. The road leading to the door of the Darbar Sahib remained constantly crowded.[73]

The increasing importance of Amritsar and the Darbar Sahib during the period of sovereign Sikh rule from 1765–1845 was reflected in the literature of the period. Kesar Singh Chhibber looked upon Ramdaspur as the Guru's city and the Harmandar as the Guru's place, his *darbār*.[74] Sant Das Chhibber dwells on the myth of amritsar as a *tīrath* in all the four cosmic Ages. All other tīraths derived their sanctity from amritsar.[75] Kavi Saundha glorifies amritsar as the favourite place of gods even before Ganga, Jamuna, Kurukshetra, Kanshi, Gaya, and Kidar came into existence. The Khalsa rose into power by bathing in amritsar. The town of Guru Ram Das was superior to heaven.[76]

Besides a mythical account of the Harmandar as Sri Darbar, Gulab Singh refers to its golden doors and its silken canopies. The Guru Granth was installed therein, and shabads were sung in various ragas to the accompaniment of musical instruments like *tāl*, *mridang*, *pakhāwaj*, dholak, *tār*, sitar, and *rabāb*. People came from far off places with offerings and received *parshad*. There were numerous Bungas in which Gurmukhs read the Granth and meditated. There were also ascetics and readers of Puranas in the Bungas around the tank.[77]

Ram Prakash Udasi praised amritsar as the source of liberation-in-life. The tall building of the Harmandar was decorated with paintings and studded with gems and diamonds. The silk and golden *bānāt* used in it were beautiful and attractive; the mirrors used in it added to its brilliance. The Granth installed in the Harmandar was read aloud by the granthīs. Shabads were sung by the *rāgīs*, and musical instruments were played. Powerful potentates bowed their heads here and placed its dust on their foreheads. They did parkarma and brought *karha* for ardas. Many *giānīs* came and explained the shabads of the Granth to the audience. Kathā and kīrtan went on day and night. The splendour of the Harmandar was beyond description.[78]

Puran Singh talks of a large number of tīraths but none of them was superior to amritsar. He refers to many other places of Sikh pilgrimage, like Anandpur Sahib, Patna Sahib, Abchal Nagar (Nander), Damdama Sahib, Muktsar, Tarn Taran, Goindwal, Khadur Sahib, Baba Bakala, Sri Gobindpur, Guru ki Vadali, Guru Nanak da Dera, Babe di Rori at Eminabad, Babe di Ber at Sialkot, and Panja Sahib. Puran Singh also refers to the services rendered to the Harmandar by Ranjit Singh.[79] The glorification of amritsar, the Harmandar, and Ramdaspur was consolidated by Sant Nihal Singh in 1863 in an anthology of the works of more than a dozen other poets.[80] Other writers of the period were influenced by the atmosphere in which the Darbar Sahib was sought to be glorified, like Ganga Ram, Kavi Kankan, Bhai Jawahar Singh, and the author of the *Gurbilās Pātshāhī Chhevīn*.[81]

Bhai Santokh Singh provides the most comprehensive statement on amritsar, the Harmandar, the Akal Takht, and Ramdaspur, weaving the growing legendary lore into a broadly historical account. He goes into much detail in order to explain the existence of almost everything in the Darbar Sahib complex, and how the town of Ramdaspur came to flourish. On points of disagreement between various sources of information, Bhai Santokh Singh says that only the Guru knows the whole truth. For a poet whose purpose was to sing praises of the Gurus, there was no need to be sceptical. Myth and legend are intricately woven into Bhai Santokh Singh's narrative.[82]

Ratan Singh Bhangu's *Guru Panth Prakāsh*, completed at the Bunga of Shiam Singh in 1841, highlights the role of amritsar, the Harmandar, and the Akal Takht in the political struggle of the Khalsa during the eighteenth century till the establishment of Sikh rule. The first act of the Khalsa was to gain control of Ramdaspur and then to retain it against the followers of Banda and to regain it from the Mughal administrators. Bathing in amritsar to wash away all sins gets linked up with the political struggle. All resolutions of vital importance for organization and political activity of the Khalsa are passed at the Akal Takht, especially on the days of Baisakhi and Diwali. Destruction of the Harmandar and its reconstruction figure prominently in Bhangu's work. Martyrdom in defence of the Harmandar and for its sanctity gets highlighted. He who dies here goes to heaven. The Harmandar and the Akal Takht are the focus of the religious and political life of the Khalsa as the most appropriate centre for *dharmyudh*.[83]

Relative Eclipse of the Akal Takht

Before the end of Sikh rule, the Darbar Sahib had become the foremost centre of Sikh pilgrimage. For Guru Arjan there was no place like Ramdaspur because of the presence of amritsar and the Harmandar, where Gurbāṇī was sung from early morning till late in the night. To this sacred space was added the Akal Takht by Guru Hargobind as the centre of temporal activity. Its sanctity and importance was never lost upon his successors. Its recovery by the Khalsa proved to be crucial in their political struggle. Its magnetic pull was reinforced by the doctrine of Guru Panth which provided the moral bond for the concerted action of the Khalsa. The Akal Takht became virtually an actor in their struggle for sovereignty. The struggle involved sacrifice. It was symbolized by the shahīdganj built in the Darbar Sahib complex itself. With the establishment of Sikh rule, the religious imagination of the Sikhs, their emotions, and their sense of piety made it the premier Gurdwara for the rulers and the ruled. At the height of his power, Maharaja Ranjit Singh felt grateful for being given the opportunity to render services to the Darbar Sahib.

The Akal Takht gained increasing importance in the eighteenth century till the occupation of territories by the Khalsa and the establishment of Sikh rule. The individual rulers had no problem with accepting a common coin as the symbolic declaration of their sovereignty and venerating the Darbar Sahib as the foremost sacred space of the Sikhs. However, they did not evolve any system in which the Akal Takht could serve as the place of their collective authority. Consequently, it remained the symbol of authority but not the centre of power. The only set of people who looked upon themselves as representatives of the Khalsa Panth as custodians of the Akal Takht were the Akalis or Nihangs.

John Malcolm noted their importance as 'fanatic priests and desperate soldiers'. They had 'the sole direction of all religious affairs at Amritsar'. Malcolm looked upon them as inheritors of the tradition of the earliest Khalsa of Guru Gobind Singh, equating them with the Tat Khalsa of the time of Banda Bahadur. They initiated converts and conducted all religious ceremonies at Amritsar where they resided, thinking of themselves as its defenders. Their Bunga was the centre of their activity. They could accuse a chief of default and fine him. If he refused to pay, they prevented him from performing his ablution ceremonies at Amritsar. Even the most powerful chief would try to conciliate them. They had a great interest in maintaining the religious and political traditions of the Khalsa as established by Guru Gobind Singh. Their role was unthinkable without Amritsar:

Should Amritsar cease to be a place of resort, or be no longer considered as the religious capital of the state, in which all questions that involve the general interests of the commonwealth are to be decided, this formidable order would at once fall from that power and consideration which they now possess, to a level with other mendicants.[84]

The importance of the Akalis had begun to decrease in the early nineteenth century. In April 1812, the Maharaja sent his special horsemen to deal with the disturbance caused by Akali Phula Singh. He was demanding 1000 rupees as his share out of the 1100 rupees received as offerings at the time of Baisakhi. He actually started fighting with the Akalis of the Darbar Sahib and a few men were actually killed or wounded on both sides.[85] In January 1814, the Maharaja ordered that the men of Akali Phula Singh should take their old fixed share and nothing more. Otherwise, they would be turned out of the city. They agreed to act in accordance with the order.[86] It was reported in November 1814 that Akali Phula Singh had risen in revolt on the pretext of helping Sada Kaur and Sardar Nihal Singh Attariwala. The Maharaja ordered Diwan Moti Ram to bring them both to his presence. This was done and Akali Phula Singh's activities across the Sutlej came to an end.[87] In 1815, Akali Phula Singh was leading the troops on Ranjit Singh's orders, virtually serving the state.[88]

Maharaja Ranjit Singh was not completely free from occasional trouble on account of the Akalis. In 1826, Raja Dhian Singh's men were obstructed by the Akali Singhs at Amritsar while seizing men for forced labour and a quarrel broke out between them. The Maharaja felt obliged to stay there for a few more days and gave some cash to the Akalis to bring about reconciliation.[89] A little later the Maharaja received the news that the Akali Singhs were creating disturbance in Amritsar and Prince Sher Singh had failed to deal with them. The Maharaja ordered Prince Kharak Singh to go to Amritsar and pacify the Akalis. He explained the royal orders to them and 'their old estate was granted to them by way of helping them in their livelihood'.[90]

As noted by Malcolm, the Akalis were hostile to the Europeans. In February 1809, they attacked the camp of Charles Metcalfe when his Muslim soldiers took out *tāzia* in Amritsar. When Charles Hugel visited the Darbar Sahib in 1836, Sardar Lehna Singh Majithia had to ensure that none of the Akalis shouted in protest.[91] On Emily Eden's visit too, Sardar Lehna Singh was ordered to ensure that none of the people, Akalis or Nihangs, uttered any rude word.[92]

For Ranjit Singh, as probably for the other Sikhs, the Akal Bunga was next in importance to the Darbar Sahib. In February 1818, the Maharaja visited the Harmandar and made offerings of large sums of money at the Akal Bunga and asked the Akalis to offer prayers on his behalf.[93] After the conquest of Kashmir, the Maharaja again made offerings at both places and showed 'humility in many ways'.[94] The last personal offering he made at the Akal Bunga was in March 1839, and the last offering he sent through Bhai Gurmukh Singh was in April 1839.[95]

The importance of the Akali Takht was reduced but not obliterated. As noted by Hugel, the Akal Bunga was 'the place of consecration' where baptismal rites were performed.[96] According to another contemporary source, the Khalsa used to come to the Akal Bunga to seek forgiveness for their errors.[97] The Akalis held darbār at the Akal Bunga and offered prayers for God's support in all situations.[98] Thus, though the Akal Takht was no longer the seat of political power, it was still a vague symbol of central authority for the Sikhs.

Notes

1. *Shabdarth Sri Guru Granth Sahib Ji*, 4 vols, Amritsar: Shiromani Gurdwara Parbandhak Committee, with the standard pagination of *Adi Sri Guru Granth Sahib*, and the advantage of annotation by Teja Singh. All the references given here are to the *Shabdarth*. For the compositions of the Bhatts, pp. 1396–1409.
2. Giani Hazara Singh, ed., *Vārān Bhai Gurdas*, Amritsar: Khalsa Samachar, 1962 (7th edn), Vār 1, pauṛīs 47–8; Vār 13, pauṛī 25; Vār 24, pauṛīs 14–17, 19–20.
3. Ibid., Vār 24, pauṛī 1. In the dharmsal at Kartarpur the sadh-sangat symbolized the abode of truth (*sachch-khand*).
4. *Shabdarth*, pp. 1011–12.
5. Ibid., p. 113.
6. Ibid., p. 493.
7. Ibid., p. 1,107.
8. Ibid., p. 1,346.
9. Ibid., p. 1,418.
10. Ibid., p. 542.
11. Ibid., p. 430.
12. Ibid., pp. 305–6.
13. Ibid., p. 624.
14. Ibid., p. 625.
15. Ibid., pp. 783–4.
16. Ibid., pp. 625–6.
17. Ibid., p. 781.
18. Ibid., p. 782.
19. Ibid., p. 626.
20. Ibid., p. 817.
21. Ibid., p. 783.
22. Ibid., pp. 73–4.
23. J.S. Grewal and Irfan Habib, eds, *Sikh History from Persian Sources*, New Delhi: Tulika/Indian History Congress, 2001, p. 57.
24. Ibid., pp. 68–9. For the author of the *Dabistān-i Mazāhib* and his work, see ibid., pp. 59–61.

25. Singh, *Vārān Bhai Gurdas*, Vār 39, pauṛī 3.
26. Grewal and Habib, eds, *Sikh History from Persian Sources*, pp. 67-8.
27. Singh, *Vārān Bhai Gurdas*, Vār 36, pauṛīs 1-10.
28. Till the late twentieth century, the descendants of Prithi Chand at Guru Har Sahai had in their possession a pothī which they claimed to have come down from Guru Nanak.
29. Kirpal Singh and Shamsher Singh Ashok, eds, *Janam Sakhi Sri Guru Nanak Dev Ji* (by Sri Miharban Ji Sodhi), 2 vols, Amritsar: Khalsa College, 1962, 1969.
30. Ibid., vol. II (Pothi Harji and Pothi Chaturbhuj), 1969.
31. Ibid., p. 118.
32. Sainapat, *Shri Gur Sobha*, Shamsher Singh Ashok, ed., Amritsar: Shiromani Gurdwara Parbandhak Committee, 1967, pp. 42-65.
33. Ratan Singh Bhangu, *Parchin Panth Prakash*, Bhai Vir Singh, ed., New Delhi: Bhai Vir Singh Sahit Sadan, 1993 (rpt), p. 47.
34. Sarwan Singh, 'Amritsar in Medieval Punjabi Literature: A Historical Analysis', PhD thesis, Guru Nanak Dev University, Amritsar, 1994, pp. 107-20. Kesar Singh Chhibber, *Bansāvalīnāma Dasān Patshāhiān Kā*, Ratan Singh Jaggi, ed., Chandigarh: Panjab University (*Parkh*, Surinder Singh Kohli, ed., vol. II), 1972, pp. 189-90.
35. Grewal and Habib, eds, *Sikh History from Persian Sources*, pp. 107-8.
36. Bhangu, *Prachin Panth Prakāsh*, pp. 104, 133-5; 163; Chhibber, *Bansāvalīnāma*, p. 187.
37. Bhangu, *Prachin Panth Prakāsh*, pp.163-70; Chhibber, *Bansavalinama*, pp. 184-5.
38. Chhibber, *Bansāvalīnāma*, pp. 183-4.
39. Bhangu, *Prachin Panth Prakāsh*, pp. 210-17.
40. Ibid., pp. 222-7; Chhibber, *Bansāvalīnāma*, p. 196.
41. Kesar Singh Chhibber mentions the occupation of Ramdaspur by the Mughals and the desecration of Darbar Sahib in the 1730s: *Bansāvalīnāma*, pp. 190- 2.
42. Bhangu, *Prachin Panth Prakāsh*, pp. 325-7.
43. Grewal and Habib, eds, *Sikh History from Persian Sources*, pp. 171-2.
44. For the occupation of territories in 1750 and onwards we now have documentary evidence: B.N. Goswamy and J.S. Grewal, eds, *The Mughal and Sikh Rulers and the Vaishnavas of Pindori: A Historical Interpretation of 52 Persian Documents*, Shimla: Indian Institute of Advanced Study, 1969.
45. Grewal and Habib, eds, *Sikh History from Persian Sources*, pp. 174-6.
46. Ibid., p. 189.
47. Ibid., pp.190-202.

48. Ganda Singh, ed., *Hukamnāme Guru Sāhibān, Mata Sāhibān, Banda Singh ate Khalsa Ji de*, Patiala: Punjabi University, 1967, pp. 232–3.
49. Bhangu, Ratan Singh, *Sri Guru Panth Prakash*, ed., Balwant Singh Dhillon, Amritsar: Singh Brother, pp. 360–5, 372–3.
50. Grewal and Habib, eds, *Sikh History from Persian Sources*, pp. 206–7.
51. Bhangu, *Prachin Panth Prakāsh*, pp. 414–25.
52. Indu Banga, *Agrarian System of the Sikhs: Late Eighteenth and Early Nineteenth Century*, New Delhi: Manohar Publications, 1978, pp. 158–9.
53. Ram Sukh Rao, *Sri Fateh Singh Partāp Prabhākar*, Joginder Kaur, ed., Patiala: 1980, pp. 68–9, 210.
54. Sohan Lal Suri, *Umdat ut–Tawārīkh*, tr., V.S. Suri, Daftar II, Amritsar: Guru Nanak Dev University, 2002, p. 43.
55. Ibid., p. 47.
56. Ibid., p. 49.
57. Ibid., pp. 74–5.
58. Ibid., pp. 82–3.
59. Ibid., p. 109.
60. H.L.O. Garrett and G.L. Chopra, tr. and eds, *Events at the Court of Ranjit Singh, 1810–1817*, Patiala: Punjab Language Department, 1988 (rpt.), pp. 31–2.
61. Ibid., pp. 60–1, 75, 100, 127, 179, 181, 227.
62. Suri, *Umdat ut–Tawārīkh*, Daftar III, parts 1–3, pp. 262, 266–7, 380; part 4, p. 135; part 5, p. 253.
63. Ibid., pp. 252, 311.
64. Ibid., pp. 242, 248, 397, 419, 647.
65. Ibid., pp. 269, 429, 500.
66. Ibid., pp. 290–3.
67. Suri, *Umdat ut–Tawārīkh*, Daftar IV, part I, pp. 70, 73–4, 105–6.
68. Ibid., part 2, pp. 168–70, 184–6; part 3, pp. 233–4.
69. Ganesh Das, *Chār Bāgh-i Punjab*, Kirpal Singh, ed., Amritsar: Khalsa College, 1965, p. 294.
70. William Moorcroft and George Trebeck, *Travels in the Himalayan Provinces of Hindostan and the Punjab in Ladakh and Kashmir; in Peshawar, Kabul, and Kundaiz; and Bokhara*, Patiala: Punjab Language Dept, 1970 (rpt), pp. 54–5.
71. Baron Charles Hugel, *Travels in Kashmir and the Punjab*, tr., T.B. Jervis, Patiala: Punjab Language Department, 1970 (rpt), pp. 389–90, 393–6.
72. Emily Eden, *Up The Country*, 2 vols, London: Richard Bentley, 1866 (3rd edn), pp. 214–18.

73. W.L. M'Gregor, *The History of the Sikhs*, 2 vols, Patiala: Punjab Language Department, 1970 (rpt), vol. I, pp. 17–20.
74. Chhibber, *Bansāvalīnāma*, pp. 35, 39–40, 182–5, 189–92.
75. Sarwan Singh, 'Amritsar in Medieval Punjabi Literature', pp. 173–95.
76. Ibid., pp. 212–29, 617–20.
77. Ibid., pp. 230–509, 621–41.
78. Ibid., pp. 482–98, 664–77.
79. Ibid., pp. 283–300.
80. Ibid., pp. 499–581, 678–724.
81. Ibid., pp. 196–211, 251–4, 301–77, 459–81.
82. Ibid., pp. 408–58.
83. Ibid., pp. 378–407. Bhangu, *Prachin Panth Prakāsh*, pp. 45–7, 104, 135, 163–70, 201–3, 214–17, 221–2, 236, 325–8, 361, 385–91, 399–400, 414–25, 470, 471.
84. Lt Col (John) Malcolm, *A Sketch of the Sikhs,* New Delhi: Asian Educational Services, 1986 (rpt), pp. 115–20, 134.
  For J.D. Cunningham, the Akalis 'peculiarly represented the religious element of Sikhism'. They acted as the armed guardians of Amritsar from time to time and took upon themselves the authority of censors. They exercised considerable influence over the Sikh rulers in the late 18th century. It cost Ranjit Singh much time and trouble to suppress them. H.L.O. Garrett, ed., *A History of the Sikhs*, Delhi: S. Chand & Co., 1955 (rpt), pp. 99–100.
85. Suri, *Umdat ut-Tawārīkh,* Daftar II, p. 72.
86. Garrett and Chopra, eds, *Events at the Court of Ranjit Singh*, pp. 37–9, 127, 189.
87. Suri, *Umdat ut-Tawārīkh*, Daftar II, pp. 172–3.
88. Ibid., pp. 173, 192–3, 195, 207–8, 244, 273, 276, 367.
89. Ibid., p. 425.
90. Ibid., pp. 428–9.
91. Ibid., Daftar III, parts 1–3, p. 354.
92. Ibid., parts 4–5, p. 345
93. Ibid., pp. 236–7.
94. Ibid., pp. 306–7.
95. Ibid., pp. 406, 419.
96. Hugel, *Travels in Kashmir and the Punjab,* p. 394.
97. Sarwan Singh, 'Amritsar in Medieval Punjabi Literature', p. 624.
98. Ibid., p. 668.

PART III
Concerns of Sikh Literature

6. An Early Eighteenth Century Janamsākhī*

Much has been written on the Janamsākhīs but no Janamsākhīs has been analysed for what W.H. McLeod calls the 'myth' of Guru Nanak, that is, the image of Guru Nanak cherished and projected by his followers at a particular time in their history. The *B40 Janamsākhī*, being dated, has special significance for such an analysis.[1]

According to Piar Singh, no two manuscripts of the Janamsākhīs are exactly alike. The number of *sākhīs* varies from manuscript to manuscript as does their sequence. He suggests that in the beginning a sākhī or a *gosht* was the unit of narrative in which a trait of Guru Nanak's personality or his teaching was meant to be conveyed to the listeners of *kathā*. Gradually the Sikh *parchāraks* began to prepare written records for use in the performance of katha. This tradition reached its culmination in the *Miharbān Janamsākhī*. In the process, several written traditions developed simultaneously.

Piar Singh identifies five such traditions: the *Bālā*, the *Purātan*, the *Ādi*, the *Miharbān*, and the Janamsākhī attributed to Bhai Mani Singh which in fact is a mixture of the Purātan, Ādi, and Bālā traditions. The *B40 Janamsākhī* too is a mixture of several traditions.[2] W.H. McLeod has classified its sākhīs as the Hafizabad version of the Purātan, Ādi, and Miharbān, miscellaneous discourses and oral traditions. The last sākhī, about the death of Guru Nanak, does not belong to either of these traditions.[3]

The *B40* manuscript was completed in 1733 by Daya Ram, an Abrol Khatri. Significantly, he refers to himself as the 'slave' of the *sangat*, which for him is the Prefect Guru's court and the Perfect

---

* 'An Early Eighteenth Century Janamsākhī' is a slightly revised version of 'The *B40 Janamsākhī*' included in my *Lectures on History, Society and Culture of the Punjab* (Patiala: Punjabi University, 2007, pp. 167–217).

Guru's tongue. The Guru resides in the sangat. Whatever is asked for is granted, especially the gift of the Name, the highest gift, which leads to liberation from the cycle of rebirth and death. Daya Ram Abrol was commissioned to write the manuscript by Bhai Sangu Mal, a devout Sikh of the Guru who was deeply attached to Gurbāṇī. The manuscript was illustrated by Alam Chand, a mason-artist, as a service to the sangat.[4]

The *B40* reflects an image of Guru Nanak that was meant to be popularized among the Sikhs in the 1730s. The fact that the Bālā tradition is not represented in the *B40*, and even the Miharbān tradition is represented only marginally, gives the impression that the sangat and its leader, Bhai Sangu Mal, were attached to the *shabad* of the Guru as non-sectarian Sikhs.[5]

SĀKHĪS OF THE PURĀTAN TRADITION

According to W.H. McLeod, eighteen sākhīs of the *B40* overlap or are similar to the Hafizabad version of the Puratan tradition. These sākhīs cover more than a third of the *Janamsākhī*, forming the largest component. They relate to Guru Nanak's birth and early life in Talvandi, his stay at Sultanpur, his travels, the invasions of Babur, and the founding of Kartarpur. A closer look at these sākhīs reveals the kind of image and the status of Guru Nanak and his message that was sought to be projected through them.

The birth of Baba Nanak is described with details of the time and place, and the name and caste of his father. More importantly, the primary purpose of his life is stated at the outset: promulgation of his own *panth* in the Kaliyuga. The thirty-three crores of Gods, twenty-four Siddhs, nine Naths, sixty-four Jogins, fifty-two Bīrs, and six Jatīs, who salute him at his birth, know that the Formless One had come to redeem the world. Outwardly he began to play with children but inwardly he thought of God. At the age of five he began to talk of things beyond the comprehension of ordinary people. The Hindus began to say that a veritable god was born and the Musalmans began to say a *sādiq* of God was born. These were the early signs of his divinity.[6]

Taken to the *pāndhā* for education at the age of seven, Nanak asked the pāndhā what he could teach. The pāndhā replied that he could teach the Vedas and Shastras, and the keeping of accounts. Nanak recited a verse to the effect that all kinds of learning was useless without the

Name of God and His praises. Another verse he recited refers to the honour received in God's court as the sole objective of life. This, said the pāndhā, could bring no material gain or social recognition, asking significantly would anything happen to those who wielded power, did evil deeds, and did not remember God? Nanak assured the pāndhā that such rulers would suffer like clothes thrashed by the washerman, the sesame seeds crushed by the oil-press, and the grain ground by the millstone. The mighty who did evil would be punished and even the beggars who remembered God would be honoured. This statement had a strong political implication in the 1730s when the Sikhs were being suppressed by the Mughal authorities. Anyway, the pāndhā reminded Nanak of his worldly responsibilities. Nanak replied that even the *sultān*s and *khān*s had to leave the world; hence, there was no point in attaching oneself to what is transient and false. The pāndhā saw that Baba Nanak was a 'perfect person'. He saluted him and said, 'do whatever you like'.[7] Apart from the political implication, Guru Nanak's preference for devotion to God over traditional learning and a professional career is portrayed in this sākhī; the pāndhā implicitly gives recognition to him, and explicitly states that he could do what he had in mind.

Vested with the sacred thread (*janjū*), at the age of nine, Nanak was sent to learn Persian (Turki). After some time, however, he sat at home. The people suggested to his father that he should get his son married. At the age of twelve he was married to the daughter of Mula, a Choṇa Khatri. But, instead of taking interest in the affairs of the family, he began to associate with *faqīr*s.[8] The idea of his parents was to induce him to take interest in domestic affairs but they failed in their purpose. Baba Nanak was not attracted by sensual pleasures, just as he was not attracted by traditional piety or worldly success.

On his father's suggestion, Nanak agreed to graze buffaloes. On the second day he left the buffaloes alone and slept on the edge of a field of wheat. The buffaloes ruined the crop, and the Bhatti owner of the field demanded compensation. Nanak said that God would increase the yield from the field which had fed the buffaloes. But the owner brought him to Rai Bular, the Bhatti chaudharī of Talvandi, who summoned Nanak's father, Kalu, and told him to give adequate compensation. He also threatened to complain to the state administrators if Kalu did not comply with his order. The threat held out by the chaudharī acquired a political dimension in the context of the early eighteenth century in view of the hostility of the Mughal administrators towards the Sikhs. Anyway, Kalu pleaded that his son was a *majzūb dīwāna*, with no worldly sense due to his preoccupation with God. But Rai Bular insisted on compensation. Nanak said that no crop had been ruined. Rai Bular sent his men to verify, and they found that not a single blade had been eaten. Rai Bular told the landowner that his accusation was false.[9] The message is clear: God had intervened to protect the honour of Nanak who had uttered that no crop was ruined. This was an indication of Nanak's status with God.

Through God's will, two sons were born to Nanak's wife: Lakhmi Das and Sri Chand. However, this did not put an end to his detached state (*udāsī*). He would go to groves or forests to sit in solitude. One day Rai Bular was out hunting and saw that the shadow of a tree under which a man was asleep had not moved away. He asked his men to wake him up. When he saw Nanak he was reminded of the incident of the ruined crop and said that God was gracious to Nanak. He told Kalu not to scold his son on any account: 'He is a great man (*mahā purakh*) and it is due to him that my town is flourishing'.[10] The sākhī projects Baba Nanak's nearness to God who was gracious to him and intervened in the natural course for his sake.

Baba Nanak's parents were keen that he should take up some gainful occupation such as cultivation, shopkeeping, trading in horses, or service. In response to their insistence, he uttered verses which implied his preference for the path of liberation over all such worldly occupations and professions. True trade, for example, should bring truth as the profit through true Name as the goods.[11] Nothing was comparable to the service of the True Lord whose greatness is beyond description.

The Bedis were distressed over the unworldly attitude of Kalu's son. They insisted that Kalu should consult a physician to treat him. The *vaid* came and checked Nanak's pulse. Nanak told him that the trouble was in his heart and not in his arm. He did not need any medicine since he was attached to God. Instead, the vaid himself was in need of the Name. The vaid told the people that Nanak was ordained to be a great healer who would help in removing sorrow and suffering.[12]

The news of Nanak's indifference to worldy affairs reached his sister's husband, Jai Ram, who was the *modī* of Nawab Daulat Khan at Sultanpur. He asked Nanak to visit Sultanpur. He recommended Nanak to Daulat Khan for a job as a well-educated person. Daulat Khan entrusted all his affairs to Nanak and appreciated his work. His kitchen was open to all, and all joined him in *kīrtan* until the last quarter of the night when he would go to the river for bath and meditation. One day he took a servant with him and entrusted his clothes to him before entering the water. He did not come out for several hours and the servant informed Daulat Khan who ordered a thorough search. The boatmen cast their nets everywhere but found nothing. Baba Nanak reappeared after three days, came to his *derā*, distributed everything he possessed, and joined the faqīrs. On the second day he began to utter: 'None is Hindu, none is Musalman'. The people reported it to the Khan who told them to ignore him, saying that Nanak was a faqīr. But the *qāzī* took notice of the utterance. Daulat Khan's men went to Baba Nanak and told him that the Khan had ordered him to be present. Baba Nanak said, 'I do not care for your Khan'. The people thought he had gone mad. Baba Nanak asked Mardana to play on the *rabāb* and sang a shabad to the effect that he was mad in the love and fear of God.

Whenever he spoke, he uttered the same words: 'None is Hindu, none is Musalman'. The qāzī approached the Khan again. This time the Khan asked Baba Nanak to come for the sake of God. Baba Nanak said, 'now that my Master has called I will go'. Guru Nanak's changed attitude towards the Khan is not without a political significance. Now that Guru Nanak had found the True Lord he did not have to care about earthly lords. Anyway, the qāzī asked him why he had said that there was no Hindu and no Musalman. Baba Nanak recited the *shalok* in which the way of the *auliya* is recommended for Musalmans: to accept God's will, to recognize His power so as to think nothing of oneself, and to be kind towards all human beings. The qāzī was nonplussed. The Khan told the qāzī to leave Nanak alone: 'he is some auliya of God'.

It was the time of midday prayer and the qāzī led the prayer. Baba Nanak smiled at his performance. The qāzī complained to the Khan and he asked Baba Nanak why he was smiling. He said that the qāzī's prayer was not accepted by God because he was thinking of his colt at home all the time. The qāzī fell at Baba Nanak's feet and said that God was gracious to him. The significance of this acknowledgement cannot be missed. A representative of Islamic orthodoxy is made to see the spiritual status of Guru Nanak. Baba Nanak then recited a shalok in which Muslim beliefs and practices are interpreted in highly ethical and spiritual terms. All present in the assembly were surprised to hear this: the *sayyidzādā*s, the *shaikhzādā*s, the qāzī, the *muftī*, and the Khans. Daulat Khan told the qāzīs and muftīs that Baba Nanak had attained to God; there was no need to question him any more. All the Hindus and Musalmans requested the Khan to keep Baba Nanak in Sultanpur. The Khan requested him to stay at least for a month so that his city would be blessed. Nanak said that his city had been blessed already, and agreed to stay for a week.[13]

One day the qāzī, on his way to the court, met Baba Nanak and asked him: 'departure or stay'. Baba Nanak said: 'departure'. The qāzī went home to prepare for travel. The Khan noticed the qāzī's absence and sent for him. When he asked the qāzī why he had not attended court, he said that Baba Nanak had told him of the order for 'departure', so he went home to get ready. The Khan said that he had given no such order. The qāzī said that Baba Nanak should be asked why he had told a lie. The Khan called Baba Nanak. He sang a shabad to the effect that nothing stays forever except God. The whole assembly was stunned into silence. At the end of seven days, Daulat Khan made the same request but Baba Nanak told him that he had to leave.[14]

The Sultanpur sākhī is rich in significance. In the first place, Nanak performed his duties well, so well indeed that Daulat Khan was sorry to be deprived of his services. Second, Nanak showed charity towards all and his dedication to God. Then, his experience at the river carries the implication of a great revelation, which enabled him to see clearly that there was no true Hindu and no true Musalman. His presentation of Islamic beliefs and practices convinced even the qāzī and the muftī, the acknowledged representatives of Muslim orthodoxy, that Baba Nanak was a friend of God. They accorded him the status of a *walī*. Finally, his critical experience at Sultanpur led to a change in the course of his life.

Baba Nanak took to wilderness, avoiding all roads and habitations. Mardana was with him. Unlike Baba Nanak, he suffered from hunger, and complained that he was being kept in the wilderness. Baba Nanak said that there could be no wilderness where there is the Name. Baba Nanak told him to eat the fruit of a particular tree. Mardana found it so delicious that he could not help keeping some for future. When he ate it again he found it to be poisonous. Baba Nanak told him that it was made sweet by God's grace for the moment. Mardana insisted that he would stay with Baba Nanak only if he was blessed to sustain himself on what sustained Baba Nanak. Baba Nanak said that he was already blessed. Mardana stayed with Baba Nanak for twelve years.[15] This sākhī underscores the presence of God everywhere and the efficacy of the Name. Mardana's devotion to Guru Nanak became the means of his liberation.

Baba Nanak returned to the Punjab after twelve years. He sat in a wilderness near Talvandi. Mardana went home and saw Baba Nanak's parents. They expressed anxiety about their son. Mardana lied that he had not seen Baba Nanak and left in a hurry. Baba Nanak's mother followed him into the wilderness. There she saw her son and expressed her deep affection for him. He sang a shabad expressing his dedication to God. She offered sweets and new clothes to him and he sang a shabad in which metaphors from food and dress emphasize the importance of loving devotion to God. Baba Nanak's father also reached there and asked him to ride the mare and stay in their newly-built house for some time. Baba Nanak sang a shabad in which the metaphors of mounting a horse and residing in a house underline the importance of ethical qualities, the Name, and God's grace. Baba Nanak assured his parents that he would come to them, but not just now. He was still in a state of udās.[16] This sākhī projects the spirit of detachment from worldly things and attachment to God and loving devotion to him.

Travelling through a wilderness Baba Nanak came upon a monster (*rākshasa*) who had a number of captives beside a huge cauldron of boiling oil. He threw one of them into it and then took Baba Nanak straight to the cauldron. The oil became cold when Baba Nanak put his finger in it. The monster fell at his feet. Baba Nanak sang a shabad in which metaphorically the boiling cauldron becomes cool through the Name and one attains liberation. Baba Nanak showed his grace to the monster and he began to recite the Name.[17] The message is obvious. Baba Nanak could overpower monsters and transform them into devotees of God as his disciples.

Bhola, a powerful and brave robber, waylaid Baba Nanak and demanded whatever he had. Baba Nanak told him to go home and ask his family members, who were the beneficiaries of his robberies, if they would share the punishment for his sins. They told Bhola that each individual would be accountable for his deeds in the hereafter. Bhola came back and sought forgiveness for his sins. Baba Nanak patted him and he was liberated. Baba Nanak sang a shabad to the effect that true friends are those who stand with one in the divine court. Appropriation of the Name removed the suffering of Bhola.[18] The message of this sākhī is simple: Baba Nanak is the redeemer of sinners; through the message of the Name, he transformed them into devotees of God to perform good deeds.

Baba Nanak entered a frightening wilderness with no habitation in sight. A dust storm arose and the sky was overcast with dark clouds. Mardana was frightened. Baba Nanak asked him to say *Vāheguru*. The storm began to assume the shape of a demon with large teeth and a huge belly, with his head touching the sky. Mardana was afraid that they would die. Baba Nanak asked him to say Vāheguru. The demon assumed human form and stood before Baba Nanak with folded hands. On being asked, he revealed that he was Kaliyuga. He offered to build a palace of pearls for Baba Nanak in his kingdom. Baba Nanak sang the shabad in which the Name of God is preferred over wealth, power and beautiful women. Baba Nanak asked Kaliyuga what else he had in his kingdom. He said that there was plenty of hunger and thirst, slander, laziness, robbery, gambling, sin, falsehood, greed, lust, and pride. Baba Nanak asked Kaliyuga not to harm his Sikh or sangat in his kingdom, and not to cast his shadow on them; they should not deviate from shabad and sākhī, *punn* and *dān*, *nām* and *isnān*. Kaliyuga said that his power was greater than that of other *yuga*s and his influence was more pervasive. This carried the implication that he could not exempt the Sikhs. Baba Nanak insisted that the only offering acceptable to him was that his sangat should live in fear of God alone. Kaliyuga reiterated that no sādhu could escape his influence. Baba Nanak persisted in his demand. Kaliyuga then submitted: 'even my life is an offering to you, my king'. He repeated his promise thrice and Baba Nanak said that his rule would be distinguished by kīrtan and kathā. Instead of austerities of a hundred years, meditation on God would be the source of liberation.[19] The message of this sākhī is loud and clear: not only would Kaliyuga have no influence on the Sikh sangats but also prevalence of the Name would be the great mark of his Age. The sākhī gives a popular form to the conviction of Guru Nanak that his path was the most efficacious, if not the only valid path, for liberation in the Kaliyuga. The exclusive efficacy of the Name in the Kaliyuga was emphasized by Guru Amar Das, Guru Ram Das, and Guru Arjan. Despite its supranatural setting, the sākhī remains true to the message of Gurbāṇī.

Baba Nanak and Mardana then went to a place where women were mourning the death of someone, uttering the words '*hai hai rājā bolo Har Har*'. Baba Nanak was deeply moved by their lamentation. He praised the town and the women who were uttering the name of God. He recited a shabad to the effect that the only source of consolation was the Name.[20] This, obviously, can be seen as Guru Nanak's instruction with regard to mourning.

Baba Nanak and Mardana went to a town where a Sikh, affected by the singing of a shabad, invited them to his place. Extremely poor, he lived from hand to mouth. His wife cooked a meal and they ate it. On the following days he sold something to keep the kitchen going. On the fourth day the Sikh cut off his long hair to sell them for money for the kitchen. His wife lighted a fire in the kitchen and went outside to fetch something. Their child fell into the fire and was fatally burnt. She wrapped the dead body in a sheet and left it inside the home. Baba Nanak sat with the Sikh to eat, and enquired about the child. The Sikhnī said that the child was asleep. Baba Nanak called him aloud and he came out. On the following day, the parents thought of selling the child to run the kitchen. Baba Nanak told the child that they were going to sell him; and he would have to grind the millstone, draw the fan, fetch water, and dance. The child replied that he would be happy to accept God's will. Baba Nanak uttered a shabad to the effect that the slave of God obeys His command and does everything for Him and in his name.[21] Projected in this sākhī is the service of *sādh*s (Sikhs), sacrifice of property and life in their service, and the willing acceptance of God's will. An entire family is visualized as Sikh.

In the mosque of Mecca, Baba Nanak slept with his feet towards the *mihrāb*. The *mujāwar* of the mosque asked him why he had turned his feet towards the house of God. Baba Nanak told him to turn his feet in another direction. The *mullā* moved Baba Nanak's feet towards the north and the mihrāb turned towards the north. He turned his feet towards the east and the south, and the mihrāb turned in the same direction. A voice from the dome of the mosque praised Baba Nanak.

He recited a shabad to the effect that God is in the heart.[22] Despite its supranatural element, the sākhī conveys a twofold message: God is everywhere in the universe, and he is also within the human heart.

Baba Nanak and Mardana went towards Multan and sat in a wilderness near Pakpattan which was well known for the *dargāh* of Shaikh Farid, the most popular Sufi saint of the Punjab. His successor, Shaikh Ibrahim, called Shaikh Brahm in Sikh literature, was Shaikh Farid's successor at Pakpattan. His disciple, Shaikh Kamal, had come to the wilderness to collect firewood. Baba Nanak sang the shalok: 'You yourself are the tablet, the pen, and the writing; talk only of the One, Nanak, not of any other'. With the wood he had already collected, Shaikh Kamal returned to Shaikh Brahm and told him that he had met a man of God. Shaikh Brahm came in a palanquin to see Baba Nanak and asked Baba Nanak to explain his position because there was one God but two acknowledged ways, namely, the Hindu and Muslim. Baba Nanak said that there was one God and only one way, that is, the realization that everything perishes and God alone remains for ever.

Shaikh Brahm recited a shalok in which silken robes are discarded in favour of the woollen blanket in order to please God. Baba Nanak responded by saying that God is pleased through loving devotion in the home. Renunciation was unnecessary. Shaikh Brahm then recited a shalok in which the woman regrets after death that she failed to meet the spouse in youth. Baba Nanak emphasized that what mattered was merit and virtue, and not age. Shaikh Brahm asked about the word, the quality, and the *mantra* which pleased the spouse to be brought close to him. Baba Nanak replied that the garb that pleased the spouse consisted of humility, patience, sweet words, and service. Shaikh Brahm asked whether grace came first or service. Baba Nanak replied that service came first. Shaikh Brahm praised Baba Nanak, saying, 'we have met an auliya of God'.

Shaikh Brahm asked for a knife to slaughter a person lawfully (halāl). Baba Nanak said that this knife was 'the truth': it removed the blood of greed. Since there could be no light without the lamp and no lamp without oil, Shaikh Brahm asked Baba Nanak how a lamp could be lighted without oil. Baba Nanak said that the lamp could be lighted by using the fear of God as the wick. Shaikh Brahm exclaimed: 'God speaks through you'. Shaikh Brahm requested Baba Nanak to recite a *Vār*. His idea was to know whom Baba Nanak would introduce as a contestant with God. Baba Nanak sang a verse to the effect that God created Himself and He created the Name. Shaikh Brahm stood up in veneration and said, 'there is no difference between you and God. Be kind to us'. Baba Nanak assured him that God would protect his honour.[23] This long sākhī raises several important issues of theology and ethics, bringing out the difference between Sufism and Sikhism, and implies the superiority of the path of Guru Nanak over Sūfism and of Guru Nanak over Shaikh Brahm.

'Guru Baba Nanak' then left the place and passing through Dipalpur, Kanganpur, Kasur, Goindwal, Sultanpur, Vairoval, and Jalalabad reached Pathanan di Kiri. There, some Pathans became his *murīds*.[24] This simple statement is important: the compiler does not see anything unusual in Guru Nanak accepting Pathans, who were associated with Muslim rulers, as his disciples.

Baba Nanak went to Saidpur, accompanied by some faqīrs. They went from door to door but got no food. The Pathans of Saidpur were busy celebrating a marriage with dance and merriment. Annoyed with their indifference to the hungry faqīrs, Baba Nanak sang the shabad which refers to Babur's 'marriage party of sin' indulging in indiscriminate rape and slaughter. A Brahman heard this shabad, brought a basket of fruit, and requested Baba Nanak to withdraw the curse. Baba Nanak said that this was no longer in his power. He advised the Brahman to save himself and his family by going to a particular pool at twelve *kos*. Baba Nanak also left the place and sat in a wilderness. On the day following, Babur sacked the town and the surrounding villages. Hindus and Muslims were slaughtered indiscriminately, their houses were plundered, and their women and children were enslaved. God listens to what the true faqīrs say. God's anger descended on the Pathans on account of the shabad recited by Baba Nanak.

Baba Nanak returned to Saidpur on the third day and saw the devastation. He sang the shabad that refers to the life of luxury and indulgence, the helplessness of the *pīr*s who claimed to blind the Mughals, the destruction of tall buildings, the princes cut into pieces, and the battle fought between the Mughals and the Pathans. Baba Nanak then went into the camp of Babur and was deeply moved to see the captives. He sang the shabad that refers to Babur's friendly treatment of Khurasan and his hostility towards Hindustan. Babur felt pleased with him, and offered *bhang* but Baba Nanak said that he remained intoxicated with the Name all the time. He sang the shabad in which the plight of the women of the ruling classes is depicted. At the end of this shabad he went into a trance. The people told Babur that, seeing the wrath of God, Baba Nanak had lost his senses. Babur asked them to pray for his recovery. Baba Nanak got up with the brightness of a hundred suns on his face. Babur saluted him and requested him to be kind. Baba said, 'if you want kindness of God, release the captives'. Babur agreed to do so and Baba Nanak said that his *pātshāhī* would last for generations.[25]

All the shabads known as '*Babar-bani*' are used in this sākhī to convey a political and moral message. Babur is God's instrument for punishing the Pathans for their misrule, negligence of duty, and their indifference to the hungry faqīrs. The men and women of the ruling class suffer for their indulgence in sensual pleasures in forgetfulness of God.

Baba Nanak settled on the bank of the River Ravi and his fame began to spread far and wide as a great devotee of God. People began to come in crowds and many of them became his followers. Among the visitors were all classes and categories of Hindus and Musalmans. They returned satisfied and praised Baba Nanak. The Karori in the neighbourhood did not relish his fame. Baba Nanak, he thought, was misleading the Musalmans. He rode out, intent upon action against Baba Nanak, and was blinded. People told him to recognize Baba Nanak as a great pīr. He began to praise Baba Nanak. But when he mounted the horse, he fell down and the people said that he should go on foot if he wished to be forgiven. He did so and he was treated kindly. He requested Baba Nanak to allow him to demarcate a piece of land for founding a village, and maintaining a *dharmsāl*. When the village was founded, Baba Nanak's father Kalu also came with his family. Baba Nanak's cot (*manjī*) was set under a pīpal tree where the sangat used to meet. Contributions came regularly from *kār*, *bhet*, and *mannat*.[26] The sākhī highlights the popularity of Guru Nanak among the people, both Hindu and Muslim, both religious and secular, and the founding of a centre with a dharmsal. Baba Nanak assumed the formal position of a guide; he gave regular sermons to large audiences, and admitted disciples. Thus, a fair degree of institutionalization was introduced by Guru Nanak in his lifetime.

The last sākhī from the Purātan tradition relates to Raja Shivnabh. A poor Khatri came to Baba Nanak for help to perform the marriage of his daughter. Baba Nanak sent his disciple Bhagirath to Lahore with a list of articles needed for the wedding, with the instruction that he should return the same day. The *bāṇiā* who supplied all but one article asked Bhagirath to wait for a day. Bhagirath said that if he did not do what his Guru had told him he would lose the only chance of his life. The bāṇiā was impressed by the reply and wanted to meet Baba Nanak. Before they came into his presence, they heard Baba Nanak chiding Bhagirath for having taken too much time. The bāṇiā fell at the feet of Baba Nanak who showed kindness to him. He stayed with Baba Nanak for three years and recorded much of his bāṇī and prepared *pothīs*.

The bāṇiā took leave of Baba Nanak to go back to Lahore. With a ship load of goods he went across the sea, and settled in the city of Raja Shivnabh. There, his daily life was marked by kīrtan at night, bath in cold water before dawn, and reading of shabad-pothī before eating anything. He kept no fasts, offered no *pūjā* in the temple, and followed no other practice of the people of the city. He came to be regarded as a grave defaulter. The complaint reached Raja Shivnabh and he asked him why he did not conform to the practices of Hindus. He replied that he had already obtained all that was believed to be the fruit of their practices. He explained further that he had been liberated by a mahā purakh whose name was Guru Baba Nanak and whose *darshan* was the source of liberation. Then he recited the bāṇī of Guru Nanak and the Raja became 'a Sikh of the shabad of the Guru Baba'.

Raja Shivnabh wanted to have the Guru's darshan. He was told that if he earnestly lodged the Guru in his heart the Guru would meet him in his own city. The Raja now began to think of meeting the Guru. He ordered his courtesans to attend to every sādhū who came to the city, and even to tempt him. Baba Nanak came to the city of Raja Shivnabh as a faqīr and entered a garden that had withered years ago. The garden suddenly became green. When the gardener came to see it, he found a faqīr sitting there in meditation. He told the Raja of what had happened. The Raja ordered his courtesans to lure the faqīr. Baba Nanak sang a couple of shabads and the courtesans started reciting 'Guru, Guru'. They told the Raja that he was now like a father to them. Their meeting with the mahā purakh had brought them liberation. The Raja was keen to discover his identity. A shabad of Nanak with the epithet 'Nanak' at the end revealed his identity. The Raja felt gratified to have found the Perfect Guru. He addressed Baba Nanak as pātshāh. He built a dharmsāl for singing the shabad of the Guru and established a *langar* in which nine maunds (over 3 quintals) of salt were used every day. After disseminating bāṇī in that part of the world, Baba Nanak returned to Kartarpur.[27]

Several features of this sākhī demand attention. Baba Nanak enables a poor man to perform his daughter's marriage; a disciple of Baba Nanak looks upon liberation as the greatest boon that only he can give; complete obedience to the Guru is the means of liberation; his personality is the source of inspiration; the daily pattern of the life of a follower of Guru Nanak is different from that of others; the bāṇī of Guru Nanak is efficacious in bringing people to his path; the conversion of women to the faith of Guru Nanak is a familiar matter; he is concerned with propagating the Name, and establishes dharmsāls for congregational worship in which the bāṇī of Guru Nanak is sung; a langar for all and sundry is the normal feature of a dharmsāl.

In the sākhīs of the Purātan tradition, Guru Nanak is the Formless One who came into the world for the redemption of humankind in the Kaliyuga through a new path of liberation. The signs of his divinity appeared early in his life: Hindus saw in him a veritable god and Muslims saw him as a sādiq; he preferred devotion to God over traditional learning or a professional career, and the pāndhā conceded his point; he was not attracted by sensual pleasures, either; God intervened in the natural course of things to honour his words, or to show his grace to Guru Nanak; the vaid recognized him as 'a physician' who would remove all sorrow and suffering.

Guru Nanak's experience at Sultanpur was a kind of revelation: he proclaimed that Hindus and Musalmans were not on the right path. The representatives of Muslim orthodoxy, that is, the qāzī and the muftī, who had the support of the state, took notice of Guru Nanak's assertion; he revealed a sympathetic understanding of Islam; the political representatives of the state felt convinced that Guru Nanak was a walī.

Guru Nanak underscored the merit of devotion to God and the efficacy of the Name. Devotion to Guru Nanak himself became the means of liberation. Detachment from worldly things was a corollary of attachment to God in loving devotion. Guru Nanak overpowered monsters and transformed them into devotees of God as his disciples. He redeemed sinners through the message of the Name and transformed them into pious Sikhs. His encounter with the personified Kaliyuga is meant to project the idea that the followers of Guru Nanak would not only remain unaffected by the evil influences of the age but also redeem it.

Guru Nanak's appreciation for the wailing women who remember God is the logical outcome of his message that death should be accepted as God's will. Besides the willing acceptance of God's will, a Sikh should sacrifice his life and property in the service of other Sikhs.

God is everywhere in the universe and He is within human beings, in their hearts. Some of the important differences between Sufism and Sikhism are brought out in Guru Nanak's dialogue with Shaikh Brahm; the superiority of Baba Nanak and his panth is established. The 'Babar-bāṇī' verses project Guru Nanak's consideration for Babur and his denunciation of the Afghans; the comment is ethical as well as political. The Karori who thinks ill of Guru Nanak's mission has to submit to him and serve him.

Guru Nanak was popular among the people, both Hindu and Muslim; he founded a dharmsāl for congregational worship, admitted disciples and gave his message to all and sundry. He enabled a poor Sikh to get his daughter married; his disciples looked upon liberation through the Guru as the greatest boon; his bāṇī, like his personality, serves as the means of bringing people to the Sikh fold; the Sikh way of life is different from that of the non-Sikhs around; women as well as men are influenced by his message of the Name; the institution that symbolizes and epitomizes the Sikh faith is the dharmsāl.

On the whole, the essential message of the sākhīs of the Purātan tradition remains close to that of the bāṇī of Guru Nanak. The presence of the miraculous in many of the *sākhīs* may not strictly be justified in the light of the teachings of Guru Nanak. The general belief of the people in the supranatural enabled them to catch the import of the sākhīs with supranatural settings or elements.

Sākhīs of the Ādi Tradition

About a dozen sākhīs of the Ādi tradition account for a little less than a fourth of the *B40 Janamsākhī*. Each sākhī has a distinct episode; a couple of sākhīs have more than one episode. Their sequence is not chronological.

The most remarkable sākhī of this tradition relates to the divine sanction for the distinctive path of Guru Nanak. One day Baba Nanak was called by God to his presence. 'I am unable to reach you', said Baba Nanak. He was told to close his eyes and he was transported to the abode of the Formless One. God told him that he was sent into the world to spread His Name. Baba Nanak recited a shabad to underscore the impossibility of describing God and his greatness. God said, 'Go, I have ordained a panth for you in the Kaliyuga and named you Guru. My title is the True King and your title is the Guru'. God told Baba Nanak that the salutation of his panth would be 'I fall at the feet of the True Guru' just as the Vaishnava salutation is 'Ram Kisan', the Sanyasi salutation is 'Namo Narayan', the Jogi salutation is 'Ades Ad Purkh ko', and Muslim salutation is 'Salamalaik'. The name of the Panth would be 'Nanak Panth'. Its purpose was to spread God's bhakti and *dharm*. The Nanak Panth was to have its dharmsāl like Ramsāla of the Vaishnavas, the Āsan of the Jogīs, the mosque of the Muslims. Three things were essential for the Panth: nām, dān, and isnān. The Nanak Panthīs should remain detached in their household. They should not harm anyone or think ill of anyone. They should cultivate humility and regard themselves as lower than everybody else. They should earn honestly and give charity in the name of God, and they should be truthful. Their only refuge should be God. They should think only of God's Name. God's grace shall be upon them. Finally, God tells Baba Nanak, 'you are me and I am you'. Through this sākhī are projected the distinctive status of Guru Nanak, the distinctive character of his message in the Kaliyuga, and distinctive identity of his panth.[28]

Equally significant is the sākhī in which Guru Nanak infuses his light into Angad and makes him the Guru in his lifetime. Lehna had come to Guru Nanak with a group of pilgrims on their way to the temple of Durga. On being asked who he was, Lehna said that he was a Trehan Khatri named Lehna. Baba Nanak said, 'your name is Angad; you are eternally my own, a part of my body'. Lehna bade farewell to his fellow pilgrims and stayed in Kartarpur. He returned to his village in the Harike area after three years. Soon afterwards, however, he shifted to Khadur to be nearer to Guru Nanak. Wearing a fine white dress one day, he went to Kartarpur. He was told to carry a sheaf of grass over his head and his dress was spoilt. Mata Choṇi chided Baba Nanak. He said, 'what you see on the head of Angad is not a sheaf of grass; I have placed a crown over his head; what you see as the drops of muddy water is saffron falling from an inverted bowl'. The image comes from the ceremony of a king's coronation. Then Baba Nanak infused his light into Angad to the full, and placed five *paisa*s and a coconut shell before him. The entire sangat fell at his feet, knowing that Baba Nanak had made him the successor to his pātshāhī.[29]

The superiority of Guru Nanak's message over yoga is demonstrated in two sākhīs. Baba Nanak had a gosht with the Siddhs at Sumer, the legendary mountain beyond the reach of human beings. 'What is happening in the world of the mortals?', asked Gorakh Nath. Baba Nanak recited a shalok which says that there is the famine of truth, without loving devotion to God, and human beings cannot be regenerated just as the split seed cannot sprout. It was followed by two other shaloks on the sad state of affairs in the Kaliyuga. Bharthari told Baba Nanak that there was no guru like Gorakh Nath who made great Siddhs of men like Isar Nath, Gopi Chand, Charpat Nath, Machhandar Nath, and Bharthari himself. The Siddhs then talked of yoga, each from his own perspective. Guru Nanak talked of the Name and absorption in the Formless One. He sang a shabad on true yoga in terms of his own message: liberation through *giān*, *dhiān*, *karnī*, *bhāo*, *prem*, *sachch*, shabad, sākhī of the Guru, and God's grace. The only boon Baba Nanak wanted was that he may never forget the creator. He had no desire for power, wealth or long life. Gorakh Nath stood up and said with his hands folded that there would be no Guru like Baba Nanak in the Kaliyuga.[30]

At the time of the Shivratri fair at Achal, to which eighty-four Siddhs came, Baba Nanak found some pilgrims complaining that someone had concealed their pot. The Siddhs suggested that a Nanak Panthi should discover it. A Sikh discovered the pot and the Siddhs were surprised. Bhangar Nath taunted Baba Nanak for having put on the garb of a householder. Baba Nanak retorted that Bhangar Nath remained alien to the truth even in the garb of a renunciant. The Siddhs challenged Baba Nanak to reveal his power. He told them to hide themselves and he would find them out. Baba Nanak found them out from wherever they had hidden themselves in all the three worlds.

Baba Nanak, in turn, concealed himself in the four elements: earth, air, water, and fire. The Siddhs looked for him in all the three worlds but failed to find him and admitted their defeat. Baba Nanak recited a shalok to the effect that the True Name is preferable to supranatural powers. The Siddhs asked him to enlighten them and Baba Nanak recited the *SiddhGosht*.[31]

Several sākhīs associate austerities and asceticism with Guru Nanak. In one sākhī, he covers a distance of four kos every day on foot reciting the *Jap*, and subsists on a single pod of *akk* and a handful of sand. He continues these practices for several years till the divine voice comes that his austerities have been accepted. He is also told to adopt a guru to benefit fully from his efforts.[32]

Consequently, Baba Nanak went to *tīrath*s for finding a guru. He came first to the Ganges where thousands of people had come to bathe in the sacred river. Baba Nanak saw no merit in their ritual. While all others threw water with their faces towards the rising sun, he threw out water with great vigour towards the west. On being asked what he was doing he said that he was watering his fields. They told him that he was trying in vain. He told them that if water could not reach his fields on the earth, how could it reach their ancestors in heaven? They realized that he was no fool. They came out of the river and started reciting God's name. Baba Nanak told them that their mind was wandering elsewhere. They marked the eating square or *chauka* and invited Baba Nanak to eat food with them. He told them that pollution had already entered the chauka with them in the form of *kumatt, kudaya, parninda*, and *krodh*. These traits were comparable to Dumni, Kasain, Chuhri, and Chandali, all of whom were untouchable or *nīch* women. On their insistence then, Baba Nanak gave them the gift of the divine Name. 'These were the first Sikhs of Baba Nanak'.[33] The import of the sākhī turns out to be dramatic. Setting out to find a guru, Baba Nanak started acting as the Guru. This could be seen as a result of the acceptance of his austerities by God.

Even at Kartarpur Guru Nanak did not dispense with austerities. He adopted a regular routine: meditation in a cell, kīrtan in the congregation and the Arati Sohila at night as the last act of worship for the day. It is evident that the recitation of the Arati Sohila was an essential part of the daily routine of worship among the Sikhs in the early eighteenth century. He would then go to the river and stand in the water till sunrise. He would see that meals were cooked in the kitchen but personally subsisted on a handful of sand and a pod of akk. The fame of Baba Nanak spread far and wide. Thousands of Sikhs flocked to him wherever he went.[34]

In another episode in this sākhī Baba Nanak is bathing in the river and Angad falls senseless due to extreme cold. Baba Nanak comes out and kicks Angad; he regains consciousness and tells Baba Nanak that his soul now has the power of millions of suns. Baba Nanak says that he performed austerities for the sake of his Sikhs. Whosoever becomes a Nanak Panthi would be liberated.[35]

The criterion for the choice of a successor is asceticism by implication. Baba Nanak went out one day and saw Gorakh Nath sitting alone. He asked Baba Nanak if he had found a true companion, that is, a disciple who was exactly like him and understood him completely. As if to test them, Baba Nanak asked his Sikhs to take to the plough. Many of them left him. Then he ordered that only one meal should be served. Many more left him. On further imposition of austerities, only a few of the Sikhs were left with him. When the crop was cut and stacked, Baba Nanak told them to burn it all. Some Sikhs were still left with him. In the third episode of the sākhī Baba Nanak assumed the form of a *dhānak* in order to frighten his followers.[36]

Some of the sākhīs relate to the way in which Guru Nanak spread his message. In one sākhī, he adopts the mixed appearance of a Vaishnava *bairāgī* and a Sūfi faqīr so that none could say he was a Hindu or a Musalman. Responding to Hindus and Musalmans in terms of their own understanding, he began to preach the way of God. He established dharmsāls and propagated nām, dān, and isnān among all.

Baba Nanak went to a land where there were no men. Inhabited by women, it was ruled by a woman. Mardana was keen to see the country. The moment he reached a habitation he was surrounded by women. A charmed thread was tied to his arm and he became a ram. Baba Nanak went in search and the women tied the charmed thread on his arm too but nothing happened. Feeling helpless, they said that Baba Nanak could get his man. He untied the thread and Mardana took his human form again. The women thought that Baba Nanak was 'a god'. They fell at his feet, wishing for men. Baba Nanak blessed their silent prayer. They gained peace and began to worship God.[37] Spiritual power triumphed over magic. Women became Guru Nanak's followers.

One day, Baba Nanak said to Angad that he wanted to see his old friend Mula. When Mula's wife saw Baba with faqīrs, she told Mula to hide and lied to Baba Nanak that he had gone out. The Baba went away but Mula experienced severe pain. He wanted to see Baba Nanak. People carried him on a cot and prayed to the Baba to be gracious. Baba Nanak told them that since Mula had seen the Guru he was liberated. They took him back to his house and he died in peace.[38] Mula's greed was the cause of his death but the Guru's darshan was the source of his liberation.

Baba Nanak went to a country where people knew nothing of God and believed in the king's power to bring rain for their crops. The king's power failed him on Baba Nanak's arrival and people eventually flocked to him. He told them to pray to God, who was invisible but who could be known from his power. The people sowed the crop in the name of God and it sprouted. After the harvest, they dug the field and found live fire underneath. They fell at Baba Nanak's feet. Dharmsāls were established in all the villages of the king. His country became beautiful with the gift of bāṇī, and the practice of nām, dān, and isnān.[39] Baba Nanak's extraordinary power once again became the means of spreading his message.

Only one sākhī relates to Muslims, and its message is not clear. On the way to Mecca, Baba Nanak met a group of faqīrs. They asked him if he was a Hindu and he affirmed this. They told him that the Sayyids who ruled the country killed the Hindus who tried to go to Mecca. Fearing for themselves, they asked Baba Nanak to leave them. They reached Mecca after a year and found Baba Nanak sitting there. The people of Mecca said that he had been there for a year. The faqīrs praised God for showing such grace to a Hindu. The people said that he was a *dānishmad* or philosopher and a leader in the prayer. The faqīrs thought that God was graceful to him because he was a Musalman. The shabad composed by Baba Nanak in Mecca shows preference for the Name despite the dominance of Islam.[40]

In the sākhīs of the Ādi tradition Guru Nanak's panth has divine sanction, with its unique validity in the Kaliyuga. The message of Guru Nanak is seen as superior to the yoga of Gorakh Nath who himself is made to acknowledge the superiority of Guru Nanak in the Kaliyuga. Guru Nanak's superiority over the Siddhs and of his path over yoga is well demonstrated. However, there is great emphasis on

Guru Nanak's austerities, in contradiction to his own compositions. His extraordinary powers become the means of spreading his message. All magical powers are shown to be futile against the spiritual power of Guru Nanak; his path is accepted by women. The light of Guru Nanak is fully infused in Angad when he is chosen to be Guru Nanak's successor. The darshan of Guru Nanak is seen as the means of liberation. On the whole, the sākhīs of the Ādi tradition move a little away from the message of Guru Nanak's bāṇī, with greater emphasis on ascetical practices and use of miracles.

Two Sākhīs of the Miharban Tradition

The two sākhīs from the Miharban tradition relate to Angad at Kartarpur. In one of these, Baba Nanak recites a shalok on the great merit of meditation on God in the last quarter of the night. It has the merit of bathing at all the sixty-eight sacred places. Angad says that the men of the world can concentrate on God only in the last quarter of the night but what about the men of God? With Baba Nanak's permission then, he goes on to say that those who have been made perfect by Baba Nanak as the Perfect Purkh remain in the same state throughout the eight quarters of the day and night and attain liberation. They remain detached from the world like the lotus in water. Only those who have God's grace and meet the Perfect Purkh like Baba Nanak attain the state of liberation in the Kaliyuga.[41]

In the second sākhī, Angad asks Guru Baba Nanak that if a person keeps awake in the last quarter of the night out of compulsion would he earn any merit? Guru Baba Nanak recites a shalok (of Guru Angad) which says that in the last quarter of the night a desire springs up in the heart of those who have friendship with the rivers and who have True Name in their hearts and on their lips. Voluntarily they bathe in the early hours and meditate on God. They are made perfect. The human body is the ninth *khand* which contains the treasure of the Name of God. It is discovered through the grace of the Guru. Then Guru Nanak says that his grace is upon Angad. Through him the world would turn to the Name. Angad touches the feet of Guru Baba Nanak.[42] In this sākhī the words of Guru Angad are spoken by Guru Nanak by way of instruction to Angad himself. The essential message comes through Angad.

In these sākhīs of the Miharban tradition Guru Nanak is extolled in a manner that extols Angad a little more; the successor is not only one with the founder but a little ahead of him. This may be seen as a subtle projection of the sectarian position of the original compilers.

THE MISCELLANEOUS SĀKHĪS

Eight sākhīs in the *B40 Janamsākhī* belong to the 'miscellaneous category' of W.H. McLeod. They relate to Guru Nanak's meeting with different kinds of religious personages, four of whom were representatives of Islam.

Shaikh Sharaf at Baghdad received enlightenment from Guru Nanak. Baba Nanak found Shaikh Sharaf dressed like a female and singing *kāfī*s. His purpose was to meet the Beloved by pleasing Him. Baba Nanak told him that God was not pleased with a garb. Liberation depended entirely upon his grace. In contrast with Shaikh Sharaf's theme of separation, Baba Nanak sang of union. The Shaikh fell at his feet. Baba Nanak showed his grace and the Shaikh was enlightened. He could see God in every human being and under every veil.[43]

At Multan, Baba Nanak's position was implicitly recognized by Shah Rukandi, the grandson of Shaikh Bahauddin Zakariya. Shah Rukandi expressed his happiness over the honour of meeting a beloved of God who was like God himself. On his request, Baba Nanak recited a *Sī-harfī* in which each verse started with a letter of the Persian alphabet.[44] This composition gave expression to Sikh and Sūfī ideas in a language understandable to an average Muslim.

At Bhatinda, Baba Ratan Haji was honoured by the visit of a beloved of God. He requested Baba Nanak to recite some of his verses to make his visit memorable. Baba Nanak recited a *ghazal* (actually an epigrammatic composition), on the subject of right conduct.[45]

At an unknown place, Shah Abdul Rahman was happy to have been honoured by the sight of a beloved of God. However, his disciple, Mian Miththa, was not so happy. He complained to Abdul Rahman that he was praising a person who talked of a hundred skies against the firm belief of the Muslims that there were fourteen *tabak*s. Abdul Rahman pointed out that the thrust of Baba Nanak's shabad was on the impossibility of describing God's greatness. On an earnest request from Abdul Rahman, Baba Nanak forgave Mian Miththa and continued to sing the shabad.[46]

In a gosht with Gorakh, the questions and answers are in verse. Kal also joins the discourse. Gorakh was satisfied with the answers to his riddles and Kal submitted to Baba Nanak who recognized the sway of Kal.[47] The message relates to the divine word, recognition of the One True Lord, detachment and discipline. However, no authentic verse of Guru Nanak is used.

In a gosht with Kabir, verses attributed to Kabir and Guru Nanak are presented as questions and answers. Kabir speaks as a disciple and Baba Nanak as the Guru. In the last stanza, Kabir says that he is set free by the Name of God imparted by the Guru and he has found enlightenment by abandoning the world. Not Ramanand, but Baba Nanak is seen as the giver of salvation.[48]

A gosht with a philosopher-faqīr is merely a statement of Baba Nanak on real renunciation which is inward, like a grain in the husk. With the core of renunciation, it does not matter whether one is a householder or a celibate. If one dons the garb of a faqīr, one's actions should conform to the ideals symbolized by each of the articles: abandoning all worldly desires, selfishness and greed, and turning away from all pleasures, symbolized respectively by the *khafnī*, the *phauṛī*, and the begging bowl. Only if the worldly fire is quenched can one become a faqīr, a pīr, a murīd, a sikh, or guru.[49] Celibacy appears to have an edge over the life of a householder.

In his discourse with Ajita Randhawa, Baba Nanak tells him that the Master enters the four Yugas in the garb of men but remains distinct from his creation. There were many incarnations of Rama and Krishna. Guru Nanak, by implication, has this status in the Kaliyuga. The Guru is considered no different from God. Those who do not meditate on the True Guru would be cast into hell. Those who have set up manjīs without understanding the Guru's shabad and his sākhī would be punished by God. A true follower of the Guru's teaching follows the dictates of truth, utters no falsehood, remains free from lust, and does not indulge in slander.[50] The references to the ninth *mahal*, that is, Guru Tegh Bahadur, indicate that this sākhī came into currency in the late seventeenth or the early eighteenth century.

In the sakhis of the miscellaneous category, Guru Nanak is presented as a mentor of shaikhs, and he bestows enlightenment on them; the ideas attributed to him have the implicit approval of the successor of an eminent Sūfī Shaikh; a popular saint recognizes the greatness of

Guru Nanak and looks up to him; a saintly Muslim recognizes Guru Nanak's nearness to God and the validity of his message despite its literal variation from Islamic belief. The importance of the divine word, worship of the One True Lord, detachment and discipline are sought to be conveyed, but without using any composition of Guru Nanak. He is deliberately exalted in comparison with Kabir and Ramanand. Renunciation is given an edge over householding. Guru Nanak's position in the Kaliyuga is compared to the position of avatārs in previous Yugas, especially Rama and Krishna. The heads of sectarian groups among the Sikhs are virtually denounced, which carries the implication that this gosht refers to a situation in the later history of the Sikhs, perhaps in the late seventeenth century.

Sākhīs of the Oral Tradition

Eighteen sākhīs from the oral tradition account for almost one-fifth of the *B40 Janamsākhī*. Most of these sākhīs relate to what may be regarded as the propagation of Guru Nanak's message. The last two relate to Gurbāṇī though Gurbāṇī is not quoted anywhere in these sākhīs.

In Kabul, Baba Nanak sat in a mosque but the Muslims objected to it because he was not a Muslim. Baba Nanak ascended the mosque and moved it all round the city. They saw a great pīr in Baba Nanak who was close to God. Both Hindus and Muslims served him. Some of them became his Sikhs and the tradition of nām, dān, and isnān was introduced.[51]

In another sākhī, Baba Nanak met Abdul Rahman in the *pargana* of Kalanaur. After polite salutations, Baba Nanak started saying 'as the juice is squeezed out of the lemon and the skin is thrown away', and with the uttering of these words, Abdul Rahman was squeezed of his power. He called another pīr but he too was shorn of his power. Baba Nanak told them that men's miracles added nothing to God's glory. Nevertheless, Abdul Rahman showed to Baba Nanak small pieces of pottery and stones turned into gold and Baba Nanak showed him large clods of earth turned into gold. Similarly, Baba Nanak showed his greater austerities. Abdul Rahman sought forgiveness.[52] His presumption about his superior position and power yielded place to humility. Guru Nanak's superiority was thus acknowledged.

In the country of the Rohela Pathans, strangers were enslaved and sold in the market. Seeing a Pathan, Baba Nanak assumed the form of a handsome boy of twelve years. The Pathan took him home and sold him in the market. His Mughal master ordered him to fetch water but all the wells dried up. Baba Nanak worked hard but did not eat or drink. The people began to think that he was a mahā purkh. They agreed to become Sikhs in return for water. Baba Nanak constructed a dharmsāl and introduced the practice of nām, dān, and isnān. He got himself caught again to be sold in slavery, with the same result. This feat was repeated with appropriate variation in the situation. When the Rohela Pathan brought him home for the fourth time, he also realized that Baba Nanak was a mahā purkh. He sought forgiveness and Baba Nanak told him to abandon the practice of enslaving people. He fell at his feet and became a Sikh.[53]

Two of the sākhīs bring Guru Nanak into confrontation with Jogīs and Sanyāsīs. Baba Nanak went to Achal and all the people flocked to him. A large number of birds had died in a hail storm and fallen in the *dhāb*. Its waves carried them towards the bank where Ajita Randhawa was sitting. He took them out, uttered *Vāheguru*, and the birds began to fly in the air. Baba Nanak was told that his own disciple Ajita Randhawa was giving life to the dead birds. He was shorn of his power. The Siddhs fell at Baba Nanak's feet.[54]

However, the sākhī does not end there. Baba Nanak went to the Tilla, and people flocked to him. The Siddhs invited him to a contest. Baba Nanak asked them to demonstrate their powers. They tried but failed. Their power was neutralized by Baba Nanak. Then Baba Nanak asked Sangatia, who had become a Sikh on that very day, to sit in a fire set ablaze. For several hours he remained unharmed. On his request, Baba Nanak restored the power of the Siddhs.[55]

In Himachal, Baba Nanak found Datt sitting with thousands of sanyāsīs, and four sanyāsīs caught hold of another to dip him in the ice cold water of the stream. Some of them survived but others died. Baba Nanak took three strides down the mountain which was seven kos in height. He bathed in the stream at the foot of the mountain where the water was not cold. Then the sanyāsīs were fed with rice, raw sugar and *ghee* which came from Baba Nanak's *chādar* spread over a bush. Datt wanted to demonstrate his power but he was bereft of it. He fell at Baba Nanak's feet and said that he was the divine light in the form of a human being. All those who heard or read and enabled others to read his shabad attained liberation.[56]

In two other sākhīs, the countries visited by Guru Nanak are named. In Kashmir, a local shepherd entertained the suspicion that Baba Nanak and Mardana were thieves or robbers in the garb of faqīrs. Hence, he did not offer any food to them. When he went back to his sheep he found them all dead. He came back to Baba Nanak who told him to utter Vāheguru. He uttered Vāheguru and the sheep became alive. The shepherd stayed on with Baba Nanak. The masters of the sheep came in search of the sheep and found them abandoned. They too came to Baba Nanak and the shepherd explained to them what had happened. They also became his Sikhs. They told other people who, too, became Sikhs. The King became a Sikh. A dharmsāl was established and the practice of nām, dān, and isnān was introduced.[57]

In Bhutant Des, Baba Nanak sat in a garden and people flocked to him. The king of the country came to see him and Baba Nanak told him to abandon the custom of keeping the newly-wed girls with him for the first night before sending them to their spouses. Baba Nanak offered him a boon of his choice. On his request, Baba Nanak provided the country with minerals of all kinds, cloth, fragrant flowers, fruits, silk, and musk. The king and his subjects were introduced to the life of nām, dān, and isnān.[58]

In the case of Ajita Randhawa, supranatural power is used to rid him of greed. He was worried about a debt he had to settle. Baba Nanak told him to lift a particular clod and take as much money as he needed. Ajita tried to grab more than what he needed. But when he counted the money it fell short by two rupees. He admitted his greed, and Baba Nanak told him to get two rupees from a particular place.[59]

In an unknown country, Guru Nanak demonstrated the futility of wealth for spiritual pursuit. A rich *sāhūkār* had preserved four treasures, and tall banners flew over each. They were meant to be taken with him after his death. Baba Nanak gave him a needle with the request to take it to the next world as a trust. When the rich man realized that he would be unable to take the needle with him after death, he ran after Baba Nanak to return the needle. Baba Nanak said, 'if you cannot carry my needle then how would the four treasures of wealth go with you?' The sāhūkār's eyes were opened; he distributed all his wealth to become a Sikh, and practise nām, dān, and isnān.[60]

In many other countries supranatural powers were used for propagating the Sikh faith. Baba Nanak and Mardana went to a country where they received rice and flour for food but no water or fire to cook. They sat down at a place and a pool of water appeared. Baba Nanak told Mardana to utter Vāheguru and cook *rotīs* and rice in the pool. He did so, and the people were surprised to see the food being cooked in water. They saw in Baba Nanak a mahā purkh. They fell at his feet and became Sikhs.[61]

Baba Nanak came to a country in which there was no fire and no grain. The people subsisted on meat, cooked in solar heat, and they were extremely hospitable. Baba Nanak's host slaughtered a ram and offered its meat to him. After eating the meat, Baba Nanak put the bones into the skin of the ram and told it to get up and graze. The master of the ram was very impressed. On Baba Nanak's suggestion he brought an eminent person of the place who was asked to sow some grain. The crop was harvested on the same day. He was told to store the grain as an inexhaustible source of distribution among the people. Baba Nanak gave them fire too, and the whole country became Sikh, with a dharmsāl established in every home.[62]

Baba Nanak went to a country adjoining the sea. The people received him well. He came to know that a huge wave used to wash away their homes every six months and they had to build their houses all afresh. Baba Nanak asked them to become his Sikhs so that their homes would not be destroyed. They agreed to do so. They left the place and when they came back they found their homes intact. They became Sikhs, a dharmsāl was established in every home, and the practice of nām, dān, and isnān was introduced.[63]

In another country, a monster used to set fire to people's houses. Baba Nanak told them to become his Sikhs in order to save their homes. They agreed. When the monster came, Baba Nanak looked at him and he was blown like a feather in the whirlwind. When he fell senseless in front of Baba Nanak, he touched the monster's forehead with his foot. The monster got up and fell at Baba Nanak's feet. He was forgiven and asked to fetch water for the dharmsāl. The practice of nām, dān, and isnān was introduced and people were instructed to serve all the guests well.[64]

Baba Nanak went to a country with two young boys, Uttam Bhandari and Sultan Gujjar. He took care of their needs even though they were indifferent to his wishes. Baba Nanak told them to utter Vāheguru and lift a stone. They refused to do so and Baba Nanak used his stick to remove the stone. Water gushed forth and people were surprised. The king came to him with food, clothes and cash. Baba Nanak accepted only food which was distributed among the people. The king and his subjects became Sikhs, a dharmsāl was built, and the practice of nām, dān, and isnān was introduced.[65]

Baba Nanak went to the town of a thug and stayed in his house. The other thugs of the town told him to get all the wealth of his rich guest. But no one in the town could wake up for several hours after daybreak. Baba Nanak left the place early in the morning. He was overtaken by four of the thugs. He asked them to get fire for cooking something to eat. Two of the men went to a place from which smoke was rising. They had earlier seen a prisoner being carried by force, and now they saw the same person riding a palanquin like a rich man. The thugs wanted to know the reason for this strange phenomenon and learned that this man was bound for hell because of his misdeeds but now he was going to heaven because the smoke of his pyre had been seen by a sādh. The thugs realized that Baba Nanak was that mahā purkh. They brought him back to the town, and the whole town became Sikh, a dharmsāl was established and the practice of nām, dān, and isnān was introduced. They took to other professions and occupations and attained liberation.[66]

Baba Nanak went to a land of thieves. Their *bhūmia* leader owned hundreds of horses and cattle. He invited Baba Nanak to his place and served him well. Baba Nanak asked him about his profession and he said that it was known to Baba Nanak. He requested Baba Nanak to make him a Sikh and Baba Nanak made him a Sikh with three injunctions: always to speak the truth, never to think ill of a person whose salt he had eaten, and never to harm the poor. The bhūmia thief resolved to leave his profession after stealing the wealth of the king. He told the guards of his palace that he was a thief. They took it as a joke and allowed him to enter. While collecting precious articles from the palace in the darkness he tasted salt and left all the bundles behind. The king proclaimed a reward for the thief if he presented himself. The bhūmia went to the court and told him everything. The king praised his faith in the Guru, and gave him the office of *wazīr*. The king himself became a Sikh.[67]

The sākhī does not end there. The king was keen to get a darshan of the Guru. His wife was the daughter of a Sikh and below his palace was a dharmsāl where kīrtan was regularly performed. One day she suggested to the king that they should request the sangat to pray for them so that they could have a son. The sangat performed the *ardās*. However, the child born was a girl. The king refused to believe this. She was brought up as a prince. At the time of her marriage to a princess, the courtiers were worried. Baba Nanak assumed the form of a golden deer and appeared in front of the marriage party. The princess in the garb of a prince pursued the deer and was separated from the rest of the party. The deer entered a garden. The princess also went there to find a mahā purkh sitting there. She fell at his feet, and the mahā purkh said that her wishes would be fulfilled. The features of the princess were transformed into those of a male. The king reached there with the rest of the party and discovered that the mahā purkh was the Guru. The king fell at his feet and expressed his gratitude for his darshan. The entire marriage party became Sikh.[68]

One sākhī demonstrates the spiritual status of a Sikh. Baba Nanak goes to a city for the sake of a Sikh who loves the Guru. He used to serve the Sikhs and then ask them: 'What is the merit of serving a sādh?' But he never got a satisfactory answer. He served Baba Nanak too and asked the same question. Baba Nanak sent him to a particular place and he found two crows there, a male and a female. He was asked to go again and he found a pair of cranes. He was asked to go again and he found two swans. He was asked to go again and he found a man and a woman. They told him that they were sinners reborn as crows. His first darshan turned them into cranes, the second into swans, and the third into human beings. 'Great is your Guru that we have attained this state by seeing you'. They all came to Baba Nanak, and the Sikh said that he had met God. Baba Nanak introduced the practice of nām, dān, and isnān, and left the city.[69]

Two sākhīs relate to Gurbāṇī. One of these underscores the importance of Arati Sohila in the daily devotion of the Sikhs. One day Baba Nanak was bathing and Angad observed that his body was marked by bruises. Baba Nanak told him that a particular Sikh, a goatherd, used to graze goats and at the same time recite the Arati Sohila with great devotion. Baba Nanak had vowed to be present wherever Arati Sohila was recited or sung. The Sikh was called and told to recite the Arati Sohila at the time of going to sleep at night.[70]

The other sākhī underlines the unity of Guru Nanak with his successors and their bāṇī. One day Mardana was performing kīrtan. Baba Nanak asked him how much of the bāṇī he had committed to memory, and Mardana replied that he remembered the entire bāṇī. Meanwhile a caravan of camels arrived and Baba Nanak asked Mardana to find out what goods they were carrying. The leader of the caravan told him that the camels were loaded with pothīs and granths of the bāṇī of Guru Baba Nanak. Mardana discovered with great surprise that he had never seen or heard this bāṇī before. Baba Nanak told him that this bāṇī would be uttered by *bhagat*s who would be a part of his body.[71]

In the sākhīs of the oral tradition, Guru Nanak triumphs over the representatives of Islam and asceticism. Though he disapproves of demonstration of supranatural powers, he shows his own power and restores the supranatural powers of the Siddhs. The use of supranatural power, generally in the interest of the people, is the chief means of inducing them to accept the message of Guru Nanak. The Sikhs are assumed to be under divine protection. The formula of nām, dān, and isnān sums up the Sikh way of life, and the dharmsāl is the central Sikh institution. God's will and the Guru's grace result in the transformation of thugs into pious Sikhs. The values of truth, loyalty to one's benefactor, and consideration for the poor are projected. The merit of faith and trust are projected through a heavy dose of the supranatural. A rich man realizes the futility of riches for liberation and turns to the way of Guru Nanak. The spiritual status of the Sikh is highlighted. The great importance of the Arati Sohila is underlined. The unity of the bāṇī of Guru Nanak and his successors is underscored. Despite the strong dose of the supranatural the essential message of these sākhīs, on the whole, is more authentic than that of the miscellaneous sākhīs.

THE LAST SĀKHĪ

The last sākhī of the *B40 Janamsākhī* relates to the death of Guru Nanak. Baba Nanak told Baba Kamla to bring grass from the river bed for the horses and buffaloes. There, three persons in the garb of *jogī*s gave a pinch of ash to him as a message for Baba Nanak. 'You have done well to bring the message', said Baba Nanak thrice. He understood the message and told Sidharan that an order had come for him from the divine court. He took Sidharan to his field in the river bed to show him the spot for his cremation. The chaudharīs and *muqaddam*s were asked to bring wood for the funeral pyre.[72] Guru Nanak thus welcomed God's will and went about calmly and deliberately to prepare for the last event of his earthly life.

Mata Choṇi came to know. She called Sidharan and told him that Baba Nanak had told her to make preparations for the *shradh* on the *naumī*. Baba Nanak agreed to stay alive for fifteen more days. This carried the implication that Guru Nanak could decide the time of his departure. After the shradh, preparation was made afresh for his cremation. Baba Nanak laid down and passed away.[73]

His sons, who were out hunting, came back and wailed that their father should have talked to them for a few *gharī*s. 'Baba Guru Karta Purkh' got up and asked them to speak. Sri Chand said that Baba Nanak had given Guruship to a low Khatri, 'what would they do now?' Baba Nanak said that it was so ordained. Furthermore, *sikhī* 'would flourish in the future and you will get whatever you ask for'. 'Even the dogs of *guru*s and *pīr*s are well fed, and you are my sons'.[74] This part of the sākhī focuses on the provisions made for his descendants. In the 1730s, some of the descendants of Guru Nanak were probably affluent. At any rate, the Sikhs were expected to care for them.

Baba Nanak told the people present not to perform any traditional rite or ceremony after his death. The chaudharīs said that this would not reflect well on his descendants. Baba Nanak said that they could do as they liked but there should be no lamentation. Then Baba Nanak departed. Thus, a compromise is suggested on the issue of funerary rites,. Baba Nanak got up yet again to tell the people that he had fulfilled the wishes of all his Sikhs in his lifetime. Then he expired for the last time.[75]

When the body of Baba Nanak was being carried for cremation, the Turks stopped the proceedings, saying that Baba Nanak was a Muslim. A chaudharī came and told people that he had seen Baba Nanak going in a *pālkī*. They lifted the sheet and found nothing underneath. The Turks went home. Baba Nanak's sheet was taken away for cremation. He appeared to be sitting calmly on the flames of fire. At midnight the air became fragrant, and sounds of sweet music were heard. 'Baba Parmesar' sat in meditation. For four gharīs he sat there, his long beard waving in the breeze. Then Guru Baba ascended towards the divine court. When the ashes of Baba Nanak were collected there were no bones. His ashes were thrown into the river. Now everyone knew that he had eluded them.[76] This comes as a confirmation that Guru Nanak went bodily to the divine court.

In this last sākhī, the pinch of ash is a message of death. It is welcomed by Guru Nanak as a part of God's will. He goes about calmly and deliberately to prepare for the last event of his life. Being one with God, he can decide about the precise time of his departure. He fulfils all the wishes of his followers. There is a suggestion that his descendants would be, and should be, well looked after by the Sikhs. A compromise is suggested regarding the funerary rites. Guru Nanak's body was not burnt; he went bodily to the divine court. The essential import of these episodes is the divinity of Guru Nanak.

CHARACTER OF THE *B40 JANAMSĀKHĪ*

In many sākhīs of the *B 40 Janamsākhī* no use is made of any composition attributed to Guru Nanak. In many more, his compositions are used, often with slight variations. There are some sākhīs in which the verses used are of other Gurus. Then there are many others in which the compositions attributed to Guru Nanak are not there in the Granth Sahib. The largest number of Guru Nanak's authentic compositions occur in the sākhīs of the Purātan, followed by the Ādi tradition. The verses not found in Guru Granth Sahib figure mostly in the sākhīs of the miscellaneous category. No verses are quoted in the sākhīs of the oral tradition and the last sākhī.

There is a broad chronological order in the *B40 Janamsākhī*. However, each sākhī constitutes a separate unit. A few sākhīs contain more than one episode, each with its own import. As a composite compilation, the *B40 Janamsākhī* does not present a unified and coherent image of Guru Nanak in terms of his basic position, doctrines, ethics, or his attitude towards the contemporary systems of religious belief and practice. Some post-eventum elements get associated with the image of Guru Nanak.

The divinity of Guru Nanak is taken for granted and reinforced. His path is shown to be new and his followers to be distinct from others. Their peculiar piety is marked by nām, dān, and isnān and their distinctive institution is the dharmsāl where the Sikhs meet for congregational worship and community meal. The superiority of

Guru Nanak's message and his own superiority is recognized by the representatives of the Brahmanical, ascetical and Islamic traditions. Guru Nanak is equidistant from them all but not without a certain degree of respect towards the Sūfis and the Siddhs. His austerities are overemphasized and his supranatural powers often serve as the means of the propagation of his message. On the whole, however, Guru Nanak of the *B40 Janamsākhī* remains rather close to Guru Nanak of the Guru Granth. Two features go against the spirit of Gurbāṇī: austerities and miracles. The former are obtrusive in sākhīs of the Ādi tradition and the latter, in the miscellaneous and oral sākhīs. However, the essential 'myth' of Guru Nanak remains a popular version of his doctrines and ethics, linked closely with the belief in his divinity. The remarkable importance given to the sangat and the shabad, and the political implications of a few of the sākhīs, make the *B40 Janamsākhī* a document of the non-Singh Khalsa of the early eighteenth century.[77]

Notes

1. For W.H. McLeod's treatment of Janamsākhī, see J.S. Grewal, 'The Janamsakhi Traditions', *Lectures on History, Society and Culture of the Punjab*, Patiala: Punjabi University, 2007.
2. Piar Singh, ed., *Janam Sakhi Sri Guru Nanak Dev Ji*, Amritsar: Guru Nanak Dev University, 1974, pp. 7–8, 10, 13.
3. W.H. McLeod, tr., *The B40 Janamsākhī*, Amritsar: Guru Nanak Dev University, 1980, pp. 13–15.
4. Singh, *Janam Sakhi Sri Guru Nanak Dev Ji*, pp. 78, 148.
5. Apart from the groups known as Miṇas, Dhir Mallias, Ram Raiyas and Niranjaṇias, there were the Keshdhārī Singhs and Sahajdhārī Sikhs in the fourth decade of the eighteenth century.
6. Singh, *Janam Sakhi*, p. 33.
7. Ibid., pp. 33–5.
8. Ibid., pp. 35–6.
9. Ibid., pp. 36–7.
10. Ibid., p. 37.
11. Ibid., pp. 37–9.
12. Ibid., pp. 39–41.
13. Ibid., pp. 41–5.
14. Ibid., pp. 45–7.
15. Ibid., pp. 47–9.

16. Ibid., pp. 49–51.
17. Ibid., pp. 53–4.
18. Ibid., pp. 54–5.
19. Ibid., pp. 55–7.
20. Ibid., p. 57.
21. Ibid., pp. 58–9.
22. Ibid., pp. 59–60.
23. Ibid., pp. 63–8.
24. Ibid., p. 68.
25. Ibid., pp. 69–73.
26. Ibid., pp. 73–4.
27. Ibid., pp. 105–12.
28. Ibid., pp. 98–9.
29. Ibid., pp. 83–6.
30. Ibid., pp. 79–83.
31. Ibid., pp. 95–8.
32. Ibid., pp. 74–5.
33. Ibid., pp. 75–7.
34. Ibid., pp. 87–8.
35. Ibid., pp. 88–9.
36. Ibid., pp. 89–92.
37. Ibid., pp. 77–9.
38. Ibid., pp. 86–7.
39. Ibid., pp. 100–2.
40. Ibid., pp. 102–3.
41. Ibid., pp. 138–40.
42. Ibid., pp. 140–2.
43. Ibid., pp. 133–5.
44. Ibid., pp. 60–2.
45. Ibid., pp. 62–3.
46. Ibid., pp. 51–3.
47. Ibid., pp. 137–8.
48. Ibid., pp. 103–4. W.H. McLeod regards this sākhī as an example of the heterodox form of discourse. The purpose of exalting Guru Nanak is negative. *The B40 Janamsākhī*, p. 151 n. 650. It is more important to note that there were some Sikhs who were not prepared to concede any parity between Guru Nanak on the one hand and Kabir and Ramanand on the other.
49. Singh, *Janam Sakhi*, pp. 136–7.
50. McLeod, *The B40 Janamsākhī*, pp. 122–3, n. 543. Singh, *Janam Sakhi*, pp. 92–5.

AN EARLY EIGHTEENTH CENTURY JANAMSĀKHĪ 157

51. Singh, *Janam Sakhi*, pp. 112–13.
52. Ibid., pp. 123–4.
53. Ibid., pp. 116–20.
54. Ibid., pp. 124–5.
55. Ibid., p. 125.
56. Ibid., pp. 127–8.
57. Ibid., pp. 115–16.
58. Ibid., pp. 113–14.
59. Ibid., p. 123.
60. Ibid., pp. 128–9.
61. Ibid., pp. 114–15.
62. Ibid., pp. 120–1.
63. Ibid., pp. 121–2.
64. Ibid., p. 122.
65. Ibid., pp. 126–7.
66. Ibid., pp. 129–30.
67. Ibid., pp. 130–2.
68. Ibid., pp. 132–3.
69. Ibid., pp. 135–6.
70. Ibid., pp. 142–3.
71. Ibid., p. 143.
72. Ibid., pp. 143–5.
73. Ibid., pp. 145–6.
74. Ibid., pp. 146–7.
75. Ibid., pp. 147.
76. Ibid., pp. 147–8.
77. McLeod states that the *B40 Janamsākhī* points plainly to 'a non-Khalsa sangat at a point in time when according to tradition Sikh orthodoxy had assumed the form and discipline of the Khalsa': *The B40 Janamsākhī*, p. 20. However, in the early eighteenth century the 'Khalsa' and 'Singh' were not yet identical. Only those among the Khalsa to whom baptism of the double-edged sword was administered added the epithet 'Singh' to their names. Therefore, a *sangat* could be 'Khalsa' though not yet 'Singh'.

7. The *Prem Sumārg*: A Sant Khalsa Vision of the Sikh Panth[*]

Of all the extant *Rahitnāma*s, *Prem Sumārg* has received perhaps the most serious attention from scholars during the past five or six decades. In the 1950s, the historians of Punjabi literature, like Mohan Singh and S.S. Kohli, took notice of *Prem Sumārg*. Mohan Singh characterized the period from 1708–80 as the age of *Prem Sumārg*: 'long before a Punjabi king rose in the person of Maharaja Ranjit Singh, this artist of vision had imaginatively conceived of a state, which would simultaneously take up and solve the linguistic, ethical, cultural, political, military, and financial problems of the people'.[1] Kohli asserted that a manuscript of 1718 was in existence.[2] In 1953, Bhai Randhir Singh published the text of the *Prem Sumārg* with a long introduction. In his view, this work was all the more important for being the only authentic and early Rahitnāma.

In his introduction to *Prem Sumārg*, Bhai Randhir Singh tells us that he used two manuscripts for preparing the text for publication. One of these was incomplete and undated but old. The other was a copy of 1874 in the Public Library at Lahore. Bhai Randhir Singh had subsequently found a manuscript dated 1801. Baba Ram Singh

---

[*] 'The *Prem Sumārg*: A Sant Khalsa Vision of the Sikh Panth' is a new version of 'A Theory of Sikh Social Order' included in my *Sikh Ideology, Polity and Social Order* (New Delhi: Manohar, 2007, pp. 248–57). An analysis of the *Prem Sumarg* was first published in the *Punjab History Conference Proceedings* (Patiala: Punjabi University, 1965, pp. 100–111). A revised version was published in my *From Guru Nanak to Maharaja Ranjit Singh: Essays in Sikh History* (Amritsar: Guru Nanak Dev University, 1972, pp. 72–83, 162–3) and it was reprinted in *The Punjab Past and Present: Essays in Honour of Dr. Ganda Singh* (Patiala: Punjabi University, 1976, pp. 165–75). It was also included in the first edition of my *Sikh Ideology, Polity and Social Order* (New Delhi: Manohar, 1996, pp. 152–61).

recommended *Prem Sumārg* to his followers in 1877. Pandit Tara Singh Narottam included it in the list of Rahitnāmas in his *Sri Gur-Tīrath Sangreh*. Bhai Kahn Singh Nabha gave its gist in his *Gurmat Sudhākar*. He also commented that, though at the beginning of this work were written the words '*sri mukhvāk pātshāhī 10*', it was composed by a devout Sikh in 1823 or 1828.[3]

Bhai Randhir Singh argued, however, that *Prem Sumārg* was composed in the early eighteenth century. In the first place, the situation of the Khalsa depicted in it was that of the early eighteenth century, and not the early nineteenth, as reflected in a letter of Bhai Mani Singh addressed to Mata Sundari and Mata Sahib Devi, depicting the plight of the Singhs after the death of Banda Bahadur. The language of *Prem Sumārg* was also similar to the language of this letter. The Singhs in the eighteenth century had a firm belief in Guru Gobind Singh coming to their aid personally and this belief figures prominently in *Prem Sumārg*. Finally, the form of *ardās* used in *Prem Sumārg* is rather simple, suggesting an early period after the time of Guru Gobind Singh.[4]

Bhai Randhir Singh argued further that Guru Gobind Singh could not be the author of *Prem Sumārg*. Internal evidence showed clearly that it was written after his death. Moreover, it contains references to verse numbers, carrying the implication that the author was making use of a work written in verse. It could, therefore, be a prose version of a kind of *Khalsa Smriti* written in verse during the time of Guru Gobind Singh. The author of *Prem Sumārg* had a good knowledge of religious and worldly affairs. He was a learned person, well-versed Persian and well familiar with Mughal administration. It seems, probable, that he was a professional writer in Guru Gobind Singh's court.[5]

The second edition of Bhai Randhir Singh's *Prem Sumārg Granth* appeared in 1965. He was kind enough to give me a copy. I found it extremely interesting and presented its analysis at the Punjab History Conference in 1965 as 'theory of Sikh social order'.[6] This essay was included in a collection of my articles in 1972.[7] In 1976, it was reprinted in *Essays in Honour of Dr. Ganda Singh*.[8] In 1982, Surjit Hans presented a paper at the Punjab History Conference, arguing that the *Prem Sumārg* was a modern forgery, a work of the British period.[9] His argument was based entirely on internal evidence and, at best, made a case for interpolations but not forgery. In a slightly modified form my essay on *Prem Sumārg* was included in the *Sikh Ideology, Polity and Social Order* in 1996.[10] A revised version of the essay is included in a revised and enlarged edition of *Sikh Ideology, Polity and Social Order* brought out in 2007.

In 1990, Nripinder Singh took serious notice of the *Prem Sumārg Granth* in his *Sikh Moral Tradition*. For him, it was a 'singularly significant' work, like the *Chaupa Singh Rahitnāma*. Both of these, 'by far the longest' and more reliable than the others, were 'assuredly eighteenth-century products'. Nripinder Singh suggested that the content of the Rahitnāmas had to be analysed carefully. For example, the statement of *Prem Sumārg* about opium eating cannot be invoked in justification of insobriety or intemperance. Similarly, in Sikh polity, the emphasis was on justice. To collect revenues or taxes 'from those who do not have enough for their own subsistence is tantamount to fraud'. Providing protection to his people was the primary duty of the Sikh ruler. He would be called upon to answer in the court of the Sachcha Pātshāh for the condition of his people. Whether or not he had said, or failed to say, his daily prayers were not relevant in this context. Economic deprivation was a form of stealing and, therefore, destructive of community.[11]

According to Nripinder Singh, the items of *rahit* in *Prem Sumārg* were 'not only a product of the consciousness that evolved out of the period of travail and exile but also of the *misl* period which culminated in the reign of Maharaja Ranjit Singh'. It was difficult 'to analyse the reciprocal impress of document and historical process' but a careful evaluation of the concepts 'rendered in the document would lead to circumstances witnessed in the historical process'. In any case, political scientists and historians could align with the students of comparative ethics to promote a common knowledge of the conception of equality, justice and statehood in the eighteenth century.[12]

McLeod's View of the *Prem Sumārg*

W.H. McLeod has taken the most persistent interest in the Rahitnāmas. In 1982, he wrote on the problem of the Punjabi Rahitnāmas, pointing out that *Prem Sumārg* was one of the three extended Rahitnāmas in prose, the other two being Chaupa Singh's Rahitnāma and the *Sau Sakhiān*. *Prem Sumārg* was 'more detailed and expansive' than the Rahitnāma of Chaupa Singh, and its material was ordered in a rigorous pattern of sections and sub-sections. In both these Rahitnāmas there was an apocalyptic vision, declaring Kalki avtār to be the final deliverer.[13] In 1986, McLeod wrote another essay, 'The Khalsa Rahit: The Sikh Identity Defined', in which *Prem Sumārg* was seen as belonging to the middle years of the nineteenth century' because of the author's 'obvious knowledge' of the rule of Ranjit Singh and his 'evident nostalgia' for the period. It was composed either shortly before or shortly after the British annexation of the Punjab.[14] In 1989, however, McLeod placed *Prem Sumārg* in the reign of Ranjit Singh.[15] In 1997, he talked again of 'the middle portion' of the nineteenth century in which *Prem Sumārg* originated.[16]

In his *Sikhs of the Khalsa: A History of the Khalsa Rahit*, McLeod paid more serious attention to *Prem Sumārg*. It was available to Major R. Leech in 1844. A portion of this work was included in an article he published in the *Journal of the Asiatic Society of Bengal* in 1845.[17] McLeod refers to Bhai Randhir Singh's argument in favour of the early eighteenth century as the period of the composition of *Prem Sumārg*.[18] This view was supported by several other scholars: Mohan Singh, S.S. Kohli, Bhagat Singh, Gurbux Singh, Fauja Singh and Mohinder Singh Kohli. J.S. Grewal had placed it in the early eighteenth century in 1972 but retracted this opinion in 1982 because of an article by Surjit Hans. Some other scholars placed the composition of *Prem Sumārg* in the late eighteenth century.[19] However, McLeod suggested that 'it should be placed in the middle or later years of Ranjit Singh's reign'.[20]

McLeod noted, however, that in some respects *Prem Sumārg* reached back to the eighteenth century, to the Rahitnāma of Chaupa Singh. Two features stood out. One was the belief in the gods of the Hindu tradition. The other was the apocalyptic setting which was drawn largely from the 'Nihakalanki Avatar' of *Dasam Granth*. McLeod asserted that *Prem Sumārg* belonged undoubtedly to the traditional camp of the Sikhs, as opposed to the radical camp of the Tat Khalsa. It was 'very much a Sanatan statement'.[21]

Special stress was laid by the author of *Prem Sumārg* on the rites of passage. In the context of 'Sanatan Sikhs Versus Tat Khalsa', McLeod observed that the marriage ceremony recommended in *Prem Sumārg* was traditional: the couple walked round 'a sacred fire', and not round the Granth Sahib. In connection with 'Anand Marriage', McLeod underlines the exceptional character of the *Prem Sumārg* in devoting a lengthy chapter to the Khalsa marriage. 'It involves superstition; it takes account of caste; Anand is not recited; the physical circumstances for the ritual are alien; it has a sacred fire fed by ghee; and the *lavan* are performed around this fire instead of around Guru Granth Sahib'. The *Prem Sumārg* reflects the time when the Panth was subject to Hindu influences. In connection with 'The Five Ks', McLeod noted that *Prem Sumārg* mentions 'five weapons' rather than 'the Five Ks'. In the context of 'jhatka meat versus vegetarianism', the author of *Prem Sumārg* recommends meat in the daily diet of the Khalsa as 'the noblest of foods'. Rather hesitantly, *Prem Sumārg* allowed the use of alcohol secretly when one had leisure. *Prem Sumārg* made no reference to the five excommunicated groups known as the *panj mel*. In the context of 'the place of women in the Khalsa', McLeod notes the exceptional message of *Prem Sumārg*: baptism by the double-edged sword was to be administered to a daughter at her birth; the epithet 'devi' was to be added to her name; her nose and ears were to be pierced. The fourth chapter of the *Prem Sumārg*, on marriage, is included in the second part of the *Sikhs of the Khalsa*.[22]

More recently, McLeod's has published an English translation of the work as *Prem Sumārag: The Testimony of a Sanatan Sikh*. The subtitle obviously sums up the character of *Prem Sumārg* for McLeod. The views expressed by scholars about the date for this work range from the early eighteenth to the late nineteenth century. About his earlier view of locating it within the first half of the nineteenth century, McLeod now says that it 'should be treated as tentative': the period seemed likely but 'certainly not definitive'.[23] A composite manuscript, dated 1815, contains the first chapter of *Prem Sumārg*. The manuscript used by the copyist was obviously older. Therefore, the *Prem Sumārg* could be placed 'at least' in the early years of the nineteenth century, and probably predated even to the eighteenth century.[24]

Talking of the manuscripts of *Prem Sumārg*, McLeod notes that Shamsher Singh Ashok has catalogued three. One of these, in the library of Bhai Kahn Singh, was stated to be an eighteenth century manuscript. However, no importance could be attached to this estimate because Ashok made decisions generally on the basis of tradition or conjecture. Another manuscript dated 1872–3 was stated to be a copy of another one dated 1701–2. The year 1701–2 was unlikely 'to the point of being an impossibility'. McLeod does not say why. The third manuscript held by Pritam Singh in 1963 was said to be 125 years old, which placed it in the first half of the nineteenth century. Two other manuscripts in Khalsa College, Amritsar, contained only the first chapter. Bhai Randhir Singh claimed to have acquired a *sanchī* dated 1801, but he did not actually describe it. Thus, there was no known manuscript of the eighteenth century. Nevertheless, *Prem Sumārg* could be seen as presenting 'an ideal of the Panth during the eighteenth century'.[25] In a footnote to the translation, McLeod says that reference to the destruction of Muslims in the near future pointed to 'the early or mid eighteenth century as the date of composition'.[26]

McLeod's reluctance to go far back into the eighteenth century appears to be linked up with his understanding of the character of *Prem Sumārg* as 'a Sanatan work'. He refers the reader to Harjot Oberoi's *The Construction of Religious Boundaries* as the most important work on the subject of Sanatan Sikhism. For Oberoi, the Sanatan Sikh tradition makes its appearance with the establishment of Sikh rule in the late eighteenth century and becomes dominant in the early nineteenth. However, the conclusion finally drawn by McLeod is not clear. *Prem Sumārg* 'presents an ideal of the Panth during the eighteenth century', and 'as an interpretation it is much closer to the society which it describes'.[27]

McLeod says that the Sanatan period followed the first recording of *Prem Sumārg*. However, Sanatan views certainly existed during the eighteenth century, and were likely to have been expressed by members of the Khatri caste. He suggests that *Prem Sumārg* was written by a Khatri. However, in the footnote he merely states that it represents 'an elite view of the Khalsa'. It does not represent popular religion with its devotion to pilgrimage, sacred places, idols, celebrated saints, and beliefs in miracles.[28] It is interesting to note that in Harjot Oberoi's conception of Sanatan Sikhism popular religion was tolerated by the elite. In *Prem Sumārg*, popular religion is explicitly rejected.

What exactly makes *Prem Sumārg* 'the testimony of a Sanatan Sikh' is not clear. Apart from the work of Harjot Oberoi, McLeod refers to his own *Sikhs of the Khalsa* for a statement on Sanatan Sikhism in which the Sikh form of marriage is specifically mentioned.[29] In *Prem Sumārg* the couple walk round the sacred fire and the Anand is not recited. This distinguished Sanatan form from the Tat Khalsa form in which the couple walk round Guru Granth Sahib, and the Anand is recited.[30] McLeod fails to see the basic difference. Nowhere in the whole ceremony prescribed in the *Prem Sumārg* is there any role for a Brahman. The baptism by the double-edged sword is made compulsory for the couple. Thus, the more significant features of the ceremony are overlooked by McLeod.

Another point specifically mentioned by McLeod is the traditional Sanatan view that the Sikh faith could be practised by 'a variety of modes'.[31] The text of *Prem Sumārg*, however, insists on the Sant Khalsa way of life. The Sahajdhārīs are not even mentioned. There is no redemption outside the Khalsa order. This takes care of the second specific point mentioned by McLeod that Sikh identity for the Sanatanist was not exclusively, or even primarily, Khalsa.[32] *Prem Sumārg* is meant exclusively for the Khalsa. There is no other Sikh identity for its author.

For a different purpose though, McLeod refers to the injunction about listening to the Vedas.[33] The words used in his translation are 'exposition of the Vedas' and 'scholars should read from the Vedas'.[34] The text has the words '*katha-baid*' and '*vidyāvān baid uchran*'.[35] The context is the royal court. It could be visualized as a courtly ritual. For the Khalsa in general, the injunction underscored is exclusive devotion to *Shabad-Bāṇī* which is equated with the Guru.

On the whole, McLeod appears to emphasize a few features of minor importance more than the basic ideas and attitudes prescribed in *Prem Sumārg* for the Khalsa. The work as a whole is anything but a Sanatan document. Sanatan Sikhism even in the work of Harjot Oberoi remains an ambiguous concept. Since McLeod uses it to contrast with the Tat Khalsa, everything pre-Tat Khalsa appears to be equated with Sanatan.

We may agree with McLeod that the language of *Prem Sumārg* is not always clear. It is not surprising that the task of translation presents difficulties, particularly the eighth and ninth chapters.[36] The difficulties of language also leave ample scope for differences in understanding of the text. In the opening paragraph of McLeod's translation there is a statement about the Panth to be created by God: 'One in which *dharam* has made its abode, [one in which] error is destroyed and true wisdom exalted'. The text appears to be talking of a Panth 'that would be instrumental in establishing dharm and destroying error so that right thinking was spread [in the world]'. A little later, the translation reads: 'To the shame of all who inhabit the world error still remains'. The text appears to say 'even now the error has not vanished due to the worldly concerns of the people'. In the second paragraph of the translation there is: 'would produce a mighty tome'. A small thing, but the text seems to say: 'the volume would increase'. In the next paragraph: 'King will supply nothing for their subjects to eat'. In the text: 'the rulers will not allow the subject people even to eat'. In the fourth paragraph of the translation: 'This is but one of a thousand things [which must be declared] spoken by the Satguru because he knew what was to come'. The text appears to say: 'Equal to a thousand things is the one thing said by the Satguru due to his concern for the people'. Understandably there are serious differences in our understanding of the text as a whole. I do not read *Prem Sumārg* as a Sanatan document. I also entertain the possibility of its composition early in the eighteenth century.

Embedded in the Early Sikh Tradition

Prem Sumārg is recorded in the form of a prophecy or, to use Mohan Singh's phrase, a prevision. God tells Guru Gobind Singh what he has ordained for the future. This form gives ample freedom to the author to see the past, present and future as intermeshed into a single whole. His work does not remain simply a reflection of the empirical Sikh social order. His vision of the Sikh future is combined with Sikh ideology and Khalsa praxis to project an elaborate picture of the Sikh community, partly as it was and partly as it should be. Contrary to the general impression, the author uses the term rahit for the injunctions embodied in his granth.[37] These injunctions give us an insight into the ideal Sikh social order conceived by the author.

In the familiar terms of the *Bachittar Nātak*, God tells Guru Gobind Singh that he has been created in God's image to spread dharm through the Panth nurtured by the ten Gurus with their message of the shabad and the worship only of the Supreme Being. Many people were under the sway of the Kaliyuga. The true Guru assumed the form of the Ten Gurus for the redemption of the people and created the Guru's Panth. The Khalsa is instituted by Akal Purkh so that by joining the Khalsa men are saved from the clutches of the Kaliyuga. For the protection of the Sant Khalsa and the destruction of the *mlechh* panth, 'the disciple of Man' (*mard kā chelā*) and 'the slave of the Supreme Being' (*parmpurkh kā dās*) would appear. All the *manjīs* and false gurus would be removed, including those who say 'we are the sons' and those who claim 'we have been authorized, ordered'. This book of injunctions is a boon for those who would be saved by the Guru and kept under protection. Whosoever believes, hears, and acts according to it would be redeemed. The Khalsa of Sri Akal Purkh will not believe in any other Guru and will not worship anywhere except where there is the light of the shabad.[38]

This opening statement is followed by four formal sets of instructions. The first relates to the early morning worship: to wake up in the last quarter of the night, to bathe with fresh or warm water from head to foot, and recite *Jap, Jāp*, and *Anand* five times. Even for an urgent business, one should recite the *charan kamal āratī* and offer ardās and then proceed. Otherwise, one should read Gurbāṇī from the *Pothi Granth* and attend to one's regular occupation, never forgetting the bāṇī-shabad.[39]

At midday, one should wash hands and feet all afresh and read both *Jap* and *Jāp*. If this were not possible, one should concentrate on Akāl Purkh and recite the *paurī 'pākī nāī pāk'*, utter seven times 'Sri Vāheguru Akal Purkh Ji, I have taken refuge with you', and recite the first *savvyyā* of Guru Gobind Singh. One must do this in spite of all pressing business.[40]

Two *gharī*s before sunset one should read *SoDar Rahrās*. At the time of the closing ceremony or *bhog*, one should bow one's head after reading *Jap* and *Jāp*. One should make a personal prayer: 'I am a sinner, you are *birad*; keep me as you wish. May I relish your *bhāṇā*, and think of the Name. I have taken refuge with you'.[41]

When one is free from all worldly business at the fall of night, one should read the bāṇī of all the ten Gurus, the *Bachittar Nātak* and Gurbāṇī from the Granth. One should perform kīrtan. One should recite the *Kīrtan Sohilā* before going to sleep. The person who observes the rahit, whether man or woman, would attain liberation.[42] Besides this daily routine of worship, an important feature of the rahit is to avoid falsehood. A man should not associate with any woman other than his wife, and a woman should not associate with any man other than her husband. One should not entertain *lobh, moh, krodh*, and *ahankār*, nor indulge in slander. One should not utter such a truth that harms others. One should speak to everyone sweetly. One should treat honour and dishonour, joy and sorrow, as the same. One should not covet another's wealth but earn one's living through honest work. One should concentrate one's mind on the feet of Sri Akal Purkh and shun all Brahmanical, ascetical, Islamic and popular practices (*matt, marhī, devī, devtā, butt, tīrath, barat, pūjā, archā, mantar, jantar, pīr pursh*, brahman, *tarpan, gaytarī*, and *sandhya*. One should love the fellow Sant Khalsa who have dedicated their body, mind, and wealth to Sri Akal Purkh, and who keep their senses under control. One should think that Sri Akal Purkh is always present with one. One should share one's food and clothes with others. If one is in a position to do something for another, one should leave one's own work to help him. The Guru is pleased with this. One should eat frugally and remain detached, regarding oneself as a wayfarer in a *sarāi*. One should remain attached to the Creator.[43]

The fourth set of instructions has several other articles. One should keep one-tenth of one's earnings for Sri Akal Purkh. In addition to this, *mannat* and *ardās* too should be kept apart, preferably in a separate room in the house, to help a Sikh, a *sādh*, a poor or a needy person. If a Khalsa receives such help he should return it to the Guru's treasury whenever he is in a position to do so. The Khalsa of Sri Akal Purkh should cultivate humility.[44]

A Sikh should never put his weapons away. Normally he should behave like a cow, but in a desperate situation he should resort to the use of arms and never show his back. Regarding the Guru as his protector, he should save himself if there is a chance. If there is no chance, he should abuse the founding fathers of the enemy's faith so that they kill him at once. He dies thus to save his own faith. The mlechh would exercise oppression for some time more and then their end would come. The Khalsa should love one another and stick together in all circumstances. They should support a Sikh who is in trouble. Guru Baba Sri Akal Purkh will come to their aid in person. There is no doubt about this.[45]

A Khalsa of Sri Akal Purkh should be addressed as 'Singh Ji' and treated with respect. A Khalsa of the Guru should keep his *kesh* uncut and never resort to *bhaddan*.[46]

He who follows these instructions would become one with the Guru. Others will benefit from him. He should say that the Guru may enable him to follow them so that he is redeemed. The Guru will save him in the end. He who does not follow these injunctions or rahits will have nothing in common with the Sikhs of Sri Akal Purkh. Those who do not believe in Akal Purkh, will receive punishment in the end. The others will be saved; they will join the Khalsa. Akal Purkh has assumed the form of Guru Baba and he will redeem all.[47]

The Sikhs of the Guru shall have his *darshan* all the time. His physical form shall not remain forever but the light in the form shall never depart from the world. Satyayuga will prevail in the Kaliyuga due to this light. The Sikhs of Guru Sri Akal Purkh will remain firm in their faith. The Khalsa has been instituted for conforming to Gurmat in the Kaliyuga. A Sikh should have complete trust in Akal Purkh and lovingly follow these injunctions.[48]

On the whole, the religious beliefs and practices of the Khalsa, their ethics, and their political stance projected in this prophecy remain embedded in the Sikh tradition as it evolved till the early eighteenth century.

INITIATION AND OTHER RULES AND CEREMONIES

The concern of the second chapter is how to initiate a person into the order of the Khalsa. The essential feature of initiation is *khande dī pahul*. It should be sweetened before it is administered to the volunteer. He should put on a white dress, including a *kachh*, and should wear five arms. The number of the Khalsa present at the time of initiation should be at least five. Five pauṛīs of *Anand* should be recited, followed by ardās: 'This Sikh has come to Sri Guru Akal Purkh and the Khalsa for refuge. He may be given the gift of the faith of the Khalsa of Sri Akal Purkh. His mind may remain steady and all his wishes may be fulfilled'.[49]

A Khalsa should treat others with love and respect in all matters. They should all cherish bāṇī-shabad, and cultivate the moral virtues of *jat, sat, santokh, dayā,* dharm, and *khimā*. Fasting means no indulgence in sensuality. One should not look at another's woman or property, should not tell lies or indulge in slander, should avoid all misdeeds.[50]

The essence of the Sikh faith is service and loving devotion, which lead to liberation-in-life. Māyā should be regarded as poison. A Sikh should serve another Sikh as he serves the Guru. The relationship between a Sikh master and a Sikh servant should be that of father and son. A Sikh should regard shabad-bāṇī as the Guru. Whatever is said in the shabad is the Guru's *hukam*; it should be obeyed. If he wishes to speak to the Guru, he should read the shabad. If he wishes to see the Guru, he should go to a gathering of the Khalsa and see the Guru in the Khalsa. About this, there is no doubt whatsoever.[51]

The Khalsa should avoid *nindia, bisvās-ghāt, la-itbārī, chori, bakhīlī, hirs, hinsā,* hankār, *kām,* krodh, and lobh or *tama*. An untruth spoken for the benefit of someone else is justified. One should be grateful to the Guru that one has been enabled to do something for another. A Sikh should not look down upon any occupation or profession.[52]

A married woman should take pahul from a Gurmukh. After the ardās, she should be instructed that 'she should have education in Gurmukhi, read and love *shabad-bāṇī*'. The baptized Sikhnīs should associate with one another and reflect on the shabad. They should serve their husbands and obey them. A widow could also take pahul. No *kesar* was to be sprinkled in her case; she should wear an iron ring on her finger, and observe jap and sat. The injunctions given in the first and the second chapter are meant for both men and women.[53] Thus, women are placed at par with men in religious matters.

The ceremonies connected with the birth of a child start with conception. The features to figure in these ceremonies are pahul for the mother, the sight of weapons like khandā, bow and arrow, and the sword, and at the time of the delivery, utterance of 'Sri Vāheguru, Sri Guru Sri Akal Purkh, I seek your protection'.[54]

If a son is born, he should first be made to bow to arms and the Granth-Pothi; the first bit of feed (*guṛhtī*) to be given to him should be touched with a khandā. The following ardās should be made: 'This living being who has come as sent by you is under your refuge. May he enjoy good health, have courage, and do service. He has come on a happy conjunction; we have no worldly relationship with him except that of Sikhī'. Then, *parshad* should be distributed among the Khalsa and among the kins on the same day.[55] Other ceremonies for the son relate to pahul administered to him by five Sikhs, piercing his ears for golden or silver rings, keeping his *kesh* intact, naming him with the epithet Singh, and feeding the Sikh men and women present on the occasion. The *bhatt* or the *nāī* has a minor role in these ceremonies but there is no role for the Brahman priest.[56]

The same ceremonies are to be performed on the birth of a daughter, with appropriate variation in detail. The daughter should also be administered pahul and bear the epithet devī. Not only her ears but also her nose should be pierced.[57] There are some differences in detail but the similarities are far more important.

The chapter on marriage is much longer. The daughter should be married at a young age. She should be married to a good Sikh even if he is poor. Wealth should not be the criterion for the choice of a groom.[58]

Marriage (*sanjog*) should be preceded by a betrothal ceremony one and a half months before the marriage. The bride should pray to Sri Akal Purkh for a happy union; she should not invoke the blessing of any god or goddess. The marriage ceremony should be performed very early in the morning. The bridegroom should wear arms while riding to the bride's home for wedding. The marriage ceremony should be performed by a Sikh of the Khalsa of Sri Akal Purkh. He should ask both the bride and the bridegroom for their consent to marry each other, and also for the consent of their elders. Fire is to be lighted as a witness to the wedlock, like Sri Bhagauti Ji and Sri Khalsa Ji. An ardās should be made to Sri Guru Akal Purkh for a happy and pious life for the couple married in accordance with his hukam. They should go round the fire clockwise, with the bridegroom leading the bride. Each time, a stanza of the *Lāvān* should be sung and some ghee thrown into the fire. After the lāvān, baptism by the double-edged sword should be administered to the couple. Five pauṛīs of the *Anand* should be sung and then *kaṛhā* should be distributed. The couple should pray to Sri Vāheguru Akal Purkh only and worship no god or goddess; they should not resort to any jantar, mantar or any magical device.[59] Despite the differences in detail, this marriage ceremony comes very close to the 'anand marriage'.

At the time of their first union, the newly wed should think of Guru Gobind and the Name. If the wife becomes pregnant by God's grace, she would give birth to a Gurmukh. Both the boy and the girl should be at least seventeen years old. The new tie should not inhibit the bride's parents from eating at the place of her Sikh in-laws. The Khalsa must eat in all Sikh homes. Sri Guru Akal Purkh has sanctified commensality among all the Khalsa.[60]

The bride and the groom may be from the same caste (*baran*) but no further distinction should be made on the basis of *gotra*s within the caste, like the Sarin, Bavanjai, Bahri, and Adhai Ghar among the Khatris. The daughter should be married into a family superior to one's own. The father of the groom should not pay any heed to this fact as a Khalsa. All the castes of the Khalsa are equally pure. There are no distinctions among the Khalsa of Sri Guru Akal Purkh. They all belong to one caste.[61] The ideal is stated emphatically.

However, it may not be possible to conform to the ideal. If so, alliances could be restricted to jātīs close to one another. In case of difficulty for the marriage of the daughter, a group close to one's own may be selected: as between Khatri and Brahman, Arora and Khatri, Suniar and Arora, Sud and Arora, Kambo and Kaith, Kambo and Suniar, Jatt and Kambo, and Chhimba, Dhobi, Kambo, and Kalal. In the long run, all would become one caste. If anyone asks the Khalsa about his gotra, he should say 'Sodhi Khatri'. The Khalsa boys and girls must get married. Marriage within the gotra and within three degrees of kinship on both paternal and maternal sides was to be avoided. There was no other restriction.[62] There was no insistence on endogamy, though compromises were allowed.

In matters of commensality, there was no restriction: *ek panth ek prashad*. In the first place, all human beings are God's progeny. The Khalsa is their essence, and there was no question of shunning any Khalsa. The Chuhras, Halal-khors, Chamiars, Sansis, Dhanaks, and the Kalals who distill alcohol (but not others), could pay to a person of another caste for getting the food prepared so that everyone could eat. Uncleanliness was due to occupations and not due to birth. All are one in the eyes of Guru Akal Purkh. Therefore, in his Panth also everyone who professes to be the Khalsa of Sri Guru Akal Purkh should be regarded as equal.[63]

A widow should lead a life of self-control and contentment (jat, sat, sīl). The author of *Prem Sumārg* gives expression to the popular idea that a woman's sexual urge is seventy times more than that of a man. If men cannot live without women, it is far more difficult for women to live without men. The women have a weak understanding and they do not know their interest; they are essentially stubborn, which is the source of all their good or bad deeds. If a widow cannot keep her sexual urge under control she should enter into matrimony with a collateral of her deceased husband or even with an outsider, avoiding only her paternal gotra and that of her mother. A widow whose son or daughter is alive should not get married. If she has sexual relations with a man, both of them should be excommunicated for good.[64]

That the author of *Prem Sumārg* is serious about widow re-marriage (*par-sanjog*) is evident from his detailed prescription.[65] The issue from a re-marriage should be treated like an issue from a marriage. There was no restriction on marriage between them. Those who talk disapprovingly of such a union should be excommunicated by the Khalsa. A Khalsa could marry a slave girl or even the daughter of a mlechh, initiating her into the Khalsa faith. Incidentally, a Muslim male could also be initiated into the Khalsa faith. Sri Guru Akal Purkh would be gracious to those who follow these injunctions.[66]

One should concentrate on God on the eve of death so that one may attain liberation. On the death of a Sikh there should be no beating of the breasts by women: all men and women should instead sing the compositions called *Alahniān*. The men should not remove their turbans. A new kachh should be put on the corpse after it has been washed. A sword should be placed on its right. God's will should be accepted without any sign of grief. The wife who is left behind should adopt simplicity and restraint, think of the deceased as present with her, and read *Pothi Shabad-Bāṇī*.[67]

Cremation of the dead is essential, even for a child. On a death anniversary, kīrtan should be performed and all kinds of food should be served to the hungry and the Khalsa. The essential procedure in all situations, with appropriate variation in detail, was the same for men and women, for young and old, for the married and unmarried, for mothers and childless widows. There was to be no mourning. The ashes of the Khalsa were to be consigned to a nearby stream or buried in the earth. In matters of condolence, there was to be no association with Masands and their followers, and with those who practised bhaddan after the death of their parents because all the three have turned away from the Guru.[68]

In no rite of passage is there any role for a Brahman. Gurbāṇī, and ardās figure everywhere.

Occupational and Personal Life

The occupation of a Khalsa Sikh should be honest in accordance with his dharm. He should not perform *chākarī* or sit in a shop. There is nothing wrong with manufacturing goods at home and selling them in the market. The best thing for the Khalsa Sikh is *saudāgarī*. Next to that is cultivation of land. A part of what a Sikh earns should be contributed to the Guru's treasury and a part should be spent on food for the Khalsa; a part should be saved and the rest spent on his parents and on his own food, dress, and toilet. The expenditure should always be less than the income. The only kind of chākarī that a Sikh may take up is soldiering or *sipāhgarī*. He should fight valiantly for his master, and should not plunder the property of people.[69]

All food and drink is pure for the Khalsa; they should not bother about *chauka*. A Sikh should share his food with others or keep a portion apart for a hungry person, whether a Khalsa or a Hindu or a Musalman. If made possible by the Guru's grace, he should eat meat every day. This *mahāprashād* purifies the one who eats it. No food is prohibited except the one that does harm to the body. The meat of a diseased animal should not be eaten. The meat of an animal killed in hunting is preferable over purchased meat or fish. In certain situations, halāl meat can be 'purified' and eaten. A Sikh should not eat the food from one who has turned away from the Guru. He should not eat the sacred food (prashad) offered to a god or goddess. The only prashad that a Sikh should take is that of Sri Guru Akal Purkh.[70]

A Sikh should not use any intoxicant. He who drinks alcohol will go to hell. If necessary, one should eat opium of good quality and in a small quantity, equal to a bean of *mung*. If one drinks *post*, one should use only two and a half pods. Intoxicants are prohibited because they cause laziness; under their influence, one cannot worship or work properly. Intoxicants induce sensual urge. One should use an intoxicant after the day's business is over, and do it privately. If one eats bhang, it should not be more than two and a half *masa*, and it should be mixed with nutritious ingredients.[71]

The Ideal Sikh Ruler

The characteristic term used for the ruler is Maharaja, though the terms Raja and Patshah are also used. That the Maharaja rules over a vast territory is evident from the territorial units for administration. The smallest administrative unit, called *pargana*, covers an area within twenty-five *kos* of its administrative centre in a town or a city. The next unit called *tarf*, consists of twenty-one parganas. Twelve tarfs constitute a *disā*. The number of disās is not mentioned but, assuming the number to be at least four, we have more than a thousand parganas in the territory under the Maharaja, and each pargana is much larger than the largest British district and many times larger than the pargana of the Mughal or Sikh States.[72] This is an empire of the future.

All authority of the state is vested in the Maharaja and he is advised to be extremely jealous of his authority. If his order is disobeyed, the culprit should be put to death, even if he happens to be his son, father, wife or mother, or his wazīr. The order of the Maharaja should be received respectfully at a distance of seven kos from the headquarters of the noble or *amir* to whom it is addressed.[73]

The Maharaja is not to share his authority with anyone: he must delegate it partially to others who exercise power on his behalf. Foremost among them is the wazīr who shares the burden of government. The Maharaja should regard him as his own deputy. No one else should be his equal, neither the Maharaja's brother, father, mother or wife, nor anyone else. The Maharaja should consult him in all important matters, and no one should be allowed to interfere in his work. The wazīr should be able to run the affairs of the state in the absence of the Maharaja, if necessary.[74]

Among other functionaries of the state is a *dīwān* who looks after the royal house-hold and *karkhāna*s, a *sipāhsālār* or *Bakhshī* who looks after the army, both infantry and artillery, a *Biskarmvanta* in charge of the palace, the gardens and the wardrobe of the Maharaja, a Smīpī to remind the Maharaja of his religious and secular duties as a Gurmukh.[75]

All the servants of the state should be given a rank or *mansab*. One with a mansab of Panjahi should maintain fifty horsemen. Each horseman should be paid thirty rupees a month and the Panjahi should receive fifty rupees a month. Revenues worth a total amount of Rs 18,600 should be assigned to him from a pargana. He should be ordered not to collect more than the amount assigned and to be considerate towards the actual cultivators. Like the Panjahi, the Hazari should have 1,000 horsemen, each paid one rupee a day. All the *balwantkārī*s, that is, the '*umarā*, should be appointed on this pattern. The *kāmvant*s, that is, *ahdī*s, and the *muhrkhā*s, that is, *gurz-bardār*s, should be paid in cash and their mansab should never be reduced.[76]

The highest 'umarā were to be appointed as *disāvant*s. In each *disā*, a dīwān was to be appointed to keep account of the revenues from tarfs and parganas. He was to function in consultation with the disāvant. A *khabar-likhtā* was to keep the Maharaja informed about all good or bad things happening in the disā. Another functionary, called *niāonkār*, was to look after justice. In each tarf there were to be a *faujdār-umda*, a niāonkār, a *khabar-navīs*, and a *hisābkār*. Similarly, in each pargana there was to be a faujdār, a dīwān, a khabar-navīs, and a niāonkār. Every city was to be placed under a *nagardār*, that is, *kotwāl*.[77] Thus, the major concerns of government and administration were related to the army, the revenues, the intelligence, and justice. The dominant systems of the state were to be *mansabdārī* and *jāgīrdārī*. A broad similarity with the Mughal empire can hardly be missed. The Khalsa empire is envisaged as vaster and its administration more elaborate.

The assessment of land revenue was to be made in cash, taking into account every relevant factor. The village was to be treated as a unit for this purpose. This could be helpful in assigning revenues of villages to mansabdārs in jāgīr in lieu of their salary. The settlement made in each pargana was to be reviewed after ten years for reassessment to help the cultivators. An excessive collection meant injustice to the cultivators. The jāgīrs could also be readjusted after reassessment.[78] Out of seven shares of the harvest, the state was to appropriate three; the cultivator was to have three shares. Half of the seventh share could be kept for charitable purposes. The remaining half could be distributed among various functionaries connected with revenue administration.[79]

All accounts of the state were to be kept in Gurmukhi. All correspondence was to be in Gurmukhi. Sikh boys and girls were to learn Gurmukhi and receive education in Gurmukhi. At the same time, the learned in other languages from every country were to be present in the Maharaja's court. He should keep at his court astrologers, good painters, excellent performers of kīrtan, and the learned in the Vedas and Shashtras. The Maharaja was also to keep *patra*s to sing the praises of Sri Akal Purkh. They should be beautiful and attractive so that they could be employed to test the genuineness of *jogī*s, digambars, sanyasīs, *bairāgī*s, *udāsī*s, pīrs, and all others in the garb of *faqīr*s. One who was lured by them should be ordered to take up some occupation and householding. One who was not lured by them should be patronized. The Maharaja should patronize the valiant warriors as well. He should ensure that none of his subjects suffers from any deprivation. The Maharaja should be a 'remover of suffering' (*dukhkh-bhanjan*).[80]

The Maharaja should fix his daily routine. He should light lamps on the night of *amāvas*; he should order the subjects to celebrate

Hola from the day of Basant Panchmi to the first day of Baisakh. His subjects should worship only Sri Akal Purkh. They should shun all non-Sikh forms of worship: *maṛhī*, *gor*, *masīt*, *dehurā*, *tīrath*, and *bart*. Their dharm and *karam* should be *nām*, *dān*, and *isnān*, and the only form of worship should be praise of Sri Akal Purkh, who alone is the True Master. All men and women, boys and girls, should participate in the celebration of *pūranmāsī*; they should participate in the kīrtan of Sri Akal Purkh and pray for the long reign of the Maharaja.[81]

The Maharaja should be concerned with matters sexual. No one should remain unmarried, whether man or woman. No woman, except the prostitute, was to be allowed to move unveiled in public. Men and women who indulged in illegal sexual intercourse were to be seated on a donkey and paraded in public, with their faces blackened. If one of them happened to be an outcaste, they were to be ordered to marry as a punishment. The prostitutes were to have separate quarters. Sexual intercourse with the prostitute was legal; she sold her body with the consent of her people; association with her was as good as 'half a marriage'. It would be better than indulging in illegitimate sex. But the best thing was to remain chaste before marriage and then to cohabit only with one's spouse.[82]

The Maharaja was to ensure that no one slept at night without food or clothes. In every village and town, the state functionaries were to provide adequate support not only to those who were without food or clothes but also to those who were without work, or who needed help to get their daughters married. The Maharaja was to pay special attention to the needs of the householders. No occupation was to be looked down upon. 'To work with one's hands is a form of bhakti'. The only tax on goods was to be imposed at the time of their purchase by the trader. The people were to be warned against any kind of deceit in trade.[83] In several ways, the monarchical state was seen as a sort of welfare state, much ahead of the times.

The grand order (*mahā hukam*), bearing the signatures and impression of the seal of the Maharaja, was to be addressed to mansabdārs of the rank of 3,000–80,000 for something important; it was to be carried by a mansabdār of 1,000. The disāvantkār was to receive it at seven kos from his headquarters and offer *taslim* five times from a distance of half the length covered by the arrow shot from a fully drawn bow, and again from a shorter distance. He was to place the document over his head and take it to his headquarters. He was then to read it and implement it without delay. The order written on behalf of the Maharaja on his oral direction, called *hukampāi* or *hasbul hukam*, was to be carried by a kāmvant and to be received by the addressee outside the city, to be read and implemented. If a state functionary did not obey an order, his house was to be plundered and he was to be executed as an example to others.[84]

On the death of a servant of the state, his property was to be taken over so that any demand of the state could be adjusted. If any debt was pending, it was to be paid to the creditor. The rest of the property was to be given to the legal heirs of the deceased. Similarly, in the case of a *sāhūkār* the amount due to the state and any creditor was to be deducted and, if he had no legal heir, the remainder was to be deposited in the treasury for charitable purposes.[85]

The author of *Prem Sumārg* gives detailed description of the standards to be given to mansabdārs of various ranks: 50, 100, 200–1,000, 2,000–5,000, 6,000–12,000. The rank of a prince and the vazīr could be upto 80,000. The heir apparent was to be distinguished from everyone else. The Maharaja was to ride in state and hold his court sitting on a high throne.[86]

The Maharaja was to have only one wife and was not to associate with a woman other than his wife. However, if he found her unsuited to his nature, he could marry another woman of equal status. Also, if he did not have a male child he could have upto seven wives. The Maharaja was never to marry for sensual pleasure. He was not to associate with a slave girl if his wife was with him. However, if he was overpowered by sexual desire in the absence of his wife he associate with a slave girl. This was considered better than associating with another woman. The general ideal stated in *Prem Sumārg* is: he who has only one wife is a jatī. He who is content with one wife is a great man.[87]

The author of *Prem Sumārg* attaches great importance to justice. The Maharaja should think that he has been given rulership to perform justice, and he should do justice impartially without fear or favour. In the divine court a ruler would not be asked about worship but about justice. None should remain disconsolate or *dukhī* in his dominions and the powerful should not be allowed to oppress the poor. The Maharaja alone will be accountable to God. The ruler who oppresses people goes to hell. Even worship does not equal justice. The essence of justice is not to appropriate what belongs by right to another, and not to allow such misappropriation. As far as possible, no one was to be harmed, nor allowed to be harmed.[88] The Maharaja was to appoint judges for each disa, tarf, and pargana in every city. The chief justice (*niāonvant*) installed by the Maharaja was to function absolutely independently and impartially. He could hear complaints even against the Maharaja and also summon him to court. If there was an appeal against the niāonvant himself, the Maharaja, or the wazīr, or a disāvant could do justice. The seal of the niāonvant should bear the words: 'through the order of Sri Guru Akal Purkh'.[89]

A whole chapter on justice relates to what the Maharaja should do for his kith and kin, his domestic economy, the property of the deceased, inheritance, servants of the state, unowned wealth or goods discovered by someone, disputes about property, the rights of wives, *amānat*, debts, matrimonial alliances, sale of slaves and animals, immovable property, *biswedārī*, and interest on loans. Daughters and sisters could inherit in certain situations, which is somewhat unusual and a little radical. At the end of the chapter it is emphasized that impartial justice enables the Maharaja to attain liberation. No worship or bhakti has an equal merit with justice. One who is unjust for any reason shall be born as a dog or a hog.[90]

THE PANTH OF LIBERATION

The last chapter of *Prem Sumārg* is on *sahāj jog*. The intoxication of the state of sahaj is superior to the intoxication of power, youth, wealth, and alcohol or opium. The state of sahaj is also called '*ek nām*', and 'hukam'. It is devoid of fear and anxiety. Only a few attain this state. The total acceptance of God's will is the hallmark of this state. Equal in the eyes of one who has attained this state are acquisition of power and its loss, nectar and poison, honour and dishonour, gold and dust, hell and heaven, and purity and impurity. The path of sahaj is easy and difficult at the same time.[91]

Sahaj jog is the antidote to *haumai* which induces people to make special efforts in a hurry. In the state of sahaj one does everything at ease: sleeping and waking up, eating and drinking, speaking and keeping silent, in domesticity and worship. The state of sahaj comes when haumai departs. All fear and anxiety vanish and the light of the Name becomes manifest.[92]

What is written in the other chapters remains related to 'the three qualities' which mark the life of a mere householder. The treasure of liberation is not there in 'the three qualities'. This chapter is on the *parm marg*. He who follows its injunctions would attain *rāj jog*, like Raja Janak, Prahlad, and Babhishan. And then he would be born to reach the state of sahaj. The sahaj jog is 'the fourth quality'. It is meant for the Kaliyuga. The panths of the Hindus and the mlechh would deviate from their dharm and the whole world become oblivious of all social norms in matrimonial and sexual matters. Dharm would fly away like a bird. The parm marg would save the Khalsa of Sri Akal Purkh, all of whom belong to the 'Chhatri Sodhi' caste. This path has been created through God's grace as the only efficacious path in the Kaliyuga. The Sikhs of the Guru worship only the one God and this '*ek angī*' bhakti is the means of liberation. The foundation of this bhakti is service or *seva*. To fulfil the wants of the hungry, the naked, and the needy is real service. Kindness is superior to everything else. The contents of the *Prem Sumārg Granth* are not meant for everyone. They are meant for those who have faith and not for the sceptics. Mard kā Chelā would promulgate the path enunciated in this granth. Those who follow this path would attain peace and liberation.[93] Thus, sahaj jog gets equated with the path initiated by Guru Nanak and Guru Gobind Singh.

Character of the Envisioned Order

The injunctions of the *Prem Sumārg Granth*, like the Khalsa Panth, have divine sanction and they are meant for the Khalsa of Sri Akal Purkh. The Sikh, the Khalsa, and the Singh refer to the same entity, and there is no other category of Sikhs. The injunctions are meant for both men and women, with some modifications. The ideal of equality is modified in some other ways too, but it remains the hallmark of the Khalsa and their distinctive identity. They are emphatically distinct from Hindus and Muslims.

No compromise is to be made with regard to the religious beliefs and practices of the Khalsa of Sri Akal Purkh. Belief in Akal Purkh to the strict exclusion of all gods and goddesses, and worship of Akal Purkh through Shabad-Bāṇī to the strict exclusion of all other forms of worship define the basic position of the Khalsa. They believe in ten Gurus and after them, in shabad-bāṇī as the Guru; it is embodied essentially in the Pothi Granth. To converse with the Guru one could read his shabad. To see the Guru, one could go to a gathering of the Khalsa to see the Guru in the Khalsa. No living person is to be regarded as Guru.

The daily life of the Khalsa is marked by early morning worship after bathing, recitation of *Japjī, Jāp, Anand, SoDar Rahrās* and Kīrtan *Sohilā*, reading of Gurbāṇī from the Granth, and participation in the kīrtan. The initiation of a person into the order of the Khalsa involves khande dī pahul, wearing a kachh and five weapons, an ardās, and instruction in the essentials of belief and ethics. A married woman and a widow can also take pahul. Apart from some other differences in detail, a baptized male is to bear the epithet 'Singh' and a baptized female the epithet 'Devi'.

The ceremonies of birth, naming, betrothal, marriage, and death do not have any role for the Brahman. To figure largely in these ceremonies are Gurbāṇī, ardas, pahul, and arms. For the marriage ceremony, fire is to be a witness, like the sword and the Khalsa; it is to be fed with ghee at proper moments. On the death of a Khalsa, no traditional mourning is to be observed; there should be no wailing; the ashes are not to be taken to the Ganges.

Ideally, the Khalsa belong to one caste and there are no distinctions of high and low between them. However, the traditional attitudes may be partially accommodated but only temporarily. Marriage within the same caste or occupational group is one such compromise. Not eating with the unclean outcastes is another. Remarriage is not allowed for a widow with children. The ideal is underscored without ambiguity: 'All are one in the eyes of Guru Akal Purkh'; everyone professing to be the Khalsa should be regarded as equal.

All honest occupations are sanctified. However, preference is given to saudagārī and cultivation of land; petty shopkeeping and service are forbidden, except soldiering. A Khalsa must save for the Guru's treasury and spend a portion of his income on the welfare of others. He should share his food with others, whether they are Khalsa, Hindu or Musalman. Meat is the most preferred item of food. In certain situations, a Khalsa can eat halāl meat. Alcohol is forbidden but, if necessary, opium or *bhang* can be taken privately in small quantities.

The form of government in the ideal Sikh state is monarchical. The authority and the orders of the ruler can be disregarded only at the cost of life. The vast territory of the state occupies an imaginary space; its primary, secondary and tertiary divisions have several common departments. The primary concerns of the state are the army, revenues, intelligence, and justice. The dominant institutions of the state are mansabdārī and jagīrdārī, both of which remind us of the Mughal state. Many terms used for offices and officials come from Mughal practice. The share of the cultivator in the produce from land is less than half, which is regarded as lenient. The language of education and administration is to be 'Gurmukhi'. The ruler is expected to ensure the worship only of Akal Purkh and the propagation of nām, dān, and isnān. Chastity and fidelity in marriage are cherished; illegal sexual intercourse is a criminal offence; prostitution is officially recognized. Monogamy is the ideal, but the ruler can have more than one wife for various reasons, including the need of a male child. In certain situations he can have sexual intercourse with slave girls. The ruler will be judged ultimately on the basis of justice, and not piety. Justice is the *raison d'etre* of the ideal Sikh state.

The path initiated by Guru Nanak and elaborated by Guru Gobind Singh is sahaj jog which stands for the total acceptance of God's will. It is an antidote to haumai. It leads to liberation, the state of raj-jog. Its essence is the service of others as a sort of selfless social commitment.

The *Prem Sumārg* does not appear to bear any clear imprint of the late eighteenth or early nineteenth century. There are a few similarities between the ideal Sikh state and the state of Maharaja Ranjit Singh, but the differences between them are more marked. Gurmukhi was not the language of government and administration under Ranjit Singh. The conception of the ideal Sikh state put forward in the *Prem Sumārg* does not appear to represent a reaction to the state in existence. The ideal Sikh social order of *Prem Sumārg* is more egalitarian than the Sikh social order of the early nineteenth century. There is no role for Brahmans in the Sikh social order which is exclusively Khalsa.

The scope of *Prem Sumārg* is quite comprehensive. It does present a conception of the ideal Sikh state, but more than that it relates to the ideal Sikh social order. Its author was a learned person, keen perhaps to influence his fellow Sikhs in the interest of the Sikh faith and community. The adoption of the form of prophecy, which could make his granth authoritative, also gave him the freedom to bring in the past in a big way. His work does not remain a reflection of his own historical situation because of his concern for the future as well as the past. His vision of the Sikh community and Sikh state was informed largely by the Khalsa ideology. The *Prem Sumārg* is essentially a Sant Khalsa document.

NOTES

1. Mohan Singh, *An Introduction to Punjabi Literature*, Amritsar: Nanak Singh Pustakmala, 1952, pp. 111–42.
2. S.S. Kohli, *Punjabi Sahit da Itihas*, Ludhiana: Lahore Book Shop, 1955, p. 216.
3. Randhir Singh, ed., *Prem Sumarg Granth*, Jalandhar: New Book Company, 1965(2nd edn), pp. 81–3, 88–9.
4. Ibid., pp. 90–110.
5. Ibid., pp. 83–8.
6. J.S. Grewal, 'The Prem Sumarag: A Theory of Sikh Social Order', *Punjab History Conference Proceedings*, Patiala: Punjabi University, 1965, pp. 100–11.
7. J.S. Grewal, 'A Theory of Sikh Social Order', in J.S. Grewal, *From Guru Nanak to Maharaja Ranjit Singh: Essays in Sikh History*, Amritsar: Guru Nanak Dev University, 1972, pp. 72–83.
8. Harbans Singh and N. Gerald Barrier, eds, *The Panjab Past and Present: Essays in Honour of Dr Ganda Singh*, Patiala: Punjabi University, 1976, pp. 165–75.
9. S.S. Hans, 'Prem Sumarg: A Modern Forgery', *Punjab History Conference Proceedings*, 1982, pp. 180–8.
10. J.S. Grewal, 'A Theory of Sikh Social Order', in J.S. Grewal, *Sikh Ideology, Polity and Social Order*, New Delhi: Manohar, 1996, pp. 152–61.
11. Nripinder Singh, *The Sikh Moral Tradition*, New Delhi: Manohar, 1990, pp. 187 n. 78, 125, 137–8, 141.
12. Ibid., p. 328.
13. W.H. McLeod, 'The Problems of the Panjabi Rahit-Namas', in W.H. McLeod, *Exploring Sikhism: Aspects of Sikh Identity, Culture, and Thought*, New Delhi: Oxford University Press, 2000, pp. 103–25.
14. W.H. McLeod, 'The Khalsa Rahit: The Sikh Identity Defined', in W.H. McLeod, *Exploring Sikhism*, pp. 126–35.
15. W.H. McLeod, *Who is a Sikh? The Problem of Sikh Identity*, Oxford: Clarendon Press, 1989, pp. 30n, 68.
16. W.H. McLeod, *Sikhism*, Harmmondsworth: Penguin Books, 1997, p. 121.
17. W.H. McLeod, *Sikhs of the Khalsa: A History of the Khalsa Rahit*, New Delhi: Oxford University Press, 2003, p. 149. Major Leech translated

two sections of the *Prem Sumarg* and Nripinder has translated small portions. Ibid., pp. 18, 20.
18. Ibid., p. 149. McLeod refers elsewhere to Randhir Singh postulating the possibility of a *Khalsa Smriti* having been prepared by Guru Gobind Singh, which has not survived. Ibid., p. 23.
19. Ibid., pp. 150, 156n 16.
20. Ibid., p. 150.
21. Ibid., pp. 148, 150–1.
22. Ibid., pp. 153, 160, 169, 206, 227, 230, 241–2, 244–5, 433–4 nn.
23. W.H. McLeod, *Prem Sumarag: The Testimony of a Sanatan Sikh*, New Delhi: Oxford University Press, 2006, p. 5. McLeod refers to the 'interesting case' of Jagtar Singh Grewal, 'interesting because he has twice changed his opinion' concerning the dating of *Prem Sumārg*. McLeod has changed his opinion more than twice, but he takes shelter in the afterthought of 'tentative' and 'definitive'. Even now his opinion is tentative.
24. Ibid., p. 6.
25. Ibid., pp. 7, 9.
26. Ibid., pp. 19 n. 11. In favour of the early eighteenth century, apart from the similarities with the Chaupa Singh's *Rahipnāma* pointed out by McLeod, we may refer to the similarities between *Prem Sumārg* and *Sakhi Rahit Ki* on the issues of Sikh rites and Sikh identity. Even more important in this connection is the *Nasihatnāma* mentioned elsewhere in this volume. If the idea of '*Raj Karega Khalsa*' could become current in the early years of the eighteenth century, someone could think of writing elabortely on the future Sikh state.
27. Ibid., pp. 1, 2, 9.
28. Ibid., pp. 2, 6.
29. Ibid., p. 1. The reference is to pp. 158–65 of McLeod's *Sikhs of the Khalsa*.
30. McLeod, *Sikhs of the Khalsa*, p. 160.
31. Ibid., p. 163.
32. Ibid., p. 164.
33. McLeod, *Prem Sumarag*, p. 8.
34. Ibid., pp. 92, 100.
35. Randhir Singh, *Prem Sumarg Granth*, pp. 107, 119.
36. McLeod, *Prem Sumarag*, p. 2.
37. Randhir Singh, *Prem Sumarg Granth*, pp. 4, 12.
38. Ibid., pp. 1–4.
39. Ibid., pp. 5–6.
40. Ibid., pp. 6–7.

41. Ibid., p. 7.
42. Ibid., pp. 7–8.
43. Ibid., pp. 8–10.
44. Ibid., pp. 10–11.
45. Ibid., pp. 11–12.
46. Ibid., p. 12.
47. Ibid., pp. 12–13.
48. Ibid., pp. 13–14.
49. Ibid., pp. 15–16.
50. Ibid., pp. 16–17.
51. Ibid., pp. 17–18.
52. Ibid., pp. 19–20.
53. Ibid., pp. 20–1.
54. Ibid., p. 22.
55. Ibid., pp. 22–3.
56. Ibid., pp. 23–5.
57. Ibid., pp. 25–6.
58. Ibid., p. 27.
59. Ibid., pp. 27–39.
60. Ibid., pp. 39–42.
61. Ibid., pp. 42–4.
62. Ibid., pp. 44–5.
63. Ibid., pp. 45–6.
64. Ibid., pp. 46–8.
65. Ibid., pp. 49–56.
66. Ibid., pp. 56–69.
67. Ibid., pp. 79–85.
68. Ibid., pp. 85–93.
69. Ibid., pp. 73–4, 77.
70. Ibid., pp. 66–7.
71. Ibid., p. 67.
72. Ibid., pp. 97, 98, 99.
73. Ibid., p. 94.
74. Ibid., pp. 94–5, 101.
75. Ibid., pp. 100–1.
76. Ibid., pp. 102–3.
77. Ibid., pp. 97, 98, 99, 100.
78. Ibid., pp. 98–9.
79. Ibid., pp. 96–7.
80. Ibid., pp. 105–7.
81. Ibid., pp. 107–8.

82. Ibid., pp. 108–9.
83. Ibid., pp. 109–11.
84. Ibid., pp. 111–13.
85. Ibid., p. 113.
86. Ibid., pp. 113–20.
87. Ibid., pp. 121–3.
88. Ibid., pp. 95–6.
89. Ibid., pp. 98–9, 104–5.
90. Ibid., pp. 124–5.
91. Ibid., pp. 146–7.
92. Ibid., p. 148.
93. Ibid., pp. 148–51.

PART IV
Norms of Equality

8. Caste and the Sikh Social Order[*]

Two Views of Caste in Relation to the Sikh Social Order

Kapur Singh was the first Sikh scholar to assert that the Sikh doctrine repudiates 'the bases as well as the institutes of the Hindu caste system' and lays down 'secure foundations' for a liberal democracy and an egalitarian society.[1] The *varnashramadharma* was a twofold division of the social order into *varna* or class, and *jātī* or caste proper. The former was believed to be ordained by God and hence eternal. The latter was a system of groups within the varna, each characterized and perpetuated through endogamy, commensality, and craft-exclusiveness.

The principle enunciated in the *Manusmriti* is given by Kapur Singh in the following words:

He, the Resplendent, for the sake of protecting all the creatures, assigned separate duties to those born of His mouth, arms, thighs and feet. Teaching and studying the Vedas, making sacrifices and assisting others in so doing, making gifts and receiving of gifts: these He assigned to Brahmans. The protection of the people, sacrificing and studying of Vedas, non-attachment to sensual pleasures and giving of gifts: these He prescribed for the Kshatriyas. The protection of the cattle, giving of gifts, sacrificing and study of Vedas, trade, banking and agriculture to the Vaishyas. God allotted only one duty to the Shudras: to serve without demur, the members of all the classes mentioned above.[2]

---

[*] 'Caste and the Sikh Social Order' is a revised version of the lecture included in my *Lectures on Sikh History, Society and Culture* (Patiala: Punjabi University, 2007, pp. 320–34). The theme was briefly discussed in my *Guru Nanak in History* (Chandigarh: Panjab University, 1969, pp. 188–92). It was amplified in 'The Ideal of Equality and the Sikh Social Order' included in *Relevance of Khalsa Value System in the 21st Century* (Chandigarh: Anandpur Sahib Foundation, 2000, pp. 66–81), and revised for the lecture at Patiala.

The greatest calamity that could fall on the social order was *varnashankara*, the confusion of castes, due to one class assuming the duties and obligations of another, or one jātī interloping into the economic reserve and monopoly of the other.

According to Kapur Singh, the teachings of the Gurus destroy all superstitions about varna and jātī. A common ethical code was to be followed by all the four varnas. All human beings had equal social rights, and none was to be discriminated against. The true conscience of mankind tells us that birth and caste do not count. 'Do not recognize *jāt* and do not ask one's jātī; there is no jāt in the hereafter'. 'All human beings have the same refuge; jātī and *nao* are nonsense (*phakkar*)'. 'Whether good or bad, all human beings have sprung up from the same light'. 'Distinctions of varna and order are against the will of God'. In these quotations there is enough evidence that Sikhism unreservedly repudiates the religious sanctions or theological validity of birth distinctions, refuses to admit that social gradation determines social ethics and civic obligations on individuals, and unambiguously declares that class and caste distinctions are of no consideration. The Semitic concept of 'divinely codified laws' is also thrown overboard when it is declared that the Veda and the Kateb do not possess any validity (*Ved kateb iftrā bhāī*).[3]

Kapur Singh tries to make a convincing case for the ideal of equality in Sikhism. But he does not take into account the social order called the Sikh Panth or the Khalsa Panth.

W.H. McLeod includes the outcastes or the untouchables in 'the classical model' of the caste system. Appropriate for dealing with the Sikh social order were also *zāt* and *got*, corresponding to caste and sub-caste in English. The former consisting of a number of the latter was an endogamous group while the latter was exogamic. The most relevant issues for discussion were commensality and connubium.

For the Sikh Gurus, caste had no meaning in the matter of access to spiritual liberation. The Brahman and the outcaste were equal in this respect. If anything, access to the Divine Name may be more difficult to the Brahman because of his pride than to the humble outcaste. The message of the *langar* was loud and clear: everyone sat in the same line *pangat* and ate the same food. The ritual of the Khalsa initiation made the same point: all who take initiation drink from the same bowl. The *karhā prashād* in the Gurdwara communicated the same message of equality. It may be prepared by any Sikh and brought to the Gurdwara for mingling with the general offering. Thus, on the sacred territory of the Gurdwara, the actual ground dedicated to Vāheguru, there was no possibility of distinctions of caste. Outcaste was equal to Jat and Jat was equal to Khatri. 'Every caste is equal to every other caste within the Panth'.

However, all the Gurus were Khatri and married their children in strict accordance with caste prescriptions. McLeod suggests that the Gurus were prepared to retain caste as a social convention once it was shorn of all its discriminatory features. In other words, the Gurus were opposed to the vertical distinctions of caste but accepted it in terms of horizontal linkages. The notion of hierarchy, thus, stood rejected. McLeod does not say so but this rejection implies that there can be no 'caste system' in the Sikh social order.

On the ground, Khatris constituted only two to three per cent of the Panth, but they continued to have an influence out of all proportion to their numbers. The majority of Khatris in the Punjab were Hindu, and the Khatri Sikhs intermarried with them. Very similar was the position of the related group of Aroras. The Khatris and Aroras among the Sikhs formed the bulk of the urban Sikh population.[4]

The Sikhs were an overwhelmingly rural community. The most important group in terms of numbers and influence was that of the Jats, forming more than 60 per cent of the total Sikh population. The Ramgarhias were next in importance to the Jats, representing a disntictively Sikh caste consisting of village carpenters (Tarkhāns), blacksmiths (Lohārs), masons (Rāj), and barbers (Nāīs). The Mazhabīs corresponded to the Hindu Chūhras or sweepers, and the Ramdāsias or Ravidasīs corresponded to Hindu Chamārs or leather workers. A small group was represented by Kalāls or brewers of country liquor. They experienced an upward mobility during the Singh Sabha movement of the late nineteenth and early twentieth centuries and emerged as the Ahluwalia caste. Each of the Sikh castes was divided into gots or subcastes. Both caste and sub-caste were regarded as of utmost importance for marriages, perpetuating the existence of castes among the Sikhs in spite of the fact that no superiority could be claimed by any caste and no inferiority could be attached to any caste.

McLeod talks of the ideal of equality and its partial application in social matters. Besides equality in the sacred space, there was no hierarchy of castes among the Sikhs. However, castes existed in the Sikh social order for the purpose mainly of matrimonial alliances. McLeod does not say anything about commensality outside the sacred space. Though the ideals are derived from the Gurus, McLeod appears to talk mostly of the modern Sikh social order, modifying the ideal position stated by Kapur Singh. However, Kapur Singh and McLeod do not say anything about the social order prevailing in the Punjab in the early sixteenth century or later which provided the context for the emergence of the Sikh social order. Nor do they talk of the composition and character of the early Sikh community.[5]

SOCIAL ORDER OF THE TIME OF GURU NANAK

Writing in the early eleventh century, Alberuni observed that there were four varnas among the Hindus: the Brahman, the Kshatriya, the Vaishya, and the Shudra. In each varna there were a number of sub-castes. However, all the four varnas put together did not account for the entire social order. Certain crafts and professions were placed below the Shudras. Among these are mentioned occupations like that of the weaver, the washerman, the basket-maker, the sailor, the fisherman, the hunter, the juggler and the shoemaker. Still lower, almost outside the pale of the society, were others, like the Chandāls. The duties of the first three varnas given by Alberuni are more or less the same as in the *Manusmriti*. However, the duty of the Shudras was to serve the Brahmans. It is also stated that an infringement of the Brahman's privileges was not merely a sin but also a crime punishable by the state.[6]

Though the society did not conform to the varnashrama ideal, the ideal itself was not discarded even in the later centuries. Writing towards the end of the seventeenth century, Sujan Rai refers to the Ahl-i Brahma as the people who subscribe to the varna order, that is, the hierarchical order consisting of the Brahman, the Kshatriya, the Vaishya and the Shudra.[7] Similarly, Ganesh Das in the mid nineteenth century looks upon the varna order as the ideal Hindu social order.[8]

The social order in northern India underwent important changes during the period of Turko-Afghan rule from the eleventh to the fifteenth century. For example, the Kshatriya of the varna order was no longer there. The Rajput ruling class, which came close to the old Kshatriyas in political power and social status, had been dislodged.

CASTE AND THE SIKH SOCIAL ORDER 193

A few of the Rajputs accepted Islam; many others migrated to other areas. Those who stayed in the Punjab were politically subordinate to the Turko-Afghan rulers. In contemporary literature they figure mostly as Rāis or Rāos.

Older than the Rajputs were the people known as Khatris who traced their origin to the days of Rama, the hero of the Ramayana. But the profession of arms was no longer important to them. Some of them served the Turkish and Afghan rulers at subordinate levels of administration. The majority of them pursued trade and shopkeeping in towns and villages. In larger cities they acted as bankers and *sarrāfs* as well. If they were to be assigned to any varna, it could be the Vaishya and not the Kshatriya. There were other trading communities like the Aroras and the Bāṇiās. Most of them lived in towns and cities but they were represented in the countryside too.

The Jats, who are mentioned by Alberuni as Shudras in the early eleventh century and by the author of the *Dabistān* as the lowest of the Vaishyas in the middle decades of the seventeenth century, were numerous in all the five *doābs* of the Punjab and between the Sutlej and the Jamuna. Mostly cultivators, they had their *muqaddams* and *chaudharīs* who acted as intermediaries between the rulers and the cultivators.[9] They lived almost entirely in villages, like several other agricultural castes in the countryside.

Both in villages and towns there were artisans and craftsmen, clean outcastes and the untouchables. The bulk of the non-Muslim population consisted of the lower castes and the outcastes. The Brahmans had lost state patronage with the fall of the Rajputs. The Turko-Afghan rulers had some need of astrologers but not of priests or learned Brahmans. As Alberuni observed, the learned Brahmans had already moved into other areas where they could seek patronage. Those who remained in the Punjab had to consolidate their hold over a humbler but a more numerous class of patrons in villages and towns. They expounded scriptures, looked after the temples, taught in *pāthshālas*, and performed ritual services for individual families. Their influence was subtle and pervasive. Socially, however, it is difficult to visualize them as being on the top of the social pyramid. The varna order had become 'confused', which was seen as a sign of the Kaliyuga.[10]

Furthermore, the social order did not consist of Hindus alone. For nearly five hundred years, Muslim soldiers, administrators, traders, scholars, men of letters, and men of religion had been coming to the Punjab from Persia, Afghanistan and Central Asia. They were to be found not only in all the cities and towns of the Punjab but also in many places in the countryside. To their number was added a much larger number of indigenous people who were forcibly converted to Islam or accepted Islam voluntarily. These converts consisted of tribes like the Gakhkhars, Janjuas, Kharals and Sials, and many clans of Jats and Gujjars. To them were added landless labourers in the villages and artisans and craftsmen in the urban centres. Muslim weavers, dyers, ironsmiths, oil-pressers, shoemakers, leather-workers, and slaves could be seen in all cities and towns.

The social order among Muslims was not based on any principle of inequality but horizontal stratification was quite visible among them. The members of the ruling class were at the top, and the erstwhile outcastes were at the lowest rung. Legally, the slaves, whether men or women, possessed no rights whatsoever. In the middle rungs were professional classes, traders, landholders, and religious classes represented by the *'ulamā* and the *mashāikh*. The Sayyids enjoyed a special status among the Muslims, followed by the *shaikhzāda*s and *pīrzāda*s. The Muslims of foreign origin, like the Persians and Afghans, thought of themselves as superior to Indian Muslims. Among the Indian Muslims, themselves, the families coming from the higher castes of the Hindu social order regarded themselves as superior to others. Thus, the Muslim social order was far from being egalitarian. The society of the days of Guru Nanak did not conform to any ideal, whether Hindu or Muslim. Taken as a whole, it provided a good example of varnashankara of the traditional Hindu conception.[11]

Guru Nanak was familiar with the ruling class, the *'ulamā* and the mashāikh among the Muslims. But he had no appreciation for the first two and only a limited appreciation for the *mashāikh*. He was familiar with Muslims as subjects and slaves. Since Guru Nanak identified himself with the common people. There is no reason to think that the Muslims were not included in that category.

However, Guru Nanak had more to say about the Hindu component of the contemporary social order. He refers to the four varnas, and specifically to the Brahman, the Khatri, the Vais, and the Shudar. He was aware of many jātīs and the presence of the outcastes or the *nīch* and the chandāl. Many a profession figures in the compositions of Guru Nanak: the *purohit*, the *pāndhā*, the *jotishī*, the sāhūkār, the moneylender, the merchant, the trader, the shopkeeper, the sarrāf, the *banjāra*, the bāniā, the goldsmith, the ironsmith, the dyer, the fisherman, the seller of bangles, the broker, the horse dealer, the singer, the poet, the dancing girl, the domestic servant, the menial, the beggar, the cultivator, the day labourer and the slave. Moreover, the Brahmans and the Khatris were no longer performing the duties assigned to them in the varna order. They imitated the rulers whom they served and yet regarded them as *mlechh*. As members of the ruling class at the middle or lower rungs, they were bracketed with oppressors.

The Early Sikh Panth

The contemporary social order appeared to Guru Nanak to have lost its legitimacy. A new social order could be created on the basis of equality. The path of Guru Nanak was open to all, irrespective of caste and creed. He addressed himself to all categories of people and not merely to the trading and agricultural communities as it is generally but wrongly believed. It was yet to be seen who would respond to his message and how the idea of equality would become operative.[12]

Bhai Gurdas is the first Sikh writer to present some meaningful information on the Sikh Panth. He mentions the names of the well-known Sikhs of the time of each of the Gurus from Guru Nanak to Guru Hargobind. He was familiar with the Sikhs at Goindwal and Ramdaspur. He refers to several other *sangat*s in the Punjab, notably those of Lahore, Patti, and Sultanpur. There were eminent Sikhs in Sirhind, Thanesar, and Delhi. There were prominent Sikhs in Kabul, Kashmir, Agra, Allahabad, Bihar, Bengal, Rajasthan, Malwa, and Gujarat. Bhai Gurdas refers to Chaddhas, Sehgals, Handas and Nandas in Agra, to Sonis in Gwalior, to Dhirs in Ujjain, to Wadhawans in Burhanpur and to Behls in Raj Mahal. They were all Khatri traders. Bhai Gurdas refers to Bhabara Sikhs in Gujarat who too were traders.[13]

The Khatris formed the most important constituent or group of the Nanak Panth in the Punjab. Among the prominent Sikhs of Guru Nanak and his successors figure individuals belonging to some of the well-known Khatri sub-castes of the Punjab: Sehgal, Ohri, Uppal, Julka, Bhalla, Passi, Khullar, Vohra, Vij, Kapur, Chaddha, Behl, Kohli, Marwaha, Mehra, Soni, Jhanji, Sodhi, Beri, Nanda, Wadhawan, Tulli, and Puri. There are several other less familiar sub-castes of the Khatris.

However, there were prominent Sikhs belonging to other varnas and jātīs. There are some Randhawa, Khaira, Dhillon, and Pannu Jats. Among the Brahmans are mentioned Tiwari and Bhardwaj. There were Sūds and Aroras. Then there were Lohārs, Naīs, Chhīmbas, Mochīs, Dhobīs, Kumhārs, Telīs, masons, goldsmiths, and chandāls.[14] At one end of the scale there were rich merchants, *seth*s and sarrāfs in cities and towns and chaudharīs in villages; on the other, there were labourers and slaves, with artisans and craftsmen, petty shopkeepers and peasants in between. It is evident that the social background of the eminent Sikhs of the Gurus covered a wide range of the social order. It is also clear that the Sikh Panth was not exactly egalitarian in terms of the economic means of its members.

The social background of the Sikhs did not matter for Bhai Gurdas. Guru Nanak addressed himself to all the four varnas, and individuals from all the four varnas could accept his path; they all met in the sangat as equals.[15] Just as betel leaf, areca nut, and lime produce one colour, so the individual members coming from different backgrounds acquired one colour in the Sikh sangat. The Guru transmuted eight metals into one. All the four varnas became one and acquired the *gotra* of Gurmukh. The eight metals became gold with the touch of *pāras*. The low castes who joined the Sikh Panth were raised to equality with others.[16] In theory, all Sikhs were equal as brothers in faith. The true Sikh of the Guru did not bother about the distinctions of caste. The notion of hierarchy was completely discarded. Bhai Gurdas is emphatic about total equality among the Sikhs in the sangat in the *dharmsāl*.

Equality in the Khalsa Order

The doctrine of Guru Granth ensured equality within the sacred space and the doctrine of Guru Panth extended it to the Sikh social order. From the very beginning the Guru was equated with the Word, and the Word came to be equated with the *bāṇī* of the Gurus. When Guru Arjan compiled the Granth, it was highly venerated even in the presence of the Guru because of the equation of the bāṇī with the Guru. The fact that Guru Angad was a Sikh of Guru Nanak before the latter installed him as the Guru made every Sikh a potential Guru and suggested an equation between the Guru and the Sikh. Bhai Gurdas' idea that the Guru dwelt in the sangat and that God was present where five Sikhs were present gave a peculiar sanctity to the collective body of the Sikhs.

According to *Gursobha*, composed by Sainapat in 1711, only a day before his death Guru Gobind Singh told his followers that the Khalsa represented his own form or *rūp*, and he would dwell in them; they were to seek inspiration in *bāṇī* as the eternal Guru.[17] The doctrines of Guru Panth and Guru Granth crystallized in the eighteenth century. All Sikhs were equal in the presence of Guru Granth as in the personal presence of the Guru. Each Sikh was equal to another as a member of the Guru Panth.

The doctrine of Guru Panth reinforced the ideal of equality in the sphere of religion and introduced the ideals of equality rather emphatically in social and political terms. The belief that the Guru was present among the Khalsa aided the evolution of the institution of Gurmata which played a vital role in their political struggle. Gurmata was a resolution adopted by the Khalsa in the belief that the Guru was present among them. It was normally binding on all the participants, and also on the Khalsa who were informed about it. The most important Gurmatas were passed at Amritsar. They related to measures of defence and aggression against the opponents. The Dal Khalsa came into action when all the leaders of the Khalsa voluntarily pooled their resources under the command of a single leader. The individual Khalsa had the right to counsel, to fight and to conquer, irrespective of his former *jātī* or occupation, or his present position in the Dal. It was largely through the institution of Gurmata that the Khalsa established themselves as rulers. Included among them were individuals who were outcaste in terms of their social background. Not only Khatris and Jats but also carpenters and vintners of the traditional social order became rulers.

However, the scope of the Gurmata was not extended to cover the government and administration of the territories conquered and occupied. From the very beginning, the individual Sikh ruler was completely autonomous in the internal administration of his principality and his relation with others. The principle of hereditary succession was adopted by all the Sikh rulers. Just as there is no doubt that the politics of the Khalsa were egalitarian, so there is hardly any doubt that the government of the Khalsa rulers was monarchical. In a monarchical form of government the social order could not remain egalitarian.

Apart from the implications of the new situation, a writer like Kesar Singh Chhibber could argue in 1769 that equality was not meant to be extended to the social sphere. The erstwhile Brahmans, Khatris, Vaishyas, and Shudras were a part of the Sikh Panth. They all shared a common faith, bound together by the ties of *sikhī*. Kesar Singh does not hesitate to state that the Sikhs who had consecrated their lives to the cause of the Panth did not bother about the distinctions of caste even for matrimonial alliance. All that was insisted upon was that a Sikh should marry a Sikh. Similarly, they put aside the sacred thread and *dhotī* and disregarded ritual purity in eating. Chhibber argues that this was not justified any longer. A Brahman Sikh should marry a Brahman Sikh and a Khatri Sikh should marry a Khatri Sikh. No one should be forced either to wear or to remove the sacred thread. A Brahman Sikh need not put it aside. In support of the ties of caste, Kesar Singh sought support from the Ādi Granth. For him, each varna had its own peculiar dharma which was not affected by the common bond of the Sikh faith. He cites the case of an outcaste Mazhabi Sikh who ate with Sandhu Jats by pretending to be a Jat Sikh. For infringing the rules of commensality of the traditional caste order, he was put to death. In Kesar Singh's view, social distinctions were to be upheld because there was no contradiction between the equality of faith and differentiation in social practices.[18] It is interesting to note that just as social stratification had begun to appear among the Khalsa with the establishment of Sikh rule, a Sikh writer was advocating the maintenance of social differentiation among the Sikhs.

It must be pointed out that Kesar Singh Chhibber presents a contrast with Ratan Singh Bhangu who wrote his well-known *Guru Panth Prakāsh* in the 1840s. The Khalsa Panth, according to Ratan Singh Bhangu, was meant to be egalitarian. More than a score of social groups are mentioned as constituting the Sikh Panth: Brahmans, Bhatts, Khatris, Aroras, Bāṇiās, Bakāls, Karārs, Sūds, Jats, Gujjars, Kambos, Sainīs, Lohārs, Tarkhāns, Kumārs, Sunārs, Jhīwars, Nāis, Chhīmbas, Kalāls, Behrūpiyas, Chūhṛas, and Chamārs. They obviously included not only the low caste but also the outcaste. Among the cherished five, Bhangu mentions a Khatri, a Jat, a Chhīmba, a Nāī, and a Jhīwar to underline that persons from all the varnas were included in the Khalsa Panth. When the Singhs drank from one vessel, all distinctions were abolished, the notion of varnas and ashramas was discarded, and the sacred thread and the sacred mark were put aside. The fortress of Ram Rauni at Ramdaspur was constructed with the labour of all the Singhs, irrespective of their political importance in the Panth. Apart from ideology, the difference of caste and the notion of ritual purity did not suit the conditions of war, defence, hardship, and hunger.

Among those who died fighting by the side of Tara Singh, the martyr, there were Brahmans, Naīs, and Tarkhāns as wells Jats; there were also Multani and Peshawari Singhs who were presumably Khatris or Aroras. The leaders of the five *jathā*s constituted by Kapur Singh in the 1730s consisted of two Jats, two Khatris and one Ranghreta. Bir Singh Ranghreta is mentioned elsewhere also as the leader of 1,300 horsemen who always fought in the van. Throughout the period of political struggle, we find incidental references to Khatris, Jats, Tarkhāns, Lohārs, Ranghretas and Mazhabīs as active members of the Khalsa Panth. The preponderance of Singhs from the countryside is implied in the tendency among the leaders of the Khalsa to occupy their own villages and the surrounding territory first. The preponderance of Jats among the Sikhs is evident from a casual remark of Jassa Singh Ramgarhia that the number of Jats in the Khalsa Panth was a hundred times more than that of the Tarkhāns. Jat preponderance is assumed in fact by Ratan Singh Bhangu when he says that the provinces wrested from the Mughals by Ahmad Shah Abdali were in turn wrested from him by 'the Jatts'.

Nevertheless, the difference of caste was discounted by the Jats themselves. Sukha Singh, a Tarkhān, was 'brought up' by Shiam Singh who was a Sandhu Jat. Jassa Singh Ahluwalia, a Kalāl, was similarly 'brought up' by Kapur Singh who was a Virk Jat. Just as the service of the Panth led Charhat Singh Sukerchakia to the pinnacle of eminence among the Khalsa, so did the service of the Panth make Jassa Singh Kalal the Pātshāh of the Panth. However, the difference between the 'caste' and the untouchable 'outcaste' groups was not completely abolished. Ratan Singh Bhangu admires Sardar Shiam Singh for giving pahul to everyone who came to him. Also, he ate with them all. But one distinction remained: he simply patronized and protected those who had a low (*nīch*) background. The implication is that he did not eat with them.[19]

The evidence of Chhibber and Bhangu suggests that no hierarchy of caste was recognized within the Sikh Panth. As brothers-in-faith all

Sikhs were equal. The author who advocates the observance of varna-dharma for matrimony and commensality is Kesar Singh Chhibber, a Brahman Sikh. But even he states that in the early eighteenth century the Khalsa did not observe traditional practices in matters of food and matrimony. The author who advocates almost total equality in the Khalsa Panth is Ratan Singh Bhangu, a Jat Sikh. He is silent about matrimonial patterns but he mentions the case of a Brahman woman abducted and molested by some Muslims who was nevertheless married by a Singh. Bhangu leaves no doubt that commensality was extended to the lowest of the clean castes in the traditional social order. The only exception were the erstwhile Chūhṛas and Chamārs. The evidence of these two writers also indicates that they looked upon the Sikh Panth as distinctly more egalitarian than the contemporary society around.

Sikh Rule and the Sikh Social Order

Prem Sumārg, an anonymous work of the eighteenth century recommended by Baba Ram Singh as the code of conduct for his Sant Khalsa, can be considered as 'a theory' of Sikh social order in so far as the author expresses his views on the purpose and goal of this social order, and presents the ideal norm to which the private and public life of the members of the society should conform. The spirit of the Sikh *rahit* was as important as the form. The essence of the Sikh way of life could not be reduced to formal observances. A Sikh should be a proof against sensual temptations and indulgence. He should always speak the truth (except when it was likely to cause harm to somebody). The watchwords of a Sikh should be continence, truth, contentment, mercy, humility, and service. He should not live on charity; he must earn his own living through honest means.

A Sikh should associate himself with the Sant Khalsa and should serve them as he would serve the Guru. The Sikhs should love one another and work in harmony. They should all come to the aid of a person who is in danger. For a Sikh, communal brotherhood was more important than the ties of kinship. A Sikh should always be ready to share his food, clothes, and other belongings with the needy; and if he were in a position to be of any service to others, he should regard it as a sign of God's grace. The best way to please the Guru was to serve his Sikhs.

Indeed, all men and women were equal in the eyes of their Creator. All mankind is the progeny of the Immortal Being.[20] There was to be no distinction between the high and the low among the Khalsa and there was to be only one caste, that of the Sodhi Khatri, the caste of Guru Gobind Singh, to which one came to belong immediately on one's initiation into the order of the Khalsa. This, however, was the ultimate objective and, meanwhile, some concessions could be given to prejudice in favour of caste and sub-caste. Marriage was permissible within the same caste and sub-caste as much as an inter-caste marriage. There were some Sikhs from whom the Khalsa should not eat, from the Chūhṛa, the Chamār, and the Sānsī, for instance. But this exception was made due to the nature of their occupations; otherwise there was nothing bad about their caste. Whoever belonged to the Khalsa could dine with them: *ek panth, ek parshād*.[21]

The Khalsa Panth was a unique community in so far as it possessed undiluted religious truth. All other religions, though ordained by God for the salvation of mankind, had deviated from the true purpose and were doomed to disappear sooner or later. It was not for the Khalsa, however, to become active agents of their destruction. It was open to the adherents of other religions to join the Panth to save themselves. They could co-exist with the Sikhs in amicable relationship. A Sikh was never expected to eat alone; if he did so, then he should keep a meal for the first visitor, whether a Khalsa, a Hindu, or a Muslim. If *jhatka* meat was not available, a Sikh could eat *halāl*. With a few minor and specific exceptions, all food as a rule was pure for the Khalsa, whether it came from a Hindu or a Muslim. The Sikh girls must be married into Sikh families but the Sikh boys could be married to non-Sikh girls, whether Hindu or Muslim. In all cases, however, the girls must be initiated into the order of the Khalsa.[22]

In spite of the author's insistence on equality, the Khalsa Panth he visualized had a social stratification of its own. The ruler and his kinsmen were at the top of the social pyramid. The civil officials, with their large *jāgīr*s, formed the social elite: they were instructed to live in a good style. The best of all occupations was trade; petty shopkeeping was not permitted to the Khalsa. That the traders were expected to be prosperous is evident from the plan recommended for their houses in cities, and their way of living. Next to trade was agriculture. But the condition of the peasant was probably not expected to be better than that of the artisan. There are indications that the artisans formed a numerous class at subsistence level. They were required to stick to their family occupations; no new openings were allowed to them. However, they were not to be addressed by their occupational names; the deriders of their occupations were to be severely dealt with. No petty service was allowed to the Sikhs except in the army, but mention is made of Sikh domestic servants. The keeping of slaves, both male and female, was permissible. Thus, stratification based on differences in economic means is built into his presentation of the Sikh social order. In the political sphere he does not see any relevance of the ideal of equality for Sikh institutions. The ideal Sikh state is not democratic or republican. It is a benevolent but authoritarian monarchy in which there is no institutional check on the power of the ruler and the use of his power.

We know from contemporary evidence that social differentiation had begun to appear among the Khalsa even before Ranjit Singh imposed a unified rule over Punjab. The process continued under Ranjit Singh. The bulk of the Sikhs still belonged to the former lower jātīs, with an overwhelming majority of Jats. But the world of the Jat ruler, or the *jāgīrdār*, was different from the world of the Jat peasant. Though individual carpenters and kalāls joined the ruling class, the majority of their erstwhile kinsmen remained in their older lowly occupations. The Akalis and Nihangs, the professed representatives of the Khalsa, who regarded themselves as equals of the rulers and collectively thought of themselves as even superior, received stipends and jāgīrs from Ranjit Singh. Occasionally they could strain his patience by postures of defiance, but they were little more than a political nuisance. Like every other subject of the kingdom of Lahore they accepted the authority of Maharaja Ranjit Singh. In this situation, the idea of Guru Panth which embodied an uncompromising ideal of equality tended to become more and more irrelevant and ineffective.

With the doctrine of Guru Panth being relegated to the background, the doctrine of Guru Granth became more important than ever before. It could enable the Sikhs to preserve partial equality among themselves: they were all equal in the presence of the Guru Granth. The established usages of religious congregation were observed by the pauper and the prince alike. Unlike the doctrine of Guru Panth, the doctrine of Guru Granth did not have obtrusive implications for the social order. The concentration of political power in the hands of one person, who shared it at will with others at subordinate levels, did not find any explicit opposition in the doctrine of Guru Granth, particularly if the ruler was just and considerate. This enabled the individual Sikh chief to rule on behalf of the Khalsa with a clear conscience.[23]

EQUALITY, CASTE CONSIDERATIONS, AND SOCIAL DIFFERENTIATION

We may conclude that Guru Nanak and his successors discarded the caste system based on the principle of inequality and they did not uphold inequality of any kind; they founded institutions based on the principle of equality, obliterating the distinctions of caste and social status; the doctrine of Guru Panth obliterated social differences by ensuring equality of all members of the Khalsa order. There was no ban on inter-caste marriage but in actual practice the old patterns did not appreciably change. There was no restriction on commensality, but inter-dining was not extended to the 'unclean' outcastes. The ideal of equality was realized fully in religious matters; it was realized partially in social and political matters. But it was not seen as relevant for matters economic. By implication, differences in wealth remained outside the operation of the egalitarian ideal. It is not surprising that horizontal stratification began to appear in the Sikh social order, both before and after the institution of the Khalsa, especially with the establishment of Sikh rule. Differences of wealth and caste were not obliterated but there was no caste system among the Sikhs. The ideal of equality was never abandoned in theory, but it was only partially realized in practice. In the early nineteenth century, differentiation in terms of classes was as important as the existence of caste considerations. Both of these were diffused more or less by the sentiment of Sikh brotherhood which was strengthened by the existence of the Sikh sacred space.

NOTES

1. Kapur Singh, *Parasharprashna: An Enquiry into the Genesis and Unique Character of the Order of the Khalsa with an Exposition of Sikh Tenets*, Piar Singh and Madanjit Kaur, eds, Amritsar: Guru Nanak Dev University, 1989, pp. 261, 278–80. This book was first published by the Hind Publishers of Jalandhar in 1959 as *Parasharprasna or the Baisakhi of Guru Gobind Singh (An Exposition of Sikhism)*. A revised edition was

204   THE SIKHS

published by the author in 1975. The language of the present edition is not exactly that of the author.
2. Ibid., p. 393.
3. Ibid., pp. 258-60, 260, 278-9.
4. W.H. McLeod, *Sikhism,* Harmondsworth: Penguin Books, 1997, pp. 228-34.
5. In his other works, McLeod emphasizes the predominance of the Jat component in the Sikh Panth from the time of Guru Arjan.
6. Edward C. Sachau, tr., *Alberuni's India 'An Account of the Religion, Philosophy, Literature Geography, Chronology, Astronomy, Customs, Laws, and Astrology of India about AD 1030,* 2 vols, Delhi: Low Price Publication, 1989 (rpt), pp. 99-104. London: 1914, pp. 100-2.
7. Sujan Rai Bhandari, *Khulāsa ut-Tawārīkh,* M. Zafar Hasan, ed., Delhi: 1918, p.24.
8. Ganesh Das, *Chār Bāgh-i Punjab,* Kirpal Singh, ed., Amritsar: Khalsa College, 1965, p. 288.
9. J.S. Grewal, *Guru Nanak in History,* Chandigarh: Panjab University, 1969, pp. 49, 51-4.
10. Ibid., pp. 50, 54.
11. Ibid., pp. 31-47.
12. Ibid., pp. 171-2, 187-91, 196.
13. Bhai Gurdas, *Vārān Bhai Gurdas,* Giani Hazara Singh, ed., Amritsar: Khalsa Samachar, 1962, *Vār* 8, *paurī* 23; Vār 11, paurīs 16, 21-3, 25-7, 29-31.
14. Ibid., Vār 11, paurīs 13, 14, 19-20, 22-3, 25; Vār 13, paurī 19.
15. Ibid., Vār 1, paurī 23; Vār 3, paurī 16; Vār 6, paurī 6; Vār 7, paurī 1; Vār 9, paurī 1; Vār 14, paurī 2; Vār 16, paurī 18; Vār 19, paurī 14; Vār 24, paurī 2, 5; Vār 26, paurī 18; Vār 29, paurī 1. The reference to all the four varnas by Bhai Gurdas should not be taken literally. It was a metaphor for the entire social order.
16. Ibid., Vār 7, paurī 5; Vār 11, paurī 7, 10; Vār 12, paurī 12; Vār 15, paurī 12; Vār 16, paurī 13; Vār 23, paurī 15; Vār 27, paurī 4; Vār 29, paurī 5.
17. Sainapat, *Sri Gur Sobha,* Shamsher Singh Ashok, ed., Amritsar: Shiromani Gurdwara Parbandhak Committee (SGPC), 1967.
18. Kesar Singh Chhibber, *Bansavalinama Dasan Patshahian Ka,* ed., Ratan Singh Jaggi published as vol. II of *Parkh*: Research Bulletin of Panjabi Language and Literature, S.S. Kohli, ed., Chandigarh: Panjab University, 1972, pp. 153-64.
19. Ratan Singh Bhangu, *Prachin Panth Prakash,* Bhai Vir Singh, ed., New Delhi: Sahit Sadan, 1993 (rpt).

20. Bhai Randhir Singh, ed., *Prem Sumārg*, Amritsar: Shiromani Gurdwara Parbandhak Committee (SGPC), 1965, pp. 3-4, 6-24, 42-5, 48-52, 61, 66-7, 84-96, 98-103, 111, 127-8, 131-3, 137.
21. Ibid., p. 44.
22. Ibid., p. 12.
23. For social change in the late eighteenth and the early nineteenth century, see Indu Banga, *The Agrarian System of the Sikhs*, New Delhi: Manohar 1978 and J.S. Grewal, *Maharaja Ranjit Singh: Polity, Economy and Society*, Amritsar: Guru Nanak Dev University, 2001.

9. Sikhism and Gender*

Status of Women in Medieval Indian Society

The historians of medieval India have commented on the inferior status of women in the society of the times and their subordinate position in the family. Clearly symptomatic of their position was the prevalence of polygamy, the practice of satī and *jauhar*, and the harsh treatment of widows. The principle of absolute fidelity on the part of women was deeply rooted in patriarchy.[1]

The contemporary writers bear witness to this principle. Alberuni was familiar with the practice of satī in the eleventh century. It was regarded as a meritorious act. The widow who refused to become satī was ill treated as long as she lived. Amir Khusrau expressed great appreciation for the supreme sacrifice of the Hindu woman for her husband. Ibn Battuta was horrified to see the actual incidents of satī, but he knew that the act was regarded as honourable and meritorious; the widow who did not become satī was despised for her lack of fidelity, and forced to live a miserable life. Writing towards the end of the seventeenth century, Sujan Rai quotes Amir Khusrau with approval. In the early nineteenth century, Ganesh Das placed satī above the martyr. He refers to actual instances of satī, and the worship of satīs. Conversely, no respectable Khatri could ever think of marrying a widow, or a divorced woman.[2]

* 'Gender in Sikhism' is a slightly revised version of the lecture included in *Lectures on Sikh History, Society and Culture of the Punjab* (Patiala: Punjabi University, 2007, pp. 335–55). The subject had been treated briefly in my *Guru Nanak in History* (Chandigarh: Panjab University, 1969, pp. 192–94). Detailed attention was given to it in my *Guru Nanak and Patriarchy* (Shimla: Indian Institute of Advanced Study, 1992). A new version appeared as 'Gender Perspective on Guru Nanak', in Kiran Pawar, ed., *Women in Indian History: Economic, Social, Political and Cultural Perspectives* (Patiala: Vision and Venture Publishers, 1996, pp. 141–58). The lecture at Patiala was an extended treatment of the subject.

Scholarly Views of Gender in Sikhism

Kapur Singh observed in the early 1950s that the law of *karma* had a close bearing on the position of women. In the Hindu texts the woman is treated with great reverence and tenderness but her social position was always inferior and subordinate to man. In the best of *Smriti*s, 'the woman is always 'a minor', that is, without the rights of an adult male. Sikhism repudiates the nexus between karma and social inequalities based on inequities and declares a woman to be 'the very essence of social coherence and progress'. Any suggestion of 'relegating her to an inferior status in any manner' is condemned. In support of this view, Kapur Singh thought it was enough to cite two lines from Guru Nanak's *Vār Āsā*: 'Why condemn her who gives birth to *rājān*. A woman is born of woman and there is none who is independent of woman'.[3]

W.H. McLeod makes the general statement that patriarchy is far from dead even in the societies which 'loudly proclaim the necessity of equal opportunity'. Sikhism as a religious system teaches that women are 'completely equal to men in all respects'. McLeod refers to the often quoted verse from the *Āsā dī Vār* which seems to uphold complete equality for women with men. Guru Amar Das took a clear stand against satī. In all respects the views of the Sikh Gurus were vastly ahead of their contemporaries.

However, Sikh history and society present 'a radically different impression'. In the first place, all the Gurus were men. Sikh history consists almost wholly of five hundred years of doings of men. Even the contemporary Sikh society and Sikh institutions are overwhelmingly male-dominated. A close examination of the teachings of the Gurus shows that they certainly conferred equal opportunity on both women and men in terms of access to spiritual liberation. A woman's place was in the home. Patriarchy was shorn of its domineering aspects but it was still intact. The equality advocated by Guru Nanak marked a considerable step forward but it did not mean 'a reordering of society'. The most that can be said is that Sikhism presents an ideal and devout Sikhs try to live up to it. Even so, if the Sikh doctrine makes women equal to men, the Sikh society provides a different picture: 'Women are institutionally subordinate to men, or at least their social status marks them as such'.

According to McLeod, the implicit recognition given to caste in the Sikh society was one reason for the firm hold of patriarchy reflected in the contemporary Sikh society. Even the *Rahitnāma*s of the eighteenth and early nineteenth centuries contained explicit prohibition of female infanticide, testifying to the practice among some members of the Panth. Hypergamy and inheritance patterns could explain its existence. It is necessary to investigate customs regarding the transfer of property by different groups within the Sikh Panth to see the influence of the ownership of land on questions of gender.

McLeod talks of Jat attitudes to gender differences. Except in rare cases, land passed to the sons of the owners. 'If land was to pass to daughters' it would mean that the daughters' husbands would have a claim on the property with the result that villages held by one Jat *got* would increasingly become the domain of several different *got*s'. A daughter's claim to a share in the family property might well be recognized, but her portion would probably be accounted for by the transfer of a dowry of cash and goods rather than property. The payment of dowry would not necessarily be the responsibility of the father alone. Uncles might also contribute. To obviate property passing out of the family, a Jat widow would be married by one of the brothers of the deceased husband. 'Land had to be retained by the immediate family if at all possible'.

McLeod comes to the conclusion that 'the sociological patterns governing the beliefs and behaviour of most Sikhs do not permit equal treatment of men and women'. Among the Jats, the issue of gender has to be decided in favour of the male. 'Women may be kindly and respectfully treated, and their lives may be rendered thoroughly satisfactory by the consideration which may be shown to them, but power rests with the males and patriarchy indisputably rules'. Talking mostly of contemporary Sikhs, McLeod visualizes four possible directions in the future: no change; a fairer and more equitable treatment to women within the patriarchal framework; greater access to public professions for women, notably in business, politics and education; overturning of patriarchy to be replaced by a completely different order. The last two possibilities would carry the Sikhs 'further than the message of the Sikh scriptures, which understandably are silent on this particular issue'. The Gurus were not confronted by any such situation. It could be argued, however, that the Gurus gave women complete equality with men in matters of ritual and in the present times the message should be extended to all aspects of Sikh society.[4]

The 'major focus' of *Relocating Gender in Sikh History: Transformation, Meaning and Identity* by Doris R. Jakobsh is construction of gender in the nineteenth and early twentieth centuries but an overview of gender formation during the Guru period is taken up for a more substantial understanding of the subject. She suggests that four principles have guided writings on women in Sikhism: silence, negation, accommodation, and idealization. In all such works, the approach to the history of women is descriptive, indicating the paucity of historical knowledge about women. The authors do not confront the issue of 'how the hierarchy of male/female, dominant/subordinate is constructed and legitimized throughout history'.[5]

Jakobsh, admittedly, is not a scripture scholar and, therefore, she relies heavily on the contributions of scripture scholars from the discipline of Sikh studies.[6] She has relied on a few secondary works and translations, notably of the Ādi Granth, the Janamsākhīs, the *Pakhyān Charitra*, and the *Chaupa Singh Rahit Nama*. According to Jakobsh, Guru Nanak maintained that women were not in any way barred from attaining enlightenment, the highest purpose of human life. However, procreation was central to his vision, especially the procreation of sons, as in the verse about the woman giving birth to rājān. Jakobsh goes on to add that by placing rājān at the top of the contemporary hierarchical order, Guru Nanak indicates his support for 'the dominant social and political order of his time'.[7] It may be pointed out that the reference to rājān is contextual: it reflects a contemporary value and carries the implication that even the rājān are not independent of women. Also, there is ample evidence to suggest that Guru Nanak denounced the political and social order of his time in very strong and clear terms.[8]

According to Jakobsh, women are often associated with *māyā* in the compositions of Guru Nanak, indicating his apprehension of the female as a barrier to the attainment of emancipation.[9] It may be pointed out that the husband is also a part of māyā and the woman is a dupe as well as a part of māyā. The view taken by Jakobsh is partial and, therefore, misleading. She goes on to say that there are negative images of women, compounded by ambivalent messages towards the outcastes: 'Evilmindedness is a low woman, cruelty a butcher's wife, a slanderous heart is a sweeper woman, wrath which ruineth the world a pariah woman'.[10] However, the images of outcaste women are used here contextually for a moral message: to regard evilmindedness, cruelty, slander, and wrath as 'untouchable'.[11]

Jakobsh observes that Guru Nanak grieved over the rape of women during the invasions of Babur but he did not show any concern about the plight of the widow, the practice of satī, or female infanticide. His silence is seen as his acceptance of the prevailing system, with the implication that he accepted women's inferiority. Thus, the 'inferiority' of women coexisted with their 'ability to attain salvation'.[12] This formulation is self-contradictory. A person who has attained liberation cannot be inferior to any other. In fact a woman who attained liberation would be superior to all men who had not.

With regard to the use of the female voice by Guru Nanak, Jakobsh observes that it means little more than a rejection of orthodoxy represented by the Dharmashastras. She appears to think that rejection is not necessarily based on a positive value. The use of female voice is also seen as indicative of Guru Nanak's elevated caste position.[13] But use of the female voice was not peculiar to individuals belonging to elevated castes. In any case, the masculine identity of God allowed by the use of female voice does not make him less accessible to women.

Formally under 'the early Guru period', Jakobsh talks only about Guru Nanak but elsewhere she refers to Guru Amar Das, Guru Ram Das, and Guru Arjan. Guru Amar Das's comment on the practice of satī is quoted: 'They are not satis who are burnt alive on the pyres; rather satīs are they who die of the blow of separation (from their husbands)'. This is seen by Jakobsh as the first instance of social criticism in Gurbāṇī 'beyond that of religious ineptitude'.[14] Her explanation is that by this time the number of Sikh men and women had increased and among them were the Khatris who generally subscribed to the ideal of satī. This does not explain, however, the emergence of a value. Dedication to a human being was futile in comparison with dedication to God.

Guru Ram Das is quoted to show that men are ridiculed when they are not dominant: 'Men obedient to their womenfolk are impure, filthy, stupid; men lustful, impure, their womenfolk counsel follow'.[15] Elsewhere in the book the verse is translated as: 'Sinful men, licentious and stupid, act as their women command. Lust abounds; thus do impure men take orders from their women and act accordingly'.[16] Guru Ram Das talks of the *manmukh* in contrast with those who act in accordance with the Guru's instruction; the sinful and ignorant men are those who listen to their women out of lust as a moral weakness, and ignore the Guru's instruction. The reference is not so general as it is made out to be. Moreover, the emphasis is on the importance of following the Guru's teaching. The statement made by Jakobsh about the increasing assertion by women in the Sikh community is based on two assumptions: one, that the number of Jats in the Sikh community had increased largely and two, that Jat women were much more assertive than the others.[17] Guru Arjan is not quoted, but he is seen as 'a regal leader' under whom the Sikhs became a separate state within the Mughal dominion. The heightened politicization of the Panth would have relegated women to positions more in line with the traditional female roles.[18] This observation is made on the assumption that women had been given a role in leadership in the time of Guru Amar Das. But the evidence to support this assumption is extremely thin and incredible.

In the Janamsākhīs there is little criticism of the society with regard to the status of women beyond Guru Nanak's disagreement with established religion and religious mores. Jakobsh herself says that the Janamsākhīs 'cannot be understood as necessarily biographical but rather as responding to the needs of the later community within which this genre developed'.[19] In other words, the compilers of the Janamsākhīs do not appear to have been seriously concerned with gender relations. But they do show concern with the basic issue: the path of liberation was open to women.

For 'the later Guru period', Jakobsh talks of the growing gulf between men and women in the Sikh Panth. The institution of the Khalsa introduced 'a novel construct of gender difference' in the development of Sikhism, transforming the ethos of the Panth from masculine to hypermasculine. This change is seen reflected in the *Pakhyān Charitra* which depicts essentially the wiles of women. In some stories women play no part and in some others they are heroic and honourable, but most of the tales relate to love, sexual intrigue, and violence. In the depiction of debauchery, women are often the seducers. The *Pakhyān Charitra*, thus, contains 'condemnation of what was understood to be implicit in womanhood'. This can be seen as the popular image of women. But women symbolize in this work 'the ultimate antithesis of the warrior-saint norm' which Guru Gobind Singh was trying to construct. 'Women had the power to turn the warrior-saint away from his true calling'.[20] But the warrior-saint was a householder who could be instructed to remain firm in marital fidelity. Jakobsh accepts the view that the *Dasam Granth*, which contained the *Pakhyān Charitra*, was held at par with the Ādi Granth. But there is no contemporary evidence to support this view. Moreover, these tales were not seen as religious in character, and not read or recited in sacred spaces.

Far more popular than the wiles of women among the Sikhs was the *Chandī dī Vār*, and the other two versions of Durga's exploits. Jakobsh does not agree with Nikki-Guninder Kaur Singh that the incorporation of the goddess was indicative of the positive Sikh attitude towards the feminine. Since the Great Mother is explicitly rejected in the Ādi Granth, Guru Gobind Singh is seen by Nikki Singh 'as an insightful artist' and not as a devotee of the goddess.[21] Jakobsh points out that the *Dasam Granth* contains the following statement: 'The sovereign deity on earth, enwrapped in all the regal pomp, to you be the victory. O you of mighty arms'.[22] Therefore, the Sikhs had the goddess in their midst in the Durga mythology but Nikki Singh does not fully explore the implications of this mythology for the Sikh tradition at large.[23] However, the goddess is rejected in the *Dasam Granth* as explicitly as in the Ādi Granth. Jakobsh is not aware of this. She leaves the impression that the tales of 'the wiles of women' were far more important than the Durga lore in the Sikh tradition. However, Guru Gobind Singh himself appears to have given great importance to Durga as God's creation. She stands bracketed with Krishan and Ram as a champion of righteous war, demonstrating an unmatched martial prowess. Moreover, their position is close to that of Guru Gobind Singh himself.[24] Jakobsh is more keen to establish Durga as an object of Sikh faith than to see her relevance for gender relations.

In the *Chaupa Singh Rahit-Nama*, according to Jakobsh, we can trace remnants of the attitudes reflected in the tales of 'the wiles of women'. However, the statements she selects indicate possibly a difference of degree and not hypermasculinity. The women were not included in the 'regular' discipline outlined for the Khalsa. They were not baptized. Anyone who administers baptism by the double-edged sword to a Sikh woman 'must offer penance'. This injunction does not imply that religious life was not open to Sikh women. In the injunctions which imply that the place of Sikh women was in the home, there is hardly any new emphasis. She is instructed to go to the *dharmsāl* twice a day but not to read the *Granth Sahib* in an assembly of Sikhs. However, she could read it in a gathering of Gursikhnīs. This suggests a sort of segregation which affirms, nonetheless, that spiritual life was open to women. The most telling injunctions cited by Jakobsh in support of her view are the notions of impurity, censured by Guru Nanak and now associated with women; penance required of a man who ate food left over by a woman; and no trust in any woman, whether one's own or another. A true Sikh should not wear red, dye his hands with henna, or apply collyrium to his eyes—all these were reserved for women. Even the male Sikhs who refused to heed the Guru's call were considered as womanly.[25] Jakobsh comes to the conclusion that the women became 'secondary' Sikhs with the ascendancy of the Khalsa. She has not analysed the Rahitnāma as a whole for gender relations. It is possible to argue that women remained respectable members of the Khalsa social order as much as of the earlier Sikh social order.

Gender in the Compositions of Guru Nanak and Guru Angad

Many verses in the compositions of Guru Nanak state the ideal of equality. God has no gender. He is in all living beings. The one who created the 'vessels' placed the same light in all. His light is in every 'heart'. God created both 'man and woman'; God's light is in both 'man and woman'. There are both female and male devotees of God.[26] Thus, at one level Guru Nanak upholds woman's equality with man.

However, God's creation is impermanent in contrast with his eternal existence; it is 'false' in contrast with God's 'truth'. The whole universe is God's māyā, 'the other play' or *dūjā khel*. It is a 'deceit', it is poison. Māyā is like an attendant in a temple dedicated to God; the man who remains devoted to the attendant never sees the Lord. The opposition between God and māyā, between truth and falsehood, is more clearly posed in another verse in which both man and woman belong to the realm of falsehood. Like many other things, there is 'pleasure in women'. Beautiful women induce men to forget God. So does the wife. The conjugal bed and beautiful women are among the objects of attachment.[27]

However, the conjugal bed is enjoyed not only by men but also by women. In a well-known verse of the 'Babur-bāṇī', the women of the ruling class suffer punishment because they had forgotten

God due to indulgence in the luxuries of this world, including the enjoyment of conjugal beds. They are the counterpart of men who suffer a similar fate for the same reason, including their enjoyment of beautiful women 'whose sight banished sleep'. The woman wishes to be beautiful and to have as much sensual pleasure as she can. The son is an object of attachment for the mother. Significantly, woman is as much a dupe of māyā as man.[28] There are unregenerated women just as there are unregenerated men. Logically, if unregenerate men can attain to liberation so can unregenerate women. Theretically, therefore, liberation is open to women as well as to men.

Guru Nanak defends women against denigration and discrimination. A longish stanza on the pandit's prejudice against the use of meat can be taken in a light most favourable to women. The verse in which he emphatically defends the woman relates to the custom of observing *sūtak*, involving the notion of pollution which is denounced in rather strong terms.[29] Not only for the indispensability of women for reproduction, womanhood per se is defended and appreciated.

Guru Nanak expresses great appreciation for the householder, and most of his metaphors come from the relationship of conjugality. He talks of the *suhagan*, the *duhagan*, and the woman in separation from her spouse. In a longish stanza the young girl is told to adorn herself with fear or *bhai* and devotion or *bhāv* to receive the love of her husband or *shauh*. Immersed in māyā due to avarice and pride, she cannot meet the spouse. If she asks the sūhagans how to meet the spouse, they would tell her to welcome whatever he does and to obey his command. She should do what he says and dedicate her body and mind to him. 'Sacrifice your "self" to attain to the Lord, for there is nothing else that works'. Auspicious is the day when he chooses her for his grace. She becomes respectable in her family when she becomes a suhagan by receiving her husband's love. Drenched in love and intoxicated with *sahaj* she is dyed in his colour to become both beautiful and wise.[30] The metaphors refer simultaneously to two parallel situations: the devotee accepting the will of God and uniting with him through his grace, and the wife dedicating herself to the husband to be enjoyed by him at will. It can be argued that the woman's subordination to her husband is reinforced. It is equally clear that she can attain liberation.

The path offered to a woman is the same as the one offered to a man. Guru Nanak is seldom so immersed in femaleness as to lose his discrete identity for long. It is easy to paraphrase his metaphors in terms of the human soul. The diction used by Guru Nanak appears to work simultaneously at two levels even when the woman expresses her pangs of separation. In many such verses it is not easy to remember that Guru Nanak is using the female voice. In a rather longish stanza in the female voice Guru Nanak dwells on the state of separation. God's grace is emphasized through the woman's total dependence on her spouse for a union. In another verse, virtue as much as grace is emphasized. Cultivation of virtues as much as grace becomes necessary for union. The woman who accepts the Guru's instruction is dear to her spouse and enjoys the peace of sahaj: she becomes suhagan by finding God as her spouse; she discards all demerit to become a *bairāgan* in search of the eternal spouse, Hari; through God's grace she is now beyond sorrow and separation. The boon of the Truth, the Name and the Shabad is obtained only through God's grace.[31]

The goal is the same for men and women. No season is good or bad in itself; without the Name there is no season of happiness. To quench the thirst, it is necessary to see the lover-God; on seeing Him the mind blossoms like the lotus in water. However, to meet Him it is necessary to have the merit of 'fear' and to recognize divine will, that is *hukam*. One cannot meet him through mere talk. The light mingles with Light only through love. To die in the service of the Lord is praiseworthy. Peace comes through meditation on the Name. The woman with merit enjoys her spouse, but the one without merit only cries in distress. When a woman loves her spouse, he too turns to her. She adorns the home when through appropriation of the Truth she is loved by her spouse. Meeting with him is an occasion for rejoicing. The sorrow of death and rebirth ends on meeting him. All desires are fulfilled.[32]

On the whole, the woman in the compositions of Guru Nanak is at par with the man in relation to God. Attached to māyā, her kith and kin, the pleasures of the senses, and a life of luxury, she is a victim of the 'five adversaries' (*kām, krodh, lobh, moh, hankār*), very much like Guru Nanak's *manmukh*, the self-willed fool of a man. She can appropriate the Truth, the Name and the Word through the mediacy of the Guru, like the Gurmukh of Guru Nanak's conception. No human being can 'achieve' or 'earn' emancipation: in the last analysis it depends on God's grace. The ultimate objective for woman as for man is sahaj, a state of eternal bliss in union with God, the mingling of light with Light.

Paradoxically, however, Guru Nanak creates spiritual space for women without discarding the inegalitarian patriarchal framework. He takes the institution of family for granted. Built into this social institution was inequality and subordination. The use of metaphors from conjugality results actually in reinforcing the institution. For the study of gender relations in the Sikh social order we have to grapple with the tension between the normative ideal of equality and the inegalitarian institution of the patriarchal family.

The *shalok*s of Guru Angad reinforce Guru Nanak's basic position. The ideal of equality is underscored. The human body, ungendered, is the *khand* which has the nine treasures of the Name. The shabad of the Guru is meant for everyone. All have only one Master, and none can be regarded as inferior. There is the same nectar within everyone; it is found through the Guru's grace. Those who appropriate the Name may receive grace. One who has the desire to meet God may find the reward for good deeds. The ideal of equality among human beings is consistently stated.[33]

Guru Angad talks of conjugal love. He talks of dedication to the beloved, and of the human frame with and without yearning for a meeting with the Master. The feet as fear, the hands as love, and the eyes as concentration may enable a wise woman to meet the spouse. There is always spring for the woman who has her spouse at home. Miserable is the woman whose spouse is in foreign lands. 'Every woman has a support of one kind or another but I have no support other than you. I cry and die if I do not lodge you in my heart'. The way to meet the spouse lies in remembering him in sorrow and comfort, all the time. The duhagan remains in misery because she is attached to some one else, and not to her spouse. The suhagan is in peace because she loves her spouse.[34] Guru Angad takes the family for granted.

There are only two other images of women in the shaloks of Guru Angad. In one, the false woman is in the forefront in the Kaliyuga, just as the mischievous man is the *chaudharī*. Both the positions infringe the ethical ideals of the Guru. In another shalok, earth is the mother, just as water is the father and air is the Guru. Bracketing the mother with the father and the Guru is not without significance. On the whole, Guru Angad appears to treat men and women alike. It is highly significant in this context that he makes the explicit statement that the *bāṇī* of Guru Nanak, unlike the Vedas, does not uphold the inequality of caste and gender.[35]

Genders in the *Vars* of Bhai Gurdas

Bhai Gurdas compares the Sikh of the Guru with a suhagan, a woman who was loved by her mother and father as a girl, treated as a beloved sister by the brothers in both the maternal and paternal families; lacs were spent on her marriage when she was loaded with ornaments and given a large dowry; she is respected in her marital home which is made honourable by her presence; she enjoys the bridal bed with her beloved husband, eating all kinds of delicious foods and always adorned with ornaments; she is rightly regarded as an equal half and the means of liberation.[36]

The Gurmukh of Bhai Gurdas is a householder. Detached-in-attachment, he becomes liberated-in-life. The house-holding Sikh of the Guru, who regards the sacred thread and the tuft as dirt, is devoted to one woman, his wife; superior to a celibate, he looks upon other women as daughters and sisters. He does not go near another woman. The Sikh of the Guru does not touch a woman other than his wife. The man who sleeps with another woman is a thief: his nose and ears are cut off. The husband of two women, like the wife of two men, remains in misery.[37] Bhai Gurdas stands clearly for monogamy and mutual fidelity.

Bhai Gurdas uses the metaphor of divorce contextually for abandoning the pleasures of the senses. He refers to a woman abandoned by her husband due to demerit. The abandoned woman is welcome nowhere. Worse than her position is that of the prostitute who entertains many men and indulges in sin; herself ruined she ruins others; her son gets no family name; she is outside the norms of the society. The prostitute adorns herself and sings to attract all and sundry; she has no husband and her son has no maternal or paternal name. The man who goes to a prostitute incurs sin and suffers from disease. The married state alone is commendable. Marriage is necessary: the Sikh of the Guru regards this world as the natal home, like the young girl who knows that she has to leave it sooner or later. Equally necessary is to beget children. He who does not go to the *sādh-sangat* is like the wife of a Raja who does not beget a child. Bhai Gurdas refers to the practice of sati for underscoring the merit of going to the sādh-sangat. Just as the family of a widow who becomes a sati is respected and honoured, so the Sikhs are respected and honoured for eradicating their *haumai* in the sādh-sangat.[38]

A few other references to women in the Vārs of Bhai Gurdas are not without interest or significance. He refers to the importance given by women to signs regarded as auspicious or inauspicious. This is not commendable. Deviation from the norm is not necessarily denounced in public by those who are closely connected with the defaulter. The mother's affection stands in her way of acknowledging in public the crime of her son who is a thief: she cries in privacy. The son dislikes his mother for having a lover but he keeps quiet; if the wife comes to know that her husband is unfaithful to her, she does not start going to other men.[39] Deviation is deplorable nonetheless.

Above all, a woman's primary obligation is towards the Guru and God. Without the perfect Guru, a beautiful woman, enjoying her conjugal bed and other pleasures of māyā, goes to hell. The only true relation in the world is that of the Sikh with the Guru, and not with the kith and kin belonging to the family of one's parents, or in-laws. People appreciate and admire the love of Laila and Majnun, Sorath and Bija, Sassi and Punnun, Mahiwal and Sohni, and Ranjha and Heer, but preferable over these is the love of the Sikh for God. The husband and wife, engrossed in mutual love but forgetful of God would suffer in the end.[40]

Bhai Gurdas takes it for granted that women could be redeemed through devotion to God. In an hour of crisis, Daropati invoked the aid of Krishan and he saved her from the dishonour of being disrobed. Gautam's wife Ahaliya succumbed to Indra's lustful attention. He was cursed, and she too was turned into a statue of stone. Lying on the bank of a stream, she was touched by the foot of Raghupati and went to heaven. Even a sinful prostitute went to heaven in the process of teaching a parrot to utter the name of Ram.[41] Like the outcaste men, outcaste women may receive God's grace. The sādh-sangat of Bhai Gurdas was not confined to men. The term 'Sikh' applies equally to men and women.

Reflection of Gender Relations in the *B40 Janamsākhī* and the *Chaupa Singh Rahit-Nama*

About a hundred years later, the *B40 Janamsākhī* makes it unambiguously explicit that the path enunciated by Guru Nanak was open to women. It is obvious that in the early eighteenth century, the Sikhs were familiar with the presence of women in the sangat. In the sākhī of Raja Shivnabh the courtesans are so affected by the bāṇī of Guru Nanak that their meeting with him becomes the source of *brahm-giān*; they start reciting 'Guru, Guru' and become intoxicated with the love of God; they tell Raja Shivnabh that henceforth he would be like their father, and that they and their generations have been liberated by a Great Man. In the sākhī of Guru Nanak's visit to a country inhabited by women, they use their magical powers to turn Mardana into a ram but they are powerless against Guru Nanak. Impressed by his spiritual power, they wish that their country too should have men. They are blessed by Guru Nanak and they gain peace. They begin to recite the name of God. Another sākhī visualizes a dharmsāl close to the palace of a Raja whose wife is the daughter of a Sikh. They visit the dharmsāl and the sangat performs an *ardās* for the birth of a son. Eventually, the Raja also becomes a Sikh. In another sākhī, Guru Nanak praises the women who recite the name of God. In yet another sākhī, the father, the mother, and the son are praised as good Sikhs; the term used for the mother is *sikhnī*.[42]

Turning to the *Chaupa Singh Rahit-Nama* it is interesting to note that it contains injunctions for three categories of Sikhs: the *keshdhārī* Singhs, the *sahajdhārī* Sikhs, and the Sikh women. They all belong to the Sikh or Khalsa community. They are not supposed to have any association with the Miṇas, Dhir Mallias, Ram Raiyas, the Masands, and their followers. Only the keshdhārīs among the Khalsa are baptized through the rite of the double-edged sword.

Injunctions with regard to women are scattered in the *Rahit-Nama*. The Sikh of the Guru is instructed not to have any association with a woman other than his wife. This injunction is repeated several times. A Sikh of the Guru must get married. He should never kill a girl child and should not associate with those who resort to this practice. This injunction too is repeated several times. A Sikh of the Guru should never receive any money for giving away his daughter in marriage. He should not give his daughter in marriage to a *mona* (clean shaven). But he may marry the daughter of a mona, initiating her through the baptism of the Granth Sahib. A Sikh who does not have the means to perform the marriage of his daughter to a Sikh should be helped. There should be no female quarters in a dharmsāl. A Sikh in the service of the state was exempt from all but three obligations: he should not smoke, should not observe *bhaddan* (which involved shaving of the head), and he should not kill a girl child. A Sikh of the Guru should not trust any woman; should never share a secret with her. A woman should be seen as a betrayer of secrets. In support of this injunction a verse of Guru Ram Das is quoted. This verse, as we noted earlier, actually talks of a man who listens to his wife rather than to the Guru. Since the opening lines of this verse do not indicate the context, the import is missed by the author of the *Rahit-Nama* (like Jakobsh). A Sikh of the Guru, or a Sikhnī, should wash his or her hands for kneading dough. They should not allow fingernails to grow long, and should not speak while kneading. To be afraid of a woman other than one's wife is praiseworthy like the conjugality of a good woman, the family of a good woman, and service of one's mother and father. A Sikh who goes to a Muslim prostitute and enjoys the dance performance of a prostitute at the time of marriage is a defaulter. Liable to corrective punishment would be a Sikh who administers baptism by the double-edged sword to a woman. A Sikh woman should not read Granth Sahib in a *darbār* of Sikhs; she should only listen. But a Sikh woman could read Granth Sahib in a gathering of Sikh women. An unwedded woman giving birth to a child is a sign of Kaliyuga.[43]

Apart from these scattered injunctions with regard to gender, there are injunctions addressed explicitly to Sikh women at one place. Some of these injunctions have been noticed by Jakobsh. A Gursikhnī should not abuse or berate a man; she should not fight with men. A Gursikhnī should sustain a docile and dutiful disposition, and regard her husband as her lord. Other male relatives should be treated like father, brother, or son, in accordance with their age and position. A Gursikhnī should not prepare or serve food if she is not clean. A Gursikhnī should not keep the company of men other than those of her own family, and she should not sit with women to exchange gossip. Most of the injunctions are on the whole what may be called the counterpart of the injunctions meant for men. A Gursikhnī should not bathe naked; she should not stand naked in water and cast it towards the sun. Both the water and the sun are like her father. A Gursikhnī should sit in a *satsang* with her head covered. A Gursikhnī should learn how to read the Granth and she should abandon singing of popular or vulgar songs. A Gursikhnī should instruct her husband in the Sikh faith. The men of the Kaliyuga have a weakness for women. Therefore, the instruction imparted by a Sikhnī is more effective. A Gursikhnī should serve better food to a Sikh in need than to a member of her own family. A Gursikhnī should learn portions of the Guru's scripture by heart. Twice a day she should visit a dharmsāl and pay homage to the Granth Sahib. She should weave cloth with the cotton she has herself spun and, depending upon her resources, offer it either as a wrapping-cloth for the Guru Granth Sahib or as a covering for the floor. A Gursikhni should set aside a handful of flour from the family's daily supply and offer it to the Guru by giving it either to dharmsāl or to a needy Sikh. The True Guru shares the satisfaction when a Gursikh has food to eat.

A Gursikhnī should always ensure that she has cleaned herself. She should keep herself physically pure and avoid those actions which defile. She should cleanse herself with water and fresh earth, before cooking. While kneading dough, or cooking food, in the cooking square she should refrain from talking in order to avoid emission of spittle. While preparing food, a Gursikhnī should wash her hands after clearing her nose or scratching her body. Small children should not be brought into the cooking area; they should be carefully watched until the food is ready. A Gursikhnī should neither attend the mourning observed by any one of the five proscribed groups nor should she exchange gifts with them.

When ceremonies requiring giving of gifts are held in her own home she should make an offering at the dharmsāl. She should not indulge in ridicule, mockery, or coarse songs at weddings. The songs of nuptial blessing which she sings should be wholesome. A Gursikhnī should bathe, or perform the five ablutions, before reciting the Guru's mantra. She should not pray at tombs and cenotaphs. She should accept only the guidance of the Guru and believe in none but the Guru, her husband, and the true congregation. She must sustain loyalty towards her husband and look for no other. This is her true duty, made clear by the Granth Sahib. Let her be dutiful, cooperative, wise, virtuous, careful of reputation, and kind-hearted.

The injunctions of Chaupa Singh's Rahitnāma are meant for Gursikhs and Gursikhnīs as equally important components of the Khalsa Panth. The essential message for both is that birth as a human being is a gift of rare value; it should not be senselessly squandered.[44]

Gender Relations in the *Prem Sumārg*

Jakobsh refers to the Rahitnāma known as the *Prem Sumārg* but she does not use its evidence, presumably because it was not yet translated into English. The author of this work may appear to take a very dim view of women when he states that they have low intelligence; they do not know what is good or bad for them; their essence is obstinacy which is the source of all good or bad they do. The woman has a much greater sexual urge than the man. Even a mother should not sleep in the same room as her grown up son. However, this traditional or popular view of the woman is used to argue that if a man cannot live without a wife, how can a woman live without a husband? Therefore, a widow should be allowed to get remarried if she cannot control her sexual urge. Not only a widow who is childless but also a widow who does not have any surviving children may get remarried. But the widow who has a daughter or a son should not remarry.[45] Though guardedly, the author of the *Prem Sumārg* does advocate the necessity of remarriage for a widow who has no son or daughter.

Common injunctions for men and women are the most striking features of the *Prem Sumārg*. It is explicitly stated that whoever follows the *rahit*, whether man or woman, shall receive the reward in this life. The first chapter relates to religious beliefs and practices and the second, to *nām*, *dān*, and the *sikhī* of Akal Purkh Ji. Not only men but also women, both suhagans and widows, are initiated into the Khalsa Panth through baptism by the double-edged sword. They are expected to acquire learning in Gurmukhi and to read and love shabad-bānī. They should gather together and reflect on the shabad.[46]

The rites and ceremonies to be performed at the birth of a daughter are similar to those to be performed at the birth of a son. The female child, like the male, is to be administered baptism by the double-edged sword. At one place a girl is to be married at a young age to a poor but good and earnest Khalsa; at another place, she is to be married at the age of seventeen years into a superior family. The author is keen to emphasize that considerations of caste and status are a temporary compromise. There are no distinctions among the Khalsa of Sri Guru Akal Purkh Ji: they all belong to one and the same caste, and shall become one in the future. The author talks of 'Khalsa Sikhnīs'.[47] There is hardly any doubt that the woman is an equal member of the Khalsa Panth for the author of the *Prem Sumārg*.

There is no prohibition against marrying a girl from another caste, or a slave girl, or even the daughter of a *mlechh*. The wife is expected to remain physically clean and to adorn herself; the injunction with regard to sexual intercourse carries the implication that it is meant for procreation. The author visualizes a part of the house used exclusively by women. The rites after death for women of all ages are similar to those for men: common to both are kīrtan and ardās.[48]

In the Sikh state visualized by the author of the *Prem Sumārg*, no one should remain unmarried. The parties to adultery should be publicly humiliated. The quarters of the prostitutes should be clearly marked and separated from others. Between adultery and going to the prostitute, the latter was preferable. The prostitute sells her body voluntarily and her heirs also consent to the practice. Association with the prostitute amounts in fact to half a marriage. The best thing is to avoid both. The ruler of the Sikh state should give greater attention and consideration to the householders.[49]

There are special injunctions for the Maharaja of the Sikh state. He should marry one woman and have no association with any other. If he finds the woman unsuitable for any reason, he may marry another woman. If the wife does not give birth to a male child, the Maharaja may marry several women in turn. But the preferable position is to have only one wife. To be content with one wife is to be a celibate. In the absence of the wife, the Maharaja may have sexual intercourse with a slave girl, but only if he is overpowered by sexual urge. It is a bad thing to do, but it is better than adultery. The maid-servants in the Maharaja's palace should preferably be married women. The life of an unmarried woman is a veritable hell. Only that woman should stay single, whether a virgin or a widow, who can subdue and control her sexual urge.[50]

If a man dies without a son, his property should go to his daughter or her son or daughter. If there is no daughter either, it should go to his sister.[51] The idea of a daughter or sister's right to property in certain situations was a radical one in the context of the times.

The *Prem Sumārg* clearly negates Jakobsh's hypothesis of increasing differentiation between men and women after the institution of the Khalsa. In the ideal Sikh social order the woman is not exactly at par with the man. But the degree of equality between Khalsa men and Khalsa women makes them far more equal than the empirical realities.

The degree of equality postulated by the author appears to come from Sikh ideology.

Notes

1. J.S. Grewal, *Guru Nanak in History*, Chandigarh: Panjab University, 1998 (rpt), pp. 55–7.
2. Ibid., pp. 55–7.
3. Kapur Singh, *Parasharprashna: An Enquiry into the Genesis and Unique Character of the Order of the Khalsa with an Exposition of the Sikh Tenets*, Piar Singh and Madanjit Kaur, eds, Amritsar: Guru Nanak Dev University, 1989, pp. 251–2.
4. W.H. McLeod, *Sikhism*, Harmondsworth: Penguin Books, 1997, pp. 241–50.
5. Doris R. Jakobsh, *Relocating Gender in Sikh History: Transformation, Meaning and Identity*, New Delhi: Oxford University Press, 2003, pp. 1–21.
6. Ibid., p.4.
7. Ibid., pp. 24–5.
8. Grewal, *Guru Nanak in History*, pp. 151–65.
9. Jakobsh, *Relocating Gender*, p. 25.
10. Ibid., pp. 25–6.
11. Grewal, *Guru Nanak in History*, pp. 190–2.
12. Jakobsh, *Relocating Gender*, p. 26.
13. Ibid., pp. 26–7.
14. Ibid., p. 29.
15. Ibid., p. 12.
16. Ibid., p. 34.
17. Jakobsh accepts W.H. McLeod's view that militancy in the Sikh Panth resulted from the very induction of martial and armed Jats into the Panth. She assumes equality between Jat men and Jat women, which made the Sikh women assertive. There is no credible evidence to support these assumptions.
18. Jakobsh, *Relocating Gender in Sikh History*, pp. 35–6.
19. Ibid., pp. 27–9.
20. Ibid., pp. 44–5.
21. Numerous verses in Guru Granth Sahib reject belief in the Goddess.
22. Numerous verses in the *Dasam Granth* reject belief in the Goddess.
23. Jakobsh, *Relocating Gender in Sikh History*, pp. 15–16.
24. The common features of the *Krishan Avtār*, *Ram Avtār*, *Chandī di Vār* and the autobiographical *Bachittar Nātak* are: aligning with the good, using physical force, demonstrating martial prowess.

25. Jakobsh, *Relocating Gender in Sikh History*, pp. 46–8.
26. Ādi Granth, pp. 13, 19, 62, 223, 228, 580, 663, 879.
27. Ibid., pp. 14–15, 72, 142, 222, 229, 351, 416, 468, 728, 1,288.
28. Ibid., pp. 417, 596, 1,187.
29. Ibid., pp. 472, 1,289–90.
30. Ibid., pp. 225, 730, 772, 1,329, 1,332.
31. Ibid., pp. 54, 557, 843, 1,232.
32. For the foregoing paragraphs, J.S. Grewal, *Guru Nanak and Patriarchy*, Shimla: Indian Institute of Advanced Study, 1993.
33. Sahib Singh, ed., *Slok Guru Angad Sahib Steek*, Amritsar: Singh Brothers, 1992 (rpt), pp. 59, 78, 114, 117, 121, 124.
34. Ibid., pp. 51, 57, 96, 99–100, 127.
35. Ibid., pp. 62, 130.
Significantly, a *shalok* of Guru Angad contains a general statement on gender. Guru Angad refers to the Vedic tradition with its ideas of good and bad actions, the doctrine of karma, transmigration, the concept of hell and heaven, and inequalities based on caste and gender. By contrast there are no such illusions in the bāṇī of Guru Nanak. Ibid., p. 122.
36. Bhai Gurdas, *Vārān Bhai Gurdas*, Giani Hazara Singh, ed., Amritsar: Khalsa Samachar, 1962, *Vār* 5, *pauṛī* 16.
37. Ibid., Vār 6, pauṛīs 8, 12, 18; Vār 12, pauṛī 4; Vār 33, pauṛīs 3, 7.
38. Ibid., Vār3, pauṛī 19; Vār5, pauṛī 17; Vār 17; pauṛī 10; Vār 19, pauṛī 7; Vār 31, pauṛī 14; Vār 33, pauṛī 9; Vār 34, pauṛī 6; Vār 35, pauṛī 13.
39. Ibid., Vār 5, pauṛī 8; Vār 30, pauṛī 14; Vār 34, pauṛī 14.
40. Ibid., Vār 15, pauṛī 7; Vār 29, pauṛī 7; Vār 35, pauṛī 20.
41. Ibid., Vār 10, pauṛīs 8, 18, 21; Vār 27, pauṛī 1.
42. *Janamsakhi Sri Guru Nanak Dev Ji*, Piar Singh, ed., Amritsar: Guru Nanak Dev University, 1974, pp. 57–8, 78–9, 109–10, 132–3.
43. W.H. McLeod, ed. and tr., *Chaupa Singh Rahit–Nama*, Dunedin: University of Otago, 1987, pp. 59–60, 66–7, 69, 75, 77–8, 105, 111, 113, 127.
44. Ibid., pp. 188–90.
45. Bhai Randhir Singh, ed., *Prem Sumārg Granth*, Jalandhar: New Book Company 1965, pp. 46–8, 84, 85.
46. Ibid., pp. 8, 17, 20–1.
47. Ibid., pp. 25, 27, 41, 43–4, 49.
48. Ibid., pp. 56–7, 74–5, 77, 86–90.
49. Ibid., pp. 108–10.
50. Ibid., pp. 121–2.
51. Ibid., pp. 126, 131.

PART V
New Socio-cultural Orientations

10. Contest over the Sacred Space

British Presence in Amritsar

Writing historical and descriptive sketches of the places of interest for tourists and administrators, David Ross took notice of Amritsar as the largest and wealthiest city of the Punjab, next to Delhi in population but second to none in commercial or political importance. It was the holy city of the Sikhs in the same way as Benares was of the Hindus, Mecca of the Muslims, or Jerusalem of the Jews and Christians. What made the city so sacred was the Darbar Sahib, called the Golden Temple. Among the many objects of interest in its precincts was the Bunga of the Akalis which treasured the weapons of the Gurus, was the place of rest at night for the Granth Sahib, and served as the baptistery of the Sikhs.[1] Close to the Golden Temple was the Guru's Garden or *Guru kā Bāgh* and the tank called Kaulsar. A dip in Kaulsar was regarded by the pilgrims as a necessary prelude to a bath in the tank of the Golden Temple. Another sacred tank was Santokhsar.

In the Golden Temple, a service was kept up before the Granth Sahib all day by singers and instrumentalists. The people cast votive offerings in front of the Granth Sahib. All Sikhs rested their foreheads on the ground, and kissed its threshold. Everything connected with the Granth Sahib and the Darbar Sahib was held in veneration. Among the curious sights on the pavement around the Golden Temple were comb-makers, sellers of steel ornaments, writers of Sikh books, Hindu bathers and *faqīr*s.

The city of Amritsar was changing. David Ross refers to the 'English station', the British cantonment, and the railway station outside the walled city of Amritsar. Within the walled city were the Town Hall, the Hall Bazar, the government school, and the Mission school. Close to the Ram Bagh Gate was the City Mission House and the Normal School of the Christian Vernacular Education Society. The strong wall of the city had been replaced by a new one, with some new gates, and the old moat had been filled up. The fort of Gobindgarh was occupied by a battery of British artillery. Though the old gateway, corner towers, palace, and pleasure houses of Ram Bagh were still standing, its wall had been nearly all pulled down and its central building was used as the station library and reading room. The old *dhāb*s in the city were filled up and converted into public gardens. There were new rulers and a new kind of administration in the city. David Ross does not say anything about the new administration, or its bearing on the control and management of the Darbar Sahib.[2]

British Anxiety to Retain Control over the Darbar Sahib and the Akal Takht

The city of Amritsar was exceptionally important for the British administration. Robert Montgomery, Judicial Commissioner of the Punjab, observed in 1858 that Amritsar was to the Sikhs what Mecca was to the Muslims and Benares to the Hindus. He went on to add, 'On Amritsar, as the pivot, might be said to turn the loyalty of the Khalsa'. Montgomery's successor, E. Thornton, stated in 1859 that though crime and vice was prevalent in the temples of Mathura, the government did not like to have any control over them. But, 'were we to abstain equally from surveillance over the Amritsar institution' it would lead to 'dangerous political intrigue'. The Commissioner of Lahore, Robert Needham Cust, whose Christian conscience allowed little room for official association with non-Christian religious institutions, admitted nonetheless that there was a difference between the affairs of 'an effete and purely ceremonial worship, such as that of the Hindus, which had no political significance or aims, and those of the high spirited and excitable Khalsa, where nationality and religion have been cemented together by the uncontrolled enjoyment of power and wealth'.[3]

Evidently, the political importance of the Darbar Sahib made its control a matter of exceptional importance to the British administrators. The Namdhari leader, Baba Ram Singh was interned in his village in 1863 so that Amritsar should become inaccessible to him. Even in 1879 it was thought that the 'Kuka militancy' might have taken a dangerous turn if the Darbar Sahib had been the centre of the movement. This official view carried the implication that the government should control such movements 'by retaining its influence over the Darbar Sahib'.[4]

The British administrators had taken over the control and management of the Darbar Sahib as a matter of routine when they took over the administration of the dominions of Ranjit Singh's successors. The Treaty of Bhairowal, imposed by the British on the minor Maharaja Dalip Singh on 22 December 1846, empowered the British Resident at Lahore 'to direct and control the duties of every department'.[5] The existing arrangements for the management of the Darbar Sahib were allowed to continue. However, Henry Lawrence, the British Resident at Lahore, began to take decisions with regard to the matters of state allowances for the Darbar Sahib, its revenue-free lands, and the *jāgīr*s of its functionaries in 1847.[6] The short phase before the annexation provided a smooth transition from the Sikh to the British regime in 1849.

The first manager of the Golden Temple, Sardar Jodh Singh, had held various positions during the time of Ranjit Singh and his successors. After the Anglo-Sikh War of 1845-6 he was posted at Amritsar as a judicial officer (*'adālatī'*) and he supported the British during the Anglo-Sikh War of 1848-9. He was appointed Extra Assistant Commissioner at Amritsar, primarily to manage the affairs of the Darbar Sahib. A General Committee was appointed, with Raja Tej Singh as its President, to oversee the affairs of the Golden Temple. However, the real power was exercised by Sardar Jodh Singh as the executive officer. He listened more to the British authorities than to the president of the General Committee. He handled all cases related to the Golden Temple. He could fine the *pujārī*s for misconduct and exclude them from the precincts for up to six months. He supervised the fiscal arrangements of the Darbar Sahib which had come down from the Sikh times.[7]

After 1857-8, some of the British administrators began to object to the management of non-Christian religious institutions by the British administration. John Lawrence, the Chief Commissioner of the Punjab, circulated an order on 25 August 1858 against interference in disputes involving religious institutions. This order contained the instruction that British officers 'will have nothing to do with the management or administration of these institutions'. It went on to add that the people must manage their own religious institutions. 'If such institutions suffer from internal disputes, that is their business, not ours'.[8] R.N. Cust, the Commissioner of Amritsar Division, took this circular order of the Chief Commissioner seriously and planned 'gradually to withdraw from executive control' of the Golden Temple. He initiated a preliminary enquiry into its affairs. He mentioned his intentions casually to Raja Tej Singh, and a few days later he received instructions not to make any changes.[9] Tej Singh, evidently, had expressed his concern to the higher authorities.

It was made clear to Cust that the Darbar Sahib was not an ordinary religious institution. It was assuredly a case to which 'abstract principles must be applied with caution and moderation'. Among other things, Cust appeared to have felt exercised over the free supply of canal water to the sacred tank. The issue of the canal water was sensitive from the Sikh point of view. Therefore, he was ordered not to introduce any change. But he was told to continue his enquiry into the affairs of the Darbar Sahib.[10]

The Lieutenant Governor was keen on a thorough investigation into the affairs of the Darbar Sahib for another reason. The functionaries of the Golden Temple had resorted to litigation with regard to shares of assignment from the offerings made by the worshippers. Some sensation had already been caused among the Sikhs by the action meditated by Cust. To prevent further dissatisfaction, it was necessary 'to define clearly the arrangements by which the future management of the Darbar is to be regulated'. The government should not stand aloof and wait till the peace was broken, blood was shed, and a spirit was evoked 'of which no man can predict the consequences'. The Lieutenant Governor suggested, in fact, that the administration should be able to mediate between the contending parties so that 'the first beginnings of strife may be allayed'. This was to be done without assuming direct management and control.[11]

On 15 September 1859, Frederic Cooper, the Deputy Commissioner of Amritsar, wrote to the Commissioner that he had completed the enquiries and worked out an arrangement. A 'convocation' had been held at Amritsar on 4 September. Apart from Raja Tej Singh, who was assisted by Rai Mul Singh, there were other chiefs and gentlemen of rank, including Sardar Shamsher Singh Sandhanwalia, Sardar Dyal Singh Majithia, and Bhai Parduman Singh. The representatives and principal shareholders of all the 'colleges' and shrines attended the convocation every day.[12]

Rai Mul Singh, 'as the man of the greatest capacity', had been thoroughly acquainted with the views of the Christian government. He was told that this government 'dealt with, and legislated for society and not for religions; it was interested in the preservation of social order, not in the maintenance of heathen shrines'. The law was ready for prompt punishment of any outrage on 'the sanctity of a peaceful institution'. The government was prepared to sanction 'the ejection from office in a shrine of the scandalous or the profligate member'. The anxiety of the Deputy Commissioner was to secure unanimity among the arbitrators and full acquiescence among the disputants for the award. Rai Mul Singh made masterly arrangements to ensure that no Sardar was moved by a sense of personal prestige and honour.

There were two objectives of the meeting: to ascertain and define the exact right and privileges of each class belonging to or connected with the religious institutions, and, after oral deliberations and consultation of recorded facts and traditional usages, to draw up an administrative paper comprehending all points for the guidance of civil courts in the future adjudication of suits connected with these institutions; to decide how far the government could withdraw from direct internal management, so as to reduce its interference to a minimum needed for preserving law and order. With regard to the second point, the whole management of the public works, beautifying the edifice, and the custody of accounts was proposed to be shifted from the hands of the government officer to those of a private individual, Bhai Parduman Singh, son of Bhai Gurmukh Singh, who had held the same office in the time of Ranjit Singh and his successors. By doing so, half of the difficulty was believed to have been solved and there was a general acquiescence in his choice.

As to the first point, the most difficult issue was that of proprietary titles. While the Sardars held opposing views on this issue, there were four dangerous and turbulent pujārīs whose 'fanatic agitation' could make unanimity difficult. Ultimately, the Deputy Commissioner pointed to the views of the government in a particular circular of April 1859 and hinted that 'excommunication was within their power', with the implication that the pujārīs could uphold or impose their views in religious matters. All signatures were affixed to the award on 12 September 1859. The services of Raja Tej Singh and Sardar Shamsher Singh were appreciated. Rai Mul Singh was appreciated for displaying 'admirable tact, temper and ability'. Indeed, he was 'the master-spirit of the occasion'.[13] Rai Mul Singh, more than the old Raja Tej Singh, was the tool used by Cooper.

Appreciating Cooper for the manner in which he had conducted the delicate matter of 'the great Sikh temple', Cust conceded that 'at least a great practical advance has been achieved'. The new arrangements could work well for a decade. He was hoping that by then 'we may be enabled to withdraw entirely' as it had been done at Benares, Mathura, and other places. He also explained the grounds of his objection to the old arrangements. The government official was called upon not merely to perform the routine duties of preserving peace and order but also to take interest in the welfare of the institution. This contributed towards its respectability and stability. In Cust's view, it was 'neither right nor expedient for the government to contribute to the permanency and credit of the Sikh *panth*'; to do so was politically dangerous and morally wrong. Cust believed that, unsupported by the state, the Golden Temple would be plundered by its own guardians and fall to ruins; the Panth founded by Baba Nanak would cease to exist; the nucleus of nationality created by Guru Gobind Singh would be dispersed. The active proselytizing Sikh would fall back into the ranks of 'the lethargic and unaspiring Hindu'.[14] Cust's objection was based essentially on the principle that a government official should not be employed directly or indirectly in the management of any temple or shrine. He liked to believe that the policy he advocated would result in the decline of the Khalsa.

In Cust's view, litigation among the functionaries of the Darbar Sahib was due to the absence of a law of inheritance. Therefore, he emphasized that some rule 'must be laid down for settling the law of inheritance'. Cooper's report was 'an advance in the right direction', but Cust suggested that no suits of the pujārīs and other 'servants' should be admitted to the civil courts. A *panchāyat* presided over by the Manager could take up such cases for adjudication once in a year. Interference of the executive should be reduced to the minimum and it should be entirely of a police character. The tank should continue to be filled with canal water and the expense charged to the municipal fund as a matter of conservancy, and for the convenience of the bathers. Cust could not approve of the practice of devoting municipal funds to 'illuminations of the tank on the occasion of Sikh festivals'. The moral effect of such practices was extremely bad. In any case, the Darbar Sahib had its own income from jāgīrs and offerings. Cust expected Bhai Parduman Singh to receive a *sanad* as manager, and to be installed by the members of the Sikh Committee to whom Sardar Jodh Singh was expected to surrender his accounts, and his charge.[15]

Thornton agreed with Cust in approving Cooper's major recommendations. According to these, the proprietary title was 'solemnly negatived'. The duties of a government servant in connection with the Darbar Sahib were explained as 'purely magisterial', limited to control over the appointment and dismissal of menial offices and 'totally unconnected with the establishment in its religious character'. The officer was to be present once a year at the distribution of the collective offerings. No one but a Hindu or Sikh of the repute and probity of Sardar Jodh Singh was to be entrusted with these duties. The direct connection with 'this great central Sikh shrine' was thus resolved into 'simple magisterial and political control'. Watch had to be kept 'against national intrigues within the dark labyrinths and crowded porticos of the surrounding Bungas'. Therefore, the Extra Assistant in charge was enabled to hear reports of the arrival of any strangers at the tank. The provisions made in the 'administration paper' solemnly ratified by the convocation were final. Questions of civil rights could be decided by 'a Christian judge without reference to a Sikh opinion'. The Extra Assistant in charge could change no old procedure, nor could he institute any new observance; he could influence 'no new sect', initiate no novice, and induct no new reader.[16]

With reference to Cust's suggestion that the pujārīs and other servants of the Darbar Sahib should be excluded from the civil courts, Thornton remarked that most of them were allowed 'a right of occupancy' on the condition of good behaviour. Moreover, their exclusion would be contrary to the spirit of the orders issued by John Lawrence on 25 August 1858. With regard to Cust's suggestion for providing no municipal funds for illumination at the tank, Thornton felt that if it was an old practice he would not like to stop it now, whatever the merit of the case otherwise. He went on to add that the Sikh chiefs, and others connected with the Darbar Sahib, had exerted themselves to carry out the aims of the government at some sacrifice of their personal views. To discontinue any established practice at this time would be considered by them as 'an ungenerous return'. This was a reference to the support received by the administration from the Sikhs during the uprising of 1857–8. The Lieutenant Governor approved of the settlement.[17]

THE ADMINISTRATIVE MANUAL OF 1859

The administration paper, called *Dastūr al-'Amal*, underscores that 'the sole proprietor of this sacred institution for ever is Guru Ram Das'. No other person has 'any title to proprietorship'. The claim to the 'noviciate or chelaship' belonged to the whole body of the Khalsa. It is important to note that the right of the collective body of the Khalsa to the Darbar Sahib was thus unambiguously recognized. This recognition, among other things, would enable the Akalis in the 1920s to claim the right to control and manage the affairs of the Darbar Sahib. The pujārīs and others were to receive 'wages' for 'service performed'.

There were four grades of those who performed service for the Darbar Sahib. In the first grade were the Granthīs who were entitled to receive the proceeds of several jāgīrs recorded in their names. They could also receive personal offerings and a share in the offerings to the Darbar Sahib. In the second grade were the pujārīs who looked after the offerings, the maintenance of the accounts, and other minor offices. They received a certain fixed allowance in perpetuity out of the total collections. In the third grade were rabābīs and rāgīs who had fifteen fixed shares or *chaukī*s in all, eight for the rāgīs and seven for the rabābīs. Their names make it absolutely clear that Hindus and Muslims were included among them. In the fourth grade were bell-strikers, treasurers, key-keepers, *munshī*s, gardeners, pālkī-bearers, *khalāsī*s and others. They received certain salaries from the collections. Their appointment and dismissal was to be controlled by 'the *Sarbrah*' on report from the pujārīs.

The pujārīs now desired that 'they may receive exactly in accordance with the rules of Maharaja Ranjit Singh'. Keeping in view the practice of Maharaja Ranjit Singh, it was laid down that 'after payment of the full ten months' wages to the Rabābīs, Rāgīs and others, and defrayment of the necessary expenses, the balance, more or less, should be distributed over the six *pattī*s of the pujārī shareholders according to their several shares on condition of good behaviour. As to the rights of the Rabābīs and Rāgīs, it was clear that they were entitled to ten months' pay on condition of good behaviour in perpetuity, but subject to small traditional deductions. They were to perform their functions daily. In special circumstances, an absence of fifteen days could be allowed to them by the Sarbrah. They had to provide a substitute for these days.[18]

The convocation was unanimous that the affairs of the Darbar Sahib could never be conducted peacefully without the support of the government. Furthermore, the management of the temple was closely allied with the reputation of the government. A responsible authority must keep an eye on bad characters. An upright and honourable 'Sikh or Hindu' should perform this duty.[19]

Despite the proposal to indict Bhai Parduman as Manager after the settlement of 12 September 1859, Sardar Jodh Singh continued to function as the Sarbrah till his retirement in 1862.[20] He was succeeded by Sardar Mangal Singh Ramgarhia, apparently on the recommendation of a council of an informal nature as in 1859. An irregular executive commission was formed in 1874 to assist Sardar Mangal Singh in the management of the Darbar Sahib. On his death in 1879, Sardar Man Singh was made the Sarbrah. The state of affairs at the beginning of his tenure is briefly described in an official memorandum of 1880. His power was limited to the settlement of petty questions and disputes; he was invested with the powers of a second class magistrate to decide petty criminal cases that arose within the precincts of the Darbar Sahib. Through a *dārogha*, Sardar Man Singh collected all the revenues of the Darbar Sahib, whether from offerings, rents of houses, or money realized from contracts to supply flowers and the like. He deducted the annual expenditure, amounting to about Rs 8, 600, and the *haqq-i malikāna-i Guru*, or three per cent on the offerings; the balance was then paid to the pujārīs according to the scale fixed in 1859. The income from rent and haqq-i malikāna was spent on the embellishment of the Golden Temple.[21]

Expediency Preferred over Legality

The Government of India Act XX of 1863 did not allow the kind of arrangement made for the control and management of the Darbar Sahib. It required the provincial governments to appoint trustees to whom powers and responsibilities for the management of religious institutions could be transferred and who would thereafter be self-perpetuating, and liable to be sued for mismanagement or neglect of duty. Except as provided in this Act, no provincial government or officer could superintend any property or take any part in the management or appropriation of any endowment made to a religious institution. In short, no provincial government or officer could in any way be concerned with a religious institution.[22] The administrators of Punjab were aware of the illegality of the arrangements made for the Darbar Sahib but they were not prepared to change them.

Problems arose from time to time but they were generally shelved. The *Dastūr al-'Amal* did not put an end to disputes among the functionaries of the Darbar Sahib, or even between them and the Manager. In 1871, the Punjab Chief Court commissioned the Raja of Jind to prepare a new administration paper as the result of a suit launched by some pujārīs. The Raja observed that the income of the Darbar Sahib had become insufficient to meet the expenses. He suggested, therefore, that its resources should be increased. The Punjab government refused to increase the revenues on the plea that its income was ample if economically managed.[23] Actually, the government could not become a patron of the institution. There was a basic difference between the British and the Sikh rulers on this point.

In 1877, a different kind of issue came to the surface. A regiment of Mazhabi Sikhs was stationed at Amritsar. Some of the soldiers came with members of their families to bathe in the *sarovar* and discovered that a certain section of the sarovar was reserved for them for a certain time of the day. They protested. The European officers of the regiment were annoyed at the second class treatment given to their men. The civil administrators commented on the contradiction between the egalitarian tenets of Sikhism and discrimination against the Mazhabis. They attributed this to 'the more bigoted or more Brahmanized of the leading Sikhs connected with the temple management'.[24] The Commissioner of Amritsar suggested that the issue of the Mazhabi Sikhs could be referred to a committee of trustees constituted in accordance with the Act of 1863. The Lieutenant Governor, Sir Robert Egerton, ruled that the Mazhabi issue, being religious, could not be taken up by the government. In any case, the Darbar Sahib had 'great political importance' and it was necessary for the government to keep in its hands 'both the appointment of chief manager and that of receiver and administrator of the jāgīr funds'.[25] Political considerations were far more important than issues of legality or constitutionality.

In June 1879, the officiating Judicial Assistant at Amritsar, dismissed the case against one Mansukh Rai who occupied a house that belonged to the Akal Bunga, on the argument that Sardar Man Singh, the Manager of the Darbar Sahib, did not have any legal status under the Religious Endowment Act XX of 1863, or even otherwise.[26] The Punjab administration thought of legalizing its position. The Secretary to the Punjab government, Lepel Griffin, wrote to the Home Department that in special cases the provincial administration might be enabled to retain the control of a religious institution 'in such a manner and such a degree as may be considered expedient'. He underscored the great political and religious importance of the Golden Temple and its centrality in Sikh affairs. It was necessary to ensure that the men who managed the affairs of the Golden Temple should be 'persons of intelligence, integrity and loyalty'. Implementation of the Act of 1863 could lead to possible danger in times of popular excitement.[27]

In September 1880, the Punjab government wrote to the Home Department that legal disability was not the only argument for fresh legislation. The doubt thrown upon the legality of the government's action could lead to a gradual erosion of the authority of the Manager of the Golden Temple. Another judicial verdict in November 1880 explicitly stated that there was no legally constituted committee for the Darbar Sahib. In August 1881, Sir Robert Egerton wrote to the Governor General for such orders on the case that would enable the Punjab administration to continue the system which had worked well for more than thirty years. Ripon gave his assent to the proposed legislation. However, the Punjab government decided not to press for exemption from the Act of 1863, fearing further complications.[28]

In May 1882, the Lieutenant Governor, Sir C.U. Aitchison, wrote to the Commissioner of Amritsar, Colonel C.A. MacMahon, that the best course was to maintain the status quo, but if absolutely necessary, they would have to conform to the Act. The Golden Temple was the only institution in India over which it was thought necessary 'to maintain direct control'. But there was hardly anything peculiar to the Golden Temple to justify this treatment. It was, in fact, 'doomed sooner or later, if only left alone, to die a natural death with growing decadence of Sikhism'. MacMahon agreed that official withdrawal would result in the decline of the Darbar Sahib. But then the Sikhs would blame the government. 'Their loyalty had served the British in good stead in the past, and 'may be of the utmost consequence to us in the future'. Therefore, MacMahon strongly favoured the status quo. Aitchison agreed to the existing arrangements, but suggested that the Deputy Commissioner of Amritsar rather than the Divisional Commissioner should be 'responsible for overseeing the Temple administration'. More responsibilities could be turned over to the general committee against the long-term possibility of implementation of the Act of 1863. Sir James B. Lyall, the new Lieutenant Governor, advised that the proper practice for the Manager was 'to act in all ordinary matters subject to the advice and control of the Deputy Commissioner, and for the general committee to be only consulted on very special occasions'.[29] The Act of 1863 remained a dead letter.

Signs of Deterioration

The colonial control over the Darbar Sahib tended to make it a static institution. Its traditional resources were drying up and no new resources were created. Though known as a 'Sikh' city, the percentage of Sikhs in Amritsar was no more than 14 even in 1921. The Muslims accounted for over 44 per cent and the Hindus for over 40.[30] Whatever the form of administration in the city under the new regime, the Sikhs remained at a disadvantage. The city municipality in particular had little reason to protect the interests or resources of the Darbar Sahib.[31] The attitude of the British towards the Golden Temple could not be genuinely respectful.[32]

J.C. Oman paid more than one visit to the Golden Temple, but not merely as a tourist. He was interested in the Darbar Sahib as a religious institution. He noticed the jarring Gothic structure of the Clock Tower which the British administrators had constructed by demolishing the Bunga of Maharaja Ranjit Singh. As a symbol of the new power it was meant to overshadow the Darbar Sahib. The men who escorted Oman did not hesitate to use the stick on the crowd of visitors to clear the way for him. The open space in front of the Akal Bunga was used for various purposes, including the slaughtering of goats on the Dusehra day. A Brahman was sitting in this open space with his Shastras, interpreting them to a small knot of women and children. A couple of yogīs smeared with ashes sat on the cold pavement, seemingly rapt in contemplation. On the north side of the tank, a Brahman was worshipping tiny images of Ganesh and Krishna. At the north-east corner of the tank there was a *lingam* about four inches high, set upon a substantial brick and marble platform at the foot of a fine banyan tree. On the eastern side was a little temple sacred to the Goddess (Devi). There, one Brahman was engaged in worship, with a *saligram* before him and a picture of the temple of Badrinarain; the other was adoring a saligram with loud blasts of a conch. On the outer circumambulatory pavement, along the southern side, a Granthī was sitting with a covered-up book before him, carrying on confidential conversation with a middle-aged man who appeared to be a shopkeeper. On inquiring about such irregular teachers, Oman learnt that they were 'despicable wretches who, under the garb of religion, lent themselves to the furtherance of the most immoral practices. Sitting behind the sacred volume of their faith, they arrange illicit meetings'.

The most interesting object on the western side of the tank was an inscription in two languages which recorded a wonderful thing believed to have happened at 4.30 a.m. on 30 April 1877. Suddenly a flash of lightening had fallen from heaven, entered the holy place by the northern door, stopped before the holy book and returned to the sky through the southern entrance. This was regarded as a miracle of Guru Ram Das. It was a standing memorial to the Superintendence of Sardar Mangal Singh Ramgarhia. Above all, the inscription expressed goodwill for the British, 'praying for a daily increase in their happy influence and the destruction of all enemies of her Imperial Majesty'.[33] This was a way of inculcating loyalty among the visitors to the Darbar Sahib.

Inside the Golden Temple, signs of neglect were becoming visible. The work executed in the time of Maharaja Ranjit Singh was deteriorating. Major H.H. Cole, who visited Amritsar for the first time in January 1881, noticed that the mosaics at the Golden Temple were suffering from dirt and neglect. He recommended that they should be periodically cleaned and 'kept from cracking by careful oiling'.[34]

Teja Singh's detailed criticism of the shrinkage of resources, faulty management, misappropriation, and observance of un-Sikh practices makes a good deal of sense. The committee that was meant to manage the affairs of the Darbar Sahib was quietly dropped in the 1880s and the entire control was vested in the Sarbrah who received instructions from the Deputy Commissioner of Amritsar. The Sarbrah was never called upon to present any accounts.[35]

CRITICISM OF CONTROL

Criticism of the affairs of the Darbar Sahib started in the late 1880s. The *Khalsa Akhbār*, launched by the Lahore Singh Sabha in 1886, demanded public accountability from the managers and other functionaries of the Darbar Sahib. In 1887 it pointed out that the committee for the management of the Golden Temple was 'neither based on the principles of the Khalsa panth nor on government legislation'. All its members were not Sikh. Raja Harbans Singh (son of Raja Tej Singh) was 'a Hindu' who professed beliefs contrary to those of the Khalsa. Another committee member was a Christian. The Gurdwara belonged to the Sikh Panth but a Deputy Commissioner presided over its management. The government was not supposed to interfere in religious matters and yet a government official was appointed as 'the president of a Khalsa Gurdwara'. An appeal was made to the administration to constitute a proper committee. At the same time, the Khalsa were exhorted to show greater concern for their sacred shrines.[36] The *Khalsa Akhbār* continued to articulate such concerns nearly till the end of the century. A letter to its editor in 1897 pointed out that near the Dukhbhanjni in the precincts of the Darbar Sahib there was a room with a painting on its front wall depicting the goddess and Guru Gobind Singh: 'The goddess stands on golden sandals and she has many hands—ten or, perhaps, twenty. One of the hands is stretched out and in this she holds a *Khanda*. Guru Gobind Singh stands barefoot in front of it, with his hands folded'.[37] The correspondent, obviously, looked upon this situation as a mark of degradation.

The considerations for which the British administrators of the Punjab had infringed the Act of 1863 informed their attitude towards the growing concern of the Sikh 'reformers' for the Sikh Gurdwaras in general and the Darbar Sahib in particular. Colonel T. Lang, Commissioner of the Lahore Division, believed that Sikhism was, and had always been, centred in the Darbar Sahib. Therefore, any individual or organization claiming to present Sikhism from outside was 'schismatic' and politically dangerous. This was the position of the Singh Sabha of Lahore which stood in opposition to the Darbar Sahib in the late

1880s. Their opposition to 'the real Sikh centre at Amritsar' would do no good to Sikhism, or to the British. In Lang's view, the Lahore Singh Sabha was an 'up-start body of no account'. It was not supported by any eminent Sikh. It consisted of 'very small people' who made use of their 'English education' to air their 'loyalty' to attract the attention of the government. But, if given recognition and encouragement, they would become 'a very dangerous body'. Their association with the Darbar Sahib in any form was highly undesirable. The pujārīs of the Darbar Sahib had learnt 'manners'. A sensible and strong manager who was loyal to the government could easily manage them. His suggestion was accepted by the Lieutenant Governor, Sir James Lyall.[38]

However, the criterion of loyalty did not ensure efficiency. Colonel Jawala Singh, who was appointed Manager in 1896 with high hopes, resigned from managership for the third time in 1902. The Commissioner of Lahore Division wrote to the Chief Secretary in May 1902 that Colonel Jawala Singh had not turned out to be as much a success as it was hoped. He was too much of a martinet, wanting in tact. A more serious shortcoming was his want of education. In matters of accounts he was very much in the hands of his munshī. It came to light later that a good deal of money had 'gone into the munshī's hands, and possibly a certain amount into those of the manager'. There was clear evidence of misuse of authority and neglect of duties. However, even the Lieutenant condoned all irregularities.[39]

Introduction and Removal of Idols

Significantly, even the loyal Sarbrahs of the Darbar Sahib did not favour the worship of idols in the precincts of the Darbar Sahib. Early in 1878, Sardar Mangal Singh Ramgarhia ordered the Brahmans of Har kī Pauṛī not to worship idols in the Darbar Sahib, stating clearly that the worship of idols in the Darbar Sahib was against the old custom. He stated categorically that the only means of worship in Sri Darbar Sahib Ji was Sri Guru Granth Sahib Ji. However, external pressure enabled the Brahmans to bring idols into the Darbar Sahib once again. Towards the end of the century, over a score of Brahmans used to bring idols into the precincts of the Darbar Sahib. They were ordered again by the Sarbrah, Colonel Jawala Singh, not to bring idols but there was pressure from outside and a compromise was worked out. On 31 March 1899, all the Brahmans acknowledged in writing that the Darbar Sahib belonged to Sri Guru Ram Das and that the Sarbrah had the right to remove them any time he liked. They also undertook to abide by the conditions imposed by the Sarbrah.⁴⁰

With the increasing influence of the Singh Sabhas, the pressure of the 'reformers' also began to count. As a protagonist of the Lahore Singh Sabha, Bhai Kahn Singh emphasized in his writings at this time that worship of idols was against the teachings of the Gurus embodied in the Guru Granth Sahib. He was the tutor of Tikka Ripudaman Singh of Nabha. It is significant, therefore, that the Tikka wrote to the Lieutenant Governor of the Punjab in March 1905 that he had found 'idols of Hindus' in the inner and outer *parkarma* of the Darbar Sahib at the time of Diwali in 1904. 'The Sikhs are not idol worshippers', he stated. If the practice was allowed to continue, 'Sri Darbar Sahib will remain no longer a Sikh temple'. The Tikka went on to add that 'some orthodox Sikh possessing force of character' should be appointed as the Manager in order to ensure that such things were not allowed to happen in future.⁴¹ The meaning of 'orthodoxy' had changed.

While the administrators were making enquiries, the Sarbrah of the Darbar Sahib, Sardar Arur Singh, ordered the Brahmans not to bring idols into the Golden Temple with effect from 2 May 1905. They did not come for a few days but on 6 May they came back with idols. They were encouraged to do so by some local interests in the city. Sardar Arur Singh wrote to the Deputy Commissioner to send the police for enforcing his order and the Brahmans were persuaded on 7 May to stop their activity.⁴²

Already on 4 May a general meeting had been held by the 'Hindu Hitkari Sabha' to protest against what was regarded as the high-handed action of the Sarbrah. Addressing the meeting, Pandit Rajinder Misar, an advocate of Amritsar, sought to make the point that Guru Gobind Singh instituted the Keshdhārī Sikhs to meet a contingency. All his predecessors had subscribed to the idea of peace with all. Their attitude was inclusive and accommodating. Rajinder Misar asserted that Guru Ram Das believed in Brahmans and their *tīrath*s. The presence of a Shivala and a Devidwar in the precincts of the Darbar Sahib clearly showed that its founders were Hindus who followed Sanatan *dharm*. Both Sikhs and Hindus had worshipped in their respective ways at the Darbar Sahib since long. The larger number of Sikhs were actually

Sahajdhārīs who worshipped Hindu deities, and revered the Granth Sahib at the same time. Guru Ram Das was 'Das of Ram', a leader of all Hindus who, therefore, had an equal right to His Temple. The resolution proposed by Pandit Rajinder Misar and passed at the meeting, emphasized that all Sikh Gurus were Hindu and whatever they did was meant to support and protect Hindu dharmā. The Hindus of Amrtisar had been bathing in the tank of Darbar Sahib since olden times and observing *dhiān, sandhya, thākur-pūjan, bhajan,* and *kathā*. The Sarbrah had interfered in the matter arbitrarily. An appeal was made to the higher officials to rescind his order.[43] We can see that the question of idols was linked up with the much larger issue of 'Sikh-Hindu' identity.

The Singh Sabha and the *Khalsa Samāchār* were seen as the chief supporters of the Sarbrah's action. The Joint Secretary of the Hindu Hitkari Sabha, Khub Chand, addressed the Singh Sabha in an open circular letter, asserting that Brahmans had a legitimate right to worship their idols at the Darbar Sahib. To deny them this right was worse than '*Sikhā-shāhī'*. The Temple of Guru Ram Das did not belong to the Keshdhārī Sikhs alone. It was far less a place of the Singh Sabha Sikhs. It was really a place of the Sanatan Sikhs, both Sahajdhārī and Keshdhārī. Neither at the Darbar Sahib nor at the Akal Bunga was a *saropa* given to a Sikh who performed rites and ceremonies in accordance with the instructions of the Singh Sabhas. Thus, a large part of even the Keshdhārī Sikhs were unhappy with the Singh Sabha Sikhs. Therefore, their views could not be taken as the views of the Sikh community. Khub Chand asserted, in fact, that the place of Guru Ram Das was the common heritage of all 'Hindus'. Therefore, all Hindus had an equal right to the Temple of Guru Ram Das.[44] The Sikhs were seen as Hindus.

On 5 June 1905, Seth Radha Kishan, President of the Hindu Hitkari Sabha, signed a memorial for the consideration of the Lieutenant Governor on behalf of the Sikhs and Hindus of Amritsar. The memorial makes the points already mentioned. Brahmans had been worshipping idols in the Darbar Sahib since its very inception. The temple was held in equal veneration 'by all sects and classes of Sikhs and Hindus'. In fact, Hindu pilgrims to the temple far outnumbered the Sikh. These Brahmans performed 'indispensable' duties for the Hindu pilgrims. The vast majority of the followers of the Gurus were

Hindus 'as much by blood as by their belief, practices and sentiments'. No special importance could be attached to the views of the Tat Khalsa who had newly-risen into prominence 'on account of their iconoclastic and anti-caste tendencies'. The great bulk of the Sikhs shared the veneration of the Hindus for their gods. By law, by marriage, and other social relations as well as by faith, the Sikhs and Hindus were one as a body. Seth Radha Kishan hoped that an 'arbitrary and unwarranted interference with the established right of Hindus to worship gods in the Temple will not be allowed to stand'. If necessary, a mixed commission of recognized representatives of Hindus and Sikhs could be formed to elicit the true opinion of the 'orthodox Hindu and Sikh community' who formed 99 per cent, if not more, of the Hindu and Sikh population. The memorialists asserted that the functionaries of the Darbar Sahib, with perhaps one or two exceptions, were 'decidedly against the *Sarbarah's* action'.[45]

C.M. King, the Deputy Commissioner of Amritsar, forwarded the memorial to the Commissioner, R.E. Younghusband, on 10 June 1905. He referred to the agreement executed by the Brahmans with a former Sarbrah, admitting his right to exclude them from the Temple precincts 'whenever he thought fit to do so'. In any case, the Sarbrah had full powers to exclude 'any person or class of persons' from the temple and in this case he acted strictly within his powers. King added that the Nihangs were opposed to the idols, and their presence could cause a riot at any time. Not a single functionary of the Darbar Sahib had complained to King, which carried the implication of their tacit approval. None of the Granthīs or Pujārīs had signed the memorial. King could not see any reason why Hindus should be represented on a commission if it was to be formed at all. 'The Golden Temple is a Sikh temple as opposed to a Hindu temple. It was presumably the property of the Sikhs as a whole'. If the memorialists thought that any right had been infringed, they could bring a civil suit to establish their right. The memorial was the work of only a few agitators. Matters were now settling down, and 'we cannot do better than refuse to interfere with the Manager's action in this matter'.[46]

King wrote to the Commissioner three weeks later that the whole agitation was engineered by Seth Radha Kishan, a man of obscure origin but great ability. King strongly recommended that no action should be taken on the memorial.[47] Seth Radha Kishan wrote again to the Lieutenant Governor in March 1906, enclosing a copy of the old memorial. It appears to have been ignored.[48]

However, the interest of Raja Hira Singh in the whole affair induced Sir Denzil Ibbetson to find out what was happening. All relevant information was provided to him.[49] The records related to the Raja of Nabha make it clear that initially he was keen to remove the wrong impression that he had something to do with the removal of idols from the Darbar Sahib. In this process he discovered that the Vakil of Nabha to the Political Agency, Bhai Kahn Singh, had written an official letter to the Deputy Commissioner of Amritsar directly, which even the ruler of Nabha was not supposed to do. Therefore, Bhai Kahn Singh was dismissed from service. Tikka Ripudaman Singh tried to intercede on his behalf with the Political Agent but without any success. Raja Hira Singh was informed by a reliable person that Sardar Sunder Singh Majithia was instrumental in getting the idols removed. Since he was associated with the management of Khalsa College, to which Raja Hira Singh had promised substantial financial assistance, the Raja withdrew his offer. The Lieutenant Governor tried to persuade him not to stop the subscription but he appears to have insisted that the role of Sardar Sunder Singh Majithia in the whole affair should be investigated. One explanation for the attitude of Raja Hira Singh was supposed to be his concern for the marriage of his daughter, Princess Ripudaman Kaur, to the Rana of Dholpur, which made the issue of Sikh–Hindu identity all the more important. When the protestors against the removal of idols met Raja Hira Singh in deputation, he told them that he had nothing to do with this action and that he was not in its favour. He stated his position clearly and explicitly in an official communication: 'I like equity and not oppression and see all with one and the same eye without any distinction of caste or creed. Of course God is one but there are divisions among mankind, and it is the sacred duty of one to move within the circle he is born in'.[50]

An *ishtihār* (advertisement) circulated by Raja Hira Singh explains his views on the Sikh position in greater detail, declaring his conservative position. All the Gurus and all the Sikhs before the institution of the Khalsa were Sahajdhārī, and the Harmandar Sahib was a Sahajdhārī institution. The Granth was a Sahajdhārī scripture. Guru Tegh Bahadur had sacrificed his life for the protection of Hindus and

Hinduism. Even Guru Gobind gave equal regard to Sahajdhārīs and Keshdhārīs. He also vested Guruship in the Granth. Only in the time of Ranjit Singh, some sections of the Sikhs had begun to talk in terms of the 'Khalsa Panth' and the result was disunity and downfall. Equal regard for all sections of the Sikh community and friendly relations with the others were in Sikh interest. The rise of a new kind of Khalsa among the Sikhs was the source of trouble. Raja Hira Singh announced a reward of Rs 500 for anyone who may refute these views on the basis of the old books of the Khalsa.[51] It is interesting to note that this view of the Sikh past had been rejected by Bhai Kahn Singh in his *Ham Hindu Nahīn*.[52]

Avtar Singh Vahiria, a known protege of Baba Sir Khem Singh Bedi, presented his views in the form of a dialogue between a Tat Khalsa and a 'true Sikh'. The former was convinced that the removal of idols from the Darbar Sahib was not in accordance with the Sikh tradition and it was not in the larger interests of the Sikhs. The decision to remove the idols was not taken by Arur Singh but by higher authorities. Therefore, if the Hindus approached the Akal Takht in all humility, the idols could be allowed on certain conditions in the outer parkarma in any case.[53]

Bachan Singh, an advocate of Ludhiana, argued that the word *sahajdhārī* was unknown in the time of the first nine Gurus, and the Sikhs were not Hindu from 'the religious point of view'. For Bachan Singh, the Sikhs had an independent and distinct identity of their own. Furthermore, whatever belonged to the Gurus and the Panth 'now belonged to the Granth and the Panth'. No one else could have any claims. Bachan Singh advised Raja Hira Singh to keep himself wholly aloof from partisanship as a ruler, and not to impose his own views on the Sikhs.[54] In a Punjabi pamphlet, Bachan Singh refuted the ishtihār of Raja Hira Singh point by point.[55] Bachan Singh's views were close to those of Bhai Kahn Singh of Nabha. It may not be a coincidence that Bachan Singh later became a Judge of the High Court of Nabha under Maharaja Ripudaman Singh.

Control Taken Over by the Khalsa

The British administrators rightly looked upon Raja Hira Singh and Tikka Ripudaman Singh as representing two opposite schools or parties: the conservative (also called Sanatan) and the radical (also called Tat Khalsa). The Sikh rulers and the Sikh elite in general supported the former and the Chief Khalsa Diwan represented the latter. In the matter of the removal of idols, the British administration of the Punjab appeared to have accommodated 'the new school of Sikhs' against 'the old'.

The British authorities accommodated the new school on another issue which involved the question of Sikh identity rather directly. Tikka Ripudaman Singh was made Additional Member of the Central Legislative Council in 1907 in recognition of the services rendered to the British empire by his father, Raja Hira Singh. In 1908, Tikka introduced the Anand Marriage Bill in order to get legal recognition for the Sikh form of marriage as distinct from the Hindus. The Bill was supported by the Tat Khalsa but not by all the Sikhs or Hindus. The term of Tikka Ripudaman Singh was not extended by Lord Minto quite deliberately, but the Bill was still pending. Sardar Sunder Singh Majithia was brought in as an Additional Member on a clear understanding that he would steer the Bill and resign. On 8 June 1909, the 'Granthis, Pujaris, Mahants and Sants' made a representation on behalf of the Golden Temple, and other institutions, with regard to the Anand Marriage Bill originally introduced in the Central Legislative Council by the Tikka Sahib of Nabha on 8 October 1908. They asserted that the members of the Singh Sabhas were working for the Bill but they did not represent the main body of the Sikhs. If made a law, it would be an impolitic measure. It would 'greatly affect the religious, social and political condition of the Sikhs'.

The memorialists argued at some length that the 'Anand Marriage Bill' was a misnomer because 'Anand' referred to a composition of Guru Amar Das which was sung on various occasions and not specifically for marriage. Furthermore, the marriage ceremony introduced recently by the Singh Sabhas was an 'innovation', and even among them it was adopted by a few persons. The real purpose of 'these so-called reformers' was to gain control of the Gurdwaras to propagate their ideas more freely among the masses. Having failed in their attempts to get control of the Gurdwaras, they had resorted to legislation, hoping that through its means 'the Sikhs would generally accept their new creed'.[56] However, the Bill was passed and the Anand Marriage Act gave legal recognition to the Sikh form of marriage as distinct from the Hindu form.

Sardar Sunder Singh Majithia had written to the Chief Secretary of the Punjab in July 1909 that a deputation might be received by the Lieutenant Governor to make a representation, principally about the Darbar Sahib. His Honour was unwilling to receive the deputation. The proposal was seen as an attempt to gain control of the Darbar Sahib. The dissatisfaction that Sardar Sunder Singh articulated with the management of the affairs of the Golden Temple was seen as a part of his 'sustained endeavour' to get the management into the hands of the Chief Khalsa Diwan. The displeasure of the Tat Khalsa with the present manager of the Darbar Sahib was merely due to the fact that he was 'an orthodox Sikh'. They also knew that his successors would also be 'orthodox Sikhs' as long as the government retained the power of appointing a manager. The Golden Temple was 'the last refuge of the Sikh orthodoxy', and 'orthodoxy' was synonymous with 'loyalty'. In the Singh Sabhas and the Chief Khalsa Diwan, on the other hand, there were men of all shades: religious, 'national' (within the constitutional acceptance of the term) and downright seditious or 'revolutionary'.

It was argued further that if a nominee of the Chief Khalsa Diwan was appointed as a manager, the tone of the Darbar Sahib would change. Europeans would be unwelcome as visitors and no prayers (*ardās*) would be offered on their behalf. The struggle between the Chief Khalsa Diwan and the orthodox party had been rendered all the more acute by another issue: whether or not the 'outcaste' Sikhs should be allowed to worship at the Darbar Sahib like the 'caste' members of the Sikh community. If a decision was taken in favour of the Tat Khalsa, the Sikh orthodoxy would disintegrate, with political implications for the British administration. The government should not put its money on the wrong horse now as they had done over the Anand Marriage Bill.[57] Thus, the commitment of the administration to support 'the orthodoxy' became strong in proportion to the sharpness of the contest between 'the orthodoxy' and the Tat Khalsa.

A confidential memorandum prepared by the criminal intelligence department on Sikh politics in 1911 was also tilted against the Tat Khalsa:

The most fundamental and immediate of the evils which the present situation seems likely to produce is the dismantling of the fabric of the orthodox Sikh faith, with a consequent disregard of the loyal traditions which have hitherto powerfully affected the character of the Sikh attitude towards the British administration. There need be no hesitation in predicting that those Sikhs who affect the new faith will inevitably tend to become less and less reliable an asset as regards their loyalty to the Crown.[58]

The loyalty of the Tat Khalsa was highly suspect. Their increasing influence among the Sikhs made the administrators more and more firm in their commitment to a policy that appears to be too rigid in retrospect.

The increasing concern of the Tat Khalsa for the Sikh Gurdwaras was reflected in their reaction to the affair of Gurdwara Rakabganj in Delhi. In May 1913 the government demolished over a hundred metres of the outer wall of the Gurdwara to build a straight road to the Viceregal Lodge. A spate of protests came from many places against this 'sacrilege'. Associated with these developments, directly and indirectly, was Tikka Ripudaman Singh. Before long the leadership even of the Chief Khalsa Diwan was challenged by the more radical Sikhs. A serious agitation was brewing in the Punjab when World War I broke out in 1914. The matter remained shelved during the War. On 21 May 1920, however, a new daily was launched and given the name *Akālī*. In its issue of 2 September, Sardul Singh Caveeshar, who was actively involved in the Rakabganj issue in 1914, asked for 100 'martyrs' or *shahīd*s who would lay down their lives, if necessary, for reconstructing the demolished wall of Gurdwara Rakabganj. More than 700 people volunteered. The British authorities decided to reconstruct the wall and gave wide publicity to this decision to obviate confrontation of any kind. More significantly, the Gurdwara was taken away from the *mahant* who had worked in tandem with the government, and handed over to the Khalsa Diwan of Delhi.[59]

The Rakabganj affair was hardly separable from the Akali Movement. The declared objective of the Sikh leaders who launched the *Akālī* was to liberate all historic Gurdwaras from the direct or indirect control of the government. Soon a movement started for taking over Gurdwaras from their custodians, generally called mahants. The Sikhs who worked for this objective came to be known as Akali. Therefore, the movement for the 'reform' of Gurdwaras is also known as the Akali Movement. Its leaders upheld the idea of equality among all the Sikhs. When the priests refused to accept an offering of *kaṛhā parshād* from some outcaste Sikhs in October 1920, the Golden Temple and Akal Takht were taken over by the 'reformers' and placed under the management of a committee which was enlarged in November and named Shiromani Gurdwara Parbandhak Committee (SGPC). This can be seen as a direct outcome of the refusal of the British administrators of the Punjab to appoint a committee in accordance with the Act of 1863. However, the scope of the SGPC was much larger. Its aim was to control and manage all historic Gurdwaras. In December 1920, the Shiromani Akali Dal (SAD) was formed to coordinate the task of taking over all historic gurdwaras.

The Akali Movement has been studied in detail.[60] Clearly, it was a non-violent struggle against the British government for the control of Gurdwaras. Resistance by the mahants, with the connivance of the local British officers, resulted in the death of a few Akalis at Tarn Taran in January 1921 and the massacre of scores of Akalis at Nankana Sahib in February. However, the Gurdwaras of both these places came under the control of the 'reformers'. In October 1921, the executive committee of the SGPC demanded the keys of the treasury (*toshakhāna*) of the Golden Temple from Sardar Sunder Singh Ramgarhia, the officially appointed Manager of the Golden Temple in place of Sardar Arur Singh who had resigned under pressure from the Tat Khalsa. The agitation over the keys went on for several months, resulting in the imprisonment of a large number of Akalis till January 1922 when the keys were handed over in public to the President of the SGPC, Sardar Kharak Singh. Nevertheless, in August 1922 the government decided upon a showdown at Gurdwara Guru ka Bagh, not far from Amritsar. Thousands of Akalis suffered severe blows and injuries in passive resistance. Eventually a face-saving device was worked out by the government in March 1923, and more than 5,000 Akalis were released from jails. The government had to give in, but the war was not yet over.

Sardul Singh Caveeshar rightly called it 'the third Sikh war'. Its last battle was fought at Jaito in the state of Nabha in 1923–5. Maharaja Ripudaman Singh was removed from his throne in July 1923 for his known sympathies with the Akali movement, in addition to his persistent resistance to British paramountcy as the Tikka and the Maharaja of Nabha. The battle started over the issue of his removal and developed into a religious issue: the right of the Sikhs to hold an uninterrupted reading or *akhand pāṭh* of Granth Sahib in the Gurdwara at Jaito. At the end of a long struggle, involving suffering and imprisonment for thousands of Akalis of the princely states and the Punjab, a settlement was finally worked out. The Akali leaders skirted the issue of Maharaja Ripudaman Singh's restoration, and the government in turn passed in July 1925 the Sikh Gurdwaras Act largely in accordance with the wishes of the Akali leaders. The SGPC was constituted as the legal authority to control and manage Sikh Gurdwaras as a representative body of the Sikh Panth, elected on the basis of universal suffrage. This was little short of a revolution.

Relevance of the Doctrine of Guru Panth

The power and authority given to the Central Board (later SGPC) by the Sikh Gurdwaras Act of 1925 were never enjoyed or exercised by the British administrators, nor by Maharaja Ranjit Singh. The Act did not relate to the Darbar Sahib alone; it related to scores of other historic Gurdwaras. What remained unsaid was even more important: the SGPC could resolve all issues of Sikh belief and practice. In the course of Sikh history, there had never been a central organization to deal with all these subjects. How did this come about?

Turning to the kinds of concern articulated by the Sikhs we find the *Panth Sevak* regretting that the Golden Temple was no longer a Sikh institution: the offerings were not used for the benefit of the Sikh Panth and the management was not in the hands of the Sikhs. Were they not 'fit to look after their own shrines'? The *Punjab Darpan* stated that the British courts had no authority to decide 'who is a Sikh?' The *Sikh* lamented that the Darbar Sahib was not in the hands of 'a bonafide representative body of the Panth'. Even the task of selecting a religious guide for the Sikhs was reserved for 'a Christian Government'.[61] The basic assumption behind these comments was that the Tat Khalsa alone were the bonafide representatives of the Sikhs and that they had the right to manage the Gurdwaras associated with their Gurus. Professor Teja Singh talks of the Sikh right of Gurmata granted by Guru Gobind Singh: 'By this constitution the Sikh community assumed the position and authority of the Guru'.[62] Here we have an explicit reference to the doctrine of Guru Panth which was revived by the leaders of the Singh Sabhas. This doctrine justified the claim that all Gurdwaras associated with the Gurus belonged to the Panth.[63]

The Punjab government declared its intention in February 1921 to legislate with regard to the management and future control of

Gurdwaras. The SGPC announced in March 1921 that it would resort to passive resistance unless legislation for a satisfactory management of Gurdwaras was adopted within four weeks. What was more significant was its conception of 'satisfactory management'. The committee demanded the right to manage all Gurdwaras, and all property associated with them, as the representative of the Panth, the community of the devout made supreme in temporal matters by the Tenth Master.[64]

The proposed legislation of 1921 was meant to provide for a Board of Commissioners appointed by the Punjab government, with at least two-thirds of its members as non-official Sikhs. However, it was to be presided over by an official nominee, and the term 'Sikh' was not defined. Teja Singh expressed the views of the SGPC when he wrote to *The Tribune* on 26 March that any intervention by the government, or any non-Sikhs, in the management or administration of Gurdwaras 'will be considered as an encroachment on the religious liberty of the Sikhs'. He went on to add that 'the whole Sikh Panth' was 'the rightful owners' and the mahants were 'its servants'. Furthermore, the proposed legislation would create many Sarbrahs (like Arur Singh) and the government would control all Sikh temples (instead of one).[65] In other words, the proposed legislation was not acceptable because the Gurdwaras would not come under the sole control of the Khalsa, and there would be no central authority representing the Panth. The proposed legislation was postponed.

In the new draft bill published in September 1922, the government made vital concessions to the Tat Khalsa view, including the provision of a central body. The SGPC insisted that no legislation could be considered before the release of all prisoners arrested in the pursuit of Gurdwara 'reform'. The Bill was adopted by the Legislative Council on 18 November through official support. Its passage appeared to undermine the basis of the authority of the SGPC. The whole 'orthodox' Sikh community was solidly behind the Akalis. The word 'orthodox' now meant the Tat Khalsa. Despite the Government of India's anxiety that it 'should not be allowed to become a dead letter', neither the SGPC nor the government was keen to implement the Act.[66]

Master Tara Singh recalled in 1945 that the Guru Ka Bagh affair was the only phase of the Akali movement when 'the order of the

Shiromani Committee was obeyed by the Sikhs as the order of the Guru'.[67] The doctrine of Guru Panth appeared to be embodied in a sense in the SGPC. This made the SGPC far more important than the custodians created by the British for the Darbar Sahib.

The Bill for the Sikh Gurdwaras Act of 1925 was drafted in consultation with the leaders of the SGPC who were actually in Lahore Jail. The Bill was based on the principle enunciated by the Tat Khalsa reformers over the past two decades: responsibility for the management and control of all Sikh religious institutions was to lie with the Sikh community.[68] The Bill envisaged the establishment of a Central Board for the management of all historic Gurdwaras. The 'Sikh' was defined as a person who solemnly affirmed that he was a Sikh, that he believed in Guru Granth Sahib, that he believed in the Ten Gurus, and that he had no other religion. Furthermore, a person elected as a member of the Central Board was not to be a *patit* (equated generally with a non-keshdhārī Sikh).[69] Thus, the control of the Khalsa over the Central Board was ensured. Malcolm Hailey, who had all along avoided 'the institution of a central body' because it could be used for political purposes, saw clearly that 'the Sikhs will not agree to legislation which does not recognize a central body of some kind'.[70]

Just as the Golden Temple was the only religious institution in British India controlled directly by the government, so the SGPC was the only organization in British India to have control over all the historic institutions of the Sikh community. The age old concern of the Sikhs for the Sikh sacred space and the doctrine of Guru Panth had a direct bearing on its unique position. Equally responsible for the creation of this institution was the insistence of the British to keep the Tat Khalsa out of the Darbar Sahib, which led to a direct contest over the Sikh sacred spaces.

NOTES

1. Rajiv A. Kapur has noticed that the number of Sikhs seemed to be slightly increasing by 1856–7. The baptismal initiations at 'the Amritsar temple' (Akal Bunga) were more numerous in that year than in the preceding: *Sikh Separatism: The Politics of Faith,* New Delhi: Vikas Publishing House, 1987 (2nd impression, paperback), pp. 11–12.
2. David Ross, *The Land of the Five Rivers and Sindh,* Patiala: Punjab Language Department, 1970 (rpt.), pp. 192–6.

3. All quoted by Nazer Singh, 'Early British Attitude Towards the Golden Temple', *Journal of Regional History*, vol. III, Amritsar: Guru Nanak Dev University, 1982, pp. 88 n 3, 96.
4. Bhai Nahar Singh and Kirpal Singh, eds, *Rebels Against The British Rule*, New Delhi: Atlantic Publishers, 1995, pp. 1–15.
5. J.S. Grewal, *The Sikhs of the Punjab* (The New Cambridge History of India), Cambridge: Cambridge University Press, 1990, p. 125.
6. For some of the early decisions of Henry Lawrence, see, Ian J. Kerr, 'The British and the Administration of the Golden Temple in 1859', *The Panjab Past and Present*, vol. X, part 2, October 1976, p. 308, and Nazer Singh, 'Early British Attitude Towards the Golden Temple', pp. 88–9.
7. Kerr, p. 309 and n. 7; Nazer Singh, 'Early British Attitude Towards the Golden Temple', p. 89.
8. Quoted by Kerr, 'The British and the Administration', p. 311.
9. National Archives of India (NAI), New Delhi, Home Department Public Branch Consultations Nos 65–71, letters of 5 March, 20 September, and 4 October 1859.
10. Ibid., E. Thornton to the Secretary to Government, Punjab, dated 4 October 1857. R.H. Davies to the Judicial Commissioner, Punjab, dated 5 March 1859; E. Thornton to the Secretary to Government, Punjab, dated 4 October 1859.
11. Ibid., R.H. Davies to the Judicial Commissioner, Punjab, dated 5 March 1859.
12. Ibid., Deputy Commissioner of Amritsar to the Commissioner, dated 15 September 1859.
13. Ibid.
14. Ibid., the Commissioner of Amritsar Division to the Judicial Commissioner, Punjab, dated 20 September 1859.
15. Cust enclosed a list of jāgīrs held by the Darbar Sahib, Akal Bunga, Jhanda Bunga, Shahid Bunga, and Baba Atal, amounting to Rs 33,787, giving also the number of Granthīs, Pujārīs, Rabābīs, Rāgīs, Ardasias, and others.
16. Ibid., E. Thornton to the Secretary to Government, Punjab, dated 4 October 1859.
17. Ibid., the letter cited above and C.H. Davies to the Judicial Commissioner, Punjab, dated 13 October 1859.
18. The rules of Maharaja Ranjit Singh were that, after paying ten months' wages to the Rabābīs and Rāgīs and others, and defraying the miscellaneous expenses of the Darbar, sometimes two months, sometimes four months, sometimes eight months or twelve months' wages, according

to the balance in hand, were paid to the Pujārīs. In case of deficit, they received nothing.
19. Ibid., 'Memorandum on the Sikh Temple, Amritsar', Administration Paper.
20. Ibid., E. Thornton to Secretary to Government, Punjab, dated 3 March 1859. Commissioner of Amritsar to the Judicial Commissioner, Punjab, dated 20 September 1859. For the tussle between the supporters of Sardar Jodh Singh and the well-wishers of Bhai Parduman Singh, see Nazer Singh, 'Early British Attitude towards the Golden Temple', pp. 93–5; Kerr, 'The British and the Administration of the Golden Temple in 1859', p. 315.
21. 'Memorandum on the Sikh Temple, Amritsar', para 8.
22. Ian J. Kerr, 'British Relationship with the Golden Temple, 1849–90', *The Indian Economic and Social History Review*, 1984, vol. 21, p. 139.
23. Ibid., p. 145.
24. Ibid., p. 146.
25. Ibid., p. 145–6.
26. 'Judgement in Civil Suit of 1879 in the Court of the Judicial Assistant at Amritsar', Home Department Public Branch Consultation Nos. 65–71, NAI, New Delhi.
27. Kerr, 'British Relationship with the Golden Temple, 1849–90', pp. 147–8.
28. W.M. Young to C. Grant, dated 16 September 1880, Home Department Public Branch Consultation, Nos 65–71, NAI, New Delhi. Judgement of G. Lewis, dated 22 November 1880. Notes on the Punjab Government's letter of 16 September 1880 with regard to the 'Sikh Temple at Amristar and its Management'.
29. Kerr, 'British Relationship with the Golden Temple, 1849–90', pp. 148–9.
30. *Census of India, 1921,* vol. XV, Panjab and Delhi, Part II, Table V. Prepared by L. Middleton and S.M. Jacob, this volume was published from Lahore in 1923.
31. Anand Gauba, *Amritsar: A Study in Urban History (1840–1947)*, Jalandhar: ABS Publications, 1988.
32. Ruchi Ram Sahni, *Struggle for Reform in Sikh Shrines,* Ganda Singh, ed., Amritsar: Sikh Ithas Research Board, Shiromani Gurdwara Parbandhak Committee, n.d., pp. 11–12. Henry Lawrence had tried 'to make known to all concerned, that by order of the Governor General, British subjects are forbidden to enter the Temple (called the Darbar) or its precincts at Amritsar, or indeed any Temple with shoes on'. Nevertheless, Major Mainwaring, who was residing in the Ram Bagh,

refused to take off his shoes when requested to do so before entering the holy place.

33. John Campbell Oman, *Cults, Customs and Superstitions of India*, London: 1908, pp. 108–13, rpt, Delhi: Vishal Publishers, 1972.
34. P.S. Arshi, *The Golden Temple: History, Art and Architecture*, New Delhi: Harman Publishing House, 1989.
35. Teja Singh, *The Gurdwara Reform Movement and the Sikh Awakening*, Jullundur: Desh Sewak Book Agency, 1922, pp. 108–9, 139–41, 143–4.
36. Quoted by Harjot Oberoi, *The Construction of Religious Boundaries: Culture, Identity and Diversity in the Sikh Tradition*, New Delhi: Oxford University Press, 1994, pp. 326–7. Oberoi's references to the Darbar Sahib, on the whole, present a comprehensive picture. However, he tends to assume that there was no difference between the Sikh and colonial rule so far as its control and management was concerned. The concern of the Tat Khalsa for the Darbar Sahib is seen by Oberoi as something totally new. Ibid., pp. 24, 103–4, 107, 130–1 nn, 223, 246, 320–8, 349, 373, 385, 389–90, 392, 403 and n. 43.
37. Quoted by Kapur, *Sikh Separatism*, pp. 22–3.
38. Ian J. Kerr, 'Sikhs and State: Troublesome Relationships and a Fundamental Continuity with Particular Reference to the Period 1849–1919', in Pashaura Singh and N. Gerald Barrier, eds, *Sikh Identity: Continuity and Change*, New Delhi: Manohar, 2001, pp. 154, 160–1.
39. Home Confidential 1902, No. 669/12, Punjab State Archives (PSA), Chandigarh.
40. Copy of order by Sardar Mangal Singh, dated 29 January 1878, and copy of the agreement signed by the Brahmans, dated 31 March 1899, Home Confidential 1905, No. 668/12, PSA, Chandigarh.
41. Ibid., copy of Tikka Ripudaman Singh's letter to the Lieutenant Governor, dated 30 March 1905.
42. Ibid., copy of the order of Sardar Arur Singh, dated 1 May 1905; translation of the report submitted to the Manager by his Munshi, dated 6 May 1905; translation of order passed by the Manager on 6 May 1905; translation of the Murasila sent by the Manager to the Deputy Commissioner, dated 6 May 1905; translation of the Manager's order, dated 7 May 1905.
43. Summary of the speech of Pandit Rajinder Misar and the resolution in Urdu, Home Confidential 1905, No. 668/12, PSA, Chandigarh.
44. Ibid., an open letter for the serious consideration to Sri Guru Singh Sabha (Urdu).
45. Ibid., a copy of the memorial in print, dated 5 June 1905.

46. Ibid., C.M. King to R.E. Younghusband, dated 10 June 1905.
47. Ibid., dated 1 July 1905.
48. Ibid., Seth Radha Kishan's petition to Sir Charles Montgomery Riwaz, dated 6 March 1906. A letter addressed to Casson on 30 March 1906 refers to the need of 'quiet enquiries' to avoid giving the impression that the government had any interest in the matter.
49. Ibid., C.M. King to R.E. Younghusband, dated 17 June 1905.
50. R.E. Younghusband to Sir Denzil Ibbetson, dated 18 June 1905. There is a good deal of correspondence related to the Raja of Nabha in Home Confidential 1905, no. 668/12, PSA, Chandigarh. The most relevant records are Bhai Kahn Singh's letter of 8 May 1905 to the Deputy Commissioner of Amritsar (attested copy dated 9 June 1905); Raja Hira Singh's letter of 26 May 1905 to C.M. King; King's note of 30 May 1905 on his personal meeting with Gurdit Singh, an *ahlkar* of Raja Hira Singh; the letter of Raja Hira Singh to King, dated 31 May 1905; King's note on his conversation with Lala Salig Ram, the Canal Nazim of Nabha sent by Raja Hira Singh; several letters of Raja Hira Singh and the Political Agent, Major C.M. Dallas; Sir Denzil Ibbetson's letter to the Raja-i Rajgan, Raja Hira Singh; Raja Hira Singh's letter of 15 June 1905 addressed to the Private Secretary of the Lieutenant Governor; the latter's letter to Raja Hira Singh, dated 18 June 1905; letter dated 26 June 1905 from the Foreign Minister of Nabha to the Political Agent.
51. Ibid., translation of the ishtihār issued by Raja Hira Singh.
52. Kahn Singh, *Ham Hindu Nahin*, Amritsar: Dharam Parchar Committee, (SGPC), 1981 (rpt of the 5th edn). For a brief analysis of this work, see J.S. Grewal, 'Nabha's *Ham Hindu Nahin:* A Declaration of Sikh Ethnicity', in Pashaura Singh and N. Gerald Barrier, eds, *Sikh Identity: Continuity and Change,* New Delhi: Manohar, 2001, pp. 231–51.
53. Avtar Singh Vahiria, *Sri Darbar Sahib Amritsar De Thakaran Walae Jhagrae Di Paṛtal,* Lahore: Sri Gurmat Press, n.d. pp. 1–24.
54. Bachan Singh, *Sikhs and Idols: A Reply to the Raja of Nabha,* Lahore: Civil and Military Gazette Press, n.d. pp. 1–12.
55. Bachan Singh, *Na Ham Hindu Na Musalman: Nabhae De Ishtihār Dā Uttar Te Khandan,* Amrisar: Wazir Hind Press, n.d.
56. *English Translation of the Punjabi Text* (of the memorial submitted by the Granthīs and Pujārīs of the Golden Temple to the Secretary to the Government of India, Legislative Department), Bhai Mohan Singh Vaid Collection, Punjabi University, Patiala.

57. 'Management of the Golden Temple', Home General 1910, No. 788/14, confidential letters 65 and 66, dated 27 April 1910, PSA, Chandigarh.
58. David Petrie's *Confidential Report* quoted by Kapur, *Sikh Separatism*, p. 57.
59. For detail on the 'movement', see Harjot Singh Oberoi, 'From Gurdwara Rakabganj to the Viceregal Palace: A Study of Religious Protest', *The Panjab Past and Present*, vol. xiv, pt. 1, 1982, pp. 182–98.
60. Mohinder Singh, *The Akali Movement*, Delhi: Macmillan, 1978. Richard G. Fox, *Lions of the Punjab: Culture in the Making*, Berkeley: University of California Press, 1985. Rajiv A. Kapur, *Sikh Separatism: The Politics of Faith*, New Delhi: Vikas Publishing House, 1987 (2nd impression, paperback). For a general outline of the Akali movement, see J.S. Grewal, *The Sikhs of the Punjab* (The New Cambridge History of India), Cambridge: Cambridge University Press, 1990, pp. 159–63.
61. For quotations, see Kapur, *Sikh Separatism*, pp. 81, 95, 102, 104.
62. Teja Singh, *The Gurdwara Reform Movement*, p. 115.
63. Ibid., p. 331.
64. Kapur, *Sikh Separatism*, p. 115.
65. Ibid., pp. 118–19.
66. Ibid., pp. 157–67.
67. Tara Singh, *Merī Yād* (Pbi), Amritsar: Sikh Religious Book Society, 1945, pp. 65–6.
68. Sahni, *Struggle for Reform in Sikh Shrines*, p. 125.
69. Kapur, *Sikh Separatism*, p. 185.
70. Ibid., pp. 161, 188.

11. Colonial Rule and Cultural Reorientation*

The late nineteenth and early twentieth centuries witnessed a remarkable resurgence among the Sikhs in the Punjab. Their numbers shot up from less than two million in 1881 to more than four million in 1931. The bulk of the Sikh population was identified as 'Singhs' who generally claimed to have a distinct religious identity. Consequently, Sikh identity for many Sikh leaders became the basis of Sikh politics. This resurgence has been seen as a revival, a re-formation or a rupture in relation to the earlier Sikh tradition.[1] It is generally agreed, however, that this half century revitalized the Singh or Khalsa tradition and marginalized the non-Singh or the Sahajdhārī Sikhs. Obviously, this revitalization was the result of a social change and cultural reorientation. However, cultural reorientation was not confined to religious matters. Our present purpose is to concentrate on cultural reorientation among the Sikhs during the late nineteenth and early twentieth centuries.

A British View of the Pre-colonial Sikhs

The most perceptive among the British historians of the Sikhs, J.D. Cunningham, recorded his impressions of the Sikhs on the eve of the annexation of the Punjab to the British Indian empire. His perspective on the Sikhs in the late 1840s appears to be a good starting point for our purpose.[2]

The Sikhs were not very numerous but their strength was 'not to be estimated by tens of thousands'. What made them important was the unity and energy of their religious fervour, and their warlike temperament. The Sahajdhārī Sikhs, the '*khulāsa* Sikhs' of John

---

* 'Colonial Rule and Cultural Reorientation' is a revised version of the chapter 'Recession and Resurgence' in my *The Sikhs of the Punjab* (Cambridge: Cambridge University Press, 1990, pp. 128–56).

Malcolm, could be seen in the cities of British India, but dominant in the Punjab were the warlike Singhs of the Tenth King, Guru Gobind Singh. Cunningham noticed a number of 'sects' or 'denominations' among the Sikhs but the criteria used to distinguish them were lineal descent, occupations, and social background rather than Singh or Sahajdhārī identity. The major exception was that of the Udasis who were proud of their association with the Sikhs and held the Ādi Granth in reverence but they were essentially a 'Hindu sect'. Cunningham is quite emphatic that 'the great development of the tenets of Guru Gobind Singh has thrown other denominations into the shade'. Furthermore, a living spirit possessed 'the whole Sikh people'. They were 'wholly different from other Indians' in their religious faith and worldly aspirations. Their faith was 'still an active and a living principle'. Cunningham estimated the number of Sikhs as ranging from twelve and a half to fifteen lacs. But they were all Singhs.[3]

The Singhs figure prominently among the top most *jāgīrdārs* of the state of Lahore. A dozen of them received revenues Rs 1,000,000. On the whole the Singhs got more than 60 per cent of the total revenue alienated by the state in favour of large jāgīrdārs. The Singhs had a lion's share in Rs 5,000,000 given in smaller jāgīrs. Of the 'religious grants' too they received a very large proportion. Foremost among them were the Sodhis, getting Rs 500,000 a year. They were followed by the Bedis who received Rs 400,000. Together, they got 45 per cent of the total revenue alienated by the state as *dharmarth*. The Golden Temple and many other Gurdwaras had a fair share in the remaining Rs 1,100,000; the Akalis are mentioned as recipients of religious grants along with others. Cunningham leaves no doubt that the Singhs were active participants in the affairs of the kingdom of Lahore and formed the most important category of beneficiaries of its patronage. He does not give much detail but a detailed study confirms his general impression.[4]

Of nearly two scores of generals and commanders in the army of Lahore before the first Anglo-Sikh war, a little more than half were Sikhs. More significantly, all the Sikhs who joined the army were Khalsa Singhs. There was hardly a unit of cavalry, infantry or artillery that did not have some Singh soldiers. Cunningham appreciated their 'manly deportment' even after the defeat, which added 'luster to that valour which the victors had dearly felt and generously extolled'. Cunningham refers to the Panchāyats of Singhs from each battalion or company. Through them, the Sikh people could intervene in the nomination and in the removal of their rulers on behalf of the Khalsa.[5]

By far the most important Sikh scripture was the Ādi Granth which was regarded as the Guru. The *Dasam Granth* was almost equally sacred but it was not regarded as Guru. Personal Guruship was declared by Guru Gobind Singh to have ended with the vesting of Guruship in the Granth and 'the general body of the Khalsa'. Therefore, belief in any personal guru was not commendable. Next in importance to the two Granths were the *Vārs* of Bhai Gurdas and the *Rahitnāma*s attributed to Bhai Nand Lal and Prahlad Singh, which depicted Sikhism as a new dispensation and the Sikh Panth as a distinct entity. They also underlined Sikh belief in the sovereignty of the Khalsa (*rāj karegā khālsa*) and the vesting of Guruship in the Ādi Granth and the Khalsa.[6]

The Colonial Context

The subversion of Khalsa sovereignty in 1849 created a radically new situation for the Khalsa. The loss of political power had immediate economic and social implications, bringing in its trail the problem of readjustment. The long-term policies of the new rulers created a new social and political environment. Like other Punjabis, the Khalsa were affected by these policies, and had to face new challenges. They tried to meet them in the light of their understanding of the past and their vision of the future. In the process, they created new institutions.

The decline of the former ruling class of the kingdom of Lahore was inevitable after the introduction of bureaucratic administration by the British.[7] Jāgīrs had been given to members of the ruling class for rendering services to the state. Their services were needed no more, and their jāgīrs had to be taken back or reduced. The Khalsa jāgīrdārs suffered more than the others because of their larger number in the Sikh administration. They suffered more also because of their greater opposition to the British.[8] However, during the uprising of 1857–8 nearly all of them supported the British actively and received adequate rewards. The Sikh aristocracy as a class was rehabilitated in the eyes of the British, and came to be treated as 'the natural leaders' of the Sikh people. At least half of the aristocratic families of the 1840s survived into the twentieth century by adjusting themselves to the colonial situation and by making use of the new opportunities. Some new families became 'families of note'.[9] As a class, the Sikh aristocracy was next in importance to the ruling chiefs of the protected Sikh states like Patiala, Nabha, Jind, Faridkot, and Kapurthala.[10]

The grants given by the Sikh rulers for religious purposes were not entirely taken back by the British administrators, though they gave no patronage to religious institutions as a matter of policy. About three scores of gurdwaras continued to hold lands. A number of Sodhis and Bedis retained a part of their grants. The descendants of eminent Bhais and Giānīs of the kingdom of Lahore retained a part of their grants, like the families of Bhai Ram Singh, Bhai Gobind Ram, and Bhai Gurmukh Singh who were closely associated with the court at Lahore. Some of the former grantees joined hands with the former jāgīrdārs to help the British administration to control and manage the affairs of the Golden Temple. Regarding Amritsar as the possible source of Sikh religious resurgence, the Punjab administrators were anxious to keep the Golden Temple under their control through close supervision. A 'simple magisterial and political control' was established over it by the administrative manual (*Dastūr al-'Aml*) of 1859. The Deputy Commissioner of Amritsar continued to supervise the work of the nominated Sikh Manager till the Golden Temple was taken over by the Akalis in 1920.[11]

The worst sufferers of the change from the Khalsa Raj to the British rule were the Singh soldiers. Many of them were retrenched after the Anglo-Sikh war of 1845–6. Most of them were disbanded after the Anglo-Sikh war of 1848–9.[12] However, the uprising of 1857–8, obliged the Punjab administrators to recruit some Sikhs all afresh. Their performance was found to be satisfactory, and the Sikhs began to be recruited in large numbers. During the First World War their absolute number in the Indian Army was smaller than that of the Punjabi Muslims but their proportion in the Indian Army in proportion to their total population in India was larger than that of any other religious community.[13] There was a common assumption among the British that the Khalsa were distinguished from the other Sikhs by their martial spirit. Indeed, the Sikhs whom the British had faced in the wars of 1845–6 and 1848–9 were all Khalsa Singhs. Their martial prowess appeared to spring from their faith. The British army authorities insisted from the very beginning that all those Sikhs who joined the army should observe the Khalsa form. Thus, a tradition of the days of Ranjit Singh was perpetuated.[14]

The bulk of the Sikhs lived in the countryside as peasants, artisans, and agricultural labourers. In the colonial situation, the small Sikh landholders were less prone to indebtedness than the others, though some of them had been reduced to the status of tenants.[15] The large landholders generally began to produce for the market. This was more true of the canal colonies where Sikhs had got a good proportion of the land as good cultivators or good soldiers.[16] Some members of the Sikh aristocracy also received large chunks of land in reward for services rendered to the colonial rulers. The large landholders in general and the Sikhs in particular were the major beneficiaries of colonial rule in the countryside as commodity producers. In cities and towns, the Sikhs were mostly Khatris and Aroras. As a part of the traditional trading communities, they were among the primary beneficiaries of colonial rule in the late nineteenth century but their number and their proportion in the Khatris and Aroras of the Punjab were rather small.

The percentage of agriculturists, artisans, and traders and shopkeepers within the Sikh community did not change appreciably from 1881 to 1921. The agriculturists amounted to over 73 per cent in 1921. The Jats alone accounted for more than 60 per cent of the Sikhs. The Tarkhāns, Nāīs, Jhīwars, and other groups of the *jajmānī* system represented nearly 12 per cent of the Sikhs. The Khatris and Aroras were about 7 per cent. The percentage of the Chuhras and Chamars was a little more. Many other social groups were represented in the Sikh community but their numbers were very small.

All the Sikhs were not pursuing their traditional occupations by now. Many Khatri, Arora, and Brahman Sikhs were in civil administration and in the professions of law, medicine, engineering, teaching, and journalism. Many Jat Sikhs were in the army and the police. This does not mean, however, that there were no agriculturist Sikhs in civil administration and other professions. Nor does it mean that there were no Khatris or Aroras in the army or the police. In fact, there were some Tarkhāns, Kalāls, and Chūhṛas too in the army, and there were Labānas, Nāīs, Jhīwars, and Chhīmbas in the police. All the traditional segments of the Sikhs were represented in the professions too. But the largest representation in the professions and in the civil services was that of the Khatris and Aroras. They were also the most educated among the 10 per cent who were literate. Contrary to the general impression, the Sikhs were not given any preference over others for civil employment. Even in the police they held less than 9 per cent of the positions. They held less than 8 per cent of the positions in various departments of the government. By 1921, a number of Jat and Tarkhān Sikhs were owning about 100 factories.[17] On the whole, a small but influential middle class was emerging among the Sikhs to cooperate or compete with the Sikh aristocracy and with Hindus and Muslims.[18]

The Sikhs still formed minority in the Punjab. They were less than 14 per cent of the total population of the province in 1931. From the very beginning the British had tended to equate the Sikh with the Singh, and this tendency was reflected in the enumeration of Sikhs in 1881, 1891, and 1901. In 1911 for the first time the census officials returned all those persons as Sikhs who claimed to be Sikhs, and there was a phenomenal increase of more than 37 per cent over the total figures of 1901. This carried the implication that a large number of Sahajdhārī Sikhs too thought of their identity as distinct from that of the Hindus. The number of Sikhs was steadily increasing so that in 1931 their number was more than double their number in 1881. At the same time, the proportion of Singhs in the Sikh community was increasing due to the conversion of non-Sikhs and the increasing consciousness of Singh identity among the Sikhs.[19] The demographic change among the Sikhs underlined the importance of new religious movements, especially the Singh Sabha Movement which appears to have marked 'a new chapter in the evolution of Sikhism'.[20]

The Nirankari and the Namdhari Awakening

Two religious movements had started before the annexation of the Punjab as Sahajdhārī movements: the Nirankari and the Namdhari. The former was founded at Rawalpindi by Baba Dayal, and its influence remained confined to that region under his successors too. Their following consisted mainly of Khatri, Arora, and Bhatia shopkeepers and traders. With their uncompromising belief in the Formless (*nirankār*), which gave them the name Nirankari, they rejected all gods and goddesses of Hindu mythology and sacred literature. They recognized the line of ten Gurus from Guru Nanak to Guru Gobind Singh and looked upon the Ādi Granth as Guru Granth Sahib. The

COLONIAL RULE AND CULTURAL REORIENTATION 267

hukamnāma of Baba Darbara Singh (1853-70) makes two things absolutely clear: one, that the Nirankaris had no use whatever for Brahmans; two, that Guru Granth Sahib was central to their ceremonies of birth, death and marriage. This hukamnāma refers to Baba Dayal as 'the true *guru*', not bracketed with any of the ten Gurus, or Guru Granth Sahib, but a guru nonetheless. The Nirankari movement ignored the Khalsa tradition and its doctrine of Guru Panth.[21]

The Namdhari movement was initiated by Baba Balak Singh in the area to the northwest of Rawalpindi, but it was given a new orientation by Baba Ram Singh, a carpenter of village Bhaini in district Ludhiana. He was in the army of Lahore when he had come into contact with Baba Balak Singh at Hazro in the early 1840s. Upon his death in 1862, Baba Ram Singh inaugurated the 'Sant Khalsa' by administering baptism by the double-edged sword to his followers. Their white dress and rosary proclaimed their spotless piety, but they wore *kesh*, *kachh*, *karā*, and *kangha* like the Khalsa, and they carried some simple weapon or merely a staff. They had no place for Brahmans in their rites and ceremonies. The popularity of Baba Ram Singh in the countryside made him potentially dangerous in the eyes of the British administrators. He was allowed to visit Amritsar in April 1863 but interned in his village soon afterwards. His following went on increasing. Their number was estimated to be more than 100,000 in the late 1860s. The 'Sant Khalsa' were spread over all the central districts which had a good proportion of Sikh population. Despite their boycott of all things British, they were well organized in compact units under *sūbā*s (governors) who had their own secret means of communication. They earned the epithet Kuka because of the shrieks (*kūk*s) of individuals who became 'intoxicated' (*mastāna*) during congregational hymn-singing (kīrtan). The more staunch among the Sant Khalsa demonstrated their iconoclastic zeal by destroying idols and small structures erected over graves and cremation spots. In 1866-7, a number of them were prosecuted and sentenced to imprisonment ranging from three months to two years.

Baba Ram Singh hated the beef-eating '*goras*' for encouragement given to cow slaughter under their rule. He hoped for the return of Sikh rule, believing in prophecies rather than having a clear agenda of his own. His followers did not act directly against the rulers but they killed some butchers. Eight of them were sentenced to death for killing butchers in Amritsar and Raikot. Baba Ram Singh was suspected of encouraging them, and his removal from the Punjab was under consideration when a band of the Sant Khalsa struck at Malerkotla in the hope of getting arms to be used against more butchers. In the process they killed ten persons. In turn, sixty-five of the Sant Khalsa were blown from guns at Malerkotla by the Deputy Commissioner of Ludhiana and the Commissioner of Ambala. Baba Ram Singh and his representatives, called sūbās, were sent to distant jails. Baba Ram Singh remained in touch with his followers during his detention at Rangoon. In 1880, he was removed to Mergui where he died in 1885.

Under the guidance of Baba Ram Singh's younger brother in his absence, the Sant Khalsa, generally called Namdharis and popularly known as Kukas, settled to peaceful occupations, abandoning their iconoclastic zeal but not their spiritual 'intoxication'. They came to believe that Baba Ram Singh was the twelfth Guru in continuation with Guru Gobind Singh through Baba Balak Singh. This undermined the doctrine of Guru Panth, and reduced the importance of Guru Granth, among the Namdharis. They gave a lot of importance to ritual fire and Chandi literature incorporated in the *Dasam Granth*. Their numbers began to dwindle, increasing the proportion of carpenters among the Namdharis. Coupled with their religious doctrines, their social background made them a sect within the Sikh community.[22]

The Resurgence of Singh Sabhas

About a year after Baba Ram Singh's deportation in 1872, an association called 'Sri Guru Singh Sabha' was founded at Amritsar. The immediate cause of its foundation was the announcement of conversion of a few Sikh students to Christianity.[23] The Singh Sabha was founded on the initiative of Sardar Thakur Singh Sandhanwalia who belonged to an aristocratic family of the time of Maharaja Ranjit Singh. Thakur Singh became president of the Sabha. Its secretary was Giani Gian Singh of Amritsar (different from the celebrated author of the *Panth Prakāsh* and the *Tawārīkh Guru Khalsa*). In 1877, the Sabha petitioned the authorities of the Oriental College at Lahore to introduce teaching of Punjabi language and literature. The first publication of the Sabha was an eighty-page booklet entitled *Sri Gurpurb Parkāsh* which could help in celebrating the birth anniversaries of the Gurus. The most eminent individuals to become associated with the Sabha were Raja Bikram

Singh of Faridkot, Kanwar Bikrama Singh of Kapurthala and Baba Khem Singh Bedi. In 1886–7 they were all suspected of sympathy with Maharaja Dalip Singh, the deposed son of Maharaja Ranjit Singh, whom Thakur Singh Sandhanwalia had persuaded to return from Christianity to the Khalsa faith in order to claim his heritage.[24] The rules of the Singh Sabha were published in 1890, laying down procedures for its functioning. By this time Baba Khem Singh Bedi was its most important leader. He had the support of the government and the Sikh Managers of the Golden Temple.[25]

The second Singh Sabha was established at Lahore in 1879 on the initiative of Gurmukh Singh and Bhai Harsa Singh, both teachers at the Oriental College, Lahore. It was avowedly meant for propagating education as well as religion among the Sikhs. Its president, Diwan Buta Singh, was a publisher and its secretary was Gurmukh Singh himself. A former chief of Bhadaur, Sardar Attar Singh, began to patronize the Sabha. In the late 1880s, Jawahar Singh Kapur and Giani Ditt Singh joined the Singh Sabha after abandoning the Arya Samaj. A number of periodicals were started by Gurmukh Singh, including the best known and the most influential *Khalsa Akhbār* which was edited by Giani Ditt Singh. The Lahore Singh Sabha demonstrated their loyalty to the British in 1886–7 by telling the Sikhs to remain aloof from Maharaja Dalip Singh and his self-styled well-wishers. Gurmukh Singh died in 1898 but the Sabha remained active till the death of Giani Ditt Singh in 1901.

By 1901, more than a hundred other Singh Sabhas had been established in the Punjab: in the district towns (like Rawalpindi, Lyallpur, Gurdaspur, Ludhiana, Jalandhar, Ambala, Ferozepore, Karnal, Montgomery, Hoshiarpur, and Sialkot), in other towns (like Dera Baba Nanak, Khanna, Ropar, Dipalpur, Pind Dadan Khan, Sahiwal, Wazirabad, Hargobindpur, Muktsar, and Tarn Taran), and in villages (like Bilga, Badowal, Chamkaur Sahib, Khumano, Lidhran, and Gujjarwal). Besides the Singh Sabhas in the state capitals like Patiala, Nabha, Sangrur, Faridkot, and Kapurthala, there was an active Singh Sabha in Bhasaur, a village in the Patiala state.

Since each Singh Sabha professed to work for the entire Panth, some kind of coordination was needed. In 1880, a General Sabha was created at Amritsar for the Singh Sabhas of Lahore and Amritsar. In 1883, a resolution for starting a Sikh college was passed by the

General Sabha. It was soon reconstituted to form the Khalsa Diwan at Amritsar. More than thirty Singh Sabhas came to be affiliated with the Diwan. But there was a good deal of tension among its leaders, particularly between Gurmukh Singh and Baba Khem Singh Bedi. The Diwan split in 1885, with the rump at Amritsar presided over by Baba Khem Singh Bedi. A Khalsa Diwan was set up at Lahore in 1886 with the support of thirty Singh Sabhas. The leading members of the Diwan set up the Khalsa College Establishment Committee in 1890. Donations from Sikh rulers and landed gentry were encouraging. However, the Sikh and non-Sikh opponents of the Lahore leaders succeeded in getting the site of the college shifted from Lahore to Amritsar. Before the century ended, a school and a college were established at Amritsar to serve as models of Khalsa institutions elsewhere in the province.[26]

The death of Gurmukh Singh and Giani Ditt Singh accentuated the feeling among some new leaders that a common platform for the Panth was absolutely necessary. In 1902 was established the Chief Khalsa Diwan at Amritsar on the initiative largely of Sardar Sunder Singh Majithia who belonged to another aristocratic family of the time of Maharaja Ranjit Singh. The president of the Diwan was Bhai Arjan Singh of Bagarian, who was an aristocrat in his own right, with Sardar Sunder Singh himself as the secretary of the Diwan. This 'aristocratic' top might suggest a close link with the Amritsar Singh Sabha but the Chief Khalsa Diwan was not linked with either Amritsar or Lahore. In due course the majority of the Singh Sabhas accepted its lead to make it a representative body of the Panth. Its ideology was closer to that of the leaders of the Lahore Singh Sabha and the scope of its concerns was even wider. It was meant, among other things, to safeguard the political interests of the Sikhs. Directly or indirectly, the Chief Khalsa Diwan helped the foundation of several important organizations, notably the Sikh Educational Conference. The *Khalsa Advocate* became its official organ.[27]

The Early Leaders

Between the leaders of the Amritsar and Lahore Singh Sabhas there were several differences—social, ideological, and personal.[28] Their activities and attitudes can be appreciated in the light of these differences. Raja Bikram Singh of Faridkot patronized the Singh Sabha and the Khalsa Diwan of Amritsar, set up a Singh Sabha at Faridkot, and financed Giani Badan Singh's work on the annotation and interpretation of the Ādi Granth in order to undo the wrong done by Ernest Trumpp's *Adi Granth* (1877). Giani Badan Singh's annotation was not regarded as commendable by the leaders of the Lahore Singh Sabha. Kanwar Bikrama Singh of Kapurthala, who patronized the Amritsar Sabha and Diwan, was instrumental in founding the Singh Sabha at Jalandhar and remained its president till his death in 1887. He patronized Gurmukh Singh who later became the leading light of the Lahore Singh Sabha. Thakur Singh Sandhanwalia was closely associated with the Managers of the Golden Temple. But his activities in connection with Maharaja Dalip Singh's return to the Punjab, landed him in difficulties, and he died in Pondicherry as an exile. These leaders belonged to the ruling houses or to the old jāgīrdār families. Baba Khem Singh Bedi belonged to a Guru lineage which had become affluent and influential under Sikh rule. Though socially an equal, he was distinguished from the other leaders by his religious position. He deliberately imitated Guru Gobind Singh, and his followers 'believed him to be an avtar whose mere touch would save them'.[29] He used to distribute charms, and his influence spread all over the north-west of the province. With consummate skill he grew fabulously rich and had a number of supporters and proteges. He was knighted by the British government.

The only aristocrat to be directly associated with the Lahore Singh Sabha and Khalsa Diwan, Sardar Attar Singh of Bhadaur, was well educated and had published books in English before the Singh Sabha was founded at Lahore. He appreciated the work of Gurmukh Singh, the moving spirit of the Lahore Sabha. Gurmukh Singh's father was a cook in the royal household of Kapurthala and he was patronized by Kanwar Bikrama Singh till he became a teacher at Oriental College, Lahore. He actually belonged to a new generation, with new ideas and aspirations. He was joined by other like-minded individuals, notably Jawahar Singh Kapur and Giani Ditt Singh. Jawahar Singh remained active in support of Sikh education and employment of educated Sikhs in government services, their advancement in the new professions, and in advocating a distinctive identity for the Sikhs. Giani Ditt Singh proved to be the greatest publicist of the movement, lecturing and writing on Sikh history and theology, highlighting the achievement of the Gurus and the Singh martyrs, defining Sikh doctrines and ritual practices, denouncing and ridiculing popular religion and belief in gods and goddesses, and defending the movement against all its opponents, whether Sikh or non-Sikh.

The most formidable opponent of the Lahore Singh Sabha was Baba Khem Singh Bedi. In 1883, he had proposed that the Singh Sabhas should be called 'Sikh Singh Sabhas' to retain or win the support of Sahajdhārīs. But he had to drop this motion because of a strong opposition, presumably from the Lahore leaders and their supporters. In 1885, Gurmukh Singh objected to Baba Khem Singh sitting on a cushion or *gadela* in the presence of Guru Granth Sahib, and this demand was supported by an overwhelming majority. Bhagat Lakshman Singh, who was baptized by Baba Khem Singh Bedi but looked upon the Lahore leaders alone as 'the pioneers' of the Singh Sabha Movement, observed later that the Baba never forgave them for two reasons: one, that they 'insulted' him by removing his *gaddī* cushions and two, that they never acknowledged him as the Guru of the Sikhs.[30] After a sustained campaign to expel Gurmukh Singh from the Diwan, stopping him from addressing a congregation at Guru ka Bagh adjoining the Golden Temple, and threatening him with violence, Baba Khem Singh Bedi succeeded in getting him excommunicated through a hukamnāma issued by the Manager of the Golden Temple in 1887. A nephew of Baba Khem Singh, Bawa Udey Singh, sued Giani Ditt Singh on the plea that he had ridiculed the Baba, among others, in the *Khalsa Akhbār* in 1887. In the process of litigation, the Khalsa Press and the *Khalsa Akhbār* had to be closed down for some time.

The most articulate opponent of the Lahore leaders was Avtar Singh Vahiria, a staunch follower of Baba Khem Singh Bedi. He was secretary of the Rawalpindi Singh Sabha and editor of the *Sri Gurmat Prakāshak*, both launched under the patronage of Baba Khem Singh. Avtar Singh published eight books, relating to Sikh history, theology, religious practices and rituals. He expected a Sikh to give the same kind of allegiance to the descendants of the Sikh Gurus as a subject gave to the king. For him, Guru Nanak was an avtār, like Rama and Krishna. The Vedas and the Puranas were as authoritative as the Sikh scriptures. He subscribed to the ideal of *varnashrama*, involving the notions of purity and pollution. He stood for the worship of the Goddess, the Brahmanical rites of passage, the parity of *charan-pahul* with the baptism by the double-edged sword, and the parity of the Sahajdhārī Sikh with the Khalsa Singh, both of whom were identified as 'Hindu'. Far more conservative and compromising than the norms of Sikh belief and practice, Avtar Singh Vahiria professed to safeguard 'the ancient customs, rites and rituals of the Sikh community'. The inspiration for his ideas and attitudes came from his living guru, Baba Sir Khem Singh Bedi, and not from the Sikh scripture or Sikh history.[31]

The New Leaders and Ideologues

The new generation of leaders was in sympathy with the ideas and objectives of the Lahore leaders. Bhai Takht Singh had actually studied at Oriental College, Lahore, and remained in close association with Gurmukh Singh and Giani Ditt Singh. He was deeply interested in the education of girls and founded the Sikh Kanya Mahavidyalaya at Ferozepore which came to be regarded as the best institution for the education of Sikh girls over the decades. Bhai Mohan Singh Vaid, a leading member of the Singh Sabha of Tarn Taran, was an associate of Giani Ditt Singh. Like him, he played a vital role in defining Sikhism and propagating Khalsa rituals; he promoted the use of Punjabi in Gurmukhi script and the idea of a distinct Sikh (Singh) identity. Babu Teja Singh of the Bhasaur Singh Sabha and Panch Khalsa Diwan was more radical than the Lahore leaders in defining Sikhism and its scripture, and in advocating Sikh *rahit* for women.[32]

Some of the Sikh writers, generally associated with either Amritsar or Lahore, are better understood as spokesmen of the Singh Sabha Movement in general. Giani Gian Singh was over fifty years old when the Amritsar Singh Sabha was founded. His *Panth Prakāsh* (1880) was meant to be an improvement upon Ratan Singh Bhangu's work carrying the same title. His *Tawārīkh Guru Khalsa* in prose was more comprehensive in its treatment of the subject. The appeal of his major works lay in the spirit in which they were written to celebrate the Khalsa tradition. Similarly, Giani Hazara Singh, who belonged to an old *giani* family of Amritsar, interpreted the *Vārs* of Bhai Gurdas in a manner that made him eminently acceptable to the Singh Sabha leaders. Bhai Vir Singh articulated ideas and concerns which made him much closer to the Lahore leaders than to any of the early leaders of the Amritsar Singh Sabha. The *Khalsa Samāchār* which he edited is more of a continuation of the *Khalsa Akhbār* than a break from it.³³ In his novels too, Bhai Vir Singh valorized Khalsa ideology and Khalsa rahit.³⁴

The most important writer of the Singh Sabha Movement was Bhai Kahn Singh of Nabha. Born in 1861, he was well acquainted with Sikh literature before he came into contact with Gurmukh Singh and Giani Ditt Singh at Lahore in the early 1880s. His magnum opus *Gurshabad Ratnākar Mahān Kosh* was published in 1930 after a labour of fifteen years. It contains more than 64,000 entries, having direct or indirect bearing on things related to Sikhism and Sikh history. His *Gurmat Martand*, published posthumously in 1962, contains two of his works published for the first time in the late 1890s: the *Gurmat Prabhākar* and the *Gurmat Sudhākar*. The former contained all the teachings of the Gurus, arranged in alphabetical order and supported with relevant quotations from the Gurbāṇī. The *Gurmat Sudhākar* was meant to identify the true teachings of the Gurus in Sikh literature itself. Rejection of those elements which did not conform to the true teachings was implied in this approach. Apart from the compositions of Guru Gobind Singh, Bhai Gurdas and Bhai Nand Lal, more than a dozen major works of Sikh literature upto the time of Bhai Santokh Singh were used by Bhai Kahn Singh. The whole range of Sikh literature was used in his *Ham Hindu Nahīn* (1898) to demonstrate that Sikh doctrines and Sikh religious practices were meant to be and were clearly different from those of the Hindus. In the subsequent editions of this book, Bhai Kahn Singh developed the idea that the distinct identity of the Sikhs made them a distinct political entity.³⁵

Another writer and publicist of this generation had a peculiar importance due to his choice of English as the medium of communication. Born in 1863, Bhagat Lakshman Singh was educated at Rawalpindi and Lahore before he took up teaching History and English at the Mission Collegiate School of Rawalpindi. There he received baptism from Baba Khem Singh Bedi and started the Khalsa Dharm Parcharak Sabha. Reacting to attempts of the Arya Samaj writers, especially Bawa Chhajju Singh, to show that the Sikh Gurus were 'only Hindu reformers' who believed in the Veda, he started the first Sikh English organ *Khalsa* in consultation with Bhai Jawahar Singh. He used this weekly to disseminate the view that 'the Sikh dispensation was an independent entity and not a subsidiary system, based on Hindu philosophy'. Guru Nanak and Guru Gobind Singh had themselves made it clear that this dispensation was based on divine revelation. Bhagat Lakshman Singh had personally seen the shaving of Sikh Rahtiās by the leaders of the Wachhowali Arya Samaj and he used the columns of the *Khalsa* to carry on propaganda work on behalf of the newly formed Khalsa Sudhar Sabha to counteract the Arya programme of *shuddhī*. Bhagat Lakshman Singh had no doubt whatever that Baba Nanak himself had conceived 'the idea of establishing a separate church' and that Guru Gobind Singh gave it 'a final and distinct shape'. The protagonists of the Singh Sabha Movement, in his view, had carried forward the work of the Gurus. The recognition of the Sikh community as 'an independent political entity' was a logical outcome of that movement. In retrospect Bhagat Lakshman Singh thought that, independently of Bhai Kahn Singh of Nabha, he was preaching through the *Khalsa* the message of *Ham Hindu Nahīn*.[36] He wrote a biography of Guru Gobind Singh, placing him in the broad context of Indian civilization and pointing out his distinctive contribution in the context of the Sikh tradition. In a book on the Sikh martyrs he underscored the importance of martyrdom in the Sikh tradition.[37]

Revitalization of the Sikh Tradition

With the support of scholars, creative writers and publicists as much as through their own lectures, writings and activity on the ground, the leaders of the Singh Sabha Movement were able to evolve a general consensus. They were all agreed that the source of true Sikhism was the early Sikh tradition. This tradition was embodied in Sikh literature. By far the most important source of Sikh belief was the Ādi Granth. Of equal importance were the genuine compositions of Guru Gobind Singh. The works of Bhai Gurdas and Bhai Nand Lal conformed to Gurbāṇī and, therefore, these works were more important than the rest. The Janamsākhīs, the Gurbilās literature, and the Rahitnāmas were useful in so far as they conformed to and supplemented the genuine Sikh tradition. On these assumptions, Sikh theology, Sikh history, and the Sikh way of life were sought to be systematized, revitalized, and propagated through education and the print media.

Much that was un-Sikh in the lives of the contemporary Sikhs was to be discarded in the light of the Sikh tradition. The beliefs and practices of popular religion, which had nothing to do with Sikhism, were denounced and debunked. The cult of Sakhi Sarvar, Gugga Pir, Sitala and the like came under attack. The gods and goddesses of 'Hindu mythology' were categorically rejected. Belief in one God involved the rejection of other deities and their incarnations. Belief in the ten Gurus from Guru Nanak to Guru Gobind Singh, and in no other, involved the rejection of all personal gurus. The *Dasam Granth* was venerable because it contained the genuine compositions of Guru Gobind Singh. But Guruship was vested in the Ādi Granth alone. The Gurdwara, with congregational worship and community meal, was recognized as the most important Sikh institution. But the Gurdwaras of the Panth were controlled and managed by those who were alien or indifferent to the Sikh tradition. This accounted for un-Sikh practices in the Sikh sacred spaces. An appeal made to the Sikh community and British Government in 1887 points out that the management of the Golden Temple was based neither on legislation nor on the principles of the Khalsa Panth. The feeling was growing that only the representatives of the Khalsa were entitled to manage the affairs of the Golden Temple. This was an essential plank of the later Akali movement.

For the Sikh way of life, it was necessary first to receive pahul, adopt the epithet Singh, carry a *kirpān*, wear kachh and kara, keep uncut hair (kesh) and kangha. The formulation of '5 Ks' came handy to popularize these old features of the Khalsa rahit. Ban on smoking and insistence on eating *jhatka* meat came from the same Rahitnāma sources. The Sikh rites of birth and death and more so the rite of marriage acquired great importance in the context of shedding all Brahmanical practices. There were precedents in theory and practice, but there was no uniformity in modes and no universality in application. The institution of marriage involved issues of property as well. Therefore, it was seen as more important than the other rites of passage. This dimension of the institution was highlighted by the death of Sardar Dyal Singh Majithia. His widow contested his will that alienated his ancestral property in favour of the Dyal Singh Trust. But the Chief Court decided in favour of the trustees. This gave great impetus to the demand for legal recognition of the Sikh rite of marriage. There was an overwhelming articulation in support of the Anand Marriage Bill. It was passed in 1909 despite opposition articulated by some Sikhs and many Hindus.[38]

COLONIAL RULE AND CULTURAL REORIENTATION 277

The Anand Marriage Act had a direct bearing on Sikh identity. It may not be accidental that the leaders of the Chief Khalsa Diwan asked for separate electorates for the Sikhs for the first time in 1909 when separate electorates were created for Muslims. Political sanctity was imparted to separate electorates and weightage by the Lucknow Pact of 1916 between the Indian National Congress and the All India Muslim League. A Sikh deputation met the Governor General in 1917 to plead for separate electorates for the Sikhs. This was conceded. The Act of 1919 provided ten seats for the Sikhs in the Provincial Council of fifty-eight seats. Sikh identity was legally and politically recognized as the culmination of the Singh Sabha Movement.[39]

After the Act of 1919, politics became increasingly important for the people in the Punjab and for the rest of the people in India. Politics became the dominant concern of the Sikhs too. However, the intellectual impetus provided by the Singh Sabha Movement was not retarded by politics. Not only did writers like Bhai Vir Singh and Bhai Kahn Singh continue to write in the twentieth century, new scholars and writers of great stature appeared on the scene to study Sikh theology and Sikh history within the parameters of the Singh Sabha Movement. The most eminent among them were Teja Singh, Bhai Jodh Singh and Sahib Singh, all associated with the Khalsa College at Amritsar.[40]

In retrospect we can see that Sikhism was a living faith in the early nineteenth century, with Singh identity as the most dominant identity among the Sikhs. The doctrine of Guru Granth was the primary doctrine and the Ādi Granth was regarded as the Guru. The *Dasam Granth* was held in veneration; the Vārs of Bhai Gurdas and the Rahitnāmas were held in great esteem. The primary institution of the Sikhs was the Gurdwara, with the Harmandar Sahib as the most important place of Sikh pilgrimage, followed by Anandpur Sahib, Patna Sahib and Abchal Nagar (Nander). The doctrine of Guru Panth was not forgotten but it was overshadowed by the profession of the Sikh rulers to rule in the name of the Panth.

Before the end of Sikh rule, at least two individual groups were gaining followers in their attempt to place the Ādi Granth at the centre of Sikh religious and social life, with no role for Brahmanical rites and ceremonies in the lives of their followers: the Nirankaris and the Namdharis. During the late nineteenth century, the Nirankaris laid great emphasis on the Sikh ceremonies of birth, marriage, and death. They developed no interest in the new education. The Namdharis adopted the Singh identity and an anti-British attitude. They too had no interest in things western. They treated the Ādi Granth as their scripture, with the Chandī literature of the *Dasam Granth* as of special importance. They began to treat Baba Ram Singh and his successors as personal Gurus. Consequently, the doctrines of Guru Panth and Guru Granth had little relevance for them. They did not establish any new educational institutions, with the implication that they had no access to western science and social sciences or to English language and literature.

The Singh Sabhas were democratic and voluntary associations of Singhs who felt concerned about the affairs of the Sikh community as a whole. Understandably, they came to coordinate their efforts through the Chief Khalsa Diwan. Other institutions like Sikh Educational Conference, the Khalsa Tract Society and the Punjab and Sind Bank were established to promote what they regarded as the collective interests of the Sikhs. They made effective use of the printing press and took to Anglo-Sikh education with great enthusiasm, establishing schools and colleges for boys and girls. The Khalsa College at Amritsar came to be regarded as the premier Sikh educational institution. The leaders of the Chief Khalsa Diwan and the Singh Sabhas tried to promote Punjabi literature in Gurmukhi script. They were keen about the Khalsa rahit and acutely conscious of a distinct Sikh identity. They looked upon the Ādi Granth as the Guru, the only source of right belief and practice. They revived the doctrine of Guru Panth and demanded that no idols should be brought into the Golden Temple for worship,[41] that the demolished wall of Gurdwara Rakabganj for straightening a road to the Viceregal Lodge should be reconstructed,[42] and that all Gurdwaras associated with their Gurus and Sikh martyrs should be managed and controlled by the representatives of the Khalsa Panth.[43]

There was a great resurgence among the Sikhs in the late nineteenth and the early twentieth centuries. It was articulated through religious, social and cultural activities, as in their swelling numbers. In the early decades of the twentieth century this resurgence began to find political expression in diverse ways. Sikh identity was emerging as the basis of Sikh politics. On the whole, the Singh Sabha Movement provided a comprehensive interpretation of the earlier Sikh tradition. What is more important, this understanding of the past was combined with the adoption of modern outlook, attitudes and institutions. It was the nature of its response to the colonial environment that made it more influential than the other movements.

Secular Aspects of Cultural Reorientation

The Singh Sabha Movement did not exhaust the Sikh response to colonial environment. In the first place, the political response of the Sikhs was not based on Sikh identity alone. Even when the inspiration came partly or largely from religion, as in the case of many Ghadarites, the objective of their politics was the freedom of the country as a whole. This was equally true of the leaders of the Central Sikh League who were closely aligned with the Indian National Congress. Because of their influence, the Shiromani Akali Dal, founded in 1920 to take over Sikh Gurdwaras from the local *mahant*s, worked in tandem with the Indian National Congress. The Babbar Akalis worked and died for the freedom of India. The Sikh leaders of the Kirti Kisan Movement, the Naujawan Bharat Sabha and several Communist Sikh leaders had Indian independence in view. When the leaders of the Shiromani Akali Dal and the Central Sikh League parted company in the 1930s, the latter joined the Indian National Congress as 'nationalist' Sikhs and remained aligned with the Congress till after 1947.[44]

The emergence of secular Punjabi literature was culturally significant, produced by Sikh authors, before 1947. Bawa Buddh Singh, a descendant of Guru Amar Das, was the first Sikh historian of Punjabi literature. An engineer by profession, he published a dozen books in the second and third decades of the twentieth century. His passion was to promote Punjabi literature as such, and not Sikh literature alone. Despite his reverence for religious literature, he was criticized for bracketing revealed *bāṇī* with secular poetry. He defended himself by saying that Gurbāṇī was a form of poetry. He wrote several plays on secular themes, including love.[45] The Sikh poets, playwrights, novelists, and short story writers of the colonial period, who laid the foundations of secular Punjabi literature in the last decades of colonial rule are well known. Among those who rose to great heights after 1947 are Sant Singh Sekhon, Kartar Singh Duggal, Mohan Singh and Amrita Pritam.[46] There were a score of other major writers whose pulse was humanistic and secular. In the early decades of the twentieth century, secular historical writing emerged in response to British historical writing on the Sikhs as in the works of Bhagat Lakshman Singh.[47] *A Short History of the Sikhs* (1951) by Teja Singh and Ganda Singh is a good example of modern historiography by the Sikhs.[48] In painting, religious themes continued to be treated during the colonial period and after 1947. However, secular personalities, landscape and other secular themes became increasingly important, expressing a new kind of sensibility.[49] Cultural reorientation among the Sikhs under colonial rule was obviously not confined to the Singh Sabha Movement and its impact on Sikh social and cultural life.

NOTES

1. G.S. Dhillon subscribes to the idea of revival as it is evident from the title of his article: 'Singh Sabha Movement: A Revival', Jasbir Singh, Mann, and Harbans Singh Saraon, eds, *Advanced Studies in Sikhism*, Irvine: Sikh Community of North America, 1989, pp. 234–62). His PhD thesis on 'Character and Impact of the Singh Sabha Movement on the History of the Punjab' was submitted to the Punjabi University in 1973. W.H. McLeod subscribes to the idea of re-formation in his *Who is a Sikh? The Problem of Sikh Identity*, Oxford: The Clarendon Press, 1989. For the idea of rupture, the best example is Harjot Oberoi's *The Construction of Religious Boundaries: Culture, Identity and Diversity in the Sikh Tradition*, New Delhi: Oxford University Press, 1994. For a discussion of these views, see J.S. Grewal, *Historical Perspectives on Sikh Identity*, Patiala: Punjabi University, 1997.
2. As he points out, Cunningham had lived among the Sikh people for eight years (1837–45) when he came into contact with all classes of men: *A History of the Sikhs*, Delhi: S. Chand & Co., 1955 (rpt), pp. xxxi–ii. He was also familiar with Sikh religious literature: ibid., pp. 321–47.
3. Ibid., pp. 8–10, 12, 16, 43, 81n1, 347–9.
4. Ibid., pp. 383–6. Indu Banga, *Agrarian System of the Sikhs: Late Eighteenth and Early Nineteenth Century*, New Delhi: Manohar Publications, 1978, pp. 118–67. See also, J.S. Grewal, *Maharaja Ranjit Singh: Polity, Economy and Society*, Amritsar: Guru Nanak Dev University, 2001.
5. Cunningham, *A History of the Sikhs*, pp. 245, 289, 387–90.
6. Ibid., pp. 321–47. The perspective that we find in Cunningham is remarkably close to that of his Sikh contemporary Ratan Singh Bhangu.

For a brief analysis, see J.S. Grewal, 'Valorizing the Sikh Tradition: Bhangu's Panth Prakash', in J.S. Grewal, ed., *The Khalsa: Sikh and Non-Sikh Perspectives*, New Delhi: Manohar, 2004, pp. 103–22.

7. For the administrative framework of the colonial Punjab in the late 19th century, see James Douie, *The Punjab, North-Western Frontier Province and Kashmir*, Delhi: Seema Publications, 1974 (rpt). Not only were the departments multiplied in the new administration, with a lot of importance attached to revenue, police and justice, but also a large measure of bureaucratic rule was established in place of the jāgīrdāri system. A new kind of personnel was needed at the lower rungs of this administration. In the beginning, this personnel was brought from Bengal and the United Provinces.

8. Active participation against the British in the Anglo-Sikh wars was the main cause of the downfall of the Atariwala Sardars. They present, however, only the most conspicuous example. A similar case was that of the son of Hari Singh Nalwa. Lepel Griffin's *Punjab Chiefs* (first published from Lahore in 1865) provides information on the treatment of the former jāgīrdārs after 1849.

9. For a good perspective on the changing fortunes of the descendants of the large jāgīrdārs of the time of Sikh rule. See J.S. Grewal and Harish C. Sharma, 'Political Change and Social Readjustment: The Case of Sikh Aristocracy under Colonial Rule in the Punjab, *Proceedings of the Indian History Congress*, Goa, 1987.

10. Kapurthala was allowed to survive as a vassal principality after the Anglo-Sikh war of 1845–6, though without the territories in the Sutlej-Jamuna Divide. The states of Patiala, Nabha, Jind, and Faridkot had come under British protection in 1809. They all supported the British enthusiastically in 1857–8 to be generously rewarded. Their support to the paramount power was always more important than that of the Sikh aristocracy.

11. Ian J. Kerr, 'The British and the Administration of the Golden Temple in 1859', *The Panjab Past and Present*, vol. X, part 2, October 1976, pp. 306–21; 'British Relationship with the Golden Temple 1849–90', *The Indian Economic and Social History Review*, vol. XXI, part 2 (April–June 1984, pp. 139–51; 'Sikhs and State: Troublesome Relationships and a Fundamental Continuity with Reference to the Period 1849–1919', in Pashaura Singh and N. Gerald Barrier, eds, *Sikh Identity: Continuity and Change*, New Delhi: Manohar, 2001 (Paperback), pp. 153–5, 164–5.

12. N.M. Khilnani talks of the liquidation of the Khalsa army leading to unemployment on a prodigious scale. Thousands of demobilized

soldiers had 'no job, no work': *British Power in the Punjab, 1839–58*, Bombay: Asia Publishing House, 1972, p. 178.

13. According to Richard G. Fox, nearly 40 per cent of the combat troops in the British Indian army at the outbreak of the War were Singhs. The proportion of Sikh troops in the army was over three times larger than the proportion of the Sikhs in the Punjab population and almost twenty times their proportion in the Indian population. Fox appears to be mistaken when he says that the Sikh contingent was absolutely larger than the Hindu or Muslim. *Lions of the Punjab: Culture in the Making*, Berkeley: University of California Press, 1985, p. 143. According to Ian J. Kerr, 'Sikhs and State', p. 159, more than 97,000 Sikhs served in the First World War.

    Mustapha Kamal Pasha has argued that the shift in recruitment to the colonial army after 1857–8 underscored the new British thinking in favour of the Punjab as a whole: *Colonial Political Economy: Recruitment and Underdevelopment in the Punjab*, Karachi: Oxford University Press, 1998, p. 145.

14. The identity of the Sikhs in the army of Ranjit Singh has generally been ignored. Contemporary documents clearly indicate that they were all baptized Singhs who wore kesh and turban, and attended religious services regularly. In one case (document 157), Ranjit Singh even gave revenue-free land to a *khidmatgār* named Diwan Singh for getting baptized. J.S Grewal and Indu Banga, eds, *Civil and Military Affairs of Maharaja Ranjit Singh (A Study of 450 Orders in Persian)*, Amritsar: Guru Nanak Dev University, 1987.

    'Not only was induction into the Indian army, and into Singh identity often one and the same', says Fox, 'but also military commanders required a strict observance of Singh customs and ceremonies afterward': *Lions of the Punjab*, p. 142. What Fox looks upon as something new in the colonial period was actually not a novelty.

15. S.S. Thorburn looked upon the Sikhs as 'foremost amongst the prosperous farmers and loyal soldiers of the Empire'. He carried the impression that they were more successful than the others in meeting the challenge of the new environment. 'Their love of gain and inherited shrewdness have, since the establishment of our reign of law, enabled them to avoid the pitfalls of the system of administration which has demoralized so many of the less efficient agricultural communities of the province': *The Punjab in Peace and War*, Patiala: Punjab Language Department, 1970 (rpt), p. 265.

16. According to Imran Ali, the choice of the central Punjab as a supply area for colonization was partly influenced by the fact that it was the

homeland of the Sikhs who had a strong representation in the military services. The most marked feature of the Sohag Para Colony was the large area allotted to Jat Sikhs: 30,000 acres, forming 38 per cent of the total area allotted. In the Chenab Colony, fourteen out of eighteen lacs of acres of land were held by peasant colonists, accounting for more than 78 per cent of the total area allotted. *The Punjab Under Imperialism, 1885–1947*, New Delhi: Oxford University Press, 1989, pp. 22, 47, 50. In Lyallpur district, the percentage of Jat Sikhs in 1931 was over 33, that is, double the proportion of their percentage in the total population. Fox, *Lions of the Punjab*, p. 181.

17. For occupational change among the Sikhs, see Ethne K. Marenco, *The Transformation of Sikh Society*, New Delhi: Heritage Publishers, 1976.

18. Competition among the religious communities in the Punjab related to numbers, access to educational institutions, representation in government services, municipalities and legislative bodies. It involved concerns about conversion, language and script. N. Gerald Barrier, *The Sikhs and Their Literature, (A Guide to Tracts, Books and Periodicals, 1849–1919)*, Delhi: Manohar Book Service, 1970. Kenneth Jones, *Arya Dharm, Hindu Consciousness in 19th Century Punjab*, New Delhi: Manohar, 1989 (rpt). Spencer Lavan, *The Ahmadiyya Movement: A History and Perspective*, New Delhi: Manohar, 1974.

19. Anurupita Kaur, 'Sikhs in the Early Census Reports', in Reeta Grewal and Sheena Pall, eds, *Five Centuries of Sikh Tradition: Ideology, Society, Politics and Culture*, New Delhi: Manohar, 2005, pp. 123–50.

20. Barrier, *The Sikhs and Their Literature*, pp. xxiii–iv.

21. For the Nirankaris, see John C.B. Webster, *The Nirankari Sikhs*, Delhi: The Macmillan Company of India Ltd. for The Christian Institute of Sikh Studies (Batala), 1979. J.S Grewal, ed., *Baba Dayal: Founder of the First Reform Movement among the Sikhs*, Chandigarh: Dr Man Singh Nirankari, 2003.

22. For the Namdharis, see Ganda Singh, *Kukian di Vithia* (Pbi.), Amritsar, 1944. Nahar Singh, ed., *Gooroo Ram Singh and the Kuka Sikhs*, New Delhi: Amrit Books, 1965. Jaswinder Singh, *Kuka Movement: Freedom Struggle in Punjab*, New Delhi: Atlantic Publishers, 1985.

23. By 1873, the Christian missionaries were well entrenched in the British Punjab. See John C.B. Webster, *The Christian Community and Change in Nineteenth Century North India*, Delhi: Macmillan, 1976. The presence of Christian missionaries in the Punjab and their activities brought religion into sharp focus and largely determined the nature of response from all the religious communities.

24. Ganda Singh, ed., *History of Freedom Movement in the Punjab*, vol. III: *Maharaja Duleep Singh Correspondence*, Patiala: Punjabi University, 1977. By 1882, Maharaja Dalip Singh was dissatisfied with his position in England. He wrote two letters to *The Times* in August and September, complaining of the treatment meted out to him after his deposition. Major Evans Bell appears to have written *The Annexation of the Punjab and Maharaja Duleep Singh* on behalf of the Maharaja (reprinted by the Punjab Languages Department from Patiala in 1970). For the same purpose, another book was printed for private circulation as *The Maharaja Duleep Singh and the Government: A Narrative* (rpt by Punjabi Prakashan from Coventry). See also, Prithipal Singh Kapur, ed., *Maharaja Duleep Singh: The Last Sovereign Ruler of the Punjab*, Amritsar: Shiromani Gurdwara Parbandhak Committee, 1995.

25. Baba Sir Khem Singh Bedi held 7,800 acres of land given to him mainly on political consideration in the Sohag Para Colony, accounting for 10 per cent of the total area allotted in the colony. Imran Ali, *The Punjab Under Imperialism*, p. 17.

26. The Singh Sabha leaders accepted Western education with enthusiasm. Combining sciences, social sciences and English literature with Punjabi language and instruction in Sikhism, they evolved the Anglo-Sikh pattern of education which was sought to be popularized in schools and, later on, in colleges. The Sikh Educational Conference met regularly for promoting education among the Sikhs.

27. For factual information on Singh Sabhas and Khalsa Diwans, W.H. McLeod, *Who is a Sikh? The Problem of Sikh Identity*, Oxford: The Clarendon Press, 1989; Oberoi, *The Construction of Religious Boundaries*; Grewal, *The Sikhs of the Punjab* (The New Cambridge History of India) Cambridge: Cambridge University Press, 1990, pp. 144–50.

28. For biographical information, Joginder Singh, *Sikh Leadership, Early 20th Century*, Amritsar: Guru Nanak Dev University, 1999. Bhagat Lakshman Singh, *Autobiography*, Ganda Singh, ed., Calcutta: The Sikh Cultural Centre, 1965; Oberoi, *The Construction of Religious Boundaries*.

29. The works published by Sardar Attar Singh were of interest to the British administrators in the context of the Namdhari movement: *Sakhee Book or the Description of Gooroo Gobind Singh's Religious Doctrines*, Benares: Medical Hall Press, *The Rahit Nama of Prahlad Rai or the Excellent Conversation of Duswan Padsha* and *Nand Lal's Rayhit Nama or Rules for Guidance of the Sikhs in Religious Matters*, Lahore, 1876.

30. Lakshman Singh, *Autobiography*, p. 91.

31. Harjot Oberoi looks upon Avtar Singh Vahiria as the great defender of the Sanatan Sikh tradition, missing the significance of his connection with Baba Khem Singh Bedi. His publications reflected not so much the views and attitudes of any large number of Sikhs as of Baba Khem Singh Bedi. His bid to influence people seems to have met little success.
32. N.G. Barrier, 'Sikh Politics and Religion: The Bhasaur Singh Sabha', in Indu Banga, ed., *Five Punjabi Centuries: Polity, Economy and Culture, 1500–1990*, New Delhi: Manohar, 1997, pp. 140–56.
33. For a brief analysis of the contents of the *Khalsa Samāchār*, see Joginder Singh, 'Resurgence in Sikh Journalism', *Journal of Regional History*, Amritsar: Guru Nanak Dev University, 1982, pp. 99–116.
34. Harbans Singh, *Bhai Vir Singh*, New Delhi: Sahitya Akademi, 1972.
35. Bhai Kahn Singh Nabha, *Ham Hindu Nahīn* (Pbi.), Amritsar: Singh Brothers, 1995 (rpt of 5th edn). For a brief analysis of the work, see J.S. Grewal, 'Nabha's *Ham Hindu Nahin*: A Declaration of Sikh Ethnicity', in Pashaura Singh and N. Gerald Barrier, eds, *Sikh Identity, Continuity and Change*, New Delhi: Manohar, 2001, pp. 231–51.
36. Lakshman Singh, *Autobiography*, pp. 137, 291–2.
37. Bhagat Lakshman Singh, *A Short Sketch of the Life and Work of Guru Gobind Singh the Tenth and Last Guru of the Sikhs*, Ludhiana: Lahore Book Shop, 1963 (rpt). For a brief statement on Bhagat Lakshman Singh's works by Prithipal Singh Kapur, see J.S. Grewal, ed., *The Khalsa: Sikh and Non-Sikh Perspectives*, New Delhi: Manohar, 2004, pp. 29–32.
38. Anand Marriage Bill was introduced in the Central Legislature in 1908 by Tikka Ripudaman Singh of Nabha. He had been taught as a young prince by Bhai Kahn Singh of Nabha who was closely associated with the Lahore Singh Sabha. The Bill was passed in 1909, steered by Sardar Sunder Singh Majithia who had replaced Tikka Ripudaman Singh as an additional member. The Nirankaris and Namdharis were also in favour of the Bill. The Granthīs and Pujārīs of the Darbar Sahib were opposed to it.
39. Before the foundation of the Central Sikh League in 1919 and of the Shiromani Akali Dal in 1920, the Chief Khalsa Diwan was the major representative of Sikh political opinion. Sardar Sunder Singh Majithia was its most important leader and he continued to represent this constituency in the Unionist ministry. See, Gurdev Singh Deol, *Sardar Sundar Singh Majithia: Life, Work and Mission*, Amritsar: Khalsa College, 1992.

40. The works of Professor Teja Singh, Bhai Jodh Singh and Professor Sahib Singh on Sikhism are still the basic and essential reading in Sikh studies, especially the annotated editions of *Guru Granth Sahib* known as *Shabdarth Sri Guru Granth Sahib* (by Teja Singh) and Sri *Guru Granth Sahib Darpan* (by Sahib Singh).
41. For the removal of idols from the Golden Temple, Jones, *Arya Dharm*: p. 211; Fox, *Lions of the Punjab*, pp. 173–4; Oberoi, *The Construction of Religious Boundaries*, pp. 322–7. All three scholars tend to assume that idols were worshipped in the Golden Temple in pre-colonial times too, but there is no credible evidence for this assumption.
42. Harjot S. Oberoi, 'From Gurdwara Rikabganj to the Viceregal Palace—A Study of Religious Protest', *The Panjab Past and Present*, Patiala: Punjabi University, vol. XIV, part 1 (April 1980), pp. 182–98.
43. For the movement to take over the control and management of historic gurdwaras, Mohinder Singh, *The Akali Movement*, Delhi: Macmillan of India, 1978; Fox, *The Lions of the Punjab*; Rajiv A. Kapur, *Sikh Separatism: The Politics of Faith*, New Delhi: Vikas Publishing House, 1987 (2nd impression, paperback).
44. For Sikh participation in nationalist movements, Harish K. Puri, *Ghadar Movement: Ideology, Organisation and Strategy*, Amritsar: Guru Nanak Dev University, 1983; K.L. Tuteja, *Sikh Politics (1920–40)*, Kurukshetra: Vishal Publications, 1984; Kamlesh Mohan, *Militant Nationalism in the Punjab, 1919–1935*, New Delhi: Manohar, 1985.
45. Christopher Shackle, 'Making Punjabi Literary History', in Christopher Shackle, Gurharpal Singh and Arvinder Pal Singh Mandair, eds, *Sikh Religion, Culture and Ethnicity*, Richmond: Curzon Press, 2001, pp. 108–17. J.S. Grewal, 'The Emergence of Punjabi Drama: A Cultural Response to Colonial Rule', *Journal of Regional History*, Amritsar: Guru Nanak Dev University, vol. V (1984), pp. 115–55.
46. For modern Punjabi poetry, novel, short story, drama, prose, and literary criticism, see Sant Singh Sekhon and Kartar Singh Duggal, *A History of Punjabi Literature*, New Delhi: Sahitya Akademi, 1992.
47. For the early Sikh writers, see J.S. Grewal, *Contesting Interpretations of the Sikh Tradition*, New Delhi: Manohar, 1998, pp. 59–81.
48. Teja Singh and Ganda Singh, *A Short History of the Sikhs*, vol. I, Patiala: Punjabi University, 1989 (rpt).
49. T.S. Randhawa, *The Sikhs: Images of a Heritage*, New Delhi: Prakash Books, 2000, Kavita Singh, ed., *New Insights into Sikh Art*, Mumbai: Marg Publications, vol. 54, no. 4, June 2003.

12. The Akalis and Khalistan*

Emergence of the Shiromani Akali Dal

The Shiromani Akali Dal was founded towards the end of 1920, soon after the formation of the Shiromani Gurdwara Parbandhak Committee (SGPC). The primary purpose of both these organizations was to take control of the Gurdwaras associated with the Sikh Gurus and Sikh martyrs, and to manage their affairs as representatives of the Sikh community.

The Sikh concern for their sacred spaces can be appreciated if we realize that the Gurdwara was by far the most important institution of the Sikhs since the days of Guru Nanak.[1] There was a time when the Sikh sacred space was known as the *dharmsāl*. It was a place where congregational worship was held, sacred food (*parshād*) was distributed, and community meal (*langar*) was prepared and eaten. It was also the place where matters of common interest to the local community could be discussed from time to time. A dharmsāl where the Guru was personally present was regarded as the premier institution, like Kartarpur (Dera Baba Nanak), Khadur Sahib, Goindwal, Ramdaspur, Kiratpur, and Anandpur. The emergence of the idea that the Guru was present in the *sangat*, added a new dimension to the sanctity of the dharmsāl. The equation of *bāṇī* with the Guru reached its culmination with the doctrine of Guru Granth. The presence of the Granth in the dharmsāl enhanced its sanctity to that of the premier dharmsāls of the days of the Gurus. Gradually, the name dharmsāl was dropped

---

* 'The Akalis and Khalistan' is a revised version of 'Sikh Identity, the Akalis and Khalistan', in J.S. Grewal and Indu Banga, eds, *Punjab in Prosperity and Violence: Administration, Politics and Social Change 1947–1997* (Chandigarh: Institute of Punjab Studies, 1998, pp. 65–103). Another revised version was published in Reeta Grewal and Sheena Pall, eds, *Five Centuries of Sikh Tradition: Ideology, Society, Politics and Culture: Essays for Indu Banga* (New Delhi: Manohar, 2005, pp. 295–333).

in favour of Gurdwara, literally the door of the Guru, because of the presence of both the sangat and the Granth. The change in the name given to the Sikh sacred space was an index of its enhanced sanctity in the eyes of the Sikhs. Understandably, the leaders of the Singh Sabha Movement attached great importance to the Gurdwara.

What enabled the Akalis to put forth the claim to control the Gurdwaras and to manage their affairs was the doctrine of Guru Panth. Personal Guruship had been abolished by Guru Gobind Singh before his death in 1708, with the enunciation that the office henceforth was vested in Shabad-Bāṇī and the collective body of the Khalsa. This idea remained operative in the eighteenth century. With the establishment of Sikh rule, individual rulers began to exercise power in the name of the Khalsa, and the doctrine of Guru Panth was relegated to the background. It was revived by the leaders of the Singh Sabha Movement in the late nineteenth century. By now the historic Gurdwaras were under the direct or indirect control of the British administrators, and the custodians of the Gurdwaras were not much concerned about their traditional role. The intrinsic importance of Gurdwaras and the doctrine of Guru Panth inspired the Singh Sabha leaders to demand their control and management on behalf of the Sikh Panth. The pursuit of this objective resulted in the formation of the Shiromani Gurdwara Parbandhak Committee and the Shiromani Akali Dal.[2]

Inevitably, the Akalis came into conflict with the British government. All through their anti-British struggle from 1921–4, they received sympathetic support from the leaders of the Indian National Congress. However, they refused to merge their entity with the Congress. The Sikh Gurdwaras Act of 1925 gave constitutional recognition to a Central Board for the control and management of historic Gurdwaras. Its elected members gave it the name of Shiromani Gurdwara Parbandhak Committee to identify it with the body formed in 1920. The Shiromani Akali Dal became an independent political party, basing its politics on a distinct Sikh identity.[3]

There is a general but erroneous impression that the leaders of the Singh Sabha Movement started insisting all of a sudden that the Sikhs were not Hindu. Bhai Kahn Singh Nabha's *Ham Hindu Nahin* [We Are Not Hindus] is often referred to in this connection. However, the relevant question to ask is why in the late nineteenth century, for the first time, some people started arguing that the Sikhs were 'Hindu'.

THE AKALIS AND KHALISTAN   289

There was a time when the term Hindu referred vaguely to the people of India. This, for instance, is the usage in Alberuni's *Kitab al-Hind*. With the coming of the Turks, the term Hindu tended to be used increasingly for 'Indians' who were not Muslim. It was used in two other senses during the medieval period: first, for the socio-religious system represented and upheld by the Brahmans, and second, for the upper caste non-Muslims. These connotations were not suddenly discarded in the nineteenth century, but the religious connotation steadily gained greater currency. The presence of Christian missionaries and the movements for socio-religious reform under colonial rule had much to do with this development. Even in the late nineteenth century several different meanings were attached to the term 'Hindu'. One question began to be posed rather sharply: whether or not Buddhists, Jains, Sikhs, Kabir Panthis, the 'untouchables', and the tribal groups were to be included among Hindus. Already before the end of the nineteenth century some of the Hindus and Sikhs of the Punjab had given the answer that Sikhs were 'Hindus'.[4]

Nabha's *Ham Hindu Nahīn*, which has turned out to be a classic statement of Sikh identity, was initially written in Hindi, indicating the audience for which it was primarily intended. He is quite explicit on the point that he wrote in response to the claims being made that Sikhs were Hindus. As a literary device, he reproduces the arguments put forth by the 'Hindu' participant in the debate. Bhai Kahn Singh's arguments are quite comprehensive in scope, relating to scripture, religious doctrines, the mode of worship, the code of conduct, the rite of initiation, rites of passage, the character of the Sikh Panth, and consciousness of a separate identity. It is interesting to note that most of the time Bhai Kahn Singh invokes Sikh writings of the pre-colonial centuries in support of his arguments, covering a wide range and a strikingly large volume of Sikh literature. What is remarkable about this book is that, though his preference for the Khalsa or Singh identity is quite clear, he regards the Sahajdhārīs (who did not take *pahul* and, therefore, did not necessarily keep their hair uncut or bear the epithet Singh) as an integral part of the Sikh Panth. The implication is extremely important. A distinct Sikh identity did not start with the Khalsa: it had already emerged during the sixteenth and seventeenth centuries.[5]

Indeed, one has to trace Sikh identity back to the time of Guru Nanak. To be a Sikh was to be a follower of Guru Nanak. He told his followers what to believe and what to do, not only through his sermons in prose but also through his poetic compositions. These compositions were used by his followers for worship in congregation. He told his followers that this mode of worship was the most efficacious for attaining liberation, and for them it was the only way. His successors wrote their own compositions, in the name of 'Nanak'. All these compositions were put together in the Granth compiled by Guru Arjan. The compositions of Guru Tegh Bahadur were added later. It is now known as the Ādi Granth, and regarded as Guru Granth Sahib. The adoption of new beliefs, practices, and institutions made the Sikhs conscious of their identity quite early in their history. The institution of the Khalsa by Guru Gobind Singh appears to be a great landmark in this process precisely because it made Sikh identity unambiguously conspicuous.

There is a long historiographical tradition in which the Khalsa figure as a community distinct from both Hindus and Muslims. In eighteenth century Sikh literature itself, the Khalsa are presented as different from both Hindus and Muslims. They represent 'the third *panth*'. There is hardly any doubt that the Khalsa identity was the most dominant identity among the Sikhs of the early nineteenth century. The colonial rulers were quick to recognize this fact. The change introduced by the Singh Sabha leaders has to be understood in terms of differences of degree, coherence, magnitude, and insistence on conformity. All this was made possible by the new means of communication, including education and the press.[6]

Bhai Kahn Singh Nabha had no objection to the Sikhs being called Hindus if the term simply meant Indian, without bringing in any religious dimension. The crucial question about the Hindu–Sikh debate is why at that particular juncture so much importance came to be attached to religious identity. A part of the answer is provided by Bhai Kahn Singh. He is keen to establish that the Sikhs were a distinct *quam* (earlier, panth), like Hindus and Muslims. To recognize this was to recognize that the Sikhs were a political community, a nationality. This recognition should lead to their worldly progress. To be an appendage of another quam was to remain at a perpetual disadvantage. To say this was not to be unpatriotic. The Sikhs were prepared to struggle for the common interests of all Indians, shoulder to shoulder with other 'nations' like Hindus and Muslims. Overarching all of them was the Indian nation. In a sense, Bhai Kahn Singh subscribed to the idea of communitarian nationalism.[7]

Akali Politics Before Independence

Like Bhai Kahn Singh, the Akalis subscribed to the idea of communitarian nationalism. They were prepared to work in tandem with the Indian National Congress as an independent entity. With the transition from communitarian nationalism to secular Indian nationalism in the 1920s and the 1930s, tension began to appear between the Congress and the Akalis on various issues from time to time: as in the deliberations of the Moti Lal Nehru Committee, the award given by Ramsay MacDonald, and the issue of support to the British government in the Second World War. Much more serious than all these issues was that of Pakistan. The historical situation of the 1940s forced the Akalis to think of Sikh future in the face of the growing possibility of Pakistan being created with the consent of the Indian National Congress. In this context, we hear of 'Khalistan' for the first time in 1940.[8]

The term Khalistan was used by a doctor, V.S. Bhatti, as the title of a pamphlet, published soon after the Lahore Resolution of the All India Muslim League in 1940, popularly known as the 'Pakistan Resolution'. Bhatti's Khalistan was meant to be a counterblast to the idea of Pakistan assumed to be embodied in the Lahore Resolution. Covering much of the area between the Chenab and the Jamuna, the Khalistan of Bhatti was meant to serve as a buffer state between India and Pakistan. With the Maharaja of Patiala as its head, Khalistan was to be a 'theocratic' state, consisting of several federating units. A corridor was to link it with the Arabian Sea. Master Tara Singh, who was President of the Shiromani Akali Dal at this time, denounced the pamphlet for confounding the confusion created by the Muslim League. Two conferences were organized by Baba Gurdit Singh of Komagata Maru to popularize the idea of Khalistan. Maulana Abul Kalam Azad expressed his disapproval of Khalistan by stating that some Akalis were using the Congress platform to propagate the idea of Sikh rāj for scuttling the idea of Pakistan.

The term Khalistan was never appropriated by the Akalis. However, they came up with counterproposals in their opposition to the idea of Pakistan in the 1940s. With the prospect of freedom coming closer, their concern for the future became greater. In March–April 1942

Stafford Cripps conceded in principle that it was not obligatory for a province to join the Indian federation. This concession appeared to carry the implication that the Punjab could become an autonomous political unit outside the Indian state. The Akali leaders did not like to be subordinated permanently to Muslim majority. The Sikh All-Parties Committee submitted to Cripps the proposal of a province with different boundaries and different proportions of the three major communities of the Punjab. The name given to the province of their conception was 'Azad Punjab'. This gave the impression as if it was meant to be an independent state. Keen to sell the idea, the Akali leaders explained that this province was meant to be a part of the Indian federation. The term *āzād* was meant to suggest that each community of this province would be free of the fear of domination by another community.[9] The Muslims and Hindus of this province would account for the bulk of its population, with 40 per cent each. The Sikhs would form the remaining 20 per cent. Rooted in a genuine fear that the creation of Pakistan would place the Sikhs under the political domination of a hostile community for ever, the Azad Punjab scheme was essentially a defensive strategy adopted in response to the recognition of the idea of Pakistan by the British government through the Cripps proposals and by the Congress through its resolution of 2 April 1942. In their opposition to the idea of Pakistan, the Sikh leaders did not hesitate to share platforms with the leaders of the Hindu Mahasabha who stood for India as a single political unit. Unlike Khalistan, Azad Punjab was to be a part of India; it was also to have a democratic constitution. All that the Sikhs could hope to gain was possibly an effective collaborative role in the affairs of Azad Punjab.

Azad Punjab remained on the political agenda of the Akali leaders for about two years. After the 'C.R. Formula' and the Gandhi–Jinnah talks on its basis, the Azad Punjab scheme was theoretically modified in two ways. Its name was dropped to bring in the idea of a Sikh state and this state was meant to be sovereign. However, in terms of the religious composition of the people in this state there was hardly any change. Furthermore, its creation was conditional upon the creation of Pakistan. During the second half of 1944 the idea of this conditional sovereign Sikh state was advocated not only by the Akalis but also by many other Sikh leaders. This viewpoint was spelt out in a memorandum submitted to the Sapru Reconciliation Committee early in 1945 by Sikh leaders who represented nearly the entire community. The memorandum underlined the fact that, accounting for four million persons in British India, the Sikhs were numerically next only to Hindus and Muslims. But their political, economic, and historical importance was much greater than their numbers. Their contribution to the defence and economy of the country was unique. The Punjab was their 'holy' land as well as their homeland. Nonetheless, the constitutional reforms of 1935 had reduced them to 'a state of political subjugation'. The Hindus as well as Muslims had disowned their mother tongue in favour of Hindi and Urdu. Discrimination was exercised against the Sikhs even in matters of religion. The Sikhs were opposed to 'any partition of India on a communal basis'. However, if the Pakistan scheme was accepted they would 'insist on the creation of separate Sikh State'. The primary demand of the memorandum was a strong, united India, and weightage for the Sikhs in a reorganized Punjab.

The Sikh leaders in general and the Akali leaders in particular tried to promote their idea of a Sikh state in 1945. At the time of the Simla Conference in June–July, Master Tara Singh met Lord Wavell and emphasized that the Sikhs were strongly opposed to the creation of Pakistan. At the same time he expressed the view that if Pakistan was to be created Jinnah must agree to the creation of a separate state for the Sikhs. The Akalis fought the elections of 1945–6 in cooperation with but independently of the Congress. Opposition to Pakistan, and not a Sikh state, was the foremost item on their agenda. The landslide in favour of the Muslim League more than neutralized their own unprecedented success in the elections. From a mere possibility, Pakistan advanced now to the stage of probability. Two days before the arrival of the Cabinet Mission in March 1946, the Shiromani Akali Dal passed a resolution in favour of 'the creation of a Sikh State'. When Master Tara Singh met the Cabinet Mission he underlined the fact that the Sikhs were opposed to any division of India, but if a division was decided upon, a separate state should be created for the Sikhs with the right to federate with Hindustan or Pakistan. Giani Kartar Singh was more categorical and asked for a separate Sikh state irrespective of whether or not Pakistan was created. However, the pleas and arguments of the Sikh leaders cut no ice with the Cabinet

Mission. Its recommendations went not only in favour of the idea of Pakistan but also against any reorganization of the Punjab. The idea of a Sikh state was thus completely set aside. In theory, the Akalis had the option to seek concessions from Jinnah as the condition of their consent to opt for Pakistan. But they favoured the idea of getting the Punjab partitioned with the support of the Congress. During the last year of colonial rule, the Akalis worked in close cooperation with the Congress, and no Sikh leader talked of a Sikh state.[10]

Understandably, the most elaborate argument in support of a sovereign Sikh state was published before the recommendations of the Cabinet Mission were made public. In April 1946, Gurbachan Singh of Sikh National College, Lahore and Lal Singh Gyani of Sikh Missionary College, Amritsar, published *The Idea of the Sikh State* on the premise that the Congress would not resist the demand for Pakistan and India would be divided in the near future into Hindustan and Pakistan as two independent countries. Freedom for Hindus and Muslims would mean 'slavery' for the Sikhs who too constituted a 'nation'. The Sikhs had the right to 'self-determination', admitted to be the 'right of nations all over the world'. As stated in the then recent resolution of the Shiromani Akali Dal, no constitutional safeguards and weightage were adequate for ensuring the growth of the Sikhs as 'a nationality with a distinct religious, ideological, cultural and political character'. An autonomous Sikh state, therefore, was 'the unconditional, absolute and minimum demand and political objective of the Sikh Panth as a whole'. This proposed state was to be 'democratic in constitution'; it was to have 'a socialistic economic structure'; it was to give 'full protection' to the minorities.

Gurbachan Singh and Lal Singh go into the background of the demand for an autonomous Sikh state. Its origins could be traced to the 'historical traditions' of the Sikhs, their 'inner urges' and their 'political ideals'. So long as there was no discussion of 'any political future' there was no occasion for giving expression to the concerns of the Sikh Panth. With the Simon Commission, however, the situation began to change. The Muslims of the Punjab began to clamour for a permanent majority in the province and the Sikhs responded by suggesting to Mahatma Gandhi in 1930 that a new province should be carved out of the existing Punjab. In 1931 they made the same suggestion to the Viceroys, Lord Irwin and Lord Willingdon. This demand was presented at the Second Round Table Conference by Sampuran Singh and Ujjal Singh.

However, the Sikh demands went unheeded, and the Communal Award was given. The provincial autonomy established on its basis caused terrible hardships to the Sikhs. Their religious rights were sought to be thwarted and their 'national' language, Punjabi, was sought to be suppressed. In 1940 came the Pakistan Resolution of the All India Muslim League. The Indian National Congress sought to appease the Muslims at the cost of the Sikhs. This disillusioned the Sikhs. In this situation they put forth the 'Azad Punjab Scheme'. Its purpose was to ensure that the Sikhs held 'the balance of power' in the new province. They were canvassing support for this idea when the 'Gandhi-Raja Formula' was floated. Its acceptance would have divided the Sikhs into two parts in two different states. Therefore, the Sikhs asked for a separate Sikh state. This was the only way in which they could survive 'in the midst of aggressive communalism'.

In the present day world of total organization and mobilization of people no 'minority' could survive without 'political strength'. The aggressive communalism of Muslim and Hindu majorities presented a grave threat to the Sikhs and their identity. They needed a state in which they were free from aggression and in which they could make laws for themselves. 'The Sikhs do not seek to dominate anyone. They want to establish a secular democratic state, in which the bulk of the Sikh population may be concentrated. The economic basis of life in such a state is bound to be socialistic, in accordance with the traditions of the Sikh society, and the inner urge of the hardy, self-respecting Sikh peasantry'.

Sikh nationhood was essentially the product of Sikh history. Organized as 'the Khalsa', the Sikhs acted as a distinct and separate nation in the days of the *misl*s and Ranjit Singh. They established a theocratic political organization first and then a monarchical system. They now wanted to organize their national life on the democratic principle. The Gurdwara Reform Movement was a decisive landmark in the revival of the Khalsa. They began to run 'a kind of parallel government' in the form of the SGPC which 'issued commands and ordinances, organized *jathā*s, fought the bureaucracy and through its actions galvanized the entire Sikh people with a powerful feeling of their aroused nationhood'. With the emergence of the concept of the 'Indian Nation', Hindus, Muslims, and Sikhs came to be treated as 'communities', with the result that these 'nations' were sought to be subordinated to the Indian nation. The Sikhs had come out of this illusion 'fostered by the lust for domination by Hindu majority'. Having formed a true conception of their status, they demanded 'a National State for themselves'. No Sikh entertained any doubt about his nationality being different from that of the Hindus. The latent nationhood of the Sikhs reasserted itself.

Gurbachan Singh and Lal Singh give a whole chapter to the views of a number of political thinkers and leaders to prove their point that the Khalsa constituted a distinct 'nation'. They go on to argue that modern 'political theory has recognized in practice the principle of providing national states to the various nationalities'. More than forty new nation-states had emerged in Europe. The Jews had been promised a national home in Palestine, 'their sacred land'. The Sikhs were demanding nothing more than establishing themselves as 'a governing group, along with other groups in a democratic system'. The areas asked for the Sikh state were the areas covered by the Sikh homeland, 'a broad compact area of which the Central Punjab is the nucleus'. More specifically, this 'Sikh Zone' covered the Lahore and Jullundur Divisions, parts of the Ambala and Multan Divisions, the Sikh princely states and the state of Malerkotla, and certain hill areas in the north and north-east. 'It is in this land, which by virtue of proprietorship, development, historic-associations and religious sanctity already belongs to the Sikhs, where the Sikhs wish to find a safe home, free from interference'. More than 80 per cent of the Sikhs lived in this zone and owned more than a quarter of its land.

Gurbachan Singh and Lal Singh do not mention the percentage of Sikhs in the total population of the Sikh state of their conception. Nevertheless, they refer to 'minorities' within the Sikh state to whom a free, prosperous, happy, and contented life is promised. But if the Sikhs were to be politically dominant in the Sikh state, it could not have a democratic constitution because the Sikhs could not form a majority in the area of the Sikh state. Or, was it simply assumed that there would be no absolute 'majority' in the Sikh state? If so, the Sikh state differed from the Azad Punjab only in being sovereign. In no sense then could it be called 'a Sikh state'.[11]

We can see that the pamphlet on Khalistan had nothing to do with the Akalis. Its idea appealed to some Sikhs who were actually opposed to them. The Azad Punjab scheme involved reorganization to ensure that no religious community was in absolute majority in the reorganized politico-administrative unit of the Indian State. The relationship of this unit with the Indian State was not spelt out, but it may not be unsafe to assume that it was something like 'provincial autonomy'. The Sikh state conditionally demanded by the Akalis was different from the Azad Punjab essentially in being sovereign, rather than autonomous. This was true of their later demand for a sovereign state irrespective of whether or not Pakistan was created. With the Sikhs being no more than 20 per cent within the proposed state, this sovereign state could not really become a 'Sikh' state. The proposal was neither clear nor realistic. There was no possibility of it being taken up seriously by the colonial administrators and politicians even if some of them were sympathetic to the Sikhs.

In any case, after the elections of 1946 and the Cabinet Mission, the Akalis themselves were far more serious about the partition of the province in the hope of a better future for the Sikhs in the Indian Union. They had three basic concerns: adequate share in political power, promotion of Punjabi language in Gurmukhi script, and protection of their religious identity.

Akali Confrontation with the Ruling Congress

The partition brought about an important demographic change in East Punjab. The Hindus formed more than 60 per cent of the total population of this state. Their leaders were anxious to retain this majority status. The Sikhs formed about 35 per cent of the total population, a much higher percentage than what they had in the British Punjab. Furthermore, they were concentrated in six districts in which they were actually more than 50 per cent: Amritsar, Gurdaspur, Jalandhar, Hoshiarpur, Ludhiana, and Ferozepur. Then there were the princely states in which the Sikhs had a majority on the margin. This demographic change eventually came to have an important bearing on their politics. Used to weightage in the British Punjab, the Akali leaders thought of weightage first in free India as well. However, the idea of weightage to religious minorities was categorically discarded by the Constituent Assembly. The Akalis demanded proportionate representation on the basis of joint electorates, with the right to contest general unreserved seats. This too was rejected by the Constituent Assembly. The Akali members of the Assembly were so resentful that they refused to sign the Constitution adopted on 26 January 1950.[12]

For some share in political power, the Akali members of the Punjab Legislative Assembly joined the Congress party in March 1948. Three months later Giani Kartar Singh was included in the cabinet in place of the Congress Sikh member Ishar Singh Majhail. Within a year, Gopi Chand Bhargava was replaced by Bhim Sen Sachar as the Chief Minister of the Punjab. In consultation with Giani Kartar Singh, Sachar evolved a language formula in 1949 which is known as the Sachar formula. A Punjabi zone was created under this scheme by adding the Ropar and Kharar *tahsil*s of Ambala district to the six Sikh majority districts. Punjabi was to be the medium of education at the primary level in all schools of this zone. Hindi was to be introduced in the last year of primary education. In the Hindi zone, the position of Punjabi was to be reversed. The Akalis had some reservations about details but they welcomed the formula as a reasonable solution to the language problem. Unfortunately, this scheme was not acceptable to the Arya Samaj leaders of the Punjabi zone: they refused to implement it. In fact, the reaction among the 'Hindu' leaders was so strong that Sachar lost his Chief Ministership. Bhargava was back in office by October 1949. The Akali members became ineffective in the new ministry. Before long, the Working Committee of the Akali Dal decided to revoke the merger of the Akalis with the Congress on the grounds that the Congress leaders had belied all their hopes of constructive sympathy and support.

The idea of reorganization of states on the basis of language had been an important item on the agenda of the Congress since 1920. After 1947, however, the Congress leaders were no longer enthusiastic about it. In 1948 the Dar Commission recommended that no linguistic state be created without the consent of a substantial minority included in its area. Its report was accepted by a committee consisting of Jawaharlal Nehru, Sardar Vallabhbhai Patel, and Sitarammaya who made a recommendation of their own that, in north India, no provincial boundaries should be changed irrespective of the merit of any such proposal. The question of language appeared to carry political implications as well. In 1950 Hukam Singh tried to clarify that the demand for a Punjabi-speaking state was democratic and secular. The Working Committee of the Akali Dal passed a resolution in favour of a state on the basis of Punjabi language and culture. Some of the Hindu leaders of the Punjab reacted to the demand by telling their followers to return Hindi as their mother tongue for the Census of 1951. They had canvassed for Hindi before 1947 also, but now their idea was to thwart the formation of a Punjabi speaking state by demonstrating that there was a substantial Hindi-speaking minority in the proposed Punjabi-speaking state. In 1952 the Akalis fought the elections on the issue of the Punjabi-speaking state. They were defeated.

Before the year ended, the Prime Minister announced the separation of Andhra from Madras as a Telugu-speaking state due to the death of Sriramula on hunger strike for the creation of Andhra. The movement for linguistic states gained momentum. Before the end of 1953 it was announced that States Reorganization Commission would be formed. The Akali leaders prepared their case on the basis of pre-1947 data. According to them there was an area of 90,000 sq km in which nearly twelve million people spoke Punjabi. The Sikh population in this area was much less than a half of the total. Nevertheless, the proposal was countered by the protagonists of Maha Punjab who advocated the merger of Himachal Pradesh and a few districts of Uttar Pradesh as well as the Patiala and East Punjab States Union (PEPSU) with East Punjab. The Commission came to the conclusion that the majority of the people were opposed to the creation of a Punjabi-speaking state, and recommended the merger of Himachal Pradesh and PEPSU with the East Punjab. The Akalis rejected the Commission's report on the day following its release on 9 October 1955.

Now a formula was evolved that met the essential demands of the Akalis without the creation of a Punjabi-speaking state. This came to be known as the Regional Formula. PEPSU alone was to be merged with the East Punjab, and the whole area was to be divided into two 'regions'. One of these was to be the Punjabi region in which the medium of school education was to be Punjabi. The other region was to give the same status to Hindi. Both the regions were to have regional committees for legislation on fourteen important subjects. The Regional Formula came closest to accommodating the political and cultural interests of the Akalis. They accepted the scheme. The

Working Committee of the Akali Dal decided to have no political programme of its own and to concentrate on the religious, educational, cultural, social, and economic interests of the Sikh Panth.

The reorganized Punjab state was inaugurated on 1 November 1956 when Partap Singh Kairon was the Chief Minister. The Akali legislators joined the Congress party. The Hindi Raksha Samiti agitated against the scheme and Kairon remained reluctant to allow the regional committees to legislate. In fact, he tried to keep the former Akali leaders out of the Legislative Assembly and to dislodge the Akalis from the SGPC. Given Kairon's attitude and outlook, the Regional Formula had little chance of success. Within a few years, the Akalis felt obliged to revive the movement for a Punjabi-speaking state.

The agitation launched by Master Tara Singh in 1960 proved to be a failure. In 1962 his place was taken by Sant Fateh Singh who presented the demand as a clearly linguistic one. Both leaders demonstrated their patriotism during India's war with China. During the war with Pakistan in 1965 Sant Fateh Singh went all out to support the government. Nehru died in 1964 and Kairon was assassinated in early 1965. There were new actors on the scene. After the ceasefire in September 1965 the Union Home Minister announced that the issue of the Punjabi-speaking state would be examined all afresh. Lal Bahadur Shastri appointed a Parliamentary Committee under the Chairmanship of Hukam Singh, who was now the Speaker of the Lok Sabha. To advise the Parliamentary Committee, a Cabinet Sub-Committee was also constituted. It consisted of Indira Gandhi, Y.B. Chavan, and Mahavir Tyagi. Indira Gandhi became the Prime Minister in January 1966 after the death of Lal Bahadur Shastri. The Punjabi-speaking state was inaugurated on 1 November 1966.

Contrary to the general impression, the new state was not created in accordance with the recommendations of the Parliamentary Committee constituted by Lal Bahadur Shastri. Indira Gandhi was unhappy with this committee, especially because of the views of its Chairman. She makes it abundantly clear in her *My Truth* why she was not in favour of creating a Punjabi-speaking state: she did not wish to deviate from a well considered policy of the Congress, and she did not wish to let down the 'Hindu supporters' of the Congress in the Punjab. Both these concerns arose from electoral considerations. She did not wait for the recommendations of the Parliamentary

Committee. A resolution of the Congress in March 1966 accepted the principle of reorganization of the Punjab. The commission known as the Shah Commission was appointed. The terms of reference given to the Commission stipulated that the Census of 1961 was to be used for data on language, with the *tahsil* as the basic unit. Consequently, many Punjabi-speaking villages and Chandigarh were left out of the Punjab. Furthermore, the Union government took over the power and irrigation projects and became the arbiter of river waters in case the two new states failed to come to an agreement. Sant Fateh Singh protested against all these decisions even before the new state was inaugurated. In December 1966 he went on fast on the issue of Chandigarh, but the issue remained unresolved.

The idea of autonomy had begun to be aired before the reorganization of the Punjab in 1966. In May 1965 'Justice' Gurnam Singh, leader of the opposition in the Punjab Assembly, moved a resolution at a conference in Ludhiana in favour of a self-determined status for Sikhs within the Indian Union. It was interpreted by the language press in the Punjab as a demand for a sovereign Sikh state. In July 1965 Master Tara Singh, who was no longer influential, gave an elaborate argument in support of the idea of 'Sikh Homeland' as an autonomous state within the Indian Union. Opposing the Punjab Reorganization Bill in the Parliament, Kapur Singh referred to Nehru's statement of July 1946: 'I see no wrong in an area and a setup in the North wherein the Sikhs can also experience a glow of freedom'. Kapur Singh was in favour of a Sikh Homeland with a special internal constitution and a special relationship with the Centre irrespective of the percentage of Sikhs in this Homeland.

The experience of the Akalis as the ruling party in the new Punjab between March 1967 and June 1971 convinced them that they could not exercise power adequately, or for long, under the constitution which placed the states at a great political and economic disadvantage in relation to the ruling party at the Centre. Within three years the Punjab was twice placed under President's rule, a euphemism for a virtual rule of the ruling party. The Akalis lost the elections in 1972. A year later came the Anandpur Sahib Resolution. Its basic emphasis was on a genuinely federal system with only defence, foreign affairs, communications, and currency as the prerogatives of the Centre. Couched partly in the language of the advocates of a Sikh Homeland, it was interpreted by the opponents of the Akalis as 'secessionist'. The Akalis returned to power in 1977 and in a crowded conference held at Ludhiana in 1978, they reiterated their stand without any ambiguity in favour of a federal system.

Meanwhile the issues of Chandigarh and the river waters had got complicated. Sant Fateh Singh announced his decision to go on fast on 26 January 1970 and to immolate himself on 1 February, if Chandigarh was not given to the Punjab. Indira Gandhi awarded Chandigarh to the Punjab. The award was meant to be implemented five years later, in 1975. At the same time she awarded Fazilka tahsil to Haryana with a corridor on the Punjab border with Rajasthan to link the awarded territory with the state of Haryana.

During the Emergency of 1975, the Akalis put up the strongest opposition to Indira Gandhi. She gave her award on the river waters in 1976. The non-riparian Rajasthan was given 8.00 maf of water. Of the remaining 7.20 maf, she gave 0.20 to Delhi and divided the rest in two equal shares for Haryana and the Punjab. Thus, the Punjab was to get 3.5 maf of water, which was less than what the state was actually using. The Akalis took up this matter with the then Prime Minister Morarji Desai. He could tell the Rajasthan leaders that their state was not a part of the Indus basin but he was not prepared to change the award. He had no objection, however, to the Punjab going to the Supreme Court for adjudication. The matter was lying with the Supreme Court when the Akalis lost the elections in 1980.

In July 1981 Sant Harchand Singh Longowal presided over a World Sikh Conference which directed the Akali Dal to plan a *dharmyudh* for pursuing the Anandpur Sahib Resolution. An agitation was launched in September and memoranda of demands were sent to Indira Gandhi. She met the Akali leaders on 16 October 1981, primarily to identify issues which could then be taken up by the Foreign Minister P.V. Narasimha Rao. A meeting with him later appeared to the Akali leaders to be 'a waste of time'. They met the Prime Minister again on 26 November. Indira Gandhi was not in favour of revising her earlier decision on the river waters but she gave assurances of much larger supplies of water and energy to the Punjab in the future on the basis of more scientific exploitation of resources. Within five weeks, she added 0.72 maf of water to the Punjab's share from an estimated surplus of 1.32 maf. At the same time, she gave 0.60 maf out of this surplus to

Rajasthan, making it clear to the Akalis that their talk of Rajasthan not being a riparian state had no relevance. All the three chief ministers concerned accepted this decision. The Chief Minister of the Punjab was obliged to withdraw its case from the Supreme Court. It was decided to complete the Sutlej-Yamuna Link (SYL) canal for Haryana in two years. On their third and last meeting with the Prime Minister on 5 April 1982 the Akali leaders got the impression that she had already made up her mind to let the issues wait.

It soon became clear, however, that Indira Gandhi was keen to see the SYL canal constructed. The Akalis launched the *nahar roko* (stop the canal) *morcha*. It failed to evoke much response. Another call failed to mobilize the peasantry. On 4 August 1982, the Akalis decided at last to launch a dharmyudh morcha to get all their demands accepted. Before long, Sant Jarnail Singh Bhindrawale joined the dharmyudh morcha. It became increasingly difficult for the government to find room for the agitating volunteers in the existing jails. Indira Gandhi decided to release the Akali volunteers on Diwali day in October. Swaran Singh hammered out a mutually acceptable formula on the important issues of Chandigarh, river waters, and the Centre–State relations. A cabinet sub-committee consisting of Pranab Mukherjee, R. Venkataraman, P.V. Narsimha Rao, and P.C. Sethi accepted the formula and Swaran Singh told the Akali leaders that the government had approved of it. But the statement placed before the Parliament turned out to be materially different from what had been agreed upon. The Akalis decided to hold a demonstration in Delhi at the time of the Asiad. Amarinder Singh negotiated another mutually acceptable agreement. There was a general impression that this was sabotaged by Bhajan Lal, the Chief Minister of Haryana, with the assurance that he would not let the Akalis pass through his state. No Sikh was allowed to pass through Haryana without being humiliated.

Sant Longowal asked the Akali legislators to resign their seats with effect from 21 February 1983. He also gave a call to ex-servicemen for a meeting at Amritsar. Nearly 5,000 responded. In April 1983 the Akalis organized their *rāsta roko* (block the roads) campaign. Twenty-six people were killed in the violence that erupted in spite of their peaceful intention. In June, they organized their *rail roko* (stop the trains) campaign and the government decided not to run any trains. Yet there was some violence. The *kām roko* (stop work) campaign of August 1983 proved to be a great success. And so was the *bandh* they organized in February 1984 to demonstrate their strength and their trust in non-violent agitation. Within a week, a meeting of five Akali leaders, five cabinet ministers, five secretaries, and fifteen leaders of the opposition parties was held at Delhi. The meeting came close to a successful settlement but anti-Sikh violence was orchestrated in Haryana, and the Akali leaders returned to the Punjab. Before the end of the month, the Akalis burnt at Delhi and Chandigarh the pages of the Constitution containing Article 25 (2)(b). They were arrested, but the government also announced its willingness to amend the Article. Early in March, Indira Gandhi appointed the Sarkaria Commission to go into Centre–State relations but the Akalis did not withdraw the morcha because her decision was unilateral.[13] By this time, Indira Gandhi had decided to prepare secretly for an army action.

From the foregoing pages it is clear that the Akalis never demanded a sovereign state for the Sikhs after 1946. The demand for a Sikh Homeland, standing in a special relationship with the Centre and having a special internal constitution, was put forward by individuals or small splinter groups of the Akalis.

The Movement of Khalistan

The idea of Khalistan was advertised in the *New York Times* in October 1971 by Jagjit Singh Chauhan. He had enjoyed a short spell of power as a minister in the Cabinet of Lachhman Singh Gill in 1967–8. Living in England now, Chauhan had no following in the Punjab. His idea of Khalistan was treated as a joke but it could embarrass the Akalis. Whenever he visited India he was treated well by some eminent leaders of the Congress. About a decade later, in June 1980, Balbir Singh Sandhu announced the formation of Khalistan, claiming himself to be the Secretary of the National Council of Khalistan with Jagjit Singh Chauhan as its President. This organization existed only on paper. In March 1981, a US citizen Ganga Singh Dhillon, who was known to Chauhan, addressed the annual session of the Sikh Educational Conference organized by the Chief Khalsa Diwan, and put forth the view that the Sikhs formed a 'nation'. The implication was that an independent state could be demanded on that basis. Soon afterwards, however, the Chief Khalsa Diwan dissociated itself from Dhillon's statement.

THE AKALIS AND KHALISTAN   305

Besides the National Council of Khalistan, the White Paper on the Punjab published by the Government of India mentions another significant group, the Dal Khalsa, which operated from overseas. It had been formed at Chandigarh in April 1978. Its president was a stenographer of the Panjab University who had published a pamphlet on Khalistan. The term 'Dal Khalsa' served as a reminder of the 'national army' of the Sikhs which had succeeded in establishing sovereign Sikh rule during the late eighteenth century. In 1979 it contested elections for the SGPC, but without any success. In 1982 the responsibility for throwing the head of a cow in a Hindu temple was reported to have been claimed by the Dal Khalsa. According to Mark Tully and Satish Jacob, the founding of the Dal Khalsa is attributed to Giani Zail Singh who paid the bill for its first meeting at the Aroma Hotel at Chandigarh and who used to ask journalists to give prominence to its activities.

The Khalistan movement has been associated with Sant Jarnail Singh more than with anyone else. What has been published on his life and of his speeches enables us to notice some of the relevant aspects of his activities and attitudes. He was initially a protagonist of religious reform. At the age of thirty, he assumed the headship of Damdami Taksal on the death of Sant Kartar Singh Bhindranwale in 1977. He also inherited the legacy of an open conflict with the Sant Nirankaris who were looked upon as heretical by Sant Kartar Singh. The armed clash on Baisakhi day of 1978 at Amritsar was an extension of this legacy, underlining the religious dimension of Sant Jarnail Singh's outlook and attitude. He continued to declare till June 1984 that religion was his sole concern. For him, the Ādi Granth was the only sacred scripture of the Sikhs; Guruship was vested in this Granth, giving it the status of Guru Granth Sahib. The Khalsa code of conduct provided the only valid mode of life for the Sikhs. He believed, in fact, that the antidote to external and internal threats to Sikhism was strict conformity to the Khalsa way of life. Insistence on the maintenance of the external form and hostility to drugs and alcohol appear to flow from his religious outlook. That this concern distinguished him in his own eyes from other Sikh leaders comes out clearly in a statement he made in 1984 that he was responsible only to the cause of Sikhism, to uphold the symbols of the faith, to see that the beards of the Sikhs remained intact and their hair uncut, and that they did not go after the evil things in life, like alcohol and drugs.

However, there was another dimension to his religious outlook. To bear arms was a religious duty of the Sikhs. The choice of arms was not confined to the sword (*kirpān*) as one of the obligatory five Ks. It was extended to modern weapons, which also carried the implication that they were meant to be used. For him, use of physical force was a legitimate part of religion. If anything, his insistence on the use of arms went on increasing. He explicitly told his audience from the roof of Guru Ram Das Langar when he was virtually confined to the Golden Temple complex 'For every village you should keep one motorcycle, three baptized Sikhs and three revolvers. These are not meant for killing innocent people. For a Sikh to have arms and kill an innocent person is a serious sin. But, Khalsaji, to have arms and not to get your legitimate rights is even a bigger sin. It is for you to decide how to use these arms. If you want to remove the shackles of your slavery you must have a plan.'

In other words, you had to be up in arms against the enemies of the faith. In his mind, hostility towards the government easily got transferred to 'Hindus': 'If you do not have the five "Ks", if you are not armed with a rifle and a spear, you will be given the beating of your lives by the Hindus.' The reference here is to the killing of Sikhs but even otherwise Sant Jarnail Singh could bracket 'Hindus' with the government. 'I only finish those,' he said on another occasion, 'who are enemies of the Sikh faith like policemen, government officials and Hindus'.

The language used by Sant Jarnail Singh has been generally interpreted to support the view that he was leading an armed struggle for Khalistan. Naturally, his movement is looked upon as 'secessionist'. The White Paper issued by the Government of India refers to secessionist and anti-national activities which had the objective of establishing an independent state for the Sikhs with external support. The activities of Sant Jarnail Singh are included in this view of the situation. However, when he was asked by a journalist in 1983 whether or not he supported the demand for Khalistan, his reply was: 'I am neither in favour of it nor against it. If they give it to us, we won't reject it'. He repeated this in March 1984. In one of his morning '*darbārs*' on the roof of the Langar he asked the audience if they wanted the Anandpur Sahib Resolution implemented in full. Hands were raised by the congregation and Sant Jarnail Singh was satisfied: 'You need not say anything more'. He warned the Akali leaders that if they accepted anything less than all the demands in the Anandpur Sahib Resolution he would expose them before the Sikhs. Thus, whereas his activities and his informal responses to questions on Sikh independence may seem to point towards Khalistan, his formal stand did not go beyond autonomy for the Punjab as a part of the Indian Union.

Articulation in favour of Khalistan became pronounced after the death of Sant Jarnail Singh. For this development, it is possible to see the relevance of Operation Blue Star and the Sikh massacres in Delhi in the wake of Indira Gandhi's assassination. Even more important was the failure of the Rajiv-Longowal Accord. In any case the number of militant groups and the number of young men who joined them during seven years after the death of Sant Jarnail Singh appears to have been far larger than their number during the seven years of his own activity from 1977 to 1984. Many of the Sikhs living in Great Britain, Canada and the United States were vocal in favour of Khalistan. Many of the militants working in the Punjab made no secret of their political objective. Continuity was provided by two important organizations: the All India Sikh Students Federation (which had been closely associated with Sant Jarnail Singh under the leadership of Bhai Amrik Singh, the eldest son of Sant Kartar Singh), and the Damdami Taksal. On their initiative, a meeting of the Sarbat Khalsa (in theory, the entire body of the Sikhs) was held at the Golden Temple on 26 January 1986. A flag of Khalistan was hoisted and the Akal Takht rebuilt by the government was demolished to be reconstructed. Khalistan was proclaimed a few months later. In August 1987, at a convention called by the acting Jathedar of the Akal Takht, Darshan Singh, it was declared that the goal of the Sikh Panth was to have a political setup in an area in which the Sikhs could experience a glow of freedom (presumably within the Indian State). This did not satisfy the militants. They continued their activities for at least five years more.

An Expedient Compromise

Both the Akalis and the protagonists of Khalistan invoked Sikh identity as essentially relevant for their political programmes. It figured prominently in their political discourses and praxis. What they shared was primarily the Khalsa or Singh identity. This identity was visible in their external appearance. They wore *kesh* and a turban, kept a flowing beard and uncut hair, carried a kirpān, and wore *kaṛa* and *kachh*. These four symbols begin with the letter 'k'. The fifth 'k' is *kangha* or the comb tucked in the kesh for keeping the hair clean and orderly. The five Ks form the most important items in the Khalsa conception of *rahit*. Sant Jarnail Singh favoured the idea of bearing modern weapons in addition to a long sword. The strictest prohibition is on the use of tobacco in any form. Sant Jarnail Singh added drugs and alcohol to tobacco as strictly prohibited items. On the first point, he was closer to the Khalsa of the eighteenth century. On the second, he was more in conformity with the Ādi Granth. Whereas the followers of Sant Jarnail Singh insist on *amritdhārī* identity, involving the observance of the five Ks after baptism by the double-edged sword (*pahul* or *amrit*), the Akalis prefer this identity but do not seriously object to what may be called the Singh identity which is less exacting than the amritdhārī identity. Besides carrying the epithet 'Singh' in one's name, by far the most important item of this identity are keeping the hair uncut, wearing turban, and refraining from the use of tobacco. Ordinarily, the Singhs of this description would wear kaṛa and less frequently also kachh. Theoretical preference for amritdhārī identity is thus common to both the Akalis and the Damdami Taksal, but they differ in actual practice.

Apart from external appearance, the Akalis and the Damdami Taksal observe distinct rites of passage: ceremonies connected with birth, marriage and death. On these, as on several other occasions, the Ādi Granth is of central importance. No ceremony can be performed without it. This is because the Ādi Granth is not only the exclusive scripture of the Sikhs in the eyes of the Akalis and the followers of Sant Jarnail Singh but also the embodiment of the Guru. Therefore, Guru Granth Sahib is its proper title. This title and this attitude spring from the doctrine of the continuity of Guruship. Guru Nanak, the founder of the Sikh faith and the Sikh Panth, was followed by nine successors. Just as he chose Angad to be the Guru, and Guru Angad chose Amar Das, and so on, Guru Gobind Singh chose the Ādi Granth to be the Guru. What ended with the death of Guru Gobind Singh was personal Guruship but not Guruship itself. The reverence and regard which the Sikhs of the ten Gurus gave them are due now to Guru Granth Sahib as well. This doctrine of Guru Granth, it must be added, is nearly 300 years old, and the equation of Gurbāṇī with the Guru can be traced back to the sixteenth century. Since the Gurus have spoken through the Granth, the only valid source of Sikh ideas and ethics is Guru Granth Sahib. The known injunctions and practices of the ten Gurus are added to this source. Both the Akalis and the followers of Sant Jarnail Singh agree that the Ādi Granth inculcates monotheism or worship of One God and rejects gods, goddesses, incarnations, and idols. Sikh doctrines and Sikh worship too, therefore, are distinctive.

The basic difference between the Akalis and the Sant was the latter's conviction that the time for the use of arms had come. Even the Government of India could see this difference. At the time of the Operation Blue Star, Lt. General Sunderji was told by the government that there were two groups in the Golden Temple complex: that of Sant Jarnail Singh and that of Sant Longowal. He was instructed to ensure that there was no fighting between the two groups. The 'extremists' were to be flushed out without any damage to the Golden Temple and the least possible damage to the Akal Takht. These instructions indicate that Sant Longowal and his followers were not seen as 'extremists'.

Nevertheless, there has been a general tendency to bracket the Akalis with the militant secessionists. One reason for this could be the demand of the Akalis for political recognition on the basis of Sikh identity, especially the form in which this recognition was sought in 1945–6, that is, a sovereign state. This was never forgotten by their opponents after 1947. They saw the ultimate design of sovereignty in every important political move or demand of the Akalis. Even at the national level there was a certain degree of distrust. There was a tendency to see more in the political aspirations of the Akalis than what was actually there.

More important than the colonial background were the compromising gestures of the Akalis. One of the Akali demands in 1981 was the release of Sant Jarnail Singh. In 1982 he was persuaded to merge his morcha with the Akali dharmyudh. No one could stop him from staying in one of the 'hostels' of the SGPC, where the government also could reach him if it wanted to, but towards the end of 1983 he shifted to the Akal Takht, which carried the implication of a tacit consent of the SGPC. Many of the Akali leaders showed willingness or even keenness to participate in the mortuary rites (*bhogs*) of some known or alleged militants.

One reason for Akali ambivalence could be the politics of the party in power in trying to use Sant Jarnail Singh against the Akalis. According to Mark Tully and Satish Jacob, Giani Zail Singh had enabled Sanjay Gandhi to discover the Sant for breaking the Akali Dal after its electoral success in 1977. They looked for a religious issue that could be politicized and they identified the Sant Nirankaris. After the death of twelve Sikhs at the hands of the Nirankaris on the Baisakhi of 1978 at Amritsar, anti-Nirankari agitations were encouraged not by the Akalis but by the Congress party. The Dal Khalsa and Sant Jarnail Singh contested elections for the SGPC in 1979 against the Akali candidates. In 1980 Sant Jarnail Singh campaigned for Congress candidates, including R.L. Bhatia. Indira Gandhi herself admitted that he had supported a Congress candidate. After the murder of Baba Gurbachan Singh, the Sant Nirankari guru, in April 1980, Giani Zail Singh told the Parliament that Sant Jarnail Singh had nothing to do with the murder. After the murder of Lala Jagat Narain in September 1981, the Chief Minister of the Punjab wanted to get Sant Jarnail Singh arrested as a suspect. He was in a Haryana village at that time. Giani Zail Singh called up Bhajan Lal to tell him not to let the Sant be arrested. When the Punjab government did arrest him in October, Giani Zail Singh told the Parliament that there was no evidence of his involvement in the murder. He was released. After the murder of Jathedar Santokh Singh at Delhi in December 1981, present at the memorial service were Giani Zail Singh, Rajiv Gandhi and Sant Jarnail Singh.

Even after 1981, when the Sant fell out with the government, Indira Gandhi continued to consult Giani Zail Singh as the President of India. According to Tully and Jacob it was possibly due to his influence that Sant Jarnail Singh was not arrested after the murder of a Deputy Inspector General of Police in April 1983 in the precincts of the Golden Temple. When the government of Darbara Singh was suspended and President's rule was imposed in the Punjab due to the cold-blooded murder of some Hindu passengers in the first week of October 1983, a senior colleague of Darbara Singh claimed that President Giani Zail Singh was in daily contact with the Sant. The implication was that Darbara Singh's downfall had been brought about through the Sant's instrumentality. Indira Gandhi maintained contact with Sant Jarnail Singh through R.L. Bhatia who remained in regular contact with Bhai Amrik Singh till April 1984.[13]

Finally, the Akali hobnobbing with the militants can be seen as compromisingly expedential. For more than a decade now they have raised none of the issues which were so vital to them before the Operation Blue Star and which were sought to be resolved through the Rajiv-Longowal Accord. They do not talk even of autonomy for the states. There may be many reasons for their silence. But their silence is eloquent: they had little to do with Khalistan.

By now, the Shiromani Akali Dal is a political party with vested interests. Its leaders would rather ensure dynastic succession at all levels in the party and in the state. In this respect, they are not different from several other political parties in the country.

NOTES

1. J.S. Grewal, 'The Gurdwara', in J.S. Grewal, ed., *Religious Movements and Institutions in Medieval India*, New Delhi: Oxford University Press, 2006.
2. J.S. Grewal, *Sikh Ideology, Polity and Social Order*, New Delhi: Manohar, 1996, pp. 133–9.
3. Mohinder Singh, *The Akali Movement*, Delhi: Macmillan, 1978.
4. The arguments generally used by those who wanted to prove that the Sikhs were Hindu can be summarized thus. To start with, Guru Nanak was a 'Hindu'. The background of Sikhs was 'Hindu'. The Sikhs and Hindus intermarry and eat together. The Sikhs observe caste distinctions in matrimony and commensality, like the other Hindus. They believe in the Vedas, if not also in the other Hindu scriptures, in addition to their own *Granths*. The Ādi Granth is a popular version of Vedantic philosophy. The *Dasam Granth* composed by Guru Gobind Singh contains long compositions in praise of the Goddess and the incarnations of Vishnu and Shiva, particularly the human incarnations of Vishnu, that is, Rama and Krishna. The Khalsa was instituted by Guru Gobind Singh as a temporary measure for protecting the Hindus. The external appearance of the Khalsa did not justify a separate identity. At best these are half-truth; at worst, simple lies.
5. Bhai Kahn Singh Nabha, *Ham Hindu Nahīn* (Pbi), Amritsar: Singh Brothers, 1995 (rpt of 5th edn). For a brief analysis, see J.S. Grewal, *Historical Perspectives on Sikh Identity*, Patiala: Punjabi University, 1997, pp. 81–100.
6. The views of W.H. McLeod, Harjot Oberoi, Daljeet Singh and G.S. Dhillon on Sikh identity have been discussed in the *Historical Perspectives* cited above.

7. Nabha, *Ham Hindu Nahīn*. For a brief analysis of this work, see J.S. Grewal, 'Nabha's *Ham Hindu Nahin:* A Declaration of Sikh Ethnicity', in Pashaura Singh and N. Gerald Barrier, eds, *Sikh Identity: Continuity and Change*, New Delhi: Manohar, 2001, pp. 231–51.
8. K.L. Tuteja, *Sikh Politics (1920–1940)*, Kurukshetra: Vishal Publications, 1984.
9. Sadhu Singh Hamdard, *Āzād Punjab* (Urdu), Amritsar: Ajit Book Agency, 1943.
10. Indu Banga, 'The Crisis of Sikh Politics (1940–47)', in Joseph T. O'Connell et al., eds, *Sikh History and Religion in the Twentieth Century*, Toronto: Centre for South Asian Studies, University of Toronto, 1988, pp. 233–55.
11. Gurbachan Singh and Lal Singh Giani, *The Idea of the Sikh State*, Lahore: Lahore Book Shop, 1946. Relevant in this context are also the following: G. Adhikari, *Sikh Homeland through Hindu-Muslim-Sikh Unity*, Bombay: 1944; Harnam Singh, Punjab: *The Homeland of the Sikhs*, Lahore: 1945; Swarup Singh, *The Sikhs Demand Their Homeland*, London: 1946.
12. J.S. Grewal, *The Sikhs of the Punjab* (The New Cambridge History of India), Cambridge: Cambridge University Press, 1990, pp. 181–204.
13. Mark Tully and Satish Jacob, *Amritsar: Mrs Gandhi's Last Battle*, Calcutta: Rupa and Co., 1985, pp. 57–62, 65–72, 121.

PART VI
Cross-cultural Debates

13. Empathy with the Sikh Past: J.D. Cunningham*

REACTIONS TO CUNNINGHAM'S *A HISTORY OF THE SIKHS*
'The author has written in anti-English spirit more as a Sikh than a Christian, more as a Punjabee than an Englishman'. This was what Henry Lawrence wrote in an unfinished article on J.D. Cunningham's *A History of the Sikhs* which had appeared at the time of the annexation of the Sikh state of Lahore to British India in 1849.[1] Cunningham's sympathy with the Sikhs was evident to critics less hostile than Sir Henry Lawrence. *The Times* noted that his heart was with the Sikhs throughout the work.[2] *The Calcutta Review* remarked that he had written his history 'for the most part as a Sikh historian would write it'.[3]

The historian's qualities were also impressive, like his 'caprice of writing as a Sikh'.[4] *The Athenaeum* admired his 'scrupulous care of a man of science'.[5] *The Times* appreciated the 'fulness of detail' in his work.[6] J.W. Kaye, who deplored the misdirection of his 'plain-speaking' in discussing British policy towards the Sikhs, had no doubt about his sincerity and admired his researches.[7]

Indeed, as Kaye pointed out, J.D. Cunningham had consulted many unpublished sources of Sikh history besides a careful study of every published work.[8] He professed to introduce the Sikhs to the British

---

* 'Empathy with the Sikh Past: J.D. Cunningham' is a revised version of 'J.D. Cunningham and his Predecessors on the Sikhs' published in the *Bengal Past and Present*, 1964. A revised version entitled 'Cunningham as a Historian of the Sikhs' was published in my *From Guru Nanak to Maharaja Ranjit Singh: Essays in Sikh History* (Amritsar: Guru Nanak Dev University, 1972, pp. 123–37, 188–93). Another version was published as 'The Emergence of a Nation: The Khalsa for Cunningham' in *The Khalsa: Sikh and Non-Sikh Perspectives* (New Delhi: Manohar, 2004, pp. 123–36).

nation by tracing their early history and then to elucidate the Anglo-Sikh and Anglo-Afghan relations in their bearing on Sikh history during the early nineteenth century.[9] He described the peoples and countries under Sikh rule or influence, discussed ancient Indian religions and 'modern' reforms to elucidate the origins of Sikhism, gave the history of Sikh Gurus and Banda Bahadur, underlined the years between 1716 and 1764 as the period of Sikh struggle for independence, put forth the concept of 'theocratic confederate feudalism' to characterize Sikh polity, narrated Ranjit Singh's rise to power until his alliance with the British in 1809 and then his career of conquest until his death in 1839, gave a separate chapter to Ranjit Singh's successors, and finally, he dealt with the first Anglo-Sikh war. Thus, with almost equal interest in all its phases, he produced a comprehensive history of the Sikhs from their origin to their war with the British in 1845–6.

Cunningham's *History* remained a standard work on Sikhs for over a hundred years. Editing its sixth edition in 1918, H.L.O. Garrett recognized the 'meticulous care' with which the work had been written and he appreciated 'the breadth and variety of the author's study'. He also remarked that Cunningham's 'partiality for the Sikhs' caused many of his statements 'to be viewed with suspicion'.[10] The edition revised by Cunningham in 1849 has been reprinted very recently as 'no ordinary book'.[11]

Cunningham's chapter on the Anglo-Sikh war proved to be the most controversial. He blamed the English for bringing about the war with the Sikhs, praised the conduct of the Sikh soldiery, and denounced the treachery of Sikh generals and ministers. By implication, he reduced the success of British arms to an ill-calculated campaign against a leaderless army. Indeed, he severely criticized many of the actions of the British Indian government and its servants, bringing Lord Hardinge's policy towards the Sikhs into disrepute. In reaction, they criticized Cunningham and justified British policies. In this process a different version of the first Anglo-Sikh war was presented which was upheld by Cunningham's later critics just as his own version was accepted by his admirers.[12]

Cunningham's treatment of the Anglo-Sikh war was seen as influenced by his personal feelings towards Lord Hardinge and his favourites. Hardinge remarked: 'The book justifies the step I took in pitchforking our friend to Bhopal. It proves his Sikh partialities—and he has not forgotten that I had sent him to another agency'.[13] Henry Lawrence in his manuscript note refers to Cunningham's feeling of 'a martyr' and to his sharp disagreements with Major Broadfoot.[14] Cunningham's attitude towards the men supposed to be responsible for British policy towards the Sikhs was anything but friendly. His criticism of Hardinge and Broadfoot is reflected in the last chapter of the his book.[15]

However, Cunningham was seen not merely as an 'apologist of the Sikhs' in their war with the British but also as one who treated their religion with sympathy and appreciation. He was almost a follower of Gobind, said Kaye; 'almost is the Granth his gospel'.[16] Henry Lawrence too thought of Cunningham's treatment of Sikhism as reprehensible.[17] The editor of *The Calcutta Review* lamented that Cunningham's abilities had been wasted for a contemptible purpose: he had preferred 'the Sikh cause and the Sikh Religion to his own'. It was all the more lamentable that he seemed to do so merely from 'affectation of singularity'.[18] An empathetic treatment of the Sikh past was beyond the understanding of Cunningham's critics.

Cunningham was distinguished from his contemporaries not so much in writing with an eye on the practical politics of British India as in treating the Sikh religion with great empathy. In fact, these two aspects of his work were not unrelated to each other. To understand his position in the history of Western historical writing on the Sikhs, it is necessary to review the work of his predecessors, albeit briefly.

Cunningham's Predecessors and Contemporaries

The Sikhs had first attracted the attention of the East India Company in the late eighteenth century. Aware of their increasing importance in the politics of northern India, Warren Hastings deputed Major Browne to collect information on the Sikhs. Browne's tract on their 'origin and progress' was later printed by order of the East India directors.[19] George Forster, who travelled through northern India in 1783, combined his personal information with 'large historical tracts of the Sicques' supplied by Colonel Polier to write more than forty pages of his *Journey from Bengal to England* on the Sikhs. Forster noted that the Sikhs had raised a strong religious structure and he expected that some capable leaders would mould them into a solid political power.

William Francklin, in his *History of the Reign of Shaw Aulum* (1798), was aware of the importance of the Sikhs for the British Indian politics. He was inclined to think, however, that they were incapable of uniting their forces and, therefore, they could not become a menace for the East India Company's allies.[20]

Though politically inspired, British interest in the Sikhs was not confined to Sikh politics. Charles Wilkin's 'Observations on Seeks and their College', published in the *Asiatick Researches* in 1788, indicates his interest chiefly in 'the tenets' and 'philosophy' of the Sikhs. The source of his information were the Sikh 'priests' at Patna.[21] John Malcolm, who was with the British army in the Punjab in 1805, started collecting material for a detailed history of the Sikhs. He produced only a 'short and hasty sketch' due to lack of leisure. Its publication was justified by its usefulness 'at a moment when every information, regarding the Sikhs, is of importance'. Malcolm emphasized the practical advantage of knowing the manners, customs, and religion as well as the history of the people with whom the East India Company was likely to have diplomatic or political relations. The most 'curious and important' aspect of the Sikhs for Malcolm was their religion.[22]

Malcolm's *Sketch of the Sikhs* remained the chief source of information on the religion and early history of the Sikhs until the publication of Cunningham's work. Malcolm was able to make some use of the Ādi Granth, the *Bachittar Nātak,* the *Bhagat Mālā,* and the *Giān Ratnāvalī* through an English translation of their 'essential parts' by John Leyden. He also received help from a Nirmala Sikh at Calcutta. For Malcolm, as for most of his contemporaries, Sikhism was 'a creed of pure deism, grounded on the most sublime general truths'. However, it blended with 'the absurdities' of Hindu mythology and 'the fables' of Muhammadan superstition. Guru Nanak was a reformer rather than a subverter of Hinduism; his desire was to reconcile it to Islam. While Guru Nanak and his successors preached philanthropy and benevolence in a peaceful manner, Guru Gobind Singh made the pursuit of arms a religious duty for his followers. They were admitted from all castes and inspired with a spirit of equality among themselves. They were also inspired with a spirit of hostility towards Muslims.[23]

Malcolm's view of the religion and history of the Sikhs informed his practical conclusions. Guru Gobind Singh had given a new orientation to Sikh history. In the latter half of the eighteenth century, the Sikhs formed a 'federative republic', a theocracy governed through the *Gurmata* 'or great national council'. The spirit of equality was the vital principle of the Khalsa. It was most likely to keep the Sikh institutions intact. Sikh theocracy was 'a very serious obstacle, if not an insuperable barrier, to the designs of any of their chiefs to establish an absolute power over the whole nation'.[24] Presumably, he had written this before the Treaty of Amritsar, signed by the East India Company with Ranjit Singh in 1809, which recognized him as the sole sovereign ruler on his side of the Sutlej.

H.T. Prinsep's *Origin of the Sikh Power in the Punjab* and *the Political life of Maharaja Ranjeet Singh* recognized the Sikh ruler's achievement within twenty years of Malcolm's *Sketch*. The growth of Sikh power and the geographical position of Sikh territories had given the Sikhs a new importance in the eyes of the British. Lord William Bentinck advised the Political Agents at Ambala and Ludhiana to collect information on Ranjit Singh's political career, and Prinsep used the material collected through their personal observation and inquiry supplemented by Persian sources.[25]

Prinsep's *Origin of the Sikh Power* complemented Malcolm's work on the Sikhs. Their early history, he said, was 'pretty generally known': his object was to trace their history only from the time of Nadir Shah's invasion of India to the present when Ranjit Singh had come to possess 'a vigour of authority unknown to any other part of India, not subject to the dominion of Europeans'. Though he paid more attention to the 'Sikh Associations' or *misls*, he was not interested in all their 'petty squabbles'. His main concern was with the family of Ranjit Singh. He devoted seven of his eleven chapters to the detail of Ranjit Singh's rise to power and his relations with the English until 1831. In a separate chapter, he discussed Ranjit Singh's character, his policies, the state of his revenues and the strength of his army. In his 'general observations', Prinsep stated that there was little chance of a stable government in the Punjab after Ranjit Singh's death. The Sikh kingdom had been created and maintained under favourable circumstances by an exceptionally astute individual.[26] By implication, the successors of Ranjit Singh were not expected to handle the affairs of the state with any competence.

The volume of relevant journals, travelogues, pamphlets, periodical articles, memoirs, gazetteers, and historical works produced during the ten years after Ranjit Singh's death indicates that British interest in the Sikhs was greater than ever before. In fact, political interest in the countries to the north-west of India had begun to increase before Ranjit Singh died in 1839. The geographical position of the Sikh kingdom, the supposed instability of the government at Lahore, the Anglo-Sikh War and the general issues of determining the British Indian frontier in the north-west kept the Sikhs at the centre of British Indian politics until 1849 when the truncated dominions of Ranjit Singh were annexed to the British empire.[27]

The writers of this decade were aware of the importance of their work for British Indian politics even when they did not set out deliberately to influence the course of British policies. The publication of W.G. Osborne's journal *The Court and Camp of Ranjit Singh*, for example, was justified by the 'excited state' of the countries to the north-west of India where the Sikhs held a 'peculiar position'.[28] The East India directors sponsored the publication of Edward Thornton's *Gazetteer of the Countries Adjacent to India on the North-West* because the subject had acquired 'a new and extraordinary interest'.[29] Similarly, an English translation of Baron Charles Hugel's travels was expected to throw light on 'the proper line of policy to be pursued by the Government of India, in relation to the Punjab'.[30] Steinbach attempted to provide 'the fullest information' on the Sikhs and their country for 'the probable future possessors' of this interesting region: 'a rupture with the present rulers' of the Punjab was seen as inevitable.[31]

Three compilations of Sikh history appeared soon after the first Anglo-Sikh war. Extracts from the works of Malcolm and Steinbach were brought out by a publisher from Calcutta in 1846 as *The History of the Sikhs* with an imposing subtitle.[32] A publisher in London employed T.H. Thornton on a complete and revised edition of Prinsep's work called forth by the 'recent events in the Punjab'.[33] The second volume of his *History of the Punjab, and of the Rise, Progress and Present Condition of the Sect and Nation of the Sikhs* was devoted to the events leading to the Anglo-Sikh War and the campaign of the Sutlej. W.L. M'Gregor devoted the second volume of his *History of the Sikhs* entirely to the war of 1845–6. His work was dedicated to Lord Gough and to the officers of the Army of the Sutlej; his object was not only to record all the facts related to Sikh history but also 'to render justice to all those enlightened men and gallant spirits, whose skill and intrepidity combined to repel the insolent invasion of a rebellious army and to consolidate the British power in the north-west of India'.[34]

The writers of the time tended as a rule to support and justify the official lines of policy. Steinbach favoured an outright annexation of the Sikh kingdom to the British empire.[35] *The Calcutta Review* described the Anglo-Sikh war as a Sikh invasion of British India and characterized it as 'the violent agonies of a young and profligate state which has died by its own hand in the mad moment of a national debauch'.[36] Major-General Caulfield argued that the 'natural' frontiers of British India as well as the stability of British rule in India demanded a complete annexation of the Punjab.[37] Montague Gore grounded himself on the unprovoked aggression and flagrant perfidy of the Sikhs and argued that no trust could be placed in 'this treacherous and unprincipled race'; all their cis-Indus territories, he suggested, should be annexed.[38] *The Edinburgh Review* thought of the annexation of the Punjab as the 'consummation' of conquest and 'he must be a bold historian who would deny' its extraordinary necessity.[39]

The historians of the time glorified the success of British arms in the Punjab and justified British policy towards the Sikhs. Thornton's *History*, for example, ended with the remark on what was deliberately projected as the 'Sikh invasion' of British India, 'Sudden and unprovoked, it was brought to a rapid and glorious close by one short and brilliant campaign; in which the enemy, possessing all the advantages of opportunity, numbers, and discipline, directed by skill and backed by a desperate resolution, was overwhelmed, and a powerful kingdom was laid prostrate at the feet of its conquerors, whose forbearance, when all was in their power suffered them to exact nothing more from the vanquished than was necessary for the maintenance of peace and security against violence and rapine.'

M' Gregor's whole work may be viewed as an elaboration of this thesis.[40] He vindicated the actions of Major Broadfoot and praised Henry Lawrence. Major G.C. Smyth published Colonel Gardner's notes as *A History of the Reigning Family of Lahore* and dedicated it to the memory of Major Broadfoot. The chief reason for publishing this work was to show that no legitimate heir to Ranjit Singh was alive. He did not hesitate to say that the Sikhs did not make an 'unprovoked attack', nor that the British acted towards them with 'great forbearance', but only to conclude that there was no justification for half measures. Smyth favoured complete annexation of the Sikh kingdom.[41]

Cunningham Criticizes British Aggandizement

Far from joining his immediate predecessors in glorifying British arms and justifying British policy towards the Sikhs, Cunningham offered a serious criticism of the British in their handling of the situation which had arisen in the Punjab after Ranjit Singh's death. In his view, they had themselves brought about the first Anglo-Sikh war, because the actions of the British Indian government had convinced the Sikhs of British designs on the Punjab. Though the sincerity of the British was not to be doubted, their honesty could be admitted only 'at the expense of their judgement and knowledge of mankind'.[42]

Cunningham spoke authoritatively in unequivocal terms. He invoked his eight years' residence among all classes of the Sikhs as the means of acquiring 'accurate information' and coming to 'just conclusions'.[43] After a brilliant career at Adiscombe, he had been nominated to the Bengal Engineers in 1831 at the age of nineteen and, after professional training, he sailed for India in 1834. In 1837, Lord Auckland appointed him Assistant to Colonel Claude Wade, the then Political Agent on the Sikh frontier.[44] Until the conclusion of the first Anglo-Sikh war, Cunningham remained among the Sikhs before he was sent to Bhopal, apparently to reward his good services but actually to remove him from the Punjab where his 'partialities' for the Sikhs were not appreciated.[45] Cunningham says that he had conceived the idea of writing a history of the Sikhs before the war of 1845–6.[46] The war made the subject even more important. At Bhopal, he found the leisure to pursue his researches into Sikh history and seems to have felt the urge to influence politics in the region from which he had been removed against his wishes and where his views had been wholly disregarded.

Cunningham addressed himself to the British nation. The East India Company derived its authority from the whole nation, all its affairs in the last resort, he said, were national affairs. England's glory was great in her Eastern Dominion and her pride was justifiable by the excellence of her sway over subject nations. But this general sense of proud achievement of a rule based on wisdom, moderation and humanity must not lead the nation to assume 'that every proceeding of her delegates is necessarily fitting and far-seeing'. The proceedings of the 'delegates' of the British nation with regard to the Sikhs were neither fitting nor far-seeing. To her greater imperial glory 'England should reign over kings rather than rule over subjects'.[47] In other words, there was no need of annexation.

Cunningham's assessment of British Indian policy towards the Sikhs was based on his assumption that armed conflict with the Sikhs could have been avoided. He praised the old school which had maintained cordial but firm relations with Ranjit Singh; he criticized the new Political Agents who, were biased in handling the Sikh affairs, by views promising only immediate advantage.[48]

He had even during his short service, seen many reasons to be thankful that there is a remote deliberative or corrective body, which can survey things through an atmosphere cleared of mists, and which can judge of measures with reference both to the universal principles of justice and statesmanship, and to their particular bearing on the English supremacy in India, which should be characterized by certainty and consistency of operation, and tempered by a spirit of forbearance and adaptation.[49]

In his view, both the letter and the spirit of British treaties with Ranjit Singh, as well as the British relations with him, entitled his successors to a friendly treatment at British hands. The Sikhs were 'so inferior to the English in knowledge and resources that there was no equality of comparison between them'. It was incumbent upon the English to adopt measures obviating armed conflict.[50]

Cunningham's view that the British as a civilized imperial power had it in their hands to avert war with the uncivilized Sikh kingdom was related to the idea that the Sikhs had the right to independent existence as a people. He had 'constantly endeavoured to keep his readers alive to that undercurrent of feeling or principle which moves the Sikh people collectively', namely the urge for 'national independence'. It was this principle which could 'rise superior to the crimes and follies of individuals' among the Sikhs and which, in Cunningham's view, demanded consideration from 'the superior genius of England and civilization'.[51]

Sympathy with the Sikh Movement and Sikh Nationality

In the history of the Sikhs Cunningham saw the growth of 'a nation'. A living spirit seemed to animate the whole Sikh people and bound them together by 'a community of inward sentiment and of outward object'.

This nationality was the product of a historical process in which race and religion had played a dominant role. Indeed, 'the characteristics of race and religion are everywhere of greater importance than the accidents of position or the achievements of contemporary genius'. It was significant, therefore, that the core of the Sikh nation was provided by the Jats, 'the finest rural population of India'. Sikhism inspired them with a spirit comparable to that of 'our own chivalrous and believing forefathers'; the 'religious faith and worldly aspirations' of the Sikhs distinguished them from all other peoples of India. In the last analysis, the Sikh nation owed its origin to the religion of Nanak and Gobind.[52]

Cunningham's treatment of Guru Nanak and Guru Gobind Singh reminded J.W. Kaye significantly of Carlyle's treatment of Muhammad. Kaye remarked, however, that in hero-worship it was not given to Cunningham 'to bend the bow of Carlyle'.[53] Kaye did not realize that the 'hero' was Sikhism and not Nanak or Gobind.

In attributing a positive role to religion in history Cunningham was unique among the British historians of India. Even before undertaking a history of the Sikhs, he had shown keen interest in Indian creeds as well as in Indian history.[54] His interest in Indian architecture and sculpture was closely linked with his interest in Hinduism and Buddhism.[55] His intellectual interests in general embraced religion as much as history, literature, philosophy, and science.[56] When criticized for his 'singular' treatment of the Sikh religion, Cunningham confessed that his primary object had been 'to give Sikhism its place in the general history of humanity'.[57]

In a comprehensive context, Cunningham saw in Sikhism the chief motivating force of Sikh history. Hindu civilization had reached its highest level of achievement after the victory of Brahmanical faith over Buddhism. Shankaracharya was the last great exponent of Brahmanism and his final triumph had 'brought with it seeds of decay'. A thousand years after Christ, while Islam received a fresh impulse from the conversion of the Turks, Hinduism had lost its original fitness for 'general adoption'; its doctrines had been debased and its social efficacy, impaired. Though Islam itself was 'Indianized' in its new environment, its doctrinal purity and social dynamism did not fail to influence the static Hindu society. Thus, in the beginning of the sixteenth century, 'the Hindoo mind was no longer stagnant or retrogressive'. Already, Ramanand had preached religious equality and Chaitanya had denounced caste; Kabir had appealed to the people in their own language against idol-worship, and Vallabh was teaching religious devotion as compatible with the ordinary obligations of social life. But they succeeded in perfecting only the 'forms of dissent' and 'their sects remain to this day as they left them'. Nanak possessed all their merits but none of their grave defects.[58]

It was reserved for *Nanuk* to perceive the true principles of reform, and to lay those broad foundations which enabled his successor Govind to fire the minds of his countrymen with a new nationality, and to give practical effect to the doctrine that the lowest is equal with the highest, in race as well as creed, in political rights as in religious hopes.[59]

Cunningham marked the stages by which the core of Guru Nanak's religious and moral reformation was given a social and political orientation. Guru Amar Das succeeded in making a clear distinction between the true followers of Guru Nanak, the active and domestic Sikhs, and the followers of his son Sri Chand, the passive and recluse Udasis. Guru Arjan perceived the wide import of Guru Nanak's teachings, their applicability 'to every state of life and every condition of society'. His activities gave Sikhism a social orientation which enabled Guru Hargobind to proclaim himself as the master of *deg* and *tegh,* that is, 'grace and power'. The impulse thus given to the Sikhs finally separated them from all the Hindu sects, for 'after the time of Hur Govind the "disciples" were in little danger of relapsing into the limited merit or utility of monks and mendicants'. The Sikhs had already become a 'kind of separate state within the empire' before study, reflection, experience, judgement and persecution induced Guru Gobind Singh to awaken his followers to 'a new life' and to give precision and aim to 'the broad and general institutions of Nanuk'. He died without achieving his immediate aim of subverting a powerful empire but success was not always the measure of greatness. 'Govind saw what was yet vital, and relumed it with Promethean fire', so that, at the end of two centuries, the Sikh faith became the 'guiding principle to work its way in the world'.[60]

Cunningham described eighteenth-century Sikh history in a manner that made Ranjit Singh a national hero as well as a genuine disciple of Guru Nanak and Guru Gobind Singh. After Banda's execution, open persecution was kept up against the Sikhs. Nevertheless, 'the peasant and the mechanic nursed their faith in secret'; they reappeared on the political scene when the government of Lahore showed signs of weakness. The sole bond of their union was the 'sincerity of their common faith'. The temporary occupation of Lahore by the Sikhs in 1760 was aptly commemorated by the rupee 'coined by the grace of the Khalsa'. Cunningham characterized the Sikh sovereign rule of the late eighteenth century as 'a theocratic confederate feudalism'. When this rude system of independence and confederacy was dissolved in the early years of the nineteenth century, the 'genuine spirit of Sikhism had again sought the dwelling of the peasant to reproduce itself in another form'. While the licentious and self-seeking Sikh chiefs and their paid followers had come to think of their faith as a conventional formula, Ranjit Singh 'laboured, with more or less of intelligent design, to give unity and coherence to diverse atoms and scattered elements, to mould the increasing Sikh nation into a well ordered state, or commonwealth' just as Guru Gobind Singh had developed a sect into a people, and given application and purpose to the general institutions of Guru Nanak. Ranjit Singh appeared to be an absolute monarch over willing and obedient subjects, but 'he knew that he merely directed into a particular channel a power which he could neither destroy nor control'. The secret of his success lay primarily in his ability to give practical shape to Sikh aspirations for freedom and progress.[61]

For Cunningham, the spirit of freedom and progress, embodied in the dynamically social character of the Sikh faith, was a result of its intrinsic merit. Guru Nanak likened the deity to Truth and laid equal emphasis on faith, grace, and good conduct. He took over from Hinduism the doctrine of transmigration which was not different 'in an ethical point of view' from the doctrine of original sin. Philosophically, the two notions were 'modes of accounting for the existence of evil, or for its sway over men'. In Cunningham's view, Sikhism stood in more or less the same relationship to Hinduism as Christianity to Judaism. Just as Christianity provided the 'latent energy' for Europe, so did Sikhism possess the energy to leaven the stagnant Hindu society.[62]

With civilization and nationality as his double frame of reference, Cunningham recognized the psychological peculiarities of peoples at times and places different from his own. He admired Indian architecture, sculpture, and literature as products of the Hindu 'genius' which imparted to them a 'national character'. For all his penchant for 'parallels', Cunningham was equally impressed with the uniqueness of historical movements. Psychological peculiarities could be seen in the history of the same nation at different stages. Thus, the rise of reform movements in medieval India marked a mental change in the Hindus, which accounted for the rise of the Sikh movement. The history of the Sikhs was marked by psychological changes which accounted for the modifications of their 'feeling and principle'. Indeed, their history in all its stages unfolded their genius as a nation.[63]

Cunningham's judgements were informed partly by his keen awareness of historical relativity. India was 'far behind Europe in civilization'. Political morality or moderation as it was understood in modern Europe could be as little appreciated in India 'as it was in Christendom in the middle ages'.[64] Cunningham was reluctant to judge the 'abstract excellence or moderation' of the Sikh government, for such a judgement ignored the genius of the people and their historical circumstances. 'It is not simply an unmeaning truism to say, that the Sikh government suited the Sikhs well, for such a degree of fitness is one of the ends of all governments by ruling classes, and the adaptation has thus a degree of positive merit.'

The 'native youthful vigour' of the Sikh kingdom reminded Cunningham of the 'rising medieval Europe'. The men of 'barbarous ages' could not be judged by the standards of modern Europe, for in judging the individuals 'the extent and the peculiarities of the civilization of their times should be remembered'.[65]

The undercurrent of Cunningham's sympathy with the Sikhs was supplied by his assumption that they deserved immunity from overwhelming external circumstance as a young nation. He had no doubt that British rule in India brought some moral and material blessings to its people. The Sikhs too under the English sway were 'perhaps to be moulded to noblest purposes by the informing touch of knowledge and philosophy'. But these advantages were a poor compensation for the loss of 'national independence'. This feeling is everywhere present in the *History of the Sikhs* and is woven into the texture of its language. For example, when the English were about to enter upon schemes of navigation and trade, it

caused them to deprecate the ambition of the King of the Sikhs, and led them, by sure yet unforeseen steps, to absorb his dominion in their own, and to grasp, perhaps inscrutably to chasten, with the cold unfeeling hand of worldly rule, the youthful spirit of social change and religious reformation evoked by the genius of Nanuk and Govind.[66]

The delicate irony of such passages arises out of Cunningham's greater sympathy for the weaker of the two antagonists. In a sense, he did write like a Sikh.

However, Cunningham did not omit or distort his carefully collected facts. Even the facts considered to be derogatory to the Sikhs find their place in Cunningham's *A History of the Sikhs*: their follies and crimes, their mixed motives and their sectarian animosities as much as their heroic deeds, their devotion and their sincerity. The Sikhs remained for Cunningham, as for his predecessors, a rude and ignorant people.[67]

Unlike his predecessors, Cunningham visualized the Anglo-Sikh conflict as an act in a vast drama in which complex and huge social forces overshadowed the individual players, however important their immediate parts might appear on the stage.

The Sikhs and the English are each irresistibly urged forward in their different ways and degrees towards remote and perhaps diverse ends; the Sikhs, as leaders of a congenial mental change; the English, as the promoters of rational law and material wealth; and the individual chiefs and rulers can merely play their part in the great social movements with more or less of effect or intelligence.[68]

Cunningham's Attitude Rooted in a Strand of British Culture

Aware of the tragic complexity of large historical processes, scientific in his search for individual facts, catholic in his aesthetic tastes, liberal in his political and religious attitudes, and romantic in his conception of nationality, Cunningham was radically different from all his predecessors and contemporaries who wrote on the Sikhs. He was nonetheless rooted in the British society of the early nineteenth century. He was akin to the Liberal Anglicans who brought about 'a revolution' in English historical outlook at home.[69] In terms of cross-cultural studies Cunningham set an example which is not easy to emulate. To get into the skin of another people, another culture, is never an easy task for a historian.

NOTES

1. Eur. Mss. F. 85 (44), Henry Lawrence Collection, British Library, London. Cunningham revised his book in December 1849 and it was published posthumously from London in 1853. Edited by H.L.O. Garrett in 1915, with many additional notes but some omissions, it has been reprinted several times. Unless otherwise stated, all references are to the first edition.
2. *The Times*, 6 April 1849, p. 7.
3. *The Calcutta Review*, vol. XI, no. 22, p. 523.
4. Ibid., p. 527 n.
5. *The Athenaeum*, 24 March 1849, No. 1117, p. 293.
6. *The Times*, 6 April, 1849, p. 7.
7. *The Calcutta Review*, vol. XI, no. 22, pp. 523-4. For Kaye's authorship of the review, Eur. Mss. F. 85 (44).
8. Cunningham made a considerable use of Punjabi and Persian sources and his footnotes reveal his familiarity with almost all the relevant works of historians and Orientalists and with travelogues, journals, and periodical articles.
9. J.D. Cunningham, *A History of the Sikhs*, H.L.O. Garrett, ed., Delhi: S. Chand & Co., 1955 (rpt), preface to the second edition, p. xxviii.
10. Ibid., Introduction, p. vi.
11. Published in 2002 from New Delhi by Rupa & Co. as *History of the Sikhs* by Joseph Davey Cunningham, with a foreword by Patwant Singh.
12. As an example of a hostile critic, see Lepel Griffin, *The Rajas of the Punjab, Being the History of the Principal States in the Punjab and Their Political Relations with the British Government*, Patiala: Punjab, Languages Department, 1870, preface, pp. v-vii. For a spirited vindication of Cunnigham's version, G.B. Malleson, *Decisive Battles of India from 1746 to 1849 Inclusive*, London: Reeves and Turner, 1888, pp. xvi-xx.
13. Hardinge to Henry Lawrence, Eur. Mss. F. 85 (44).
14. Ibid., note by Henry Lawrence.
15. Cunningham, *A History of the Sikhs*, 1849 pp. 266-7.
16. *The Calcutta Review*, vol. XI, no. 22, p. 541.
17. Henry Lawrence had sent a copy of Cunningham's work to a Christian missionary at Calcutta for criticism of his treatment of the Sikh religion. He latter found that 'the author everywhere exhibits sentiments which are worthy only of reprobation'. Eur. Mss. F. 85 (44).
18. Ibid., editor of *The Calcutta Review* to Henry Lawrence.
19. Published in 1788 as a part of the India Tracts, Browne's *History of the Origin and Progress of the Sikhs* is included in the *Early European Accounts*

of the Sikhs, Ganda Singh, ed., Calcutta: Firma K.L. Mukhopadhayaya, 1962.
20. George Forster, *A Journey from Bengal to England, through the Northern Parts of India, Kashmere, Afghanistan and Persia, and into Russia by the Caspian-Sea*, 2 vols, Patiala: Languages Department, Punjab (rpt), vol. II, pp. 291-340. William Francklin, *The History of the Reign of Shaw Aulum*, London: printed by Cooper & Graham, 1798, pp. 71-8.
21. Charles Wilkins, 'Observations on Seeks and Their College', *Asiatick Researches*, Calcutta: 1788, vol. I, pp. 288-94.
22. Lt Col (John) Malcolm, *Sketch of the Sikhs*, pp. 1-6, 144.
23. Ibid., pp. 144-8, 157-72.
24. Ibid., pp. 148-57, 172-95, 196-7.
25. H.T. Prinsep, *Origin of the Sikh Power in the Punjab and Political Life of Maharaja Ranjit Singh, with an account of the present condition, religion, laws and customs of the Sikhs*, Calcutta: Military Orphan Press, 1834, preface, pp. vi, 21, *passim*.
26. Ibid., pp. 2, 21-37, 38-49, 50-177, 183.
27. See, for example, *The Calcutta Review*, vol. I, no. 2, pp. 449-507; no. 3, pp.153-208; vol. II, no. 4, pp. 469-535; vol. III, no. 6, 'Notices', pp. i-vi, xiv-xxii; vol. V, no. 10, pp. 48-72; 'Notices', pp. viii-xxii; vol. VI, no. 11, pp. 241-304; vol. IX, no. 18, pp. 511-24; vol. X, no. 19, pp. 1-21. *The Quarterly Review*, vol. LXXVIII, no. 155, pp. 175-225. *The Edinburgh Review*, vol. LXXXIX, pp. 184-221. Charles Masson, *Narratives of Various Journeys in Baluchistan, Afghanistan and the Punjab, including a residence in the countries from 1826 to 1838*, 3 vols, London: Richard Bentley, 1842. H.M. Lawrence, *Adventures of an Officer in the Punjab in the Service of Ranjit Singh*, 2 vols, London: Henry Colburn, 1846. General Caulfield, *The Punjab and the Indian Army*, London: 1846. C.M. Wade, *Notes on the State of our Relations with the Punjab and the Best Mode of their Settlement*, Ryde, Isle of Wight: 1848, R.B. Smith, *Agricultural Resources of the Punjab*, London: 1849. John Briggs, *What Are We to do with the Punjab?* London: James Madden, 1849.
28. W.G. Osborne, *The Court and the Camp of Ranjit Singh*, London: Henry Colburn, 1840, preface.
29. Edward Thornton, *Gazetteer of the Countries Adjacent to India on the North West*, London: Allen and Co., 1844, preface.
30. Baron Charles Hugel, *Travels in Kashmir and Punjab*, tr., J.B. Jervis, London: 1845, preface, p. iii.
31. Lt Col Steinbach, *The Panjaub, being a brief account of the country of the Sikhs, its extent, history, commerce, productions, government, manufactures, laws, religion etc.*, London: 1845; second edition bringing down

the history to present times and including a narrative of the recent campaign of the Sultej, London; Smith, Elder & Co., 1846, preface; also, pp. 41–2, 55, 57, 58, 129.
32. 'A concise account of the Punjab and Kashmir, its topography, climate and productions, customs, manners and character of the people, commerce, manufactures, history and religious institutions, government, administration of the laws, revenue, extent of population, etc. etc. etc'.
33. T.H. Thornton, *History of the Punjab*, London: 1846, preface, pp. x–xi.
34. W.L. M'Gregor, *The History of the Sikhs*, 2 vols, London: James Madden, 1846, preface, p. iv.
35. Lt Col Steinbach, *The Punjaub*, preface, p. iv, *passim*.
36. *The Calcutta Review*, vol. VI, no. 11, p. 241.
37. General Caulfield, *The Punjab and the Indian Army*, London: 1846, pp. 3–6, 7–8.
38. Montague Gore, *Remarks on the Present State of the Punjab*, London: John Murray, 1849, preface, pp. iii–xi, 18, 20, 25.
39. *The Edinburgh Review*, vol. LXXXIX, p. 220.
40. M'Gregor, *The History of the Sikhs*, (1870), vol. I, p. 1; vol. II, pp. 45, 308, 217.
41. G.C. Smyth, *A History of the Reigning Family of Lahore*, Calcutta: W. Thacker & Co., 1847, preface, pp. xviii–xix, xx, xxi–iii.
42. Cunningham, *A History of the Sikhs*, p. 301.
43. Ibid., preface, p. v.
44. For Cunningham's life, see D.N.B., *The Gentleman's Magazine*, vol. XXXV (New Series), pp. 555–6; Tarit Kumar Mukherji's article on his activities in India, *Bengal Past and Present*, vol. LXXVI, pt. I, no. 142, pp. 116–22.
45. Hardinge to Henry Lawrence, Eur. Mss. F. 85 (44).
46. Cunningham, *A History of the Sikhs*, preface, p. vii.
47. Cunningham, *A History of the Sikhs* (Garrett's edn), p. xxix.
48. Cunningham, *A History of the Sikhs*, pp. 152–3, 290, *passim*.
49. Ibid., pp. 152–3.
50. Cunningham, *A History of the Sikhs* (Garrett's edn)
51. Cunningham, *A History of the Sikhs*, p. 334.
52. Ibid., pp. 1, 13 and n 9, 16, 90–1.
53. *The Calcutta Review*, vol. XI, no. 22, p. 527 n.
54. *Journal of Asiatick Society of Bengal*, vol. XIII, pt. 1, pp. 172–253. This issue contains Cunningham's 'Notes' of Moorcroft's travels in Ladakh (written in 1842) which show his familiarity with Hodgson's work on Buddhism and his awareness that Csoma-de-Kiros was working on the subject. Another issue of *JASB*, vol. XVI, pt. 2, pp. 739–63, contains his

'Notes' on the antiquities of the Bhopal Agency forwarded to the editor with a note that his chief qualification was not scholarship but 'a proper degree of interest in the history of the country and of the creeds which its inhabitants have professed'.

55. *JASB*, vol. XVII, pt. 1, pp. 68–70, 154, 305–12. This issue further underlines the nature of his antiquarian interests; see the remark, for instance, on a temple: 'while it is religiously a Brahminical edifice, it is architecturally and sculpturally an adaptation from Buddhism, and serves to show how old material forms are preserved amid mental changes and the revolutions of sentiment'. Sir Henry Elliot Collection in the British Library (Eur. Mss. D. 313, 61–2) contains Cunningham's letter of 25 January, 1848 to the Resident of Indore, asking him to direct Lt. Maisey's attention to the architectural and sculptural remains at Sanchi. The results were published in General F.C. Maisey's *Sanchi and its Remains*, London: 1892, 'with remarks on the evidence they supply as to comparative modern date of the Buddhism of Gotama'. See also Cunningham, *A History of the Sikhs* (1849), p. 23 n.

56. Cunningham's footnotes to *A History of the Sikhs* alone show his familiarity with the Bible, Strauss' *Life of Jesus*, Newman's *On the Development of Christian Doctrine* and Waddington's *History of the Church* as much as with Herodotus, Tacitus, Gibbon, Grote, Thirwall and Hallam, and with Milton, Shakespeare, Homer, Dante, Virgil, Schleiermacher's *Introduction to Plato's Dialogues*, Ritter's *Ancient Philosophy*, Whewell's *History of Inductive Sciences* and Richard's *Physical History of Mankind*. For Cunningham's interest in geography and geology, see *JASB*, vol. XVIII, pt. 2, pp. 694–702 and *Selections from the Public Correspondence of the Punjab Administration*, Lahore: 1855, p. 11.

57. Cunningham, *A History of the Sikhs* (Garrett's edn), p. xxviii.
58. Cunningham, *A History of the Sikhs*, pp. 27, 32, 40, 43.
59. Ibid., p. 40.
60. Ibid., pp. 52, 53, 59 and n, 63, 70–1, 79. 89–90, 95.
61. Ibid., pp. 95, 98, 103, 105, 112–13, 141, 178, 180, *passim*.
62. Ibid., pp. 25 n, 43–4, 90–1, 334, 336, 341; also Garrett's edition, pp. xxviii–xxix. Arnold Toynbee's view of the Sikh movement is very close to this view. But, whereas Toynbee looks upon Sikh militancy as a deviation from the original purpose, Cunningham looked upon it as a corollary of the ideology of Guru Nanak. Arnold J. Toynbee, *A Study of History*, 10 vols, London: Oxford University Press, 1955(rpt), vol. VII, pp. 75–6, 414–5, 417, 532n; vol. VIII, pp. 203, 462.

EMPATHY WITH THE SIKH PAST 333

For Toynbee's treatments of Sikh history, also see J.S. Grewal, *Guru Nanak to Maharaja Ranjit Singh: Essays in Sikh History*, chapter XVIII, Amritsar: Guru Nanak Dev University, 1972, pp. 138-43, 194-5.

63. Ibid., pp. 23, 24 & n, 30 n, 31 n, 60 n, 90, 178-9, *passim*; *JASB*, vol. XVI, pt. 2, p. 744.
64. Cunningham, Ibid., p. 291.
65. Ibid., 180 n.
66. Ibid., pp. 193, 242 n, 334.
67. Ibid., pp. 59, 60, 61, 65, 109, 110, 118, 122, 126, 141, 152, 156, 187-8, 236-7, 245, 271, 281, 290, 298, 300.
68. Cunningham, *A History of the Sikhs* (Garrett's edn), pp. xxix-xxx.
69. For the stream of liberal, Christian historiography in the United Kingdom, see Duncan Forbes, *The Liberal Anglican Idea of History*, Cambridge: 1952.

14. The Contemporary Controversy in Sikh Studies*

MIXED RESPONSE TO W.H. MCLEOD'S EARLY PUBLICATIONS

Debate and disagreement is a common feature of historical writing. However, the recent controversy in Sikh studies has been rather bitter, prolonged and comprehensive. It started in a way with the publication of W.H. McLeod's *Guru Nanak and the Sikh Religion* in 1968. A strong reaction to his handling of the Janamsākhīs for the life of Guru Nanak induced Ganda Singh to write in his defence. Ganda Singh upheld the historian's right to discard 'fiction' and he defended McLeod against the charge of *mala fide* intentions. However, Ganda Singh did not accept all his conclusions with regard to the events of Guru Nanak's life. He appreciated McLeod's lucid exposition of the 'teachings' of Guru Nanak.[1] Attar Singh too thought of it as 'the most systematic, the most cogent and the most sympathetic'. He went on to add that Sikh scholars had a 'latent hostility' towards a 'rational exploration of any theme relating to Sikh faith'.[2]

McLeod's *The Evolution of the Sikh Community*, published in 1975, was seriously criticized by Fauja Singh. Ignoring the ideology of Guru Nanak in his exposition of the growth of the Sikh community, McLeod gave more importance to 'contemporary events and Jat cultural patterns'. He acknowledged Guru Nanak as the founder of the Sikh Panth but not of the Sikh faith. In Fauja Singh's view, Guru Hargobind had begun to wear the swords of mīrī and pīrī in consonance with 'Guru Nanak's system of thought' which enabled

---

* 'The Contemporary Controversy in Sikh Studies' is based largely but not entirely on two chapters 'Emergence of the Debate' and 'The Debate Continues', in the *Contesting Interpretations of the Sikh Tradition* (New Delhi: Manohar, 1998, pp. 119–31, 215–37).

the Jats to make a great contribution to Sikh history. In other words, politicization of the Sikh movement did not spring from Jat culture.[3]

McLeod's view that the doctrines of corporate and scriptural Guru appeared gradually during the eighteenth century 'in response to contemporary circumstances and cultural patterns of the Jats' was 'contrary to historical facts'. Fauja Singh refers to the *Gursobha* for the vesting of Guruship in the Khalsa. For the scriptural Guru, he refers to the *Gurbilās* of Koer Singh. We may add that the vesting of Guruship in *Shabad-Bāṇī* is there in the *Gursobha* itself.

McLeod's theory of the gradual evolution of the Sikh code of discipline during the eighteenth century was based on the assumption of late origins for the Rahitnāmas. This view was untenable so far as 'the basic code' was concerned. The confusion on this issue arose 'because all the 5Ks are not found mentioned together in contemporary or near contemporary sources'. In other words, McLeod did not make a distinction between the individual items and the formulation of 'the 5Ks'. McLeod's assumption that Jats wore uncut hair remained unsupported by evidence. If uncut hair was a cherished Jat tradition, why had it disappeared from amongst the hundreds and thousands of Hindu and Muslim Jats in the country?[4]

McLeod's essay on the Janamsākhīs was 'probably the best of the whole lot'. Besides a historical assessment of their evidence, it explained their nature, purpose, and function. The essay on Sikh scriptures contained useful information, McLeod took cognizance of 'the controversy regarding the three versions of Ādi Granth' but left the problem unsolved. In his short treatment of the *Dasam Granth*, he raised the issue of its value in assessing the impact of the hill-culture on the Jats and, through them, on the evolution of the Sikh Panth during the eighteenth century. But the issue remained unresolved. Fauja Singh appreciated McLeod's view that the Sikh Gurus had abolished the caste system in the religious sphere completely and in social matters partially. This view was closer to historical realities than the extreme view that the Sikh Gurus abolished the caste system completely and established full equality, or that they abolished caste distinctions only in the religious field. However, McLeod took 'a static' view of things. The process of 'liquidation' of differentiations was started by Guru Nanak and it reached its culmination in the Khalsa which represented a completely casteless society. The elements of the caste system in the Sikh social order reappeared subsequently, particularly under Brahmanical influences.[5]

Summing up his assessment of *The Evolution of the Sikh Community*, Fauja Singh stated that it was 'an extremely thought-provoking but tendentious study'. McLeod's formulations were far reaching as a new theory of development of the Sikh community, but they were mostly based on conjecture and some of them were not even good hypotheses. There was 'substantial ground to regard them as ill-founded' because known historical evidence appeared to contradict them.[6]

The Evolution of the Sikh Community was criticized in stronger terms by Daljeet Singh. After his retirement from civil service in 1969, he had started taking interest in Sikhism and published articles on the doctrines of *māyā* and *nām* in Sikhism.[7] In his view, McLeod's treatment of five major themes in a little over one hundred pages tended to become journalistic rather than academic. In other words, he tended to generalize on the basis of inadequate evidence. Nearly the whole structure of his book was based on the premise that 'Sikhism had no new religious thesis' to offer. McLeod's equation of Sikhism with the sant tradition did not explain how the 'quietist mysticism' of the sant tradition was suddenly transformed into the prophetic mission of Guru Nanak. Nor did it explain how an 'inert ideal' of salvation was changed into the 'dynamic goal' of carrying out the will of God. In other words, liberation for the sants was an inert and passive state of bliss; for Guru Nanak and his successors, liberation-in-life was preceded and followed by active participation in life. McLeod attributed the socio-political and military activities of the Sikhs to 'the influence of Jat elements amongst Sikh ranks'. Empirical evidence did not support this conjecture. His hypothesis about the impact of the Shakti cult of the hills ignored the simple fact that this cult never inspired the hill people to throw off the political yoke. In his hypothesis about the 5Ks, McLeod cited no evidence to show that they were Jat symbols in the region before their adoption by the Sikhs, nor does he explain why they disappeared from among all the Jats of the neighbouring regions of Haryana, Rajasthan, and Pakistan.[8]

McLeod appeared to have made 'the simplistic assumption' that Guru Nanak's mission was the same as that of the bhaktas and found it difficult to explain 'the exteriority, the organization and the socio-political objective and struggle' of the Sikh Gurus. Instead of revising his premises he proceeded to find props for his fragile structure in entities like the Jat culture and the Shakti cult. Just as the growth of Christianity could not be explained without reference to the life and teaching of Christ, so the growth of the Sikh Panth could not be explained without reference to the theses of the Gurus and their lives. Just as the deep concern of Jesus for the poor could not be attributed to the presence of poor fishermen among his followers, the sociopolitical concerns of the Gurus could not be attributed to the presence of Jats among their followers. In other words, values did not emerge from facts. Daljeet Singh remarked that it was a common failing of 'persons with mechanistic views' to ignore the role of ideology as 'a cementing and directive force in human history' and to over stretch and over estimate the significance of 'ordinary facts and routine events'.[9] More emphatically than Fauja Singh, Daljeet Singh raised the issue of ideology against the importance attached to environment in historical causation.

Besides publishing his *Sikhism: A Comparative Study of its Theology and Mysticism* in 1979 and *The Sikh Ideology* in 1984, Daljeet Singh persuaded Jagjit Singh to write his views on the history of the Sikh movement. Jagjit Singh had published an article on 'The Jats and Sikh Militarization' in the *Journal of Sikh Studies* in February 1977. His *Sikh Revolution* in 1981 was followed by *Perspectives on Sikh Studies* in 1984. The last two sections of the latter related to the issue of caste in the Sikh Panth and the role of Jats in the Sikh movement.

In 1986 came out the *Perspectives on the Sikh Tradition*, edited by Gurdev Singh, a former Judge of the Punjab and Haryana High Court. About three-fifths of this book consisted of contributions made by Daljeet Singh and Jagjit Singh on the basis of their published works. The other contributions to this volume came from Hari Ram Gupta, Ganda Singh, Harbans Singh, and Noel Q. King. Three of these four scholars had nothing to say against McLeod, but their findings appeared to be opposed to those of McLeod. The professed purpose of this publication was to present a formidable refutation of McLeod's propositions.[10]

Khushwant Singh's 'foreword' to the *Perspectives on the Sikh Tradition* gave the impression that McLeod was finally refuted. According to him, McLeod had come to the conclusion in his *Guru Nanak and the Sikh Religion* that the life story of Guru Nanak was based on fiction, and that Guru Nanak had merely stated the religious beliefs current during his time and could not, therefore, be regarded as 'the founder of a new faith'. In his *The Evolution of the Sikh Community*, McLeod expressed the view that large-scale intrusion of the Jats into the Khalsa Panth, rather than being something planned by Guru Hargobind and Guru Gobind Singh, was the main cause of the metamorphosis of the pacifist Nanak Panthis into the militant fraternity of the Khalsa. Furthermore, McLeod questioned 'the authencity of the baptismal ceremony of the Baisakhi of 1699' and discounted the Rahitnāmas as 'subsequent compilations'. McLeod was 'on weak ground' and some of his conclusions were 'erroneous'. The record had to be set right in order to establish that the Sikh religious tradition was not 'an edifice built on hot air or make believe'. This was what the *Perspectives on the Sikh Tradition* had done.[11]

Gurdev Singh dwelt on the motives of McLeod as much as on his 'misrepresentation' of the Sikh tradition. After Independence, the Sikhs were concentrated in the Punjab and settled in distant countries like Canada, USA, and UK. Wherever they went they attracted attention because of their distinctive appearance and their 'integrity, hard labour and will to work'. These moral traits evoked interest in their religion, history, and social structure. Foreign scholars became interested in Sikhism and Sikh history, and some of them made valuable contribution to Sikh Studies. However, some tendentious works also appeared to make the Sikhs 'victims of distortion, misrepresentation and misunderstanding'.[12] Even a hurried glance through McLeod's *Guru Nanak and the Sikh Religion*, his *The Evolution of the Sikh Community*, and his *Early Sikh Tradition* (published in 1980) reveals that Sikhism, in his opinion, did not deserve much consideration as it was only 'a rehash of an effete Hindu creed'. There was a deliberate design. McLeod was involved in missionary activities for a number of years in the Punjab and realized that missionary work had no future unless the faith of the new generation in its own traditions was undermined. He adopted a non-believer's approach to accept nothing that was not established to his satisfaction about Sikhism and its founder, resulting in a negative approach.[13]

McLeod's salient propositions 'belittle the Sikh faith and doctrines in the eyes of the English speaking people and other non-Sikhs'. The slow reaction of the Sikhs to his first 'tendentious work' encouraged

McLeod to come up with *The Evolution of the Sikh Community* in which he attacks 'most of the Sikh traditions, institutions and beliefs' and questions their validity in order 'to create doubt about the others'. Eight propositions are attributed to McLeod: one, that Guru Nanak belongs to the sant tradition; two, that his successors did not preach one set of doctrines, giving up at one stage his teachings in favour of militancy; three, that the Panth got armed not because of any decision of Guru Hargobind but because of Jat influx; four, that the traditional account of the founding of the Khalsa cannot be accepted; five, that the Sikh code of discipline and Sikh symbols were evolved during the eighteenth century and not promulgated by Guru Gobind Singh on the Baisakhi of 1699; six, that the Gurus denounced caste system but they were not sincere or serious in removing caste differences; seven, that the succession of Granth Sahib as the Guru after Guru Gobind Singh was a subsequent adoption and not due to his injunction; eight, that the authenticity of the current version of Guru Granth Sahib is open to question.[14]

Gurdev Singh claimed that all these propositions stand refuted in the *Perspectives on the Sikh Tradition*. Noel Q. King's essay underlines the basic fault in McLeod's methodology in dealing with the Janamsākhīs for the life of Guru Nanak. Daljeet Singh's essays establish the originality and uniqueness of the Sikh faith. Hari Ram Gupta establishes the authenticity of the baptismal ceremony on the Baisakhi of 1699. Ganda Singh and Harbans Singh prove that Guru Gobind Singh abolished the system of personal Guruship by vesting Guruship in the Granth Sahib. Jagjit Singh demonstrates that caste distinctions were abolished by the Gurus in both theory and practice, and that 'militarization' of the Sikh movement was a logical outcome of Sikh ideology and deliberate decisions of the Gurus and not of the influx of Jats, or any economic crisis or impact of the Shakti cult.[15]

Emergence of Sikh Studies in the West

By this time, interest in Sikh studies had emerged in the USA. The 'intellectual and fiscal milieu' in the US was changing even before McLeod published his first work. South Asian programmes were launched in 1962, leading to the development of interest in regional issues and regional languages in India. A few graduate students became 'Punjab Specialists'. In 1966, a Research Committee on the Punjab was formed to pursue and promote Punjab studies. Closely linked with this committee were Kenneth Jones, Eric Gustafson, Paul Wallace, and Baldev Raj Nayar, among others. The *Sources of Punjab History*, edited by Gustafson and Jones, was published in 1975. The *Arya Dharm* of Kenneth Jones was published in 1976. Among the 'Punjab Specialists' were at least two scholars who took interest in Sikh themes. N. Gerald Barrier's *The Sikhs and Their Literature* was published in 1970, and Tom G. Kessinger's *Vilayatpur* was published in 1974.[16]

The first conference on Sikh studies in the US was held at Berkeley in 1976. Its moving spirit, Mark Juergensmeyer, had worked on the Radhasoamis of the Punjab. The conference was co-sponsored by the Sikh Foundation. Its director, Narinder Singh Kapany, though a physicist, was keen to promote Sikh studies in North America. Evidently, the presence of Sikhs in the United States had become relevant for the emergence of Sikh studies. As Mark Juergensmeyer put it, the sizeable population of Sikhs living outside India could not be ignored by the scholarly community. The papers presented to the conference were published in 1979 as *Sikh Studies: Comparative Perspectives on a Changing Tradition*, edited by Mark Juergensmeyer and N. Gerald Barrier.

The major concern of the conference was how to develop Sikh studies in North America. Juergensmeyer pointed out that 'traditions of misunderstanding' of Sikhism were embodied in the textbooks on 'world religions' and 'the religions of India'. A better understanding of Sikhism was needed for various reasons. In the first place, Sikhism represented 'a rich and interesting religious tradition' in itself to form an important subject of study. Second, its study could lead to 'a more complex interpretation of the whole of India's cultural history'. Furthermore, the scholars of special fields within religious studies in general could take Sikhism into account for comparative studies in the areas of textual criticism, mythology, social studies and political thought. Thus, valuable in their own right, Sikh studies could be relevant for comparative studies and have a 'provocative' effect on other areas of scholarship.[17]

John C.B. Webster reviewed Sikh studies in the Punjab. The major figures in Sikh studies during the nineteenth century were European: J.D. Cunningham, Ernest Trumpp, and M.A. Macauliffe. In the twentieth century, the field belonged mainly to Indian scholars like Bhai Vir Singh, Bhai Kahn Singh of Nabha, and Principal Teja Singh as perhaps the most outstanding Punjabis, and Indubhusan Banerjee and N.K. Sinha as the most outstanding non-Punjabis. The Khalsa College at Amritsar, with Bhai Jodh Singh and Ganda Singh, provided a broader institutional base for the development of Sikh studies. The establishment of universities at Patiala and Amritsar and several other institutions contributed to the growing stream of Sikh studies. Books, monographs and articles were published; a number of periodicals and the *Encyclopaedia of Sikhism* were started. The only hindrance in this pursuit was the non-availability of qualified personnel. Indeed, religion and theology had not been taught as scholarly disciplines in Indian universities. The methodology in historical scholarship in the field was not strong. The expansion of Sikh studies in the Punjab was of the traditional type. Western scholars had much to gain from what was going on in the Punjab but they had to face the charge that they were foreign scholars who either did not understand or simply attacked the Sikhs and Sikhism, using methods which did not apply to Indian religious traditions.[18] This last observation alluded obviously to the criticism of McLeod's work on the Sikhs.

For a perspective on early Sikh history, I pointed out that the origins of the Sikh movement need to be traced to 'the response' of Guru Nanak to the social situation, and that his kinship with the sant tradition did not militate against his position as 'the founder of a new system of religious beliefs and practices'. The ideological, institutional and social linkages between the work of Guru Nanak and his first four successors were much closer than what the historians had thought to be. The issues of numbers, composition, and identity in relation to the sixteenth century Sikh Panth demanded more attention. Seventeenth century Sikh history was better conceived in terms of the transference of goals and transformation of the Sikh Panth and not Sikhism. The most remarkable feature of seventeenth century Sikh community was its division into an 'anti-establishment' mainstream and 'pro-establishment' dissident groups. This feature demanded a detailed study and the question of the preponderance of the Jat peasantry in the Sikh Panth deserved a more thorough investigation than what Cunningham, Banerjee, McLeod, and others had done. The institution of the Khalsa was meant to solve two interrelated problems: internal unity and external threat. On this view, the logical and historical links between the seventeenth and the eighteenth centuries became as evident as the links between the sixteenth and the seventeenth centuries. Three legacies left by Guru Gobind Singh dominated the eighteenth century: struggle for sovereign rule, the egalitarian doctrine of Guru Panth, and the principle of unity embodied in the doctrine of Guru Granth Sahib. The first provided the motivation for political mobilization; the second enabled the Khalsa to come together as equals so that even the former outcaste could become rulers; and the third provided a cushion for social differentiation under monarchical polity. The leaders of Sikh resurgence in the late nineteenth century were to 'pick up the threads which had run through the history of the period and survived the loss of political power'. Thus, it was necessary to have a perspective which took into account both the change and continuum and provided a meaningful frame of reference.[19]

Talking of the role of ideology and institution building in modern Sikhism, N. Gerald Barrier pointed out that intellectual and institutional developments of crucial importance had taken place between 1870–1920. There were four new areas for exploration: division and unity in Sikhism, the nature and function of Sikh institutions, social and political mobilization of Sikhs under British rule, and the evolution of theological and historiographic trends among Sikh intellectuals.[20]

Commenting on the perspectives presented at the conference, Engene Irschick suggested that Sikhism should not be regarded as less significant than any of the other religious traditions which were the special concerns of Indian and non-Indian scholars, nor should it be regarded as unique. To understand the ways in which Sikhism developed and the way it functioned, it was necessary to look at the social and economic bases of the movement in medieval and in contemporary society. 'If it is true that one goal of Guru Nanak was to eliminate caste and other social differentiation which was a part of Hinduism of his time we must look at the way it was achieved or fell short of its original goals'. Equally important was to know the extent to which egalitarian ideas and practices continue in present day Sikhism.[21]

Ainslee Embree pointed out that in the perspectives presented at the conference there was no reference to any sustained attention having been given to questions of the relationship between religion and social change. Direct and specific studies were needed in this connection. 'The history of Sikhism would appear to provide material for a very important contribution to all the great themes: religion and the rise of capitalism, the relationship between social dislocation and social dynamism, the creative role of minorities, even that grandest of all, the differences between western and Indian culture'. Was there any causal connection between the theological presuppositions of Sikhism and the extraordinary dynamism of the Sikhs in the twentieth century? There were clear indications that Sikh studies could provide material for exploring new frontiers to deepen our knowledge of how societies functioned.[22]

Significantly, the American scholars participating in the conference tended to assume that the views of the western scholars on the Sikh tradition were valid. For instance, McLeod appeared to have demonstrated that the indigenous elements in Sikhism were largely those customs of the tribes of Jats who made Sikhism their own. Similarly, Barrier appeared to have shown that Sikhism became a religion only in the nineteenth century, symbolized by the assertion, *ham hindū nahīn* (we are not Hindus), as an expression of the Sikh anxiety to locate their religious history, and their personal identity, outside the Hindu matrix and that Sikhism as now embedded in the structural dynamics of North Indian society was largely a product of the historical forces of the nineteenth century.[23] Both of these issues are under scholarly debate.

Apart from the 'contexts of Sikh studies', the papers presented at the Berkeley conference related to the 'origins' and the 'texts' of Sikhism, and 'the Sikhs abroad'. Kenneth E. Bryant was aware of opposing views expressed by scholars on whether or not Sikhism was a sect of Hinduism. A piece of terrain largely ignored by both sides was that of poetics, especially the canons of literary criticism applied to the works of Guru Nanak and Kabir. In his argument that an understanding of the medium can enhance our understanding of the message, Bryant made a clear distinction between Vaishnava and *sant* poetry. In the process, he bracketed Guru Nanak with Kabir.[24]

Karine Schomer pointed out that the historians of Indian religion had tended to oversimplify the medieval religious situation by classifying all important figures, movements, and literatures as representative of either *saguṇa bhakti* or *nirguṇa* bhakti. The label saguna bhakti obscured important differences between the Krishna *līlā* in the ritual life of the Vallabha sect and in the story of Rama retold by Tulsidas. Similarly, the label nirguna bhakti failed to distinguish between the individual sants and the organized sects or panths developed by their followers. Schomer compared the Guru Granth tradition with the Dadu Panthi tradition of Kabir to show that the former conforms to the 'moods and motivations' appropriate to a solid, moral, God-fearing religious community of householders, suggesting the possibility that Guru Amar Das and Guru Arjan may have 'edited out' the mystic and emphasized the teacher and preacher. This comparison appeared to bring out 'the unique features of Sikhism as an organized religion'.[25] This does not mean, however, that Schomer is contesting the placing of Guru Nanak and Kabir within the sant tradition.

Talking of 'some issues' in relation to the Sikh scriptures, McLeod declared that his concern extended to the study of all sacred texts, regardless of the tradition which accorded them sanctity. He underlined the importance of textual analysis for the Ādi Granth as for all other scriptures. There were numerous deletions in the manuscript known as the Kartarpuri Bīṛ. Three deletions in particular appeared to be important because these verses were not deleted in the recension known as the Banno Bīṛ. This suggested the possibility of the latter being an earlier recension from which the Kartarpuri Bīṛ was copied. This suggestion carried the implication that the Kartarpuri Bīṛ was not really the one compiled by Guru Arjan. Bhai Jodh Singh's *Sri Kartarpuri Bir de Darshan*, published in 1968 to establish its authenticity, left the principal problem unsolved for McLeod. Though the verses were not deleted, they were left incomplete. It was conceivable, therefore, that the Kartarpur text was in fact a later recension and that its scribe, appreciating the problem raised by the hymns, simply omitted the remainder in each case. There was surely the need of a sustained campaign of textual analysis if we were to establish 'a sure and certain text'. The traditional account that Guru Gobind Singh conferred his authority upon the corporate community and the sacred scripture, giving rise to the doctrines of Guru Panth and Guru Granth, could neither be positively affirmed nor categorically rejected.[26] McLeod was aware of the clear evidence of the *Gursobha* on this issue but he placed its composition a few decades later than 1711, the date which is generally ascribed to it.

C.H. Loehlin stated that, though the authenticity of the Kartarpuri Bīṛ appeared to be established, many scholars claimed originality for the Banno Bīṛ. A solution to such questions seemed impossible because of the inaccessibility of these manuscripts, especially the Kartarpur one. Bhai Ardaman Singh (of Bagarian) had asserted in 1975 that Guru Granth Sahib was the only scripture in the world which was written, prepared, and sealed by the founder who directly received the Word. Such a categorical statement required further study to put the issue beyond all doubt.[27] Authenticity of the Kartarpuri Bīṛ was, thus, suspect for both McLeod and Loehlin and they called for a textual study of the scripture.

Narinder Singh Kapany stated that the Sikhs had demonstrated an uncanny capability to retain their identity, beliefs, and traditions, and yet participate most actively in the American and Canadian scene. With their deep commitment to their own culture as well as to the American way of life, they formed a rich subject for scholarly studies.[28] When the second conference was held at Berkeley in 1987, there was a lot of tension. The papers presented at the conference were not published.

In Canada, the first conference on Sikh studies was also held early in February 1987. The presence of a large 'diaspora' of Canadian Sikhs in the province of Ontario, especially in Toronto, and their inclination to encourage the study of Sikh history and religion provided the general context for this conference. To serve as a 'catalyst' for the conference was the presence of W.H. McLeod who was getting recognition as the foremost scholar of Sikhism in the west. He had gone to Berkeley on sabbatical leave in 1978 and participated in a conference on the sant tradition which incidentally, reinforced his convictions about the place of Guru Nanak within the sant tradition.[29] In 1980, the Clarendon Press published McLeod's *Early Sikh Tradition* which for him is the best book he has ever written. He received a Commonwealth Fellowship from the University of Toronto in 1982 and went there early in 1986. He was to give a series of four lectures on Sikhism under the auspices of the American Council of Learned Societies and a series of seven lectures at the University of Oxford as Radhakrishnan Memorial Lectures. His presence in Toronto inspired Milton Israel and Joseph T. O'Connell to organize a conference on Sikh studies at Toronto in February 1987. Unfortunately, McLeod could not participate in the conference due to a serious stroke. The papers presented at this conference were published in 1988 as *Sikh History and Religion in the Twentieth Century*.

Apart from papers on the Sikh diaspora and comments on recent events in the Punjab, this volume contained eight papers on 'religion and culture' and seven papers on 'history and politics'. Among the former set was McLeod's paper on 'A Sikh Theology for Modern Times', outlining the topics which needed to be treated for evolving a systematic Sikh theology. He hammered the point that an integrated and comprehensive account of Sikh theology had yet to be written. It was necessary first of all to be clear about Sikh concepts and terminology: the epithets for God, like Akāl Purkh, Kartār, Vāheguru; the concepts of nām, *hukam*, and guru; the term panth; the doctrine of mīrī-pīrī; the Khalsa and the *rahit;* the term sant and the concept of sādh-sangat; the words gurdwara and dharmsāla; the five *takht*s; kīrtan, *kathā*, and *granthī*; the word *seva*. On all these, and many other related terms, a clear understanding would actually mean a new interpretation.[30]

Notable among the papers on 'history and politics' was Harjot Oberoi's 'From Ritual to Counter-Ritual: Rethinking the Hindu-Sikh Question, 1884-1915'. It opened with a bang. Oberoi asserted that Bhai Kahn Singh Nabha 'brought almost four centuries of Sikh tradition to an end' when he proclaimed in 1897 ham hindū nahīn. Oberoi argued that the religious categories 'Hindu' and 'Sikh' were ambiguous, fluid and fragile. Distinctively Sikh life style rituals were absent among the Sikhs before the influence of the Singh Sabhas became pervasive. Therefore, the Sikhs in their earlier history were encompassed in 'Hindu' society. Oberoi noticed, however, that in many ways the *Rahitnāma* literature of the pre-colonial period foreshadowed the homogeneous Sikh identity and religious boundaries of the late nineteenth century. The roots of the drive for this autonomy were traced by some scholars back to Guru Nanak, but the reasons for the consolidation of Sikh cultural autonomy lay entangled in the social history of late nineteenth-century Punjab.[31] Oberoi's paper, thus, raised the all important question of Sikh identity, with a direct bearing on Sikh politics.

I was invited to the Toronto conference to speak on the 'legacies of the Sikh past for the twentieth century'. McLeod's *The Evolution of the Sikh Community* was in a way relevant for my purpose. It could be adapted, I said, 'with only a mild disagreement here and a minor modification there'. McLeod had not discussed the issues directly and I outlined the significant developments of the pre-colonial period of Sikh history in 'slightly different terms'. The themes taken up for discussion were the doctrines of Guru Granth and the Guru Panth, *raj karega khalsa*, and social and ideological differentiation within the Sikh Panth. My treatment of these themes was quite different from their treatment by McLeod.

The emergence of interest in Sikh Studies in North America, the nature of issues raised by western scholars, and the recognition given to the scholarship of W.H. McLeod, who was the most controversial figure in the eyes of many Sikhs, induced his critics to respond to these academic activities.

CRITICISM OF WESTERN SCHOLARSHIP

Before the end of 1988, a conference was held at the California State University, Long Beach, by the Sikh community of North America. Apart from Daljeet Singh, Jagjit Singh and Noel Q. King, some scholars from the Panjab, Punjabi and Guru Nanak Dev Universities made their contributions to the conference, with some new contributors from North America and UK. In the volume published as *Advanced Studies in Sikhism* it was stated that the recent Western writings in the field of Sikh studies had generally been quite peripheral in their scope and inadequate in their approach.[32] To be criticized directly in this volume were W.H. McLeod and Harjot Oberoi.

Daljeet Singh criticized McLeod and Oberoi from the viewpoint of methodology. The tools of social sciences were inadequate for the study of religion because they related to its empirical aspects and left out the spiritual. The denial of the spiritual element in religion vitiated its study and ruled out its very need or meaning. Daljeet Singh looked upon ontology or the spiritual base of religion as essential to a proper understanding and development of any religion. McLeod's formulation of sant synthesis left out the spiritual experience of Guru Nanak. That was why he maintained that Guru Nanak made no new contribution to religious thought. Harjot Oberoi talked of Sikh religion as 'a peasant faith' or as 'rural religion', reflecting the limitation of sociological or anthropological approach to the study of Sikhism. In Sikh monotheism, worldly life was accepted as the arena for the practice of virtues for spiritual growth, underlining the importance of work and production. Rejection of monasticism, asceticism, celibacy, and *ahinsa*, and the creation of an organized and a disciplined society were the logical outcome of Guru Nanak's ideology. McLeod and Oberoi appeared to lack an understanding of these essentials of Sikhism which distinguished it from Vedanta, Vaishnavism, and Nathism.[33]

Daljeet Singh took notice of some 'oblique but incorrect' observations made by McLeod, throwing doubt on the authenticity of the Kartarpuri Bīṛ even after the publication of Bhai Jodh Singh's *Kartarpuri Bir de Darshan*. Daljeet Singh himself had delivered a lecture on 'The Authenticity of Kartarpuri Bir' at the Punjabi University in 1987, refuting all the objections raised by G.B. Singh, W.H. McLeod, and Pritam Singh. Their views had no factual or rational basis. McLeod's bias was understandable because of his association with a Christian missionary centre. Daljeet Singh's paper in the *Advanced Studies of Sikhism* is a revised version of his lecture. It was meant to establish that 'the Kartarpuri Bir is incontrovertibly the authentic Adi Granth prepared by the Fifth Guru'.[34]

In a slightly revised version of his earlier articles on the issue of the 'Jat theory of Sikh militarization', Jagjit Singh developed the argument that the Sikh social and political revolution would not have materialized without Sikh ideology, 'even if the Panth had been composed entirely of Jats'. The 'native character and mores' of the Jats could never lead to any revolution.[35]

Jagjit Singh's paper on 'the caste system and the Sikhs' was essentially the same as in the *Perspectives*. The only major work he criticized was Ethne K. Marenco's *Transformation of the Sikh Society*. Jagjit Singh underlines the obliteration of caste distinctions among the early Sikhs and the Khalsa, which enabled the erstwhile Shudras and outcastes to become the rulers of the land. Even after this 'revolutionary' phase, there were 'no religious, commensal, or other social discriminations at the Panthic level'. In the villages, the Sikhs drawn from artisan, menial and outcaste categories were decidedly better placed socially than their counterparts in the caste society.[36]

S.S. Kohli criticized McLeod's view of the evolution of the early Sikh Panth and the growth of militancy as a great misrepresentation. McLeod lacked understanding of Sikh thought. He knew that Sikhism was antagonistic towards the caste system but cleverly manipulated the issue of Khatri and Jat culture for creating a cleavage among the Sikhs on caste basis. Inderjit Singh developed an argument in support of the unity of Sikh thought without an explicit reference to McLeod.

Madanjit Kaur criticized McLeod's hypothesis that the doctrine of Guru Panth developed gradually in the eighteenth century.[37]

S.S. Kohli tried to present a correct appraisal of the *Janamsākhīs*, stating among other things that they do contain a few myths and legends but they cannot be placed in the category of 'mythical and legendary literature'. Another contributor drew a parallel between the Janamsākhīs and the four Gospels, emphasizing that the image of Guru Nanak that emerged from the Janamsākhīs was that of a kind, loving, wise and godly person 'lit with Divine knowledge, through whom God is revealed to everybody who comes in contact with him and meditated on the "Word"'. McLeod failed to appreciate the 'myth' of Guru Nanak and the significance of miracles in that 'myth'. The critique of McLeod's works by Mrigendra Singh, given in a summary form, does not make any additional point.[38]

Gobind Singh Mansukhani argued against McLeod's view that the Sikh code of discipline and the Sikh symbols were evolved in the eighteenth century as a result of 'gradual growth'. He cites a *hukamnāma* of Guru Gobind Singh, dated 23 May 1699, taking its authenticity for granted. This hukamnāma refers to only four symbols beginning with the letter 'k': there is no reference to *kangha*. Madanjit Kaur states that the Sikh tradition on this issue is strong, and it is supported by 'Sikh sources'. She refers to the *Gursobha* in which there is actually no mention of the '5 Ks'. She goes on to say that early Sikh scholars did not record Sikh history, and there was little scope of preserving 'the contemporary historical records' in the extraordinary circumstances of the post-Khalsa phase. In other words, even if there were such records they did not survive. Madanjit Kaur, thus, begins with the promise of producing hard evidence in support of the Sikh tradition but ends up by merely accepting the received tradition.[39]

Gurdarshan Singh Dhillon took notice of Harjot Oberoi's paper entitled 'Popular Saints, Goddesses and Village Sacred Rites: Re-reading Sikh Experience in the Nineteenth Century', presented at the Berkeley conference in 1987. Dhillon emphasized that the Singh Sabha was not 'a reformist movement': it made no innovations in Sikh thought and practice. The true Sikh tradition had begun to be eroded with the establishment of Sikh rule when a large number of Hindus and Muslims joined the Panth for mundane reasons. They were slow in shedding some of their old beliefs and practices, which affected the overall character of the Khalsa Panth. Then, in the early decades of British rule, Sikhs fell prey to Brahmanical Hinduism. Harjot Oberoi selected some features of the late nineteenth-century Sikhism and projected them back as an integral part of original Sikhism. There was no credible evidence that the worship of Sakhi Sarvar, Gugga Pir, Seetla Devi, and village ancestors was widely spread among the Sikhs, or that it was universally tolerated. The norms against such practices are enshrined in the Sikh scripture and in Sikh literature. Oberoi's view of Sikhism as a rural religion was lopsided. The great achievement of the Singh Sabha Movement lay in strengthening the early Sikh tradition for meeting new challenges.[40]

James R. Lewis gave a new version of his papers published in 1985 in 1987, relating to the mispresentations of Sikh tradition in world religions' textbooks in terms of factual errors, the notion of syncretism, and the contrast between the supposed pacifism of Guru Nanak and the militancy of Guru Gobind Singh. In his discussion of syncretism, Lewis appreciated McLeod for rejecting this concept and emphasizing the 'originality' of Guru Nanak.[41]

Compared with the *Perspectives on the Sikh Tradition,* there is much substantive repetition and much supplementary material in the *Advanced Studies.* There is also a basic continuity in terms of contributors, themes, and old works. However, two new themes are added to the debate: the Singh Sabha Movement and Sikh identity. The scope of the debate was, thus, extended to the modern period. The question of textual analysis was brought to the fore. The professed purpose of the *Advanced Studies* was to present a clear image of Sikhism and to create a climate for establishing a centre of Higher Learning and Research in Sikh Studies.[42] Evidently, the future direction of Sikh studies is of crucial importance.

An Early Response to Criticism

A conference held at Columbia University in 1989 resulted in the publication of *Studying the Sikhs: Issues for North America.* The editors, John Stratton Hawley and Gurinder Singh Mann, noticed the 'marked tensions between academics and believers' which had affected the field of Sikh studies in recent years and created a concern that surfaced in 'almost every chapter of the book'.[43]

Mark Juergensmeyer talked of confrontation between two views of scholarship. The subject matter of religious studies had changed dramatically in the 1960s and 1970s, and made the field of religious studies less 'religious' in its orientation and more objective and 'intellectually respectable' in terms of 'methodology'. The 'Enlightenment' ethos of secular universities had a serious implication for Sikh studies. The guardians of standards within the field looked for Sikh scholarship that was objective in approach, sophisticated in methodology, cross-cultural in significance, and contextual in historical analysis. These expectations were somewhat out of kilter with the recent trends in Sikh scholarship in the Punjab where the main concern was to show the distinctiveness of the faith rather than its connections and similarities with other traditions. Another concern of 'Sikh' scholars was to demonstrate solidarity with the community in projecting an integral, unified, and autonomous culture. Thus, a stage was set for an unhappy confrontation between the two views of scholarship.[44]

McLeod's *Guru Nanak and the Sikh Religion* still remained one of the most controversial works in this context. To most western scholars his approach seemed to be commonplace, even conservative. He had separated hagiography from historical facts and placed the historical figure of Guru Nanak in his contemporary cultural and political context. What made the issue sensitive was that a non-Sikh was examining a problem in Sikh history for an audience consisting primarily of western academics. McLeod had come to be regarded as the premier scholar of Sikhism in the West, chosen from an international pool of scholars to give nationwide lectures sponsored by the American Council of Learned Societies in 1986. It was a distinction that no other scholar of Sikhism had achieved. However, in India and elsewhere in Sikh communities, he was often presented as being hostile to the faith. This raised the issue of approach to scholarship: 'is a tradition's own understanding of its history to be explicated and affirmed or are the historical data of a tradition available for cross-cultural analysis?'[45] Juergensmeyer leaves the impression that the modern modes of analysis are enough to sanctify one's scholarship and by that token alone McLeod's work remains above criticism.

Indeed, Juergensmeyer supports McLeod's view that the Sikh tradition emerged from medieval Hinduism, deriving its origins from the sants, among whom Guru Nanak himself was to be numbered and whose verses are included in the Ādi Granth.[46] Despite serious scholarly criticism, the view taken by McLeod is seen as the correct one.

N. Gerald Barrier talked of a tension between two approaches to Sikh historiography, the one more familiar in the Punjab and the other more at home in western universities. The former tended to reinforce a respect for the Gurus, a sense of historical continuity, a clear differentiation between Sikhism and Hinduism from the time of the first Guru, and to provide an almost hagiographic treatment of Sikh historical figures. The scholars trained in Western universities questioned traditional sources and applied rigorous textual analysis in treating documents that related to other historical and religious traditions. They tended to look upon Sikhism as an evolving religious and cultural tradition, one that mirrors and in turn affects the environment in which it was evolved. They respected the authenticity of Sikhism and supported the separate boundaries of its doctrines and institutions but they did not accept some of the presuppositions of the Sikh historians. The loudest criticism of western scholarship on Sikhism revolved around the issues of unity and equality among the Sikhs. Non-Sikh scholars were charged with creating divisions, especially between Jats and non-Jats. There was also a debate between the earlier view of Sikhism as a syncretism and the recent emphasis on Sikhism as a 'synthesis'. Was this emphasis too in need of revision?[47] Barrier does not answer the question but the answer is 'yes'. On the issue of Sikh identity Harjot Oberoi's views had stirred reaction among Sikh historians who claimed a single line of authoritative practice from Guru Gobind Singh up to the present.[48] It is not clear who are these 'Sikh historians'. In any case, Oberoi's view of Sikh identity can surely be questioned.

W.H. McLeod defended his position with regard to the *Ādi Granth*. He refers to Daljeet Singh drawing heavily upon Bhai Jodh Singh's *Sri Kartarpuri Bir de Darshan* to produce an essay on the 'Authenticity of Kartarpuri Bir' in which he attacked McLeod for his contribution to the subject. McLeod insists that he had merely raised questions with the intention of promoting academic discussion. But surely, the questions he posed had raised doubts about the authenticity of Kartarpuri Bīr. McLeod states that Gurinder Singh Mann has confirmed the authentic status of the Kartarpur manuscript. 'Even so several questions still await answer'. However, if the authenticity of the Kartarpur manuscript is accepted, all other questions lose much of their importance.[49]

Joseph T. O'Connell observed that a network of vocal Sikhs evidently felt troubled by the thrust of 'critical scholarship' upon the religious history of the Sikhs. They were not confined to Delhi or the Punjab. Included among them were like-minded associates in the United States with influence in Sikh organizations and access to community publications. What seemed to unite the various papers at the Long Beach conference was 'the negative bond of being united against contemporary academic research on Sikh history and religion'. Some of the writers failed to distinguish criticizing views from imputing motives, attacking the personal integrity of those with whom they disagreed or whom they just did not fathom. There was always some degree of tension between those committed to scholarly inquiry and those committed to preserving and fostering a religious way of life.[50] On the whole, thus, two views of scholarship, or two approaches to Sikh historiography, appeared to explain the criticism of the academics by the believers, leaving little scope for any kind of meaningful dialogue.

I was invited to update an earlier lecture on the state of Sikh studies for *Studying the Sikhs*. It was published as 'A Brief History of Sikh Studies in English' outlining the developments from J.D. Cunningham's *History of the Sikhs* (1849) to W.H. McLeod's *Who is a Sikh* (1989). This outline ended with a brief comment on the controversy which had raised important issues. This controversy, I suggested, could be quite fruitful if it made the critical scholars more aware of 'the implications of their apparently innocuous findings for believers' and if it helped their critics to become 'more clearly aware of the real implications of "methodological atheism" that characterizes all rational–empirical research in the world today'.[51]

SEVEN MORE CONFERENCES

Towards the end of 1990, seven international conferences were held at London, Toronto, Vancouver, Berkeley, Chicago, Washington and New York by a number of Sikh organizations. Nearly half of the participants were those who had contributed to *Perspectives on the Sikh Tradition* and *Advanced Studies in Sikhism*. They contributed a score of papers while new scholars contributed another score. Three of the new scholars were associated with universities and the study of Sikh tradition. Others were independent scholars with or without any connection with academic institutions. Apart from old themes, some new themes were taken up for discussion. Some old and new works were criticized but, on the whole, a number of expositions were marked by positive projections. The papers were published in two volumes in 1992 as *Fundamental Issues in Sikh Studies* and *Recent Researches in Sikhism*. The consideration for publishing two volumes was logistic. The papers presented at the conference in London were published by the Institute of Sikh Studies, Chandigarh, and the papers presented at the conferences in North America were published by the Punjabi University, Patiala.

One of the reasons given for holding the conferences was the publication of literature by Oberoi and McLeod at Vancouver and Toronto with 'considerable disinformation about the religion and history of the Sikhs'.[52] Harjot Oberoi had asserted in a paper entitled 'Popular Saints, Goddesses and Village Sacred Sites: Re-reading Sikh Experience in the Nineteenth Century' that if there was any such thing as a key to historical problems in the case of the Sikh tradition it was to be found in its constituency: 'Sikh religion is first and foremost a peasant faith'. In a paper entitled 'Sikh Fundamentalism: Ways of Turning Things Over' he had asserted that fundamentalism among the Sikhs was apparently the basic cause of the political unrest then current in the Punjab. Seeking to provide 'meaning and shape' to what appeared to be 'chaotic and meaningless', Oberoi described this unrest as 'primarily a movement of resistance'. His whole discussion of the problem lent little support to his thesis of 'Sikh fundamentalism' but he was determined to put this tag on the Sikh struggle. The purpose of Kharak Singh's paper entitled 'Sikh Ideology, Fundamentalism and Punjab Problem' was to take up the Punjab problem and its genesis, which Oberoi had carefully avoided, and then to take up his observations to show its irrelevance and to expose it as a 'cover to hide the realities'.[53] Daljeet Singh's paper on 'Punjab River-Waters Dispute' was also provoked by expression given in academic publications to opinions that were 'far from being correct and factual'. His purpose was to state the factual, legal and constitutional position about the Punjab water and hydel power problem, which constituted the basic issue.[54] The scope of debate was thus expanding.

Madanjit Kaur argued that Guru Gobind Singh never worshipped Durga. Harnam Singh Shan argued at length that Sikhism is an original, distinct, revealed, and complete religion. Daljeet Singh gave a positive exposition of Sikh identity. Gobind Singh Mansukhani gave a brief and rather unsystematic account of the origin and development of Sikh studies. Kharak Singh argued for a World Institute of Sikhism as an alternative to the kind of Sikh studies pursued in North American universities. Kharak Singh and Gurdarshan Singh Dhillon argued that 'Raj Karega Khalsa' couplet is 'in consonance with the injunctions and the thesis of the Gurus'. A paper on *Dasam Granth* was specially invited from Gurtej Singh who assessed the views of D.P. Ashta and Ratan Singh Jaggi on the authenticity of *Dasam Granth*. Another paper related to gender relations among the Sikhs.[55]

In *Recent Researches in Sikhism* two papers were meant to refute Harjot Oberoi's views in 'From Ritual to Counter-Ritual: Rethinking the Hindu-Sikh Question, 1884–1915', published in *Sikh History and Religion in the Twentieth Century*. G.S. Dhillon pointed out that Oberoi 'never makes any reference to the Guru Granth' for his emphatic assertion that the Sikhs showed little collective interest in distinguishing themselves from the Hindus before the late nineteenth century. He looks upon the groups like the Udasis and the Sakhi Sarvarias, among several others, as 'living within the framework of the Sikh faith'. He makes no distinction between sanctioned and unsanctioned practices, obliterating the line between cultural practices and aberrations. He takes a narrow view of religion when he says that it was meant for the individual salvation of man. Oberoi puts forth spurious arguments in support of his view that the Singh Sabha innovators created 'a new Sikhism' entirely different from the Sikh religion and society of the earlier four centuries. In a 'critical analysis' of Oberoi's paper, Gurbakhsh Singh pointed out that Oberoi has ignored the Sikh scriptures and paid only cursory attention to early Sikh history.[56]

To refute the argument of S.S. Hans that Koer Singh's *Gurbilās Pātshāhī 10* was an early nineteenth century work, Madanjit Kaur argued at some length that it could safely be placed between 1751 and 1762. On the ideology of Guru Nanak, S.S. Hans was refuted by Kharak Singh in an exposition of Guru Nanak's position in the history of religious thought. Hans was wrong in stating that the world for Guru Nanak was 'unreal', and that his intense reaction to the politico-administrative set up of his times was 'more symbolic than realistic'. The idea of 'active asceticism' was not appropriate for Guru Nanak's position. Kharak Singh cited examples of the translation of some verses of Guru Nanak given by Hans, together with the original verses and his own translation, to show how 'major misrepresentations' were made by Hans. Furthermore, in support of his indefensible thesis, Hans made 'ample use of the art of suppression'.[57]

In another paper in this volume, Kharak Singh brought out the 'misrepresentation' of Sikhism in the encyclopaedias published in the West from 1917-77 (making it amply clear that the position was much worse than what was pointed out by Mark Juergensmeyer). James R. Lewis pointed out that it was common among western students of Sikh religion to refer to the supposedly baneful effects of orthodoxy on Sikh scholars studying their own tradition, but western academics did not necessarily bring an objective, unprejudiced perspective to their work. The seemingly neutral terms of analysis introduced value judgements embedded in them, like syncretism, neo-Sikhism, and the early pacifism versus later militancy. An important implication of this approval was a 'differential treatment' given to Sikhism by Western scholars.[58]

In a discussion of methodology for the appraisal of sources for Sikh studies, Gobind Singh Mansukhani cited examples from the works of McLeod to illustrate the limitations of 'the analytical method'. However, his own exposition of 'integrated methodology' is not very clear. G.S. Dhillon cited the works of W.H. McLeod, Richard G. Fox, and N.G. Barrier for their contention that 'the assertion of a distinct Sikh identity in the mid-nineteenth century' was mainly due to the support extended by the British. A quotation from McLeod on this point shows that Dhillon is attributing to him the view actually of Fox. Both Fox and Barrier in any case had misunderstood the attitude of the British rulers towards their Sikh subjects. The British were extremely cautious in dealing with the Sikhs. The Sikhs also knew the basis of British policy. 'While they would not mind helping and placating the Sikhs on minor and non-essential issues, they would never tolerate any sufferance of their political interests'. The British never failed to suppress the growth of Sikh political consciousness. They tried to weaken Sikh ideology through a studied patronage of Hinduized mahants and pujārīs and the control of Sikh shrines through nominated managers. In his article on 'the Sikh rule and Ranjit Singh', Dhillon emphasized the way in which Ranjit Singh employed his power to build his rule on religious foundations with due respect for all religions. The liberal and humanitarian teaching of Sikhism was reflected in Ranjit Singh's employment policy. His state was sustained by 'values and attitudes that characterised the Sikh tradition'. His rule demonstrated very clearly the historical role and impact of 'a whole-life or Mir-Piri religion on the society of its times'.[59]

Essays on the subject of Mīrī-Pīrī had been specially invited from both Daljeet Singh and Jagjit Singh. Daljeet Singh had little doubt that Mīrī-Pīrī doctrine was an essential part of the Sikh religion. Guru Nanak's system was radically different from the earlier Indian religions due to the principle that there was 'an inalienable link between the spiritual life and the empirical life of man'. The changes initiated by Guru Arjan and Guru Hargobind were deliberate and calculated. It was naive to maintain that militarization of the movement was 'in any way influenced by Jats in the Sikh society who were clearly in a small minority then'. The mission of Guru Nanak was fulfilled when a religiously motivated casteless and classless brotherhood, the Khalsa, was created to fight for righteousness and against all socio-political injustice. The later Sikh history demonstrated the fundamental validity of Guru Nanak's 'Miri-Piri or whole-life religion'.[60]

Jagjit Singh put forth the idea that acquisition of political power for a noble cause could be 'a legitimate spiritual pursuit'. Unfamiliar with the idea, most of the scholars failed to appreciate the novel doctrine of mīrī-pīrī. The hypothesis that the Sikh movement was a purely religious movement before it took a political turn with the martyrdom of Guru Arjan was a 'distortion'. Guru Arjan's 'direct political involvement' was evident from the fact that he helped the rebel prince Khusrau with money and applied *tilak* on his forehead. This was how Jahangir construed his action. Thus, it was not Guru Arjan's martyrdom which gave a political turn to the Sikh movement; rather it was the political ethos of the Sikh movement that contributed to his martyrdom. Another major misrepresentation was to say that Guru Hargobind deviated from the nām *mārg* by taking up arms. There was no common criterion for determining what was and what was not compatible with the experience of nām in its social and historical manifestation. In Guru Nanak's mission, nām mārg was inextricably joined to sharing 'responsibility of a creative and virtuous development in the world'. The distinctive Sikh view of nām mārg was not wedded to the doctrine of *ahinsa*. The obligation to bear arms and to be linked with nām were considered by the Khalsa to be complementary and not mutually exclusive. The Sikh view of nām embraced the totality of life and inspired participation in God-oriented worldly activity with a view to creating a 'meaningful, ordered totality' in the world.[61]

An essay by Gurtej Singh on the 'political ideas' of Guru Nanak was closely related to the theme of mīrī-pīrī. Guru Nanak's political ideas were intimately connected with his acceptance of this world as a real and 'legitimate sphere of activity for a man of religion'. What Guru Nanak says of God as the true sovereign constitutes the aim of all earthly political activity: dispensing even-handed justice, destroying evil doers, and promoting good, for example. Firm commitment to justice and equality alone made rulership legitimate. Guru Nanak considered politics to be the ultimate test of faith. Martyrdom in war is one of the accepted modes of attaining liberation. The state had no authority to regulate matters of spirituality or conscience. The primary allegiance of man must be to righteousness, truth and conscience. The claim of the state to rule over the souls of its citizens was denied by Guru Nanak.[62]

In one of the essays in this volume there is a non-Sikh Indian perspective on the Khalsa embodied in Tinkari Banerjee's *Guru Gobinda Singha* in Bengali, Beni Prasad's *Guru Gobind Singh* in Hindi, and Lingaraja Mishra's *Guru Gobinda Simha* in Oriya. An analysis of these works by Himadri Banerjee shows some common features. For all the three authors, the Khalsa stood for the revival of 'a militant form of Hinduism'; the Sikhs had no separate identity; the Mughals represented the enemy. Himadri Banerjee points out that all the three authors were deeply influenced by the contemporary Hindu-Muslim question in the early twentieth century.[63] Banerjee does not say so but the authors of these works can be seen as inspired by 'Hindu nationalism'.

Two New Themes

Two themes have received special attention in the recent controversy: textual criticism and Sikh identity. Piar Singh's *Gatha Sri Adi Granth* was published towards the end of 1992 in a scholarly search for the genuine text of the Guru Granth. In his considered view the Kartarpur manuscript was not the Granth prepared by Guru Arjan. Within a month, the sale of his book was suspended by Guru Nanak Dev University as its publisher. Two weeks later the Shiromani Gurdwara Parbandhak Committee imposed a ban on research on the Guru Granth. Piar Singh was summoned to the Akal Takht on 31 March 1993, and ordered to do penance for forty days. He accepted the *tankhāh*. On 13 May he requested the Acting Jathedar of the Akal Takht to apprise him of the objectionable passages in his book. He received no reply. In defence of his *Gatha* he wrote another book which was published in 1996 as the *Gatha Sri Adi Granth and the Controversy* stoutly maintaining that the Kartarpuri Bīr was 'a fake copy and not the original *Adi Granth* prepared by Bhai Gurdas'.[64]

However, two Sikh scholars working in North America have conducted equally serious textual studies and come to the conclusion that the Kartarpuri Bīr is authentic. One of them is Pashaura Singh whose doctoral thesis, 'The Text and Meaning of the Adi Granth', was supervised by W.H. McLeod and submitted to the University of Toronto in 1991. A revised version of Pashaura Singh's thesis was published later as *The Guru Granth Sahib: Canon, Meaning and Authority*, exploring the concept of scripture from the Sikh perspective and seeking to understand the processes of canon formation and the vesting of Guruship in the Ādi Granth. He has underscored the role of the Ādi Granth as the Guru in the personal piety of individual Sikhs and the corporate identity of the Sikh community.[65]

The other scholar is Gurinder Singh Mann who published *The Goindval Pothis: The Earliest Extant Source of the Sikh Canon* in 1996, arguing not only in favour of their authenticity but also in support of their use by Guru Arjan in compiling the Kartarpuri Bīr. A revised version of Gurinder Singh Mann's thesis has been published as *The Making of Sikh Scripture*, constructing a comprehensive picture on the basis of a much larger number of manuscripts and clarifying the issues far more cogently.[66] The study of the Sikh scripture that began in the early twentieth century has come a long way, becoming exceptionally intensive in the last two decades of the twentieth century.

A whole volume has been published against Pashaura Singh. The *Planned Attack on Aad Sri Guru Granth Sahib: Academics or Blasphemy*, published in 1994, contains thirty-six reviews and eight appendices, covering more than 400 pages in print. The reason for its publication is given in the introduction to this volume. Despite all evidence to the contrary, W.H. McLeod had persisted from 1975 to 1993 in casting doubt on the authenticity of the Kartarpuri Bīṛ and, by implication, on the Guru Granth. The doctoral thesis of his research student, Pashaura Singh, was seen as serving this purpose in a devious way. This explains the strong and spontaneous response to Pashaura Singh's unpublished thesis circulated by design among Sikh scholars.[67]

Balwant Singh Dhillon, in his *Early Sikh Scriptural Tradition: Myth and Reality*, published in 1999, accepts the authenticity of the Kartarpuri Bīṛ alone. The Guru Harsahai Pothi, the Goindval Pothis, and MS 1245, (a recension of the Granth in the library of Guru Nanak Dev University, Amritsar) were neither authentic nor relevant for the compilation of the Granth by Guru Arjan. Dhillon's arguments[68] are not very convincing

A senior Sikh scholar who criticized Pashaura Singh and Piar Singh was Trilochan Singh. He looked upon Pashaura Singh as 'a willing victim' of McLeod's propaganda machinery. Trilochan Singh was emphatic that the article entitled 'The Need for Textual and Historical Criticism' attributed to C.H. Loehlin was concocted by McLeod's 'clique' after the putative author's death to serve their own purpose. This article is actually an exact reprint of an appendix of Loehlin's *The Granth of Guru Gobind Singh and the Khalsa Brotherhood*, published in 1971. Much of what Trilochan says about Pashaura Singh and Piar Singh is wide off the mark.[69]

Trilochan Singh's main target was W.H. McLeod. He gives two chapters to Trumpp and twelve to McLeod in his *Ernest Trumpp and W.H. McLeod As Scholars of Sikh History, Religion and Culture*. He appreciates Trumpp amidst all his faults: 'no Sikh scholar upto the time of Trumpp, had analysed so accurately the prosody of verses of Adi Granth as this German scholar has done'. But there is no redeeming feature of McLeod's work for Trilochan Singh in what he regards as a comprehensive answer to 'all the clap-trap methods and theories' of McLeod. Trilochan Singh refers to his 'art of subterfuge and evasion', his 'naked antagonism and open malicious hostility', and his 'nefarious designs'. McLeod is 'neither honest nor rational, nor reasonable and logical in his analysis of historical events, nor does he anywhere, in any of his books follow the minimum rules of academic ethics'. Ironically, Trilochan Singh finds both Trumpp and McLeod shrill and screeching in their criticism of Sikhism under an academic garb to cover their malicious missionary intentions. McLeod 'never goes beyond what Trumpp stated a century earlier'. Trilochan Singh's critique of McLeod borders on the invective.[70] Its publication is a measure of Sikh resentment against McLeod.

The issue of Sikh identity came to a climax with the publication of Harjot Oberoi's *The Construction of Religious Boundaries: Culture, Identity and Diversity in the Sikh Tradition* in 1994 as a revised version of his doctoral thesis. The basic hypothesis put forth in this work is that the Sikhs were not unduly concerned with establishing distinct religious boundaries before the advent of colonial rule in the Punjab. Even the growing hegemony of the Khalsa did not put an end to religious fluidity within the Sikh tradition which was marked by immense diversity. The new social and cultural forces of the period of colonial rule helped the Singh Sabhas to recast Sikh tradition in a monolithic mould and to marginalize other identities. A new worldview replaced the old and transformed the earlier Sikh tradition into modern Sikhism.[71]

A critique of Harjot Oberoi's work appeared in 1995 as the *Invasion of Religious Boundaries*. It contains thirty-two articles and reviews and eight appendices (questioning the legitimacy and justification of appointing Harjot Oberoi to the Chair of Punjabi and Sikh Studies at the University of British Columbia). Some of the articles included in it had been published earlier, like those of Daljeet Singh, G.S. Dhillon, Noel Q. King, and Kharak Singh. These were meant to provide basic information on some of the issues raised in the book. Many titles of reviews indicate the drift of their argument: 'journey into obscurity'; 'academics or imagination'; 'a stranger to Sikhism'; 'an attempt at destruction'; 'scholar or saboteur'; 'an unpardonable excess'; 'mischievous propaganda is not research'. The crucial issue for all the contributors was a distinct Sikh identity which Oberoi appeared to undermine by arguing that it was almost an invention of the colonial period. His exposition of 'Sanatan Sikhism' was extremely misleading. Contemporary evidence refuted his argument that there was no distinct Sikh identity before the advent of the Singh Sabhas.[72]

In 1996, an international conference was held at the University of Michigan to explore the issue of Sikh identity. Its proceedings were published in 1999 as *Sikh Identity: Continuity and Change*.

The observations made by Bhai Harbans Lal, Pashaura Singh, and Gurudharam Singh Khalsa in this volume do not support Oberoi's interpretation of Sikh identity. Their significance lies in the fact that they are far from being polemical or even directly critical of Oberoi.[73]

McLeod's Response

If anything, this prolonged controversy appears to have enhanced the importance of the works of W.H. McLeod. A single omnibus volume of his four books and a collection of his major articles have been published by the Oxford University Press, New Delhi. His work on rahitnāmas is followed by his *autobiography as a historian*. To these have been added the translation of a Rahitnāma and another volume of his articles.[74]

In his *Autobiography*, McLeod has tried to explain his position. He says that he regards himself as a historian of religion. Trained in western methods of historical research, he adheres to western notions of historiography. His primary objective has been to communicate 'an understanding of the Sikh people and their religion to educated Western readers'. Western understanding underlines 'all that I have written and no apology is offered for it.'[75] This is McLeod's response to the charge of Eurocentrism levelled against him by his critics.

For McLeod, the western historical method confronts tradition, sometimes accepting it, sometimes doubting it, but all too frequently rejecting it. The attitude of the western historian is firmly rooted in the Enlightenment. He insists that all conclusions should be rational and based on sound sources. 'This is light years away from the attitude that takes its stand firmly on revelation and accepts as true that which is divinely revealed'. This appears to rule the 'believer' out of court. But many 'believers' in the West have been good historians. For McLeod, the Western view stands in complete opposition to 'the traditionalist view'. He appears to oversimplify both the task of the historian and the position of his critics labelled as 'traditionalist' historians. McLeod ends his statement on 'the purpose' of his autobiography with the words: 'My works stand as I have written them, and readers will need to decide whether they are acceptable or whether the comments of my critics make better sense'.[76] McLeod does not seem to visualize a third possibility. A scholar may study both McLeod and his critics and make up his own mind on controversial issues. McLeod concedes that Sainapat's evidence pointed out by Fauja Singh has a good claim of being accepted on the point that 'Guru Gobind Singh named the Khalsa as his heir'. He also recognizes that recent research on the Sikh scripture has left him far behind. On all other issues, McLeod only explains or defends his position. He thinks that the campaign against him began to decline in 1996. The attacks from 'academic sources' appeared to have lost much of their frequency and fervour. McLeod expected his *Sikhs of the Khalsa* to produce at least a brief outburst when published. But the work has created no ripples. There is hardly anything new or objectionable in the work from the viewpoint of his critics. McLeod is inclined to believe that Sikh interests have largely shifted away from 'foreign academics and their alleged allies'.[77] His critics, however, are inclined to believe that they have demolished all his hypotheses and produced a wide range of alternative reading. Thus, there has been a lot of controversy but little of dialogue. Paradoxically, a lot of good work on Sikh studies has been relegated to the background because it does not appear to be relevant for the terms in which the debate has been conducted. Even some of the works which have figured in the controversy have been seen from a constricted perspective. The scholars interested in studying the Sikh tradition would do well to come out of the grooves of this prolonged controversy and think positively for themselves.

Notes

1. *The Panjab Past and Present*, vol. IV, pt. 2 (October 1970), pp. i–x.
2. *The Panjab Past and Present*, vol. VI, pt. 1 (April 1972), pp. 234, 237.
3. *The Panjab Past and Present*, vol. XI, nos 21–2 (April 1977), pp. 178–85.
4. Ibid., pp. 179–82.
5. Ibid., pp. 182–4.
6. Ibid., pp. 184–5.
7. *Journal of Sikh Studies*, Amritsar: Guru Nanak Dev University, February 1974 and August 1975.
8. *Journal of Sikh Studies*, vol. IV, no. 1 (February 1977), pp. 166–8.
9. Ibid., pp. 168–9.
10. *Perspectives on the Sikh Tradition*, ed. Gurdev Singh, Patiala: Siddharth Publications for Academy of Sikh Religion and Culture, 1986.
11. Ibid., pp. ix–x.

12. Ibid., pp. 4–5.
13. Ibid., p. 5.
14. Ibid., pp. 8–10.
15. Ibid., pp. 14–36.
16. N. Gerald Barrier, 'The Evolution of Punjab Studies in North America', *The Panjab Past and Present*, vol. XVI, pt. 2 (October 1982), pp. 398–406.
17. Mark Juergensmeyer, 'The Forgotten Tradition: Sikhism in the Study of World Religions', in Mark Juergensmeyer and N. Gerald Barrier, eds, *Sikh Studies: Comparative Perspectives on a Changing Tradition*, Berkeley: Berkeley Religious Studies Series, 1979, pp. 13–23.
18. John C.B. Webster, 'Sikh Studies in the Punjab', ibid., pp. 26–32.
19. J.S. Grewal, 'A Perspective on Early Sikh History', ibid., pp. 33–9.
20. N. Gerald Barrier, 'The Role of Ideology and Institution–Building in Modern Sikhism', ibid., pp. 41–51.
21. Eugene F. Irschick, 'Sikhism as a Category of Study', ibid., pp. 53–4.
22. Ainslie T. Embree, 'Locating Sikhism in Time and Place: A Problem For Historical Surveys', ibid., pp. 55–62.
23. *Sikh Studies: Comparative Perspectives on a Changing Tradition*, eds, Juergensmeyer and Barrier, pp. 21, 59, 61.
24. Kenneth E. Bryant, '*Sant* and *Vaishnava* Poetry: Some Observations on Method', ibid., pp. 65–74.
25. Karine Schomer, 'Kabir in the *Guru Granth Sahib*: An Exploratory Essay', ibid., pp. 75–89.
26. W.H. McLeod, 'The Sikh Scriptures: Some Issues', ibid., pp. 97–111.
27. C.H. Loehlin, 'Textual Criticism of the Kartarpur Granth', ibid., pp. 113–18.
28. Narinder Singh Kapany, 'Sikhs Abroad', ibid., pp. 207–8.
29. Hew McLeod, *Discovering the Sikhs: Autobiography of a Historian*, Delhi: Permanent Black, 2004, pp. 85–6. For McLeod's articles, *The Sants: Studies in a Devotional Tradition of India*, eds, Karine Schomer and W.H. McLeod, Delhi: Motilal Banarsidass, 1987.
30. W.H. McLeod, 'A Sikh Theology for Modern Times', in Joseph T. O'Connell et al., eds, *Sikh History and Religion in the Twentieth Century*, New Delhi: Manohar, 1990, pp. 32–43.
31. Harjot S. Oberoi, 'From Ritual to Counter-Ritual: Rethinking the Hindu-Sikh Question, 1884–1915', ibid., pp. 136–58.
32. Jasbir Singh Mann and Harbans Singh Saraon, eds, *Advanced Studies in Sikhism*, Irvine: Sikh Community of North America, 1989, pp. vii–viii.
33. Daljeet Singh, 'Issues of Sikh Studies', ibid., pp. 16–29. 'Sikhism, Vaishnavism, Vedanta and Nathism—A Comparison', ibid., pp. 33–55.

34. Daljeet Singh, *Essays on the Authenticity of Kartarpuri Bir and the Integrated Logic and Unity of Sikhism*, Patiala: Punjabi University, 1987, pp. 1–87. Daljeet Singh, 'Authenticity of the Kartarpuri Bir', *Advanced Studies in Sikhism*, pp. 138–60
35. Jagjit Singh, 'Sikh Militancy and the Jats', ibid., pp. 214–33.
36. Jagjit Singh, 'The Caste System and the Sikhs', ibid., pp. 278–300.
37. S.S. Kohli, 'Constant Unity of Sikh Thought', ibid., pp. 98–108; Inderjit Singh, 'Unity of Sikh Thought', ibid., pp. 109–18; Madanjit Kaur, 'The Guruship and Succession of Guru Granth Sahib', ibid., pp. 121–37.
38. Surinder Singh Kohli, 'Janamsakhis—Their Value and Importance', ibid., pp. 301–16. Surjit Singh, ' A Study of W. Hew McLeod's Methodology Employed in his Work "The Evolution of Sikh Community"—The Janamsakhis', ibid., pp. 317–25; Raja Mrigendra Singh, 'A Critique on Dr W.H. McLeod's Works', ibid., pp. 326–8.
39. Gobind Singh Mansukhani, 'Sikh-Rahat-Maryada and Sikh Symbols', *Advanced Studies in Sikhism*, pp. 174–91; Madanjit Kaur, 'The Creation of the Khalsa and Prescribing of the Sikh Symbols', ibid., pp. 195–213.
40. Gurdarshan Singh Dhillon, 'Singh Sabha Movement—A Revival', ibid., pp. 234–62.
41. James R. Lewis, 'Mispresentations of the Sikh Tradition in World Religions Textbooks', ibid., pp. 265–77.
42. Manu and Saraon, eds, *Advanced Studies in Sikhism*, p. viii.
43. John Stratton Hawley and Gurinder Singh Mann, eds, *Studying the Sikhs: Issues for North America*, Albany: State University of New York Press, 1993, p. 4.
44. Mark Juergensmeyer, 'Sikhism and Religious Studies', ibid., pp. 9–14.
45. Ibid., pp . 14–16.
46. Ibid., p. 20.
47. N. Gerald Barrier, 'Sikh Studies and the Study of History', ibid., pp. 25–33.
48. Ibid., pp. 33–45.
49. W.H. McLeod, 'The Study of Sikh Literature', ibid., pp. 55–9.
50. Joseph T. O' Connell, 'Sikh Studies in North America: A Field Guide', ibid., pp. 123–7.
51. J.S. Grewal, 'A Brief History of Sikh Studies in English', ibid., pp. 161–73.
52. Kharak Singh, Gobind Singh Mansukhani, and Jasbir Singh Mann, eds, *Fundamental Issues in Sikh Studies*, Chandigarh: Institute of Sikh Studies, 1992, p. xi.
53. Kharak Singh, 'Sikh Ideology, Fundamentalism and Punjab Problem', ibid., pp. 136–59.

54. Daljeet Singh, 'Punjab River-Waters Dispute', ibid., pp. 196–228.
55. Madanjit Kaur, 'Devi Worship Story: A critique', ibid, pp. 170–8. Harnam Singh Shan, 'Sikhism, An Original Distinct Revealed and Complete Religion', ibid., pp. 41–2, 52; Daljeet Singh, 'The Sikh Identity', ibid., pp. 106–15; Mansukhani, 'Origin and Development of Sikh Studies', ibid., 127–35; Kharak Singh, 'Need for World Institute of Sikhism', ibid., pp. 238–54; Kharak Singh and Gurdarshan Singh Dhillon, 'Raj Karega Khalsa', ibid., pp. 187–95; Gurtej Singh, 'Two Views of Dasam Granth', ibid., pp. 179–86; Kanwaljit Kaur, 'Sikh Women', ibid., pp. 98–104.
56. Gurdarshan Singh Dhillon, 'Sikh Identity: A Continuing Feature', in Jasbir Singh Mann and Kharak Singh, eds, *Recent Researches in Sikhism*, Patiala: Punjabi University, 1992, pp. 226–46; Gurbakhsh Singh, 'From Ritual to Counter-Ritual: A Critical Analysis', ibid., pp. 273–85.
57. Madanjit Kaur, 'Koer Singh's Gurbilas Patshahi 10: An Eighteenth Century Sikh Literature', ibid., pp. 161–72. Kharak Singh, 'Guru Nanak in History of Religious Thought', ibid., pp. 81–8.
58. Kharak Singh, 'Misrepresentation of Sikhism in Western Encyclopaedias', ibid., pp. 335–58. James R. Lewis, 'Some Unexamined Assumptions in Western Studies of Sikhism', ibid., pp. 286–98.
59. Gobind Singh Mansukhani, 'An Integrated Methodology for Appraisal of Sources for Sikh Studies', ibid., pp. 109–21; Gurdarshan Singh Dhillon, 'The Sikh Rule and Ranjit Singh', ibid., pp. 347–72; Gurdarshan Singh Dhillon, 'The Sikhs, and the British, 1849–1920', ibid., pp. 173–225.
60. Daljeet Singh, 'Sikhism: A Miri Piri System', ibid., pp. 42–60.
61. Jagjit Singh, 'The Doctrine of "Meeri-Peeri"', ibid., pp. 136–49.
62. Gurtej Singh, 'Political Ideas of Guru Nanak, the Originator of the Sikh Faith', ibid., pp. 61–71.
63. Himadri Banerjee, 'Creator of the Khalsa: A Non-Sikh Indian Literary Perspective', ibid., pp. 152–60.
64. Piar Singh, *Gatha Sri Adi Granth and the Controversy*, Michigan: Anant Education and Rural Development Foundation, 1996, p. 114. For Piar Singh's earlier analysis of the Kartarpuri Bir, see his *Gatha Sri Adi Granth*, Amritsar: Guru Nanak Dev University, 1992, pp. 174–209.
65. Pashaura Singh, *The Guru Granth Sahib: Canon, Meaning and Authority*, New Delhi: Oxford University Press, 2000.
66. Gurinder Singh Mann, *The Goindval Pothis: The Earliest Extant Source of the Sikh Canon*, Cambridge (Massachusetts): Harvard University Press, 1996; Gurinder Singh Mann, *The Making of Sikh Scripture*, New Delhi: Oxford University Press, 2001.

67. Bachittar Singh Giani, ed., *Planned Attack on Aad Sri Guru Granth Sahib: Academics or Blasphemy*, Chandigarh: International Centre of Sikh Studies, 1994.
68. Balwant Singh Dhillon, *Early Sikh Scriptural Tradition: Myth and Reality*, Amritsar: Singh Brothers, 1999.
69. Trilochan Singh, *Ernest Trumpp and W.H. McLeod As Scholars of Sikh History, Religion and Culture*, Chandigarh: International Centre of Sikh Studies, 1994, pp. 343–76.
70. Ibid., pp. 60, 87, 294, 299, 377–90.
71. Harjot Oberoi, *The Construction of Religious Boundaries: Culture, Identity and Diversity in the Sikh Tradition*, New Delhi: Oxford University Press, 1994.
72. Jasbir Singh Mann, Surinder Singh Sodhi, and Gurbakhsh Singh Shergill, eds, *Invasion of Religious Boundaries*, Vancouver: Canadian Sikh Study and Teaching Society, 1995.
73. Bhai Harbans Lal, 'Sahajdhari Sikhs: Their Origin and Current Status within the Panth', ibid., pp. 109–26. Pashaura Singh, 'Early Markers of Sikh Identity: A Focus on the Works of the First Five Gurus', ibid., pp. 69–92. Gurudharam Singh Khalsa, 'The End of Syncretism: Anti-Syncretism in Sikh Tradition', ibid., pp. 93–107.
74. Full references to these works are given in the Bibliography.
75. McLeod, *Discovering the Sikhs*, pp. 125, 127–30.
76. Ibid., pp. 130–1, 135.
77. Ibid., pp. 148, 163, 188–91.

Glossary

abchal nagarī	an eternal city; used as a metaphor for the dispensation of Guru Nanak and his successors which was believed to be everlasting
achint	without anxiety or worry; an attribute of God
adharma	devoid of *dharm*; doing something unethical; generally used in connection with religious beliefs and practices
Ādi Granth	the Sikh scripture, compiled by Guru Arjan in 1604 (containing the compositions of the first five Gurus and a number of *bhaktas, sant*s, and Sūfīs) and authenticated by Guru Gobind Singh with the compositions of Guru Tegh Bahadur included. Now known as Guru Granth Sahib
agiān	ignorance, absence of knowledge
ahadī	a special trooper, generally used as a messenger by the emperor or assigned a special duty
ahankar	pride, conceit; one of the five adversaries of man
ahinsa	non-violence; the principle of inflicting no physical injury on a living being
Akal Takht	the platform constructed by Guru Hargobind to conduct temporal affairs. The practice was revived by the Khalsa in the early eighteenth century. A structure raised on the spot came to be known as Akal Bunga where all important meetings of the Khalsa were held. It served as the headquarters of the 'Akalis' till the early nineteenth century
akk	a plant with poisonous juice
akhbārnavīs	a writer of news or a newswriter; an intelligencer
amānat	something left in trust
amāvas	dark moonless night of the month
amrit	nectar, elixer of life; water used for baptism by the double-edged sword
amritdhārī	one who has been initiated through the baptism of the double-edged sword

GLOSSARY

amritsar	literally the pool of water of immortality; term originally used for the tank constructed by Guru Ram Das; the usage was extended to the town of Ramdaspur (Amritsar) before the end of the eighteenth century
anand	joy, happiness; the state of bliss; a composition by Guru Amar Das
Anand Kāraj	Sikh marriage ceremony in which the Guru Granth Sahib, and not fire, is used for circumambulation and in which a Brahman has no role
anna	small coin, sixteenth part of a rupee, and equal to 4 paisas or 12 pies
archā	worship or praise of a deity
ardās	prayer; a formal and collective prayer of the Sikhs, noticed by the author of *Dabistān-i-Mazāhib* in the seventeenth century; probably going back to the time of Guru Nanak
ardāsia	one who performs ardās; a person employed by Sikh rulers and *jāgīrdar*s for this purpose
ashtpadī	unit of poetry in Guru Granth Sahib
asur	demon as opposed to a god (*devta*); an enemy
auliyā	plural of *walī*; friends of God; an epithet used for Sūfī Shaikhs
avtār	'descent'; incarnation of a deity, usually the human incarnations of Vishnu
āzād	free, independent
bābā	grandfather; used also as an epithet of respect
bairāgan	female renunciant in the Vaishnava tradition; a female devotee of God
bairagī	renunciant, usually a Vaishnavite
bakhīlī	closefistedness, miserliness
Bakhshī	quarter-master general, responsible for the upkeep of the army
balwantkārī	noble of high rank, like a high *mansabdār*
bānāt	variety of good cloth
bāṇī	utterance; generally used for sacred verses
bandh	stopping all normal activity by way of protest
bāṇīa	trader or a shopkeeper
banjārā	carrier of goods, moving with a small or large caravan
bāolī	well with steps to reach the water

GLOSSARY

bart	ritual fasting
batāī	division of produce between the cultivator and the state or the proprietor
bhaddar also *bhaddan*	rite of removing hair, especially on the death of one's father
bhākhā	from *bhāshā*, language; the spoken language; a regional language in India; a vernacular
bhāṇā	whatever happens due to God's will or pleasure
bhāo	love of God
bhai	brother; a Sikh formally connected with religious affairs; also used as a title
bhajan	recitation, especially for the praise of God; a composition in praise of God or expressing devotion to God
bhagat/bhakta	devotee of God, used generally for the devotees of the human incarnations of Vishnu, that is, Rama and Krishna
bhandār	place for the preparation and distribution of food in religious institutions; a store; a storehouse
bhang	hemp, cannabis, its leaves and pistils; hashish
bhatt	Brahman poet, panegyrist, keeper of family records of his patrons
bhet	offering; an offering made to the Guru or Guru Granth Sahib
bhog	conclusion of the reading of the Ādi Granth, followed generally by singing of hymns and always by an *ardās*
bhūmia	holder of land; a synonym for zamīndar
birad	the nature of God to redeem
biskarmvanta	chief architect of the state
bisvās-ghāt	betrayal of trust
biswedārī	holding of one-twentieth share in the produce or revenue as a superior right over land
Brahm-giān	knowledge of Brahm, the ultimate reality; knowledge of God, or realization of God
brahm mūrit	one who has a godly appearance; a title used for Brahmans
bungā	structure, building; used for each of the many structures raised around the pool of nectar (*amritsar*) in Ramdaspur
butt	statue, idol

GLOSSARY

chādar — sheet of cloth worn as an article of dress by both men and women but in different ways

chākarī — service, soldiering, personal service, service for food, clothing and shelter but without wages

chakkar — term used by the Nath Panthis for a particular practice

chandāl — one of the lowest categories of outcaste; an untouchable

charan pahul — nectar of the foot; the practice of drinking the water in which the toe of the guru has been dipped, symbolizing humility and dedication on the part of the initiate; also called *charanamrit*

chaudharī — headman of a group of villages for collecting revenues on behalf of the government; (the office was generally hereditary)

chaukā — square drawn on the ground to serve as a table cloth, particularly by a Brahman to avoid 'pollution' of any kind

chaurī-bardār — bearer of fly-whisk

chhotā ghallūghārā — small carnage, with reference to an event of 1740s in which a large number of Sikhs were killed by the Diwan of Lahore in a single campaign; called small or rather smaller, in comparison with the larger (*waddhā*) massacre of the Sikhs by Ahmad Shah Abdali in 1762

chorī — stealing, thieving

dakshina — reward given to a Brahman for his services.

dal khalsa — term used for the combined forces of the Sikh leaders during the eighteenth century

dān — charity; to give away something from one's honest earnings for the use of others

darbār — royal court; used for the Harmandar, and also the Guru Granth Sahib

dargāh — place of a *pīr* who is no longer alive: a holy place, court

dārogha — superintendent or head of an organization.

darshan — the sight of a venerable person or place; used in the context of the Sikhs visiting the Guru as an act of merit

darūd — prayer; thanksgiving

darvesh — pious person, generally used for the Sūfis

Dasam Granth	term used for the compilation earlier called the Book of the Tenth King (*Dasven Pātshāh kā Granth*); its compilation is commonly attributed to Bhai Mani Singh; the authorship of its contents (a number of independent compositions) and the date of its compilation have been the subject of debate
dasvandh	one-tenth; the Sikh norm of keeping approximately one-tenth of the yearly income for the Guru or the Panth
dayā	kindness, mercy, grace
deg	cauldron for preparing food; a symbol of open kitchen for all and sundry
dehurā	structure raised over a spot of cremation
deoṛhidār	keeper of the gate; a chamberlain
derā	camp; encampment; a unit in the army of Maharaja Ranjit Singh and his successors; the place of a religious personage
devī	goddess
devtā	god
dhāb	large pool of rain water collected in a low space.
dhānak	one of the lowest outcaste groups
dharm	appropriate moral and religious obligations attached to any particular group; duty, moral obligation; a righteous cause
dharm-dhām	sacred place, a place of pilgrimage
dharmarth	granted in charity; equivalent of the Persian *madad-i ma'āsh* or aid for subsistence; a grant given to a religious institutions or individual for charitable purposes
dharm-karm	stage at which one takes up the responsibilities of one's father
dharmnash	destruction of non-Sikh beliefs and ethics cherished before entering the Khalsa Order
dharmsāl	place for earning merit; Sikh sacred space or the Sikh place of worship in early Sikh history, now generally called Gurdwara
dharmyudh	struggle or fight for a righteous cause; used by Guru Gobind Singh for his own mission
digambar	the 'sky-clad'; the Jain monks who generally went naked or almost naked

disā	direction, division
disāvant	viceroy over the provinces of a particular direction from the capital
dīwān	keeper of a treasury; the head of the finance department; a title given to Hindu nobles by Maharaja Ranjit Singh and his successors
doāb	land between two rivers; an interfluve
dohagan	woman who does not enjoy the presence or the love of her husband; an unhappy wife
dūhra	rhyming couplet
dubidha	to be in two minds due to double affiliation; affiliation to *māyā*
dusht	evil-doer; the enemy
ek angī	of one organ, refers to Sikhism as the only efficacious path to liberation in the Kaliyuga when dharm has the support only of one leg
ek nām	one name, refers to the system of religious beliefs and practices initiated by Guru Nanak and elaborated by his successors
faqīr	pious person; a devotee of God; used generally for a mendicant
farmān	a royal order used for the written orders of the Mughal emperors
fātiha	opening *sūrah* of Qur'ān used at the beginning of an undertaking, and in prayer for the dead
faujdār	one who keeps troops; a military officer under the Mughals whose duty was to maintain law and order and to assist civil authorities; the office survived into the early nineteenth century Punjab
faujdār-i 'umdah	*faujdār* of a high rank, in charge of a large territory for keeping law and order
gaddī	cushioned seat; a throne; the seat of the head of a religious fraternity
gayatrī	Rigvedic verse generally used for prayer
gharī	subdivision of *pahar* as a unit of three hours
ghoriān	verses meant to be sung at the time of wedding
ghurcharhā	trooper who rides the horse; an individual horseman in the cavalry of Ranjit Singh; a kind of gentleman-trooper
giān	knowledge; knowledge of the ultimate reality; knowledge of God

Giānī	one who has acquired knowledge or attained to divine knowledge; a learned Sikh
gosht	discourse or debate, used for an episode in the Janamsakhis of Guru Nanak
golak	treasury; a box to receive cash offerings; money saved in a home to be carried to the Guru
gor	grave
got (gotra)	branch or a sert of a caste or a distinct social group claiming to have a common descent; an exogamic group within an occupational group (*jātī*) which is endogamic
granthī	professional reader of the Granth; the functionary in charge of a Gurdwara
guṇa	quality
gurbāṇī	an utterance of the guru; compositions of the Gurus included in Guru Granth Sahib
gurbhāī	fellow disciple of the guru, given great importance in the Sikh tradition
gurbilās	poetical work written in praise of a guru or one gurus
Gurmat	instruction or teaching of the guru; used for Sikhism as the way of life taught by the gurus
gurmata	decision of a general congregation of Sikhs, generally taken in the presence of Guru Granth Sahib
Guru	epithet used for the founder of Sikhism and each of his nine successors, and also for the Granth Sahib and the Panth; preceptor; religious teacher
Guru-Murīd	special relationship of the guru and the disciple in Sikhism
gurzbardār	mace-bearer, generally sent as an important messenger from the court
hākim	one who is in command; an administrator; a ruler.
hakīm	physician
halāl	anything lawful, as opposed to *harām* (prohibited); the traditional Muslim mode of slaughtering animals for meat
hankār	pride
Harmandar	the temple of God; the central Sikh shrine in Amritsar commonly known as the Golden Temple
hasbul hukam	in accordance with the royal order
haumai	psyche of self-centredness, arising out of attributing to oneself what actually is due to God's will

GLOSSARY

hinsa	violence
hirs	greed
hisābkār	accountant, a finance officer
hom	ritual burning of incense in a fire pit
hukam	order; the divine order operative in the natural and the moral world as an expression of God's omnipotence
hukamnāma	written order; used generally for the letters of the Sikh Gurus to their followers
hukampāi	as ordered; in accordance with the royal order
hundī	document for remittance of money through a commission agent
huzūr-i anwar	his resplendent presence, an epithet used for the ruler; used also for Ranjit Singh in his orders and the Persian works of his time
huzūrī	relating to the presence, the Guru's presence; the Sikhs who lived in his presence; a work prepared at the Guru's court
ijāra	an arrangement by which a certain source of income was placed in the charge of a person on the condition of paying a stipulated sum to the state
ijāradār	holder of an *ijāra*
irādat-nishān	one who is marked by earnest loyalty
jāgīr	assignment of land revenue in lieu of salary for performing service for the state
jāgīrdār	holder of a jagir who is entitled to collect revenues from a given piece of land in lieu of service to the state
jāgīrdārī	system of jāgīrs by which payment of service to the state was made through an assignment of revenue instead of cash
jajmānī	also called *sepī,* the system in which customary payment was made for services rendered by Brahmans and others over the year; the patron is referred to as *jajman*
jal-parwāh	to throw the corpse in a running stream for its final disposal
Janamsākhī	collection of episodes associated with the life of Guru Nanak, meant primarily to depict his doctrines, ethics and his spiritual status; several traditions of this genre developed in the seventeenth and eighteenth centuries

janjū	thread worn by the upper caste Hindu as a sacred symbol
jantar	diagram used for its efficacy in a spiritual exercise
jap	silent recitation of the names or praise of God
Jāp	composition of Guru Gobind Singh
jarrāh	surgeon
jat	complete control over sexual desire and indulgence
jathā	group, band; used particularly for the fighting unit of the Khalsa in the eighteenth century
jātī	an occupational group within a larger category of caste indicating the ritual status in the *varna* order
jauhar	rite of self-immolation by women in a desperate situation in which the men have taken the decision to fight unto death
jhatka	mode of slaughtering an animal for meat with one stroke of the sword or some other weapon; the traditional Indian mode of slaughtering animals Unlike *halāl*, it carried no religious significance
jīvan-muktā	liberated-in-life; a Sikh who remains socially committed after an experience of God
jizya	tax imposed on non-Muslim subjects of an Indian state headed by a Muslim ruler; it was formally abolished by Akbar, reimposed by Aurangzeb, and abolished again by his successors
jogī (yogī)	one who practises *yoga*; a person belonging to any of the twelve orders of the followers of Gorakh Nath
jotishī	astrologer
julāhā	weaver, generally a Muslim weaver
Kabitt	stanza of four rhyming lines
kachh	short drawers of a special kind meant to be worn by those Sikhs who have been initiated through baptism of the double-edged sword
Kāfī	form of poetic composition in Punjabi, with a refrain and some rhymed lines
kāfir	infidel from the Muslim viewpoint; a non-Muslim who does not belong to the category of 'the people of the book' like the Christians and the Jews
kalāl	vintner, a distiller of alcohol; a seller of alcoholic drinks
Kaliyuga	fourth and the last of the cosmic ages traditionally regarded as the age of degeneracy

378 GLOSSARY

kankūt	method of assessment based on appraisement of the standing crop by inspection
kām	desire, sexual desires and emotions
kāmvant	functionary of the state
karā	iron bracelet meant to be worn by the baptized Khalsa
kār-bhet	offering; an offering made by a Sikh for the Guru
kardar	official; generally used for administration at the *ta'alluqa* (*pargana*) level under Sikh rule
karhā parshād	sacramental food distributed in gurdwaras to all persons present, generally prepared with equal quantities of wheat flour, sugar, and ghee
karkhāna	house of work, a manufactory, a workshop
karm-kānd	belief that certain ritual practices can lead ultimately to release; equated sometimes with the path of action, as distinct from the path knowledge and the path of bhakti
karmnāsh	destruction of the belief in the law of *karma*
karmī	through actual conduct
kathā	exposition of the guru's verses, generally in connection with the life of the guru
katra	locality; enclosed market-cum-residential quarters, with a separate entrance and internal management
kes (*kesh*)	hair of the head, uncut hair
kesar	saffron, used ceremoniously in several situations
keshdhārī	baptized Singh who maintains long unshorn hair
khairkhah-i bā-safā	one who is a sincere well-wisher; a title used for Ansari '*faqīrs*' in the service of Ranjit Singh
khabar-likhtā	newswriter
khafnī	miniature funerary box as a constant reminder of death
khālas	pure; a true devotee of God
khalāsī	peon
Khalsa	Sikh brotherhood instituted by Guru Gobind Singh; used for an individual as well as the collective body
khand	a part, a region; one of the nine divisions of the earth
khandā	double-edged sword
khande kī pahul	baptism by the double-edged sword, introduced by Guru Gobind Singh for initiating Sikhs and others into the Order of the Khalsa

kharag-jagg	refers to the fire ceremony of the sword, the double-edged sword, supposed to have been performed by Guru Gobind Singh to invoke the aid of the Goddess for instituting the Khalsa
khimā	forgiveness
khufianavis	secret intelligencer; a reporter of events
khulāsa	term used for Sikhs not initiated through baptism by the double-edged sword and, consequently, not keeping unshorn hair, and not bearing arms or the epithet 'Singh'
kirpān	sword
kīrtan	singing of hymns in praise of God, especially from the sacred scripture of the Sikhs; hence *kīrtan darbār* for an elaborate performance
Kīrtan Sohilā	composition in Guru Granth Sahib to be recited before going to sleep
kiryā	performance of a traditional Brahmanical ritual appropriate for the occasion like death, marriage or birth
koil	black sparrow known for its sad, sweet notes
kos	measure of distance equal approximately to 4 kms
kotwāl	the holder of a fort, generally the officer responsible for law and order in a city
kritnāsh	destruction of the sanctity of a hereditary occupation.
krodh	anger
kūcha	lane
kudayā	unkindness
kulnāsh	destruction of the family pride and its ties
kumatt	weak understanding
kuththā (halāl)	meat obtained by slaughtering an animal in the Muslim fashion
la-itbārī	faithlessness
langar	kitchen attached to a Gurdwara from which food is served to all regardless of caste or creed; a community meal; a kitchen
lāvān	verses of Guru Ram Das meant to be sung for the marriage ceremony among the Sikhs, called Anand Kāraj because the *Anand* of Guru Amar Das is recited or sung at the end
lobh	greed

380   GLOSSARY

madad-i ma'āsh	literally aid for subsistence; most commonly used in the Mughal times for land-revenue alienated in favour of a religious personage or institution
mahal	a place; a unit area for revenue collection in the Mughal times; used for Guru Nanak and his successors to denote their sequence as 1, 2, or 3 upto 10; an alternative usage is *pātshāhī*
mahant	head of a religious establishment, generally celibate but not in all cases; therefore, succession in some cases could be hereditary; used for the custodians of Gurdwaras to whom recognition and support was given by the British administration
mahā parshād	great food, meat
mahūrat	auspicious time
manjī	literally, a cot; used for the office of the Guru's representative to look after the affairs of a local congregation
manmukh	self-oriented; one who follows his own impulses rather than the guidance of the Guru
mannat	an offering made on the fulfilment of a wish
mansab	office, position or rank under the Mughals indicating the status, obligations and remuneration of its holder in the official hierarchy
mansabdār	holder of a *mansab* in the system evolved by the Mughals, called the *mansabdārī* system
mantra	an utterance of a sacred character; a sacred verse; popularly used for a magical formula
mārg	path, a religious path, a religion
marhī	small structure raised on the spot of cremation; treated by some people as an object of worship
māsā	twelfth part of a *tolā* which is approximately one gram
masand	representative appointed by the Guru to look after the affairs of a local congregation of Sikhs, or a number of such congregations
masānī	from *masān* or *marhī*, used for the goddess or the spirit believed to be living in the cremation ground
mashāikh	plural of *shaikh*; guide; *pīr*; *murshid*
masīt	mosque
masjid	mosque

matt	instruction, advice; a whole system of religious beliefs and practices
mazār	mausoleum; the tomb of a Sūfī Shaikh regarded as a place of pilgrimage
māyā	material world and all that is therein, treated in the Sikh tradition as 'false' in contrast with the eternal truth of God
melī	an associate, a synonym for *sahlāng*
mihrāb	principal place in a mosque, where the leader of prayer takes his stand with his face towards Mecca.
mīṇā	a derogatory epithet used for Prithi Chand, the elder brother of Guru Arjan, and also for his successors and their followers
mīrī-pīrī	leadership of both the spiritual and temporal realms associated with Guru Hargobind and his successors.
misl	combination of Sikh leaders for the purpose of defence and occupation of territories in the eighteenth century
misldār	holder of a misl as a fighting unit.
mlechh	impure; a derogatory term used for an outcaste or a foreigner, both were regarded as outside the four-tier varna order
modī	person in charge of stores
moh	attachment to earthly things
morchā	entrenchment, a battle; an agitational mode of protest
muʿatamid al-khidmat	one whose services are distinguished or who is distinguished by the good services rendered
muftī	expounder of the law in Islam
muhrkhās	special royal seal
mujāwar	one who looks after a religious establishment in Islam
muktī	release, emancipation, liberation
mūng	variety of pulses
munshī	writer, scribe, clerk
murīd	disciple, especially the disciple of a Sūfī Shaikh
muqaddam	the headman of a village or a part thereof
mushakhkhāsah	a fixed amount, used in connection with revenue
mutasaddī	accountant, official
nagardār	the holder of the city, an officer in charge of the public affairs of a city

GLOSSARY

nāī	barber who performed various other services for his patrons
nām-dān-isnān	phrase used by Guru Nanak for the essential features of the Sikh way of life, that is, meditation on God, charity, and both physical and moral purity
nāo	name
naūmī	the ninth day of the lunar month
navīsinda	writer
nāzim	administrator; governor of a province.
niāonkār	one who administers justice, a judge, a magistrate
nīch	low, the lowest; used for people below the Shudras in the traditional social order in India
nindiā	backbiting, slandering
nirbāṇ	from *nirvāṇa*, release from the cycle of rebirth and death
nirguṇa	without qualities or attributes, used generally for transcendent God who may at the same time be immanent in the universe; the term is meant actually to distinguish monotheism from belief in incarnation
nisān	mark of signature; a standard.
nusrat jang bahadur	the brave who is victorious in battle; used as title
pada	unit of poetry; stanza; hymn
pādshāh	ruler, king, emperor; used generally for the Mughal rulers instead of *sultān*; used metaphorically for the Sikh Gurus
pahul	water used for initiating a person as a Sikh (*charan pahul*) or a Singh (*khande kī pahul*)
paighambar	messenger of God; a prophet
paisa	copper coin valued at 64th of a rupee
pālkī	palanquin, litter
pancha	one of the five; the member of a *panchāyat*; the headman of a village or one of its subdivisions
pāndhā	Brahman teacher
Panth	literally a path; the people following a particular path; collectively the followers of the Gurus; the Sikh community
pāras	imaginary stone that is believed to transmute base metals like iron into gold by a mere touch; the philosopher's stone

pargana	a small unit of administration in a province under the Mughals; remained in use in the Punjab till the mid-nineteenth century and became synonymous with the *ta'alluqa*
parnindā	slandering others
parkarma	circumambulatory path on all the four sides of the tank around the Harmandar; also the path around the Harmandar, called inner *parkarma*
parm marg	path of love, synonym for *prem sumārg*
parsang	context
parshād	sacred food; simply food
parwāna-i wālā	the exalted order, used for the order of Ranjit Singh
pauṛī	stanza in a composition
pathshāla	school
patit	renegade
patras	women in the royal palace employed in various kinds of duties, including music and dance, for entertainment
pātshāhī	rulership; used also for the tenure of a Sikh guru
pattī	composition related to the letters of a script
peshkār	an official who acts as the head of secretaries
pīr (shaikh)	among Muslim mystics the guide who leads on the path of union with God; believed to be the bestower of blessings after his death too
pīr pursh	a person of exalted spiritual state
pīrzāda	the son of a pīr; descendant of a pīr
post	poppy pods
pothī	book
prem	love for God as distinguished from love for a human being
prem bhakti	loving devotion to God
pūjā	worship, adoration of a deity, veneration; homage; idol worship
punn	an act of merit, especially religious
pūran māsī	the day of the full moon
purohit	the Brahman who performs the customary duties for a family, or a number of households
qanūngo	hereditary keeper of the revenue records at the *pargana* or the ta'alluqa level
qaum	a significant social group or a particular occupation; a nationality; a nation

qāzī	judicial officer who administered Islamic law; office survived into the early nineteenth century in the Punjab
qudrat	power; divine power; nature
rabābī	one who plays on the *rabāb*, a kind of violin with three strings
rāgī	singer, particularly of the hymns of the Sikh scripture
rahit	way of life, used especially for the Sikh way of life in accordance with the philosophic and ethical principles advanced by the Gurus
rahitmaryāda	accepted norms of belief and conduct in Sikhism
Rahitnāma	written code of belief and conduct; norms laid down for the Sikh way of life in accordance with the principles of Sikhism, including penance for infringing those principles
rai'yat	subjects; self-cultivating peasant
rāj	political power, rulership
rāj-jog	attitude of remaining detached in the pursuit of temporal affairs
rāja-i kalān bahadur	great raja, a title used for Raja Dhian Singh
rāja-i rājgān	raja of rajas, title given to Raja Dhian Singh
rājgān	*rājā*s, chiefs
rākhī	literally 'protection'; in the eighteenth century a Sikh leader's claim to a part of the produce from land in return for protection against all other claimants
ramāinī	poem or a unit of verse in praise of God
sachch	truth; as the unique attribute of God
Sachchā Pādshāh	the True King
Sadd	form of poetic composition, a particular composition in Guru Granth Sahib
sādh	a person devoted to religious pursuits; a mendicant; a recluse; a Sikh
sādh-sangat	an association of the pious; used generally for the Sikh congregation for worship through kīrtan and *kathā*
sādiq	one who is truly devoted to God
sagan	a formal gift offered generally on a happy occasion
saguṇa	with qualities or attributes, used generally for the human incarnations of Vishnu

sahaj	the state of union with God
Sahajdhārī	non-Singh Khalsa; a Sikh who is not baptized as a Singh and does not observe the Khalsa code of discipline
sahlang	a part, an associate; a person admitted to the Sikh faith by a representative of the guru on his behalf
sāhūkār	rich trader who may also be a moneylender
sāj	used to rhyme with *rāj* to reinforce the meaning, alluding to government and administration
sākhī	an eyewitness; testimony; an episode bearing witness to the spiritual status of a religious guide; a statement bearing witness to the truth of God; a teaching
saligram	stone used for making idols
sālik	one who treads the path of union with God
samādh	structure raised over a spot of cremation in honour of an important person, whether secular or religious; the counterpart of a mausoleum
sanad	written document possessing legal validity
sanchī	certain number of folios to serve as a unit for binding together as a book
sandhya	meditation on a deity
sangat	assembly, religious congregation; a congregation of Sikhs; the collective body of Sikhs at one place
sankalp	vow to make an offering after a particular wish is fulfilled or for the fulfilment of a particular wish
sanskār	symbols and rites peculiar to a community of people
sant	a saint; generally a follower of the figures like Namdev, Kabir, Ravidas and Dadu; equated with Sikh in Guru Granth Sahib, and now with an eminent Sikh known to be pious
santokh	contentment; satisfaction with what one has
sarāi	halting place for caravans and other travellers
Sarbat Khalsa	the entire body of the Khalsa, a meeting of the entire body, to which every Sikh stands invited
sardār-i kasīr al-iqtidār	the leader whose honour is on the increase; title
sardārān-i kalān	great *sardār*s; nobles of the top rank
sardārān-i nāmdār	the eminent sardars; the nobles of the middle rung
sarkār-i 'ala	literally His Exalted Majesty; a form of address used for Maharaja Ranjit Singh

saropā (sirpāo)	robe of honour in Mughal times, consisting of a large number of articles of dress from the head to the feet, including even arms and horses; in Sikh practice, a simpler robe of honour, now even a single shawl, or a piece of cloth symbolic of honour
sarovar	tank, pool of water
sarrāf	money-changer; jeweller
sat	total commitment to integrity of the self
satgur	the true Guru, used for both God and the Guru in Sikhism
sat-sangat	the true association, generally used for the Sikh congregation for worship
Satjug	the first of the four cosmic ages, regarded as the best of all the four
saudāgarī	trade, especially in horses
sayyid	a descendant of the Prophet Muhammad or a person belonging to his tribe; regarded as venerable among Indian Muslims
sayyidzāda	the son of a Sayyid; generally used for a distinguished Sayyid lineage
sīel	self-control, contentment
seth	rich trader; rich person
sevak	one who performs worship or service; a Sikh
shabad	the word; a hymn; a verse of Guru Granth Sahib
shabad-guru	the belief or doctrine that the word (*shabad*) represents the guru or is the Guru
shahīd	martyr
shahīdganj	a Gurdwara built in commemoration of a martyr
Shaikh	head of a Sūfī order; a respectable Muslim
shaikhzāda	son of a Shaikh; descendant of a Shaikh
shāntī	peace
shalok/shloka	a verse, generally rather short, like a *dohā* or a rhyming couplet
shraddh	rite by which the dead ancestors are supposed to be fed through the mediacy of Brahmans
shuddhī	purification, especially in the context of reconversion
shuhdā	plural of *shahīd*, a martyr in Islamic tradition; their tombs were treated as sacred
shujā'at dastgāh	one who has access to or mastery over bravery; used as a title

siddh	person who has attained high spiritual state so as to command supranatural powers
sī-harfī	literally, of thirty letters; a composition making use of the letters of the Perso-Arabic alphabet at the beginning of each of its stanzas, approximately 30
sikh	a discipline; used generally for a follower of Guru Nanak and his successors
sikhī	the Sikh way
sipāhsālār	head of an army, a commander, a commander in chief
siyāsat	capital punishment; now used for politics in general
sūba	a province or the primary division of an empire; the governor of a province was called *subadār*, and his office *subadārī*
suhāgan	woman whose husband loves her and cares for her
sunn-samādh	the void; a concept in which God or Reality alone exists without any attribute
smīpī	person who advises the ruler in matters religious and ethical
sūtak	the notion of pollution in certain situations, especially in relation to women during menstruation and childbirth
tabak	one of the 14 worlds of Muslim belief
tahhawar panāh	one who is a refuge of majesty; used as a title
tahsīl	collection, particularly of the revenues from land; the revenue collector was called *tahsīldār*
takht	throne; one of the five Sikh religious centres of authority
tama	greed
tankha	ordinarily salary, but used by the compilers of Rahitnāmas (manuals for the Sikh way of life) for corrective punishment or penance awarded to a Sikh for infringing a particular norm
tarf	direction, division
tarpan	offer of food and other items to the image of a deity for worship
taslīm	acceptance, submission
tat-khalsa	staunch Khalsa; used for the Khalsa of Guru Gobind Singh who opposed Banda Bahadur and his followers in the early eighteenth century, and also for the Singh reformers of the early twentieth century

tāzia	procession taken out by the Shī'a Muslims during the month of Muharram to mark the martyrdom of Husain and Hasan, the sons of Ali and the Prophet's daughter
tegh	sword; sword as the symbol of power, and justice
thākur	master; a deity; an image of a deity, especially Vaishnava
thākur-pūjan	worship of a god, generally an idol
thānadār	commandant of a garrison or a fort
tilak or *tikka*	sacred mark on the forehead of a Brahman, an upper caste Hindu, or the member of any religious sect; also used for the coronation of a ruler
tīrath	sacred place; a place of pilgrimage; notionally, sixty-eight places in India
tith	phase of the moon
toshakhānia	person in charge of stores
Udasi	a renunciant belonging to an order tracing its origin to Guru Nanak through his son Sri Chand but not through Guru Angad and his successors
ujjal didār	of pure bright countenance; used as a title for the Khalsa
'ulamā	plural of *'ālim*, a person who possesses knowledge; used generally for the learned in Islamic theology and law
umarā	plural of *amīr*; a nobles
ummat	community of the followers of the Prophet Muhammad; used also for the followers of Guru Nanak and his successors, though rarely
upāsana	praise
updes	instruction, teaching
vaid	physician
vakīl	agent or deputy; envoy
vār	literary genre, generally used for heroic poetry; Guru Nanak used it for his religious compositions; the most famous Vārs in Sikh literature were composed by Bhai Gurdas in the early seventeenth century for celebrating Sikh Gurus and the Sikh Panth
varna	literally colour, used for any one of the ideal fourfold social order
varnashramadharma	the concept of the fourfold division of the social order (Brahman, Kshtriya, Vaishya, Shudra) and individual life (Brahmacharya, Grahst, Sanyās, and Vanprasta)

waddhā ghallūghārā	the great carnage of the Sikhs at the hands of the Ahmad Shah Abdali in February 1962
walī	friend, friend of God
wazīr	the first or the prime minister, next in authority and importance to the king
yasā	the manner of killing a royal or a religious person without shedding his blood
yogī	one who follows the path of *yoga* or practices believed to lead one to union with God or the ultimate reality
yuga	one of the four cosmic ages in the Indian conception of time
zamīndār	literally the holder of land; applied alike to the intermediary who collected revenue on behalf of the state, to a vassal chief and to a peasant proprietor
zāt	personal rank in the mansabdārī system
zikr	remembrance; reciting of God's names; the practice of Muslim mystics to remember God

Bibliography

Adhikari, G., *Sikh Homeland through Hindu-Muslim-Sikh Unity*, Bombay: 1944.
Adi Sri Guru Granth Sahib Ji (Sri Damdami Bir, various printed editions).
Ali, Imran, *The Punjab Under Imperialism 1885–1947*, New Delhi: Oxford University Press, 1989.
Anurupita Kaur, 'Sikhs in the Early Census Reports', in Reeta Grewal and Sheena Pall, eds, *Five Centuries of Sikh Tradition: Ideology, Society, Politics and Culture*, New Delhi: Manohar, 2005, pp. 123–50.
Arshi, P.S., *The Golden Temple: History, Art and Architecture*, New Delhi: Harman Publishing House, 1989.
Attar Singh, Sardar, *Sakhee Book, or the Description of Gooroo Gobind Singh's Religion and Doctrines*, Benares: Medical Hall Press, 1873.
———, *The Rayhit Nama of Prahlad Rai or the Excellent Conversation of Duswan Padshah*.
———, *Nand Lal's Rayhit Nama or Rules for Guidance of the Sikhs in Religious Matters*, Lahore: 1876.
Bachan Singh, *Nā Ham Hindu Na Musalman: Nābhe De Ishtihār Dā Uttar Te Khandan*, Amritsar: Wazir Hind Press, n.d.
———, *Sikhs and Idols: A Reply to the Raja of Nabha*, Lahore: Civil and Military Gazette Press, n.d.
Bachittar Singh, Giani, ed., *Planned Attack on Aad Sri Guru Granth Sahib: Academics or Blasphemy*, Chandigarh: International Centre of Sikh Studies, 1994.
Banerjee, Himadri, 'Creator of the Khalsa: A Non-Sikh Indian Literary Perspective', in Jasbir Singh Mann and Kharak Singh, eds, *Recent Researches in Sikhism*, Patiala: Punjabi University, 1992, pp. 152–60.
Banga, Indu, *Agrarian System of the Sikhs: Late Eighteenth and Early Nineteenth Century*, New Delhi: Manohar Publications, 1978.
———, 'The Crisis of Sikh Politics (1940–47)', in Joseph T. O' Connell et al., eds, *Sikh History and Religion in the Twentieth Century*, Toronto: University of Toronto, 1988, pp. 233–55.
Bani Bhagat Kabir Ji Steek, ed., Bhai Jodh Singh, Patiala: Punjabi University, 1993 (3rd edn).

Barrier, N. Gerald, *The Sikhs and Their Literature: A Guide to Tracts, Books and Periodicals, 1849–1919*), Delhi: Manohar Book Service, 1970.

———, 'The Role of Ideology and Institutions-Building in Modern Sikhism', in Mark Juergensmeyer and N. Gerald Barrier, eds, *Sikh Studies: Comparative Perspectives on a Changing Tradition*, Berkeley: Religions Studies Series 1979, pp. 41–51.

———, 'The Evolution of Punjab Studies in North America', *The Panjab Past and Present*, vol. XVI, pt. 2 (October 1982).

———, 'Sikh Studies and the Study of History' in John Stratton Hawley and Gurvinder Singh Mann, eds, *Studying the Sikhs: Issues for North America*, Albany: State University of New York Press, 1993, pp. 25–33.

———, 'Sikh Politics and Religion: The Bhasaur Singh Sabha', in Indu Banga, ed., *Five Punjabi Centuries: Polity, Economy and Culture, 1500–1990*, New Delhi: Manohar, 1997.

Bell, Major Evans, *The Annexation of the Punjab and Maharaja Duleep Singh*, Patiala: Punjab Languages Department, 1970 (rpt).

Bhalla, Sarup Das, *Mahima Prakash*, 2 vols, Gobind Singh Lamba, ed., Patiala: Punjab Languages Department, 1971.

Bhandari, Sujan Rai, *Khulāsa ut-Tawārīkh*, M. Zafar Hasan, ed., Delhi: 1918.

Bhangu, Ratan Singh, *Prachīn Panth Prakāsh*, Bhai Vir Singh, New Delhi: Bhai Vir Singh Sahit Sadan, 1993 (rpt).

———, *Sri Guru Panth Prakāsh*, Balwant Singh Dhillon, ed., Amritsar: Singh Brothers, 2004.

Briggs, John, *What Are We To Do With The Punjab?* London: James Madden, 1849.

Browne, James, *India Tracts*, London: The East India Company, 1788.

Bryant, Kenneth E., '*Sant* and *Vaishnava* Poetry: Some Observations on Method', *Sikh Studies: Comparative Perspectives on a Changing Tradition*, pp. 65–74.

Caulfield General, *The Punjab and the Indian Army*, London: 1846.

Census of India, 1921, vol. XV, Panjab and Delhi, Part II, Table V. Prepared by L. Middleton and S.M. Jacob, this volume was published from Lahore in 1923.

Chhibber, Kesar Singh, *Bansāvalīnāma Dasān Pātshāhiān Kā*, Ratan Singh Jaggi, ed., (published as vol. II of *Research Bulletin of Panjabi Language and Literature*, ed., S.S. Kohli), Chandigarh: Panjab University, 1972.

Chopra, G.L., ed., *Chiefs and Families of Note in the Punjab*, Lahore: 1940

Cunningham, Joseph Davey, *A History of the Sikhs from the Origin of the Nation to the Battles of the Sutlej*, London; John Murray, 1849.

BIBLIOGRAPHY 393

Cunningham, Joseph Davey, *A History of the Sikhs*, Delhi: S. Chand & Co., 1955 (rpt).

Daljeet Singh, *Essays on the Authenticity of Kartarpuri Bir and the Integrated Logic and Unity of Sikhism*, Patiala: Punjabi University, 1987.

———, 'Authenticity of the Kartarpur Bir', in Jasbir Singh Mann and Harbans Singh Saraon, eds, *Advanced Studies in Sikhism*, Irvine: Sikh Community of North America, 1989, pp. 138-60.

———, 'Issues of Sikh Studies', *Advanced Studies in Sikhism*, pp. 16-29.

———, 'Sikhism, Vaishnavism, Vedanta and Nathism—A Comparison', *Advanced Studies in Sikhism*, pp. 33-55.

———, 'Sikhism: A Miri Piri System', *Recent Researches in Sikhism*, pp. 42-60.

———, 'Punjab River-Waters Dispute in Kharak Singh, Gobind Sing Mansukhani, and Jasbir Singh Mann, eds, *Fundamental Issues in Sikh Studies*, Chandigardh: Institute of Sikh Studies, 1992, pp. 196-228.

———, 'The Sikh Identity', *Fundamental Issues in Sikh Studies*, pp.106-15.

———, *Essentials of Sikhism*, Amritsar: Singh Brothers, 1994.

Deol, Gurdev Singh, *Sardar Sundar Singh Majithia: Life, Work and Mission*, Amritsar: Khalsa College, 1992.

Dhillon, Balwant Singh, *Early Sikh Scriptural Tradition: Myth and Reality*, Amritsar: Singh Brothers, 1999.

Dhillon, G.S., 'Character and Impact of Singh Sabha Movement on the History of the Punjab', PhD thesis, Patiala: Punjabi University, 1973.

———, 'Singh Sabha Movement: A Revival', in *Advanced Studies in Sikhism*.

———, 'The Sikhs and the British, 1849-1920', *Recent Researches in Sikhism*, pp. 173-225.

———, 'The Sikh Rule and Ranjit Singh', *Recent Researches in Sikhism*, pp. 347-72.

———, 'Sikh Identity: A Continuing Feature', *Recent Researches in Sikhism*, pp. 226-46.

Douie, James, *The Punjab, North-Western Frontier Province and Kashmir*, Delhi: Seema Publications, 1974 (rpt).

Eden, Emily, *Up the Country*, 2 vols, London: Richard Bentley, 1866 (3rd edn).

Embree, Ainslie T., 'Locating Sikhism in Time and Place: A Problem for Historical Surveys', *Sikh Studies: Comparative Perspectives on a Changing Tradition*, pp. 55-62.

BIBLIOGRAPHY

English translations of the Punjabi Text (of the memorial submitted by the Granthis and Pujaris of the Golden Temple to the Secretary to the Government of India, Legislative Department), Patiala: Punjabi University, Bhai Mohan Singh Vaid Collection.

Eur. Mss. D. 313, Henry Elliot Collection, British Library, London.

———, F. 85 (44), Henry Lawrence Collection, British Library, London.

Events at the Court of Ranjit Singh 1810–1817, H.L.O. Garrett and G.L. Chopra, eds, Patiala: Punjab Languages Department, 1988 (rpt).

Fenech, Louis E., *Martyrdom in the Sikh Tradition: Playing the 'Game of Love'*, New Delhi: Oxford University Press, 2000.

Forbes, Duncan, *The Liberal Anglican Idea of History*, Cambridge: Cambridge University Press 1952.

Forster, George, *A Journey from Bengal to England*, 2 vols, London: R. Faulder, 1798.

Fox, Richard G., *Lions of the Punjab: Culture in the Making*, Berkeley: University of California Press, 1985.

Francklin, William, *The History of the Reign of Shaw Aulum*, London: Printed by Cooper and Graham, 1798.

'Fr. Guerreiro's Account of Guru Arjan's Martyrdom', in J.S. Grewal and Irfan Habib, eds, *Sikh History from Persian Sources*, New Delhi: Tulika/Indian History Congress, 2001.

Ganda Singh, ed., *Early European Accounts of the Sikhs*, Calcutta: Firma K.L. Mukhopadhyaya, 1962.

——— ed., *Hukamnāme Guru Sāhibān, Mata Sāhibān, Banda Singh Ate Khalsa Ji De*, Patiala: Punjabi University, 1967.

———, 'Editorial', *The Panjab Past and Present*, vol. IV, pt. 2 (October 1970).

——— ed., *History of Freedom Movement in the Punjab, vol. III: Maharaja Duleep Singh Correspondence*, Patiala: Punjabi University, 1977.

———, *Kūkiān dī Vithīā* (Pbi.), Patiala: Punjabi University, 2000 (rpt).

Ganesh Das, *Char Bagh-i Punjab*, ed., Kirpal Singh, Amritsar: Khalsa College, 1965.

Garrett, H.L.O. and G.L. Chopra, tr. and ed., *Events at the Court of Ranjit Singh (1810–1817)*, Patiala: Punjab Languages Department, 1970 (rpt).

Gauba, Anand, *Amritsar: A Study of Urban History (1840–1947)*, Jalandhar: ABS Publications, 1988.

Gore, Montague, *Remarks on the Present State of the Punjab*, London: John Murray, 1849.

Goswamy, B.N., *Piety and Splendour: Sikh Heritage in Art*, New Delhi: National Museum, 2000.

Goswamy, B.N. and J.S. Grewal, *The Mughals and the Jogis of Jakhbar*, Simla: Indian Institute of Advanced Study, 1967.

———, *The Mughal and Sikh Rulers and the Vaishnavas of Pindori: A Historical Interpretation of 52 Persian Documents*, Simla: Indian Institute of Advanced Study, 1969.

Grewal, J.S., 'The Prem Sumarag: A Theory of Sikh Social Order', *Punjab History Conference Proceedings*, Patiala: Punjabi University, 1965.

———, *Guru Nanak in History*, Chandigarh: Panjab University, 1969.

———, 'A Theory of Sikh Social Order', in J.S. Grewal, *From Guru Nanak to Maharaja Ranjit Singh*.

———, 'Cunningham as a Historian of the Sikhs', *From Guru Nanak to Maharaja Ranjit Singh*.

———, *In the By-Lanes of History*, Simla: Indian Institute of Advanced Study, 1975.

———, 'A Perspective on Early Sikh History', *Sikh Studies: Comparative Perspective on a Changing Tradition*, pp. 33–9.

———, 'The Emergence of Punjabi Drama: A Cultural Response to Colonial Rule', *Journal of Regional History*, Amritsar: Guru Nanak Dev University, vol. V (1984).

———, *The City of the Golden Temple*, Amritsar: Guru Nanak Dev University, 1986.

———, *The Sikhs of the Punjab* (The New Cambridge History of India, II. 3), Cambridge: Cambridge University Press, 1990.

———, *Guru Nanak and Patriarchy*, Simla: Indian Institute of Advanced Study, 1993.

———, 'A Brief History of Sikh Studies in English', *Studying the Sikhs: Issues for North America*, pp. 161–73.

———, *Sikh Ideology, Polity and Social Order*, New Delhi: Manohar, 1996.

———, *Historical Perspectives on Sikh Identity*, Patiala: Punjabi University, 1997.

———, *Contesting Interpretations of the Sikh Tradition*, New Delhi: Manohar, 1998.

———, 'Nabha's *Ham Hindu Nahin*: A Declaration of Sikh Ethnicity', in Pashaura Singh and N. Gerald Barrier, eds, *Sikh Identity, Continuity and Change*, New Delhi: Manohar, 2001.

———, *Maharaja Ranjit Singh: Polity, Economy and Society*, Amritsar: Guru Nanak Dev University, 2001.

———, 'Valorizing the Sikh Tradition: Bhangu's *Panth Prakash*', in J.S. Grewal, ed., *The Khalsa: Sikh and Non-Sikh Perspectives*, New Delhi: Manohar 2004, pp. 103–22.

Grewal, J.S., ed., *The Khalsa: Sikh and Non-Sikh Perspectives*, New Delhi: Manohar, 2004.

———, 'The Gurdwara', in J.S. Grewal, ed., *Religious Movements and Institutions in Medieval India*, New Delhi: Oxford University Press, 2006.

———, 'Kabir and the Kabir-Panthis', *Religious Movements and Institutions*.

———, ed., *Baba Dayal: Founder of the First Reform Movement among the Sikhs*, Chandigarh: Dr Man Singh Nirankari, 2003.

———, 'The Janamsakhi Traditions', *Lectures on History, Society and Culture of the Punjab*, Patiala: Punjabi University, 2007.

Grewal, J.S. and Indu Banga, eds., *Early Nineteenth Century Punjab (From Ganesh Das's Char Bagh-i Panjab)*, Amritsar: Guru Nanak Dev University, 1975.

———, eds, *Civil and Military Affairs of Maharaja Ranjit Singh (A Study of 450 Orders in Persian)*, Amritsar: Guru Nanak Dev University, 1987.

Grewal, J.S. and Irfan Habib, eds, *Sikh History from Persian Sources*, New Delhi: Tulika/Indian History Congress, 2001.

Grewal, J.S. and S.S. Bal, *Guru Gobind Singh (A Biographical Study)*, Chandigarh: Panjab University, 1967. Reprinted in 1987.

Griffin Lepel, *The Panjab Chiefs: Historical and Biographical Notices of the Principal Families in the Territories under the Punjab Government*, Lahore: 1865.

———, *Ranjit Singh*, Allahabad: Kitab Mahal, 1957(rpt).

———, *The Rajas of the Panjab, Being the History of the Principal States in the Punjab and Their Political Relations with the British Government*, Patiala: Punjab Languages Department, 1970 (rpt).

Gupta, Hari Ram, *A History of the Sikhs*, vol. I, Simla: The Minerva Book Shop, 1952.

Gurbachan Singh and Lal Singh Giani, *The Idea of the Sikh State*, Lahore: Lahore Book Shop, 1946.

Gurbakhsh Singh, 'From Ritual to Counter Ritual: A Critical Analysis', *Recent Researches in Sikhism*, pp. 273–85.

Gurdas, Bhai, *Vārān Bhai Gurdas*, ed., Giani Hazara Singh, Amritsar: Khalsa Samachar, 1962.

Gurdev Singh, ed., *Perspectives on the Sikh Tradition*, Patiala: Siddharth Publications for Academy of Sikh Religion and Culture, 1986.

Gurtej Singh, 'Political Ideas of Guru Nanak, the Originator of the Sikh Faith', *Recent Researches in Sikhism*, pp. 61–71.

———, 'Two Views of Dasam Granth', *Fundamental Issues in Sikh Studies*, pp. 179–86.

Hamdard, Sadhu Singh, *Āzād Punjab* (Urdu), Amritsar: Ajit Book Agency, 1943.
Hans, S.S., 'Prem Sumarg: A Modern Forgery', *Punjab History Conference Proceedings*, 1982.
Harbans Singh, *Bhai Vir Singh*, New Delhi: Sahitya Akademi, 1972.
Harbans Singh and N. Gerald Barrier, eds, *The Panjab Past and Present: Essays in Honour of Dr Ganda Singh*, Patiala: Punjabi University, 1976.
Harjot Singh, 'From Gurdwara Rikabgang to the Viceregal Palace: A Study of Religious Protest', *The Panjab, Past and Present*, Patiala: Punjabi University, vol. XIV, pt. 1 (April 1980), pp. 182–98.
Harnam Singh, *Punjab: The Homeland of the Sikhs*, Lahore: 1945.
Hawley, John Stratton and Gurinder Singh Mann, eds, *Studying the Sikhs: Issues for North America*, Albany: State University of New York Press, 1993.
Hawley, John Stratton and Mark Juergensmeyer, *Songs of the Saints of India*, New York: Oxford University Press, 1988.
Hess, Linda and Shukdev Singh, *The Bijak of Kabir*, San Francisco: North Point Press, 1983.
Home Department Public Branch Consultations Nos 65–71 (letters of 5 March, 20 September, and 4 October 1859), National Archives of India, New Delhi.
Home Confidential 1902, No. 669/12, Punjab State Archives, Chandigarh.
———— 1905, No. 668/12, Punjab State Archives, Chandigarh.
Home General 1910, no. 788/14, Punjab State Archives, Chandigarh.
Hugel, Baron Charles, *Travels in Kashmir and the Punjab containing a Particular Account of the Government and Character of the Sikhs*, tr., Major T.B. Jervis, Patiala: Punjab, Languages Department, 1970 (rpt).
Indarjit Singh, 'Unity of Sikh Thought', *Advanced Studies in Sikhism*, pp. 109–18.
Irschick, Eugene F., 'Sikhism as a Category of Study', *Sikh Studies: Comparative Perspective on a Changing Tradition*, pp. 53–4.
Jaggi, Rattan Singh and Gursharan Kaur Jaggi, eds, *Sri Dasam-Granth Sahib*, 5 vols, New Delhi: Gobind Sadan, 1999.
Jagjit Singh, 'The Caste System and the Sikhs', *Advanced Studies in Sikhism*, pp. 278–300.
————, 'Sikh Militancy and the Jats', *Advanced Studies in Sikhism*, pp. 214–33.
————, 'The Doctrine of Meeri-Peeri', *Recent Researches in Sikhism*, pp. 136–49.
Jakobsh, Dorris R., *Relocating Gender in Sikh History: Transformation, Meaning and Identity*, New Delhi: Oxford University Press, 2003.

Jaswinder Singh, *Kuka Movement: Freedom Struggle in Punjab*, New Delhi: Atlantic Publishers and Distributors, 1985.
Jodh Singh, *Varan Bhai Gurdas: Text, Transliteration and Translation*, 2 vols, Patiala: Vision and Venture, 1998.
Jodh Singh, Bhai, 'Jin Prem Kiyo Tin Hi Prabh Payo', in S.S. Amol, ed., *Ek Murit Anek Darsan*, Jalandhar: Lyallpur Khalsa College, 1967, pp. 44–5.
Joginder Singh, 'Resurgence in Sikh Journalism', *Journal of Regional History*, Amritsar: Guru Nanak Dev University, 1982, vol. III, pp. 99–116.
———, *Sikh Leadership, Early 20th Century*, Amritsar: Guru Nanak Dev University, 1999.
Journal of Asiatick Society of Bengal, vol. XIII, pt. 1; vol. XVI, pt. 2; vol. XVIII, pt. 2.
Journal of Sikh Studies, Amritsar: Guru Nanak Dev University, February 1974 and August 1975, and February 1977.
Juergensmeyer, Mark, 'The Forgotten Tradition: Sikhism in the Study of World Religions', *Sikh Studies: Comparative Perspectives on a Changing Tradition*, pp. 13–23.
———, 'Sikhism and Religious Studies', *Studying the Sikhs: Issues for North America*, pp. 9–14.
Juergensmeyer, Mark and N. Gerald Barrieer, eds, *Sikh Studies: Comparative Perspective on a Changing Tradition*, Berkeley: Berkeley Religious Studies Series, 1979.
Jones, Kenneth, *Arya Dharm: Hindu Consciousness in 19th Century Punjab*, New Delhi: Manohar, 1989 (rpt).
Kanwaljit Kaur, 'Sikh Women', *Fundamental Issues in Sikh Studies*, pp. 98–104.
Kapany, Narinder Singh, 'Sikhs Abroad', *Sikh Studies: Comparative Perspectives on a Changing Tradition*, pp. 207–8.
Kapur, Prithipal Singh, ed., *Maharaja Duleep Singh: The Last Sovereign Ruler of the Punjab*, Amritsar: Shiromani Gurdwara Parbandhak Committee, 1995.
Kapur, Rajiv A., *Sikh Separatism: The Politics of Faith*, New Delhi: Vikas Publishing House, 1987 (2nd impression)
Kapur Singh, *Parasharaprashna: An Enquiry into the Genesis and Unique Character of the Order of the Khalsa with an Exposition of the Sikh Tenets*, Piar Singh and Madanjit Kaur, eds, Amritsar: Guru Nanak Dev University, 1989.
Kavita Singh, ed., *New Insights into Sikh Art*, Mumbai: Marg Publications (vol. 54, no. 4), June 2003.

Kerr, Ian. J., 'The British and the Administration on of the Golden Temple in 1859', *The Panjab Past and Present*, vol. X, 1976, pp. 306-21.

———, 'British Relationship with the Golden Temple 1849-90', *The Indian Economic and Social History Review*, vol. XXI, 1984, pp. 139-51.

———, 'Sikhs and State: Troublesome Relationships and a Fundamental Continuity with Particular Reference to the Period 1849-1919', in Pashaura Singh and N. Gerald Barrier, eds, *Sikh Identity: Continuity and Change*, New Delhi: Manohar, 2001.

Khalsa, Gurudharam Singh, 'The End of Syncretism: Anti-Syncretism in Sikh Tradition', *Sikh Identity*, pp. 93-107.

Kharak Singh, Gobind Singh Mansukhani, and Jasbir Singh Mann, eds, *Fundamental Issues in Sikh Studies*, Chandigarh: Institute of Sikh Studies, 1992.

Kharak Singh, 'Martyrdom in Sikhism', *Abstracts of Sikh Studies*, Chandigarh: Institute of Sikh Studies, January 1994.

———, 'Guru Nanak in History of Religious Thought', *Recent Researches in Sikhism*, pp. 81-8.

———, 'Mispresentation of Sikhism in Western Encyclopedias', *Recent Researches in Sikhism*, pp. 335-58.

———, 'Sikh Ideology, Fundamentalism and Punjab Problem', *Fundamental Issues in Sikh Studies*, pp. 136-59.

———, 'Need for World Institute of Sikhism', *Fundamental Issues in Sikh Studies*, pp. 238-54.

Kharak Singh and Gurdarshan Singh Dhillon, 'Raj Karega Khalsa', *Fundamental Issues in Sikh Studies*, pp. 187-95.

Khilnani, N.M., *British Power in the Punjab, 1839-58*, Bombay: Asia Publishing House, 1972.

Kirpal Singh, and Shamsher Singh, eds, *Janam Sakhi Sri Guru Nanak Dev Ji*, 2 vols, Ashok, Amritsar: Khalsa College, 1962, 1969 (vol. I attributed to Miharban and vol. II to Harji and Chaturbhuj)

Kohli, S.S., *Punjabi Sāhit dā Itihās*, Ludhiana: Lahore Book Shop, 1955.

———, 'Janamsakhis: Their Value and Importance', *Advanced Studies in Sikhism*, pp. 301-16.

———, 'Constant Unity of Sikh Thought', *Advanced Studies in Sikhism*, pp. 98-108.

Lakshman Singh, Bhagat, *A Short Sketch of the Life and Work of Guru Gobind Singh, the Tenth and Last Guru of the Sikhs*, Ludhiana: Lahore Book Shop, 1963.

———, *Autobiography*, Ganda Singh, ed., Calcutta: The Sikh Cultural Centre, 1965.

Lal, Bhai Harbans, 'Sahajdhari Sikhs: Their Origin and Current Status Within the Panth', *Sikh Identity: Continuity and Change*, pp. 109-26.

Lavan Spencer, *The Ahmadiyya Movement: A History and Perspective*, New Delhi: Manohar, 1974.

Lawrence, H.M., *Adventures of an Officer in the Punjab in the Service of Ranjit Singh*, 2 vols, London: Henry Colburn, 1846.

Leech, R., 'Notes on the Religion of the Sikhs being a notice of their Prayer, Holidays and shrines', *JASB*, no. CIXII, 1845.

Lepel Griffin and C.F. Massy, *Chiefs and Families of Note in the Punjab*, revised and corrected by W.L. Conran and H.D. Craik, Lahore: Government Printing, 1909.

Lewis, James R., 'Mispresentations of the Sikh Tradition in World Religions Textbooks', *Advanced Studies in Sikhism*, pp. 265-77.

―――, 'Some Unexamined Assumptions in Western Studies of Sikhism', *Recent Researches in Sikhism*, pp. 286-98.

Loehlin, C.H., 'Textual Criticism of the Kartarpur Granth', *Sikh Studies: Comparative Perspectives on a Changing Tradition*, pp. 113-18.

Lorenzen, David N., 'The Kabir-Panth and Social Protest', in Karine Schomer and W.H. McLeod, eds, *The Sants: Studies in a Devotional Tradition of India*, Delhi: Motilal Banarsidass, 1987, pp. 281-303.

Madanjit Kaur, 'The Creation of the Khalsa and Prescribing of the Sikh Symbols', *Advanced Studies in Sikhism*, pp. 195-213.

―――, 'The Guruship and Succession of Guru Granth Sahib', *Advanced Studies in Sikhism*, pp. 121-37.

―――, 'Devi Worship Story: A Critique', *Fundamental Issues in Sikh Studies*, pp. 170-8.

―――, 'Koer Singh's Gurbilas Patshahi 10: An Eighteenth Century Sikh Literature', *Recent Researches in Sikhism*, pp. 161-72.

Maisey, General F.C., *Sanchi and Its Remains*, London: 1892.

Makhaz-i Tawārīkh Sikhān, Ganda Singh, ed., Amritsar: Khalsa College, 1949.

Malcolm, Lt Col (John), *Sketch of the Sikhs*, New Delhi: Asian Educational Services, 1986 (rpt).

Malhotra, Karamjit K., 'The Earliest Manual on the Sikh Way of Life', in Reeta Grewal and Sheena Pall, eds, *Five Centuries of Sikh Tradition Ideology, Society, Politics and Culture*, New Delhi: Manohar, 2005, pp. 55-81.

Malleson, G.B., *Decisive Battles of India from 1746 to 1849, Inclusive*, London: Reeves and Turner, 1888.

Mann, Gurinder Singh, *The Goindval Pothis: The Earliest Extant Source of the Sikh Canon*, Cambridge (Massachusetts): Harvard University Press, 1996.

Mann, Gurinder Singh, *The Making of Sikh Scripture*, New York: Oxford University Press, 2000.

Mann, Jasbir Singh and Harbans Singh, eds, *Advanced Studies in Sikhism*, Irvine: Sikh Community of North America, 1989.

Mann, Jasbir Singh and Kharak Singh, eds, *Recent Researhes in Sikhism*, Patiala: Punjabi University, 1992.

Mann, Jasbir Singh, Surinder Singh Sodhi, and Gurbakhsh Singh Shergill, eds, *Invasion of Religious Boundaries*, Vancouver: Canadian Sikh Study and Teaching Society, 1995.

Marenco, Ethne K., *The Transformation of Sikh Society*, New Delhi: Heritage Publishers, 1976.

Mansukhani, Gobind Singh, 'Sikh-Rahat Maryada and Sikh Symbols', *Advanced Studies in Sikhism*, pp. 174–91.

———, 'Origin and Development of Sikh Studies' *Fundamental Issues in Sikh Studies*, pp. 127–35.

———, 'An Integrated Methodology for Appraisal of Sources for Sikh Studies', *Recent Researches in Sikhism*, pp. 109–21.

Masson, Charles, *Narratives of Various Journeys, in Baluchistan, Afghanistan and the Punjab, including a Residence in those Countries from 1826 to 1838*, 3 vols, London: Richard Bentley, 1842.

Massy, Charles Francis, *The Punjab Chiefs—Historical and Biographical notices of the principal families in the different divisions of the Punjab* 2 vols, Lahore: Govt of the Punjab, 1890.

McLeod, W.H., *Guru Nanak and the Sikh Religion*, Oxford: The Clarendon Press, 1968.

———, *The Evolution of the Sikh Community*, New Delhi: Oxford University Press, 1975.

———, 'The Sikh Scriptures: Some Issues', *Sikh Studies: Comparative Perspectives on a Changing Tradition*, pp. 97–111.

———, *Early Sikh Tradition: A Study of the Janam-sakhis*, Oxford: The Clarendon Press, 1980.

———, (tr.) *The B40 Janaamsakhi*, Amritsar: Guru Nanak Dev University, 1980.

———, 'The Development of the Sikh Panth', *The Sants: Studies in a Devotional Tradition of India*.

———, ed. and tr., *The Chaupa Singh Rahit-Nama*, Dunedin: University of Otago Press, 1987.

———, *Who is a Sikh? The Problem of Sikh Identity*, Oxford: The Clarendon Press, 1989.

———, 'A Sikh Theology for Modern Times', *Sikh History and Religion in the Twentieth Century*, pp. 32–43.

McLeod, W.H., 'The Study of Sikh Literature', *Studying the Sikhs: Issues for North America*, pp. 55-9.

———, *Sikhism*, Hammondsworth: Penguin Books, 1997.

———, 'The Problems of the Panjabi Rahit-Nama', *Exploring Sikhism: Aspects of Sikh Identity, Culture and Thought*, New Delhi: Oxford University Press, 2000, pp. 103-25.

———, 'The Khalsa Rahit: The Sikh Identity Defined', *Exploring Sikhism*, pp. 126-35.

———, *Sikhs of the Khalsa: A History of the Khalsa Rahit*, New Delhi: Oxford University Press, 2003.

———, *Discovering the Sikhs: Autobiography of a Historian*, Delhi: Permanent Black, 2004.

———, *Prem Sumarg: The Testimony of a Sanatan Sikh*, New Delhi: Oxford University Press, 2006.

———, *Essays in Sikh History, Tradition, and Society*, New Delhi: Oxford University Press, 2007.

M'Gregor, W.L., *The History of the Sikhs, vol I, containing the lives of the Gurus, the history of the independent Sirdars or Misls and life of the great founder of the Sikh monarchy, Maharaja Ranjit Singh*: Vol. II, *Containing an Account of The War between The Sikhs and the English in 1845-46*, Patiala: Punjab Languages Department, 1970 (rpt).

———, *The History of the Sikhs*, London: James Madden, 1846.

Mohan, Kamlesh, *Militant Nationalism in the Punjab 1919-1935*, New Delhi: Manohar, 1985.

Mohan Singh, *An Introduction to Punjabi Literature*, Amritsar: Nanak Singh Pustakmala, 1952.

Mohinder Singh, *The Akali Movement*, Delhi: Macmillan, 1978.

Moorcroft, William and George Trebeck, *Travels in the Himalayan Provinces of Hindustan and the Punjab in Ladakh and Kashmir, in Peshawar, Kabul, Kunduz and Bokhara from 1819 to 1825*, Patiala: Punjab Languages Department, 1970 (rpt).

Mrigendra Singh, Raja, 'A Critique of Dr. W.H. McLeod's Works', *Advanced Studies in Sikhism*, pp. 326-8.

Nabha, Bhai Kahn Singh, *Ham Hindu Nahīn* (Pbi.), Amritsar: Singh Brothers, 1995 (rpt of 5th edn).

Nahar Singh, ed., *Gooroo Ram Singh and the Kuka Movement: Freedom Struggle in Punjab*, New Delhi: Amrit Books, 1965.

Nazer Singh, 'Early British Attitude Towards the Golden Temple', *Journal of Regional History*, vol. III, Amritsar: Guru Nanak Dev University, 1982.

Nahar Singh, Bhai and Kirpal Singh, eds, *Rebels Against the British Rule*, New Delhi: Atlantic Publishers and Distributors, 1995.

Nripinder Singh, *The Sikh Moral Tradition*, New Delhi: Manohar, 1990.

Oberoi, Harjot, 'From Ritual to Counter-Ritual: Rethinking the Hindu–Sikh Question, 1884–1915', *Sikh History and Religion in the Twentieth Century*, pp. 136–58.

———, *The Construction of Religious Boundaries: Culture, Identity and Diversity in the Sikh Tradition*, New Delhi: Oxford University Press, 1994.

O'Connell, Joseph T., 'Sikh Studies in North America: A Field Guide', *Studying the Sikhs: Issues for North America*, pp. 123–27.

Oman, John Campbell, *Cults, Customs and Superstitions of India*, London: 1908. Reprinted by Vishal publishers from Delhi in 1972.

Osborne, W.G., *The Court and the Camp of Ranjit Singh, with an Introcuctory Sketch of the Origin and Rise of Sikh State*, London: Henry Colburn, 1840.

Pasha, Mustapha Kamal, *Colonial Political Economy: Recruitment and Underdevelopment in the Punjab*, Karachi: Oxford University Press, 1998.

Pashaura Singh, *The Guru Granth Sahib: Canon, Meaning and Authority*, New Delhi: Oxford University Press, 2000.

———, *Life and Work of Guru Arjan*, New Delhi: Oxford University Press, 2006.

———, 'Early Markers of Sikh Identity: A Focus on the Works of the First Five Gurus', *Sikh Identity: Continuity and Change*, pp. 69–92.

Piar Singh, *Gatha Sri Adi Granth*, Amritsar: Guru Nanak Dev University, 1992.

———, *Gatha Sri Adi Granth and the Controversy*, Michigan: Anant Education and Rural Development Foundation, 1996.

———, ed., *Janam Sakhi Sri Guru Nanak Dev Ji*, Amritsar: Guru Nanak Dev University, 1974.

Prem Sumārg Granth, ed., Bhai Randhir Singh, Jalandhar: New Book Company, 1965.

Prinsep, Henry T., *Origin of the Sikh Power in the Punjab and Political Life of Maharaja Ranjit Singh, with an Account of the present condition, Religion, Laws and Customs of the Sikhs*, Calcutta: Military Orphan Press, 1834.

Puri, Harish K., *Ghadar Movement: Ideology, Organisation and Strategy*, Amritsar: Guru Nanak Dev University, 1983.

Randhawa, T.S., *The Sikhs: Images of a Heritage*, New Delhi: Prakash Books, 2000.

Rao, Ram Sukh, 'Jassa Singh Binod', M/ 772, Punjab State Archives, Patiala.

———, *Sri Fateh Singh Partap Prabhakar*, ed., Joginder Kaur, Patiala: Joginder Kaur, 1980.

Ross, David, *The Land of the Five Rivers and Sindh*, Patiala: Punjab Languages Department, 1970 (rpt).
Sachau, Edward C., *Alberuni's India, An Account of the Religion, Philosophy, Literature, Geography, Chronology, Astronomy, Customs, Laws and Astrology of India about AD 1030*, 2 vols (bound as one), Delhi: Low Price Publications 1989 (rpt).
Sachdeva, Veena, *Polity and Economy of the Punjab During the Late Eighteenth Century*, New Delhi: Manohar, 1993.
Sagar, Sabinderjit Singh, ed., *Hukamnamas of Guru Tegh Bahadur*, Amritsar: Guru Nanak Dev University, 2002.
Sahib Singh, *Slok Guru Angad Sahib Steek*, Amritsar: Singh Brothers, 1992 (rpt).
————, ed., *Sri Guru Granth Sahib Darpan*, 10 vols, Jalandhar: Raj Publishers, 1963, 1964, 1970 and 1972.
Sahni, Ruchi Ram, *Struggle for Reform in Sikh Shrines*, ed., Ganda Singh, Amritsar: Sikh Itihas Research Board, SGPC, n.d.
Sainapat, *Shri Gur Sobha*, ed., Shamsher Singh Ashok, Amritsar: Shiromani Gurdwara Parbandhak Committee, 1967.
Sarwan Singh, 'Amritsar in Medieval Punjabi Literature: An Historical Analysis', PhD Thesis, Guru Nanak Dev University, Amritsar, 1994.
Schomar, Karine 'Kabir in the Guru Granth Sahib: An Exploratory Essay', *Sikh Studies: Comparative Perspectives on a Changing Tradition*, pp. 75–86.
Schomer, Karine and W.H. McLeod, eds, *The Sants: Studies in a Devotional Tradition of India*, Delhi: Motilal Banarsidass, 1987.
Sekhon, Sant Singh and Kartar Singh Duggal, *A History of Punjabi Literature*, New Delhi: Sahitya Akademi, 1992.
Selections from Public Correspondence of the Punjab Administration, Lahore: 1855.
Shabdarth Sri Guru Granth Sahib Ji, 4 vols, Amritsar: Shiromani Gurdwara Parbandhak Committee, standard editions [ed., Teja Singh].
Shackle, Christopher, 'Making Punjabi Literary History', in Christopher Shackle, Gurharpal Singh and Arvinder Pal Singh Mandair, eds, *Sikh Religion, Culture and Ethnicity*, Richmond: Curzon Press, 2001, pp. 108–17.
Shan, Harnam Singh, 'Sikhism, An Original Distinct Revealed and Complete Religion', *Fundamental Issues in Sikh Studies*, pp. 41–2.
Smith, R.B., *Agricultural Resources of the Punjab*, London: 1849.
Smyth, G.C., *A History of the Reigning Family of Lahore*, Calcutta: W. Thacker and Co., 1847. Reprinted by the Punjab Languages Department, Patiala, in 1970.

Stienbach, L. Colonel, *The Panjaub, Being a Brief account of the Country of the Sikhs, its Extent, History, Commerce, Productions, Governments, Manufactures, Laws, Religion etc.,*. London: 1845. Reprinted by the Punjab Languages Department, Patiala, in 1970.

Sukha Singh, *Gurbilās Pātshāhī 10*, Gursharan Kaur Jaggi, ed, Patiala: Punjab Language Department, 1989 (rpt).

Suri, Sohan Lal, *Umdat-Ut-Tawarikh*, 5 vols (Daftars II–V), tr., V.S. Suri, Amritsar: Guru Nanak Dev University, 2001, 2002.

Suri V.S. (tr.) *Umdat Ut-tawarikh*, 5 vols, Amritsar: Guru Nanak Dev University, 2001, 2002. Sohan Lal Suri's *Umdat Ut-tawarikh* in Persian consists of 5 Daftars. The first Daftar was not translated by V.S. Suri. Therefore only 4 Daftars have been published by Guru Nanak Dev University. Dafter III consists of five parts. Its translation covers two volumes (parts 1–3 in one and parts 4–5 in the other). Dafters III and IV are reprints.

Surinder Singh, *Sikh Coinage: Symbol of Sikh Sovereignty*, New Delhi: Manohar, 2004.

Surjit Singh, 'A Study of W. Hew McLeod's Methodology Employed in his Work "The Evolution of Sikh Community—The Janamsakhis', *Advanced Studies in Sikhism*, pp. 317–25.

Swarup Singh, *The Sikhs Demand Their Homeland*, London: 1946.

Tara Singh, *Merī Yād* (Pbi), Amritsar: Sikh Religious Books Society, 1945.

Teja Singh, *The Gurdwara Reform Movement and the Sikh Awakening*, Jullundur: Desh Sewak Book Agency, 1922.

Teja Singh and Ganda Singh, *A Short History of the Sikhs*, Patiala: Punjabi University, 1989 (rpt).

The Athenaeum, March 24, 1849. (No. 1117).

The Calcutta Review, vol. I, nos 2, 3; vol. II, no. 4; vol. III, no. 6; vol. V, no. 10; vol. VI, no. 2; vol. IX, no. 18; vol. X. no. 19; vol. XI, no. 22.

The Edinburgh Review, vol. LXXXIX.

The Quarterly Review, vol. LXXVIII, No. 155.

The Panjab Past and Present, vol. IV, pt. 2 (October 1970); vol. VI, pt. 1 (April 1972); vol. XI, pt. 1 (April 1977).

The Times, 6 April 1849.

Thorburn, S.S., *The Punjab in Peace and War*, Patiala: Punjab Languages Department, 1970 (rpt).

Thornton, Edward, *A Gazetteer of the Countries Adjacent to India on North West including Sind, Afganistan, Beluchistan, the Punjab and the neighbouring States*, 2 vols, London: Allen and Co., 1844.

Thornton, T.H., *History of the Punjab*, London: 1846.

Thornton, T.H., *History of the Punjab and of the Rise and Progress and Present Condition of the Sect and Nation of the Sikhs*, 2 vols, London: Allen and Co., 1846.
Toynbee, Arnold J., *A Study of History*, 10 vols, London: Oxford University Press, 1955 (rpt).
Trilochan Singh, *Ernest Trumpp and W.H. McLeod as Scholars of Sikh History Religion and Culture*, Chandigarh: International Centre of Sikh Studies, 1994.
Tully, Mark and Satish Jacob, *Amritsar: Mrs Gandhi's Last Battle*, Calcutta: Rupa & Co., 1985.
Tuteja, K.L., *Sikh Politics (1920–40)*, Kurukshetra: Vishal Publications, 1984.
Uberoi, J.P.S., *Civil Society and the Sikh State*, New Delhi: Oxford University Press, 1996.
Vahiria, Avtar Singh, *Sri Darbar Sahib Amritsar De Ṭhākarān Wāle Jhagre Dī Paṛtāl*, Lahore: Sri Gurmat Press, n.d.
Vārān Bhai Gurdas, ed., Giani Hazara Singh, Amritsar: Khalsa Samachar, 1962 (7th impression).
Vaudeville, Charlotte, *The Weaver Named Kabir*, New Delhi: Oxford India Paperbacks, 1997.
Wade, C.M., *Notes on the State of Our Relations with the Punjab and the Best Mode of Their Settlement*, Ryde, Isle of Wight: 1848.
Webster, John, C.B. *The Christian Community and Change in Nineteenth Century North India*, Delhi: Macmillan, 1976.
———, *The Nirankari Sikhs*, Delhi: Macmillan/Christian Institute of Sikh Studies (Batala), 1979.
———, 'Sikh Studies in the Punjab', *Sikh Studies: Comparative Perspectives on a Changing Tradition*, pp. 26–32.
Whitehead, R.B., *Catalogue of Coins in Lahore Museum*, 3 vols, Lahore: Lahore Museum, 1997 (rpt).
Wilkins, Charles, 'Observations on Seeks and Their College', *Asiatick Reaserches*, Calcutta, vol. I (1788).

Name Index

Abdus Samad Khan 103
Adina Beg Khan 105
Ahluwalia, Fateh Singh xiv, 108
Ahluwalia, Jassa Singh 106, 107, 108, 199
Ajit Singh, Sahibzada 49, 59
Akali Phula Singh 115, 116
Ala Singh 84, 106
Alam Chand 123
Amarinder Singh 303
Amir Khusrau 206
Amrita Pritam 279
Arth Mal 63
Arur Singh, Sardar 244, 248, 252, 254, 258
Ata Khan, Haji 105
Attar Singh, Sardar 269, 271, 284, 334
Auckland, Lord 111, 112, 322
Aurangzeb 29, 59, 61, 63, 64
Azad, Maulana Abul Kalam 291

Baba Balak Singh 267
Baba Darbara Singh 267
Baba Dip Singh 45, 46
Baba Gurbachan Singh 310
Baba Gurdit Singh 291
Baba Ram Singh 158, 200, 267, 268, 278
Baba Ratan, Haji 144
Babur 124, 133
Bachan Singh 248, 259
Badan Singh, Giani 271
Bagga, Amar Singh 107

Bahadur Shah 79
Bahauddin Zakariya, Shaikh 144
Banda Bahadur 34, 35, 39, 48, 65, 79, 80, 81, 92, 102, 103, 114, 115, 326
Bawa Buddh Singh 279
Bawa Udey Singh 272
Baz Singh 79
Bedi, Baba Khem Singh 248, 269, 270, 271, 272, 273, 284, 285
Bentinck, Lord William 319
Bhagat Lakshman Singh 45, 272, 274, 275, 280, 284, 285
Bhagirath 135
Bhai Amrik Singh 309, 310
Bhai Ardaman Singh 345
Bhai Arjan Singh 270
Bhai Gurdas xv, xiv, 40, 47, 49, 52, 55, 56, 57, 58, 68, 95, 96, 100, 101, 195, 196, 204, 217, 218, 225, 273, 274, 275, 359
Bhai Gurmukh Singh 110, 111, 233, 264
Bhai Harsa Singh 269
Bhajan Lal 303, 310
Bhangi, Desa Singh 107
Bhangi, Gujjar Singh 83, 84
Bhangi, Gulab Singh 108
Bhangi, Hari Singh 83, 107
Bhangu, Ratan Singh 49, 50, 51, 63, 65, 67, 68, 69, 70, 107, 114, 118, 119, 198, 199, 200, 204, 273, 280
Bhargava, Gopi Chand 298
Bhatia, R.L. 310

NAME INDEX

Bhatti, V.S. 291
Bhindrawale, Sant Jarnail Singh
  46, 303, 305, 306, 307, 308,
  309, 310
Bindranwale, Sant Kartar Singh 305
Bikram Singh, Raja 269, 270
Bikrama Singh, Kanwar 269, 271
Binod Singh 103
Bota Singh 45, 67, 68
Broadfoot, Major 317, 321
Buta Singh, Diwan 269

Caveeshar, Sardul Singh 251, 252
Chandu Sahi 61, 63
Charhat Singh Sukerchakia 83, 84,
  108, 199
Chauhan, Jagjit Singh 304
Chhibber, Gurbakhsh Singh 103
Chhibber, Kesar Singh 61, 62, 75,
  93, 103, 112, 120, 198, 199,
  200, 204
Cooper, Frederic 232, 234, 235
Cripps, Stafford 292
Cust, Robert Needham 230, 232,
  234, 235

Dalip Singh, Maharaja 231, 269,
  271, 284
Dara Shukoh 603
Darbara Singh 310
Daulat Khan 126, 127, 128
Davies, R.H. 256
Daya Ram 123
Deva, Chaudhari 102
Dharam Chand 33
Dhian Singh, Raja 86, 116
Dhillon, Ganga Singh 364
Dhir Mal 37, 41, 63
Ditt Singh, Giani 269, 270, 271,
  273, 274
Duggal, Kartar Singh 279, 286

Eden, Emily 112, 116, 119

Fateh Shah 29
Fateh Singh, Sant 301, 302

Gandhi, Indira 300, 302, 303,
  304, 310
Gandhi, Rajiv 310
Gandhi, Sanjay 310
Gill, Lachhman Singh 304
Gobind Ram, Bhai 264
Gorakh Nath 29, 139, 141, 142,
  145
Gulab Singh 86, 113
Gurbachan Singh 294, 296, 312
Gurbakhsh Singh 82, 355
Gurbakhsh Singh, Nihang 45, 50,
  67, 69, 70, 71, 107
Gurdit Singh 108, 259
Gurmukh Singh 269, 270, 271,
  272, 274
Gurnam Singh, Justice 361
Guru Amar Das 9, 11, 13, 22, 23,
  32, 53, 54, 55, 95, 96, 101, 131,
  207, 210, 249, 279, 308, 325,
  344
Guru Angad (Angad, Lehna) 10,
  13, 15, 22, 54, 57, 95, 96, 101,
  128, 139, 141, 142, 143, 216,
  225, 308
Guru Arjan 11, 16, 17, 22, 23, 31,
  32, 41, 43, 46, 47, 54, 55, 57, 58,
  60, 61, 63, 66, 95, 96, 97, 98, 99,
  100, 101, 114, 131, 196, 210, 211,
  290, 325, 344, 357, 359, 360
Guru Gobind Singh xii, xiv, 11, 12,
  16, 22, 23, 24, 25, 26, 28, 30, 31,
  32, 33, 34, 35, 36, 37, 38, 39, 43,
  44, 47, 49, 50, 58, 59, 60, 62, 64,
  65, 66, 67, 79, 80, 81, 102, 106,
  115, 159, 165, 166, 179, 181,

NAME INDEX 409

197, 212, 234, 242, 244, 262, 263, 266, 268, 271, 274, 275, 276, 288, 290, 308, 311, 318, 324, 325, 326, 338, 339, 342, 350, 352, 355, 363
Guru Har Krishan 22, 61, 63
Guru Har Rai 22, 41, 63
Guru Hargobind 22, 23, 31, 38, 41, 55, 61, 63, 99, 100, 101, 114, 195, 325, 339, 357
Guru Nanak xi, xii, xv, 3, 4, 6, 10, 13, 14, 15, 16, 19, 20, 21, 22, 23, 24, 32, 38, 42, 43, 39, 47, 52, 53, 54, 55, 56, 57, 58, 59, 61, 65, 80, 83, 95, 97, 98, 99, 101, 123, 124, 125, 126, 127, 128, 129, 130, 131, 132, 133, 134, 135, 136, 137, 138, 139, 140, 141, 142, 143, 144, 145, 146, 147, 148, 149, 150, 151, 152, 153, 154, 155, 156, 181, 195, 196, 203, 207, 209, 210, 211, 213, 214, 215, 216, 219, 266, 275, 276, 287, 289, 324, 325, 326, 332, 336, 338, 339, 341, 342, 343, 344, 345, 350, 351, 356, 357, 358
Guru Ram Das 11, 16, 18, 22, 23, 32, 54, 57, 83, 95, 96, 101, 112, 131, 210, 220, 236, 241, 244, 245
Guru Tegh Bahadur 11, 22, 23, 24, 31, 37, 38, 43, 44, 47, 48, 49, 50, 54, 58, 59, 60, 61, 62, 63, 64, 66, 67, 70, 74, 145, 247

Hailey, Malcolm 255
Harbans Singh, Raja 242
Hardinge, Lord 316, 317, 329, 331
Harji 101
Hira Singh, Raja 247, 248, 249, 259
Holkar 108

Hukam Singh 298, 300
Husain Khan 29

Ibbetston, Sir Denzil 247, 259
Ibn Battuta 206
Irwin, Lord 294
Israel, Milton 345

Jagat Narain, Lala 310
Jahan Khan 105
Jahangir 99, 357
Jai Ram 126
Jaspat Rai 104
Jassa Singh 105
Jawahar Singh, Bhai 113, 274
Jawala Singh, Colonel 243
Jhanda Singh 107
Jnaneshvar 4
Jodh Singh, Sardar 231, 235, 237, 251

Kabir xii, 3, 4, 5, 6, 7, 8, 9, 13, 15, 18, 19, 20, 31, 38, 145, 156, 325, 343, 344
Kairon, Partap Singh 300
Kalikdas 62
Kalu 126
Kanhiya, Jai Singh 82, 83, 107
Kanhiya, Jaimal Singh 107
Kankan Kavi 113
Kapur, Jawahar Singh 269, 271
Kartar Singh, Giani 293, 298
Kavi Saundha 112
Kharak Singh, Maharaja 111
Kharak Singh, Prince 109, 116
Khudadad Khan 84
King, C.M. 246, 259
Kingra, Amar Singh 107

Lakhmi Das 126
Lakhpat Rai 104

Lal Singh 296
Lang, Colonel T. 242
Lawrence, Henry 230, 231, 315, 317, 321, 329
Lawrence, John 231
Longowal, Sant Harchand Singh 302, 303, 309
Lyall, Sir James B. 240, 243

MacDonald, Ramsay 291
MacMohan, Colonel C.A. 239, 240
Mahan Singh 84, 85, 108
Mahatma Gandhi 44, 294
Mahtab Singh, Bhai 45, 67, 69
Mai Sukhan 108
Majhail, Ishar Singh 298
Majithia, Sardar Dyal Singh 232, 276
Majithia, Sardar Lehna Singh 111, 116
Majithia, Sardar Sunder Singh 247, 249, 250, 270, 285
Man Singh, Sadar 237, 239
Mangal Singh 86
Mangal Singh, Sardar 258
Mani Singh, Bhai 45, 67, 68, 69, 70, 71, 104, 123, 159
Mardana 127, 128, 129, 130, 131, 132, 141, 148, 149, 152, 219
Massa Ranghar 104
Mata Choni 139, 153
Mata Sahib Devi 34, 39, 103, 159
Mata Sundari 34, 39, 159
Mati Das 62, 64
Metcalfe, Charles 108, 116
Mian Khan 84
Mian Miththa 144
Miharban 100, 101, 123, 143, 144
Milkha Singh 84
Minto, Lord 249
Mir Mannu (Muin ul-Mulk) 105

Mitt Singh 69
Montgomery, Robert 230
Moti Ram, Diwan 116
Mukherjee, Pranab 303
Mul Singh, Rai 232, 233, 234

Nabha Das 9, 20
Nadir Shah 81, 319
Nalwa, Hari Singh 281
Nand Lal, Bhai 34, 263, 274, 275
Nehru, Jawaharlal 298
Nihal Singh, Sant 113
Nihal Singh, Sardar 116

Ochterlony, Colonel David 109

Parduman Singh, Bhai 232, 235, 237, 257
Patel, Sadar Vallabhbhai 298
Petrie, David 260
Prince Khusrau 63
Prince Mu'azzam 29
Prince Taimur 105
Princess Ripudaman Kaur 247
Prithi Chand 37, 61, 100, 101, 102
Puran Singh 113

Radha Kishan, Seth 245, 246, 259
Rajinder Misar, Pandit 244, 245, 258
Ram Dayal, Misar 86
Ram Rai 30, 41, 63
Ram Singh, Bhai 230, 264
Rama 30
Ramanand 5, 9, 29, 148, 156, 325
Ramgarhia, Jassa Singh 83, 107, 199
Ramgarhia, Sardar Mangal Singh 237, 241, 243
Ramgarhia, Sardar Sunder Singh 252
Randhawa, Ajita 145, 147, 148

NAME INDEX

Ranghreta, Bir Singh 199
Ranjit Singh, Maharaja xiii, 12, 50, 70, 79, 85, 86, 87, 93, 108, 109, 111, 113, 114, 116, 181, 202, 231, 233, 236, 240, 241, 248, 253, 256, 265, 268, 269, 295, 316, 319, 320, 321, 323, 324, 326, 357
Ravana 25, 43, 108
Ravidas 3, 8, 20, 52
Ripon, Lord 239
Ripudaman Singh, Maharaja 252, 253
Ripudaman Singh, Tikka 244, 247, 248, 249, 251, 258, 285
Riwaz, Sir Charles Montgomery 259

Sachar, Bhim Sen 298
Sada Kaur 82, 84, 116
Sahib Chand 51
Sahib Singh 20, 225, 286
Sandhanwalia, Sardar Shamsher Singh 232, 234
Sandhanwalia, Sardar Thakur Singh 268, 269, 271
Sangatia 147
Sangu Shah, Bhai 124
Santokh Singh, Bhai 113, 114
Santokh Singh, Jathedar 310
Sarwan Singh 118
Sati Das 62
Sekhon, Sant Singh 279, 286
Sethi, P.C. 303
Shah Muhammad 94
Shahjahan 100
Shaikh Brahm (Ibrahim) 132, 133, 137
Shaikh Farid 132
Shaikh Kamal 132

Shaikh Sharaf 144
Shastri, Lal Bahadur 300
Sher Singh, Maharaja 111
Sher Singh, Prince 116
Shiam Singh 199
Sidharan 152, 153
Sirhindi, Shaikh Ahmad 47
Sri Chand 126, 153, 325
Subeg Singh, Bhai 45
Sukha Singh, Bhai 67
Sundarji, Lt. General 309
Swaran Singh, 120, 303

Takht Singh, Bhai 273
Tara Singh 199, 260
Tara Singh, Bhai 45, 67, 68
Tara Singh, Master 254, 293, 300, 301
Tara Singh Narottam, Pandit 159
Taru Singh, Bhai 45, 49, 51, 67, 69, 70, 71
Teja Singh, Principal 341
Tej Singh, Raja 321, 232, 234, 242
Tiloka 30
Tukaram 4
Tulsidas 3, 343

Vahiria, Avtar Singh 248, 259, 272, 273, 285,
Vaid, Bhai Mohan Singh 259
Vallabh 325
Venkataraman, R. 303

Wawell, Lord 293
Willingdon, Lord 294

Younghusband, R.E. 246, 259

Zail Singh, Giani 305, 310
Zakariya Khan 103, 104

Place Index

Abchal Nagar (Nander) 277
Achal 139
Amritsar 17, 20, 34, 46, 49, 69, 71, 72, 75, 81, 82, 84, 86, 92, 94, 95, 96, 97, 107, 108, 109, 110, 111, 112, 114, 115, 117, 118, 119, 155, 158, 163, 182, 197, 203, 204, 205, 224, 225, 229, 230, 232, 238, 240, 244, 245, 256, 257, 259, 264, 268, 270, 273, 277, 278, 282, 284, 285, 297, 303, 308, 311, 312, 315, 333, 341, 367; Akal Bunga xix, 103, 107, 110, 111, 116, 117, 239, 240, 225, 256; Akal Takht xiv, xvi, 82, 95, 100, 101, 102, 103, 104, 105, 106, 107, 108, 109, 113 114, 115, 117, 248, 251, 309, 359; Baba Atal 110, 11, 256; Bunga Ghariali 110, Jhanda 110, 256, Ramgarhia 107, Shahid 110, 256, Takht 66; Bunga of Sher Singh 112, of Shiam Singh 114; Bungas 109, 113, 235; Darbar Sahib xiv, xvi, 105, 107, 108, 109, 110, 111, 112, 113, 114, 115, 116, 229, 230, 231, 232, 235, 236, 237, 238, 239, 240, 241, 242, 243, 244, 245, 246, 247, 248, 250, 253, 255, 256, 258, 285; Dukh Bhanjani 110, 111, 242; Golden Temple xiv, 49, 95, 229, 231, 232, 234, 237, 239, 240, 241, 242, 246, 250, 251, 252, 253, 255, 256, 259, 260, 262, 264, 269, 271, 272, 276, 286, 306, 309, 310; Harmandar xiv, 83, 96, 97, 98, 99, 100, 101, 102, 103, 104, 105, 106, 107, 109, 111, 112, 113, 114, 116; Harmandar Sahib 70, 247, 277; Guru Ram Das Langar 306; Kaulsar 229; Manji Sahib 110; Ram Bagh 108, 230; Ram Bagh Gate 111, 229; Ram Rauni 105, 199. *See also* Ramdaspur
Anandgarh 37
Anandpur 29, 59, 67, 71, 287
Ayodhya 98

Baghdad 144
Basohli 86
Batala 84
Benares 8, 20, 229, 230, 234
Bhaini 267
Bhangani 29
Bhatinda 144

Chak Guru 102, 105, 106
Chamkaur 59

Dasuha 33
Dera Baba Nanak 10, 287
Dhaka 30, 33, 64

Faridkot 84, 264, 271, 281
Fatehgarh 71
Ferozepur 297

PLACE INDEX 413

Gaya 112
Gobindgarh 108, 109, 230
Goindwal 63, 96, 133, 195, 287
Gujarat 195
Gujjranwala 84
Gujrat 84
Gurdaspur 297
Gwalior 100

Harike 138
Haryana 304, 336
Hazro 267
Hoshiarpur 297

Jaipur 4
Jaito 252
Jalalabad 133
Jalandhar 71, 182, 203, 225, 258, 271, 297
Jammu 86
Jasrota 86
Jind 84, 85, 264, 281

Kaithal 84
Kalanaur 146
Kanganpur 133
Kanshi 112
Kapurthala 264
Karnal 79
Kartarpur 10, 96, 124, 139, 104, 143, 287
Kashmir 147, 195
Kasur 133, 134
Khadur 96, 138, 287
Kidar 112
Kiratpur 100, 287
Kurukshetra 105, 112, 286, 312

Lahore 18, 48, 69, 71, 79, 81, 85, 86, 92, 101, 102, 103, 104, 105, 106, 108, 109, 135, 158, 195, 202, 321, 262, 264, 267, 268, 269, 270, 272, 273, 274, 284, 285, 312, 326
Lohgarh 80, 100

Machhiwara 31, 33
Malerkotla 268
Malwa 195
Mathura 230, 234
Mecca 131, 142, 229
Monghyr 64
Mukhlispur 80
Muktsar 71
Multan 81, 132, 144

Nabha 84, 85, 264, 281
Nankana Sahib 252
Naushehra 33
Nirmoh 59

Pakistan 293, 294, 336
Pakpattan 33, 132
Pandharpur 19
Paonta 29
Patiala xix, 41, 42, 72, 74, 75, 84, 85, 92, 93, 95, 119, 123, 155, 158, 182, 206, 255, 264, 266, 281, 286, 311, 330, 354, 363, 365
Patna Sahib 277
Patti Haibatpur 79, 195
Peshawar 81
Pirag 33
Punjab 194, 195, 229, 231, 242, 261, 262, 269, 271, 278, 282, 301, 303, 321, 322, 340, 346, 352, 353
Puri 5

Raikot 268
Rajasthan 195, 302, 303, 336
Ram Nagar 84

Ramdaspur 17, 34, 82, 83, 95, 96, 97, 98, 99, 100, 101, 102, 103, 104, 105, 106, 107, 108, 112, 113, 195, 199, 287. See also Amritsar
Rangoon 268
Rawalpindi 267
Rupayana 33

Sadhaura 80
Saidpur 133

Sirhind 79, 81, 195
Sultanpur 124, 127, 128, 133, 195

Talwandi 125, 129
Tarn Taran 63, 252
Thanesar 195
Tilla 147

Vairoval 133

Wazirabad 84

Subject Index

Abchal Nagari 98, 99
Ādi Granth 7, 8, 11, 198, 209, 212, 262, 263, 266, 275, 277, 278, 290, 308, 309, 311, 318, 335, 344, 352
Akāl Ustat 26, 37
Akali Movement 251, 252, 254
Akalis 51, 108, 115, 116, 117, 202, 229, 236, 251, 252,253, 262, 264, 288, 291, 292, 293, 294, 297, 298, 299, 300, 301, 302, 303, 304, 308, 309
Alāhnian 172
All India Sikh Students Federation 307
Anand 170, 180
Anand Marriage Act 249, 277
Anand Marriage Bill 249, 250, 276, 285
Anandpur Sahib Resolution 301, 302, 306, 307
Āratī Sohilā 140, 151, 152
ardās 34, 70, 81, 111, 151, 170, 172, 180, 250
Āsā dī Vār 207
Azad Punjab Scheme 292, 295, 296, 297

B40 Janamsākhī xv, 123, 124, 137, 144, 146, 152, 154, 155, 156, 157, 218
Babar-bāṇī 134, 137, 213
Babbar Akalis xvii, 279

Bachittar Nātak 23, 28, 30, 37, 38, 48, 58, 59, 62, 64, 165, 224
Baisakhi 17, 30, 33, 43, 96, 102, 104, 106, 111, 114, 115, 176, 305, 338, 339
bāṇī 16, 152, 196, 219, 279, 287
bāṇī-shabad 168
Bansāvalīnāma 62
Basant Panchmi 176
Benatī Chaupaī 24, 37
Bhagvata Purana 25
bhakti xii, 3, 5, 14, 31, 176, 178, 343
Bhatts 95, 96, 117
bhog 34, 309
Bījak 6, 7
Biṛs 124
Brahma 13, 14, 25, 26, 27, 28, 37

Cabinet Mission 293, 294, 297
caste 171, 180, 192, 195, 198, 203, 216, 336
caste system 190, 191
Central Sikh League 279, 285
Chandī Charitra Ukti Bilās 25, 37
Chandī dī Vār (Vār Srī Bhagautī Jī Kī) 22, 25, 37, 212, 224
Chaupa Singh Rahit-Nama 209, 212, 219, 221, 225
Chief Khalsa Diwan 249, 250, 251, 270, 277, 278, 285, 304
Christian Vernacular Education Society 229

416 SUBJECT INDEX

City Mission House 229
Communal Award 295

Dabistān-i Mazāhib xv, 9, 12, 31, 32, 38, 40, 47, 99, 100, 117, 193
Dal Khalsa 84, 197, 305, 310
Damdami Taksal 307, 308
Dar Commission 298
Dasam Granth 22, 24, 161, 212, 263, 268, 276, 277, 278, 311, 335
Dastūr al-'Amal 236, 264
dhādīs 46, 47, 49
dharmarth 82, 262
dharmsāl xiv, 15, 16, 17, 59, 96, 102, 117, 137, 138, 141, 142, 148, 149, 150, 151, 152, 154, 213, 219, 221, 287
dharmyudh 25, 30, 62, 66, 71, 114, 302, 303, 309
Dhir Mallias 41, 37, 38, 39, 155, 219
Diwali 17, 33, 96, 106, 108, 109, 110, 111, 114, 244
duhāgan 214
Dusehra 108, 110, 111

Ganesh 241
Ghadarites xvii, 279
goddess (Adi Bhavani, Chandi, Durga, Kali, Shakti Mata) 25, 27, 28, 37, 64, 65, 66, 138, 212, 241, 272, 311, 355
got (*gotra*s) 170, 171, 190
Government of India Act XX of 1863 237, 239, 240
Granth (Granth Pothi, Granth Sahib, Guru Granth, Guru Granth Sahib, Pothi Granth, Pothi Shabad-Bani) 6, 12, 16, 31, 37, 68, 82, 95, 106, 109, 110, 112, 113, 166, 196, 197, 202, 203, 266, 267, 277, 278, 288, 290, 305, 308, 309, 339, 342, 344, 345, 347, 358, 360
Gugga Pir 276, 350
Gurbani 17, 53, 55, 57, 96, 97, 106, 108, 124, 131, 146, 151, 155, 166, 172, 180, 210, 279, 308
Gurdwara(s) xiv, xvi, xix, 16, 17, 21, 44, 46, 49, 83, 102, 105, 114, 190, 191, 242, 249, 251, 254, 262, 276, 277, 279, 287, 288
Gurdwara Rakabganj 278
Gurdwara Reform Movement 295
*gurmata*s 82, 106, 197, 319
Gurmukh 7, 52
Gurmukhi 169, 175, 181
Gurmukhi script 278, 297
Gursikhni 220, 221
Gursobha 35, 37, 39, 41, 48, 49, 59, 75, 92, 197, 335, 344, 349
Guru Panth 82, 106, 114, 196, 197, 202, 203, 255, 277, 288, 342, 347, 349
Guru Panth Prakāsh 49, 50, 198
Guruship 15, 19, 22, 39, 153, 248, 263, 276, 288, 305, 308

halemī rāj 99
Ham Hindu Nahīn 275, 288, 289, 311, 343, 346
Hindu Hitkari Sabha 244, 245
Hinduism 6, 7, 18, 20, 59
Hola 176
Holi 33
*hukamnāma*s 30, 31, 34, 38, 39, 80, 106, 267, 349

inscriptions on coins 80, 81, 86

SUBJECT INDEX 417

jāgīr(s) 83, 262, 263
Janamsākhī(s) xv, xviii, xiv, 10,
    101, 123, 175, 209, 211, 275,
    334, 349
Jap 25, 26, 37, 140
jātī 190, 196, 197, 202
Jatts 124
jīvan-muktā 57
jogī xi, 31
Jogīs 7, 20, 138, 147

Kabir Granthavali 6
Kabir Panth 4, 5, 6, 8, 18, 20
Kaliyuga 23, 38, 55, 64, 66, 124,
    130, 131, 136, 138, 139, 142,
    154, 146, 165, 168, 179, 193,
    220
Karhā parshād 34, 69, 113, 169,
    170, 251, 287
kathā 34, 96, 113, 245, 246, 346
Khalistan 291, 297, 304, 305,
    306, 307
Khalsa xiii, xiv
Khalsa Akhbār 242, 269, 272, 274
Khalsa Advocate 270
Khalsa Diwan 270, 271
Khalsa Panth xiii, 65, 66, 82, 179,
    198, 199, 200, 201, 221, 278,
    338, 350
Khalsa Raj 264
Khalsa Samāchār 245, 273
Khalsa Sikhnis 222
Khalsa Tract Society 278
kīrtan 34, 58, 96, 113, 152, 172,
    346
Kīrtan Sohilā 166, 180
Kirti Kisan Party xvii, 279
Krishan Avtār 25, 28, 37, 224
Krishna xii, 3, 14, 25, 27, 28, 37,
    145, 146, 212, 218, 241, 272,
    311, 343

langar 15, 96, 136, 287
lāvān 170
Liberal Anglicans 328
liberated-in-life 14, 56
liberation 179
liberation-in-life 53

Mahadev (Mahesh, Rudra, Shiva)
    13, 14, 25, 26, 27, 28 37, 43,
    311
Maharaja, an ideal Sikh 173, 174,
    175, 176, 177, 178, 223
mansab 174
mansabdār 176, 177
Manusmriti 189, 192
martyr(s) 45, 29, 50, 60, 67, 251
Martyrdom xiii, 37, 42, 43, 44, 45,
    46, 49, 52, 53, 56, 58, 60, 63, 67,
    68, 69, 70, 71
Masand 32, 33, 35, 36
masands 11, 31, 62, 172, 219
māyā 7, 8, 213, 215
Miṇās 37, 38, 39, 41, 155, 219,
Mīrī-Pīrī 357
misl 82
mlechh 195, 223
mullā xi, 20, 131
Mullās 7, 52

nām, dān, isnān 152, 176, 181
Nāmdhārī (Kūkas) xvii, 266, 267,
    268, 277, 278, 283
Nasīhatnāma 34, 35, 39, 41, 183
Naths 124
Naujawan Bharat Sabha xvii, 279
Nihangs 115, 202
Niranjanias 155
Nirankaris xvii, 266, 267, 277, 283

Operation Blue Star 307, 309, 311
outcastes 190, 191, 194

418 SUBJECT INDEX

Pakhyan Charitra 209, 211, 212
Pakistan Resolution 295
patriarchy 206, 207, 216
Prem Sumārg (*Granth*) xv, 158,
 159, 160, 161, 162, 163, 164,
 165, 171, 172, 177, 178, 179,
 181, 182, 183, 200, 205, 223,
 222
Punjab and Sind Bank 278
Punjabi-speaking state 299, 300
Puranas 14, 25, 26, 31, 113, 272

qāzī xi, 13, 52, 84, 128
Qur'ān (*kateb*) 14, 25, 26, 27, 190

rahit 44, 55, 200, 222, 273, 274,
 308, 346
Rahitnāma(s) xv, 44, 60, 81, 158,
 159, 160, 161, 208, 263, 275,
 335, 338, 346
rāj-jog 63, 95, 179
rāj karegā khālsā 22, 37, 93, 181,
 183, 263, 347, 355
Rajiv-Longowal Accord 307, 311
rākhī 82
Ram Avtār 25, 28, 37, 224
Ram Raiyas 37, 38, 39, 41, 155, 219
rām-rāj 98
Rama xii, 14, 25, 28, 37, 146, 212,
 272, 311, 343
Regional Formula 299, 300

sādh-sangat 52, 58, 217
sādhs xii
Sahaj jog 178, 181
Sahajdhari Sikhs 164, 219, 245, 247,
 248, 261, 262, 272, 289
Sāhibzādas 68, 69, 71
Sākhī Rahit Kī 60
Sanatan 161, 162, 163, 164, 165,
 244, 248, 285

Sanatan Sikhism 51
sangat 15, 124, 151, 55, 157, 195,
 196, 287
Sant Khalsa xv, 165, 167, 182, 200,
 267, 268
sant tradition 4
sanyasīs 147
Sarbat Khalsa 84
satī 8, 206, 210
Satluj-Yamuna Link (SY2) canal
 303
Seetla Devi 350
Sitala 276
Shabad 16, 158
shabad-bāṇī 16, 37, 39, 164, 169,
 179, 222, 288, 335
Shah Commission 301
shahīd 46, 50, 49, 52, 53, 60, 67,
 68, 69, 71, 251
shahīdganj 48, 60, 69, 71, 107
shahīdī 70
*shaikh*s (*mashaikh*) 5, 7, 14, 52,
 83, 194
Shaiva xi, 83
Shakta xi, 7, 83
Shakti 25
Shastras 14, 25, 50, 124
Shiromani Akali Dal 252, 279,
 285, 287, 288, 293, 294,
 311
Shiromani Gurdwara Parbandhak
 Committee xvi, 205, 252, 253,
 254, 255, 257, 284, 287, 288,
 295, 305, 309, 310, 359
*siddha*s (Siddhs) 26, 50, 101, 124,
 139, 142, 147, 152, 155
Siddh Gosht 140
Sikh Educational Conference 270,
 278, 284, 304
Sikh Gurdwaras Act 253, 255,
 288

'Sikh Homeland' 301, 304
Sikh (Singh, Khalsa) identity 252, 261, 266, 277, 288, 289, 311, 350, 361, 362
Sikh Panth xv, 10, 12, 13, 16, 17, 18, 19, 37, 55, 60, 138, 195, 196, 198, 204, 208, 234, 253, 273, 289, 290, 307, 308, 341
Sikh State 293, 294, 296
Sikh Studies 338, 340, 341, 343, 347, 350, 353, 355, 356, 363
Singh Sabhas xvi, xvii, 46, 51, 71, 191, 242, 243, 244, 245, 249, 258, 266, 268, 269, 270, 271, 272, 273, 274, 275, 277, 278, 279, 280, 284, 285, 288, 290, 346, 350, 355, 361
Sketch of the Sikhs 319
Smritis 14, 25, 28, 207
Sodar Rahrās 166, 180
Sri Guru Panth Prakāsh 92
Sūfīs xii, 8, 14, 18, 101, 141
Sūfism 133, 137
suhāgan 8, 214, 217

Tat Khalsa 44, 45, 46, 47, 49, 51, 161, 164, 246, 249, 250, 251, 253, 254, 255, 258
The Idea of the Sikh State 294
theocratic confederate feudalism 316

'ulamā 14, 94

Vaishnava xi, 6, 8, 83, 141
Vaishnavas 7, 9, 18, 31, 138
Vaishnavism 19, 348
Vārān Bhai Gurdas 73
Varkari 4
varna (baran, varnas) 170, 190, 196, 198
Varnashankara 190, 194
varnashrama 192, 272
varnashramadharma 189
Vārs xiv, 47, 55, 56, 101, 218, 263, 273
Veda(s) 13, 14, 20, 25, 26, 27, 31, 124, 190, 216, 272
Vishnu 13, 14, 26, 27, 28, 37, 311

World War First 264, 281